No Angel
in the Classroom

No Angel in the Classroom

Teaching Through Feminist Discourse

BERENICE MALKA FISHER

ROWMAN & LITTLEFIELD PUBLISHERS, INC.
Lanham • Boulder • New York • Oxford

ROWMAN & LITTLEFIELD PUBLISHERS, INC.

Published in the United States of America
by Rowman & Littlefield Publishers, Inc.
4720 Boston Way, Lanham, Maryland 20706
http://www.rowmanlittlefield.com

12 Hid's Copse Road
Cumnor Hill, Oxford OX2 9JJ, England

British Library Cataloguing in Publication Information Available

Library of Congress Cataloging-in-Publication Data

Fisher, Berenice M.
    No angel in the classroom : teaching through feminist discourse / Berenice
Malka Fisher.
        p.   cm.
    Includes bibliographical references and index.
    ISBN 0-8476-9123-3 (cloth : alk. paper)—ISBN 0-8476-9124-1 (pbk. :
    alk. paper)   1. Feminism and education.   2. Women—Education (Higher)—
Political aspects.   I. Title: Teaching through feminist discourse.   II. Title.
    LC197.F58   2001
    378′0082—dc21   00-057588

Printed in the United States of America

⊗ ™ The paper used in this publication meets the minimum requirements of
American National Standard for Information Sciences—Permanence of Paper for
Printed Library Materials, ANSI/NISO Z39.48–1992.

To Linda Nathan Marks
feminist comrade,
wise critic, and
light of my life

Contents

Acknowledgments

The love, encouragement, and inspiration of many people enabled me to stick with this project, but, more than anyone, my life partner Linda Nathan Marks gave me the faith that I could complete it. Through its various drafts, she shared her highly perceptive and detailed criticisms, as well as her sage advice about the work as a whole. My psychotherapist, Lee Zevy, continuously strengthened my moral and intellectual courage to undertake and persevere with this effort. Lorraine Cohen, Sherry Gorelick, and Celene Krauss, members of my writing group, helped sustain my spirit and gave me valuable suggestions in shaping the manuscript. I also want to thank the members of a number of other groups to which I belong: the Shock of Gray theater ensemble; my women's therapy, lesbian couples, and Jewish holiday groups; the NYU School of Education Women's Studies Commission (recently renamed the Commission on Gender, Race and Social Justice); and the NYU EQUAL Commission's Seminar on Teaching Social Justice. I am deeply indebted to the students in my women's studies classes, whose own struggles to learn and live with integrity have stimulated the writing of this book.

Many individuals have given their thoughtful criticisms of parts or the whole of the manuscript: Nancy Barnes, Becca Chase, Ann Diller, Carol Anne Douglas, the late Liz Durbin, Cathy Green, Mary McRae, Elizabeth Merrick, Elizabeth Minnich, Lucretia Phillips, Paula Ressler, Mary Sue Richardson, Irene Shigaki, Ellen Shumsky, Cynthia Shor, Joan Tronto, Mardi Tuminaro, and Mary Wislocki. Nancy Azara, Karen Burkhardt, Pam Fishman, Eve Maged, Ellen Shumsky, and Kathy Stillson generously talked with me about their consciousness-raising experiences.

Four friends in particular patiently followed my ongoing struggles to create this text and have never failed to cheer me on: Lila Braine, Roberta Galler, Donna Gould, and Miriam John. My sister Judy Winograd gave loving encouragement throughout the process. The support of many other friends, relatives, colleagues, helpers, and healers was crucial as well:

Carol Alpert, Amy Bauer, Carol Bay and Margot Fitzgerald, Darla Bjork, Naomi Braine, Denslow Brown, Sandy Butler, Paulette Caldwell, Suzanne Carothers, Claudette Charbonneau and Pat Lander, Tom Colwell, Portia Cornell and Lynne Kimmel, Alice Deakins, Beverly Decker and Suzanne Iasenza, Laima Druskis and Jane Jennings, Skipper Edwards and David Silberberg, Marnie Evans, Michelle Fine, Charles and David Fisher, Mark Fishman, Miriam Frank, Lucy Freund, Stephanie Glickman, Karen Humphrey, Debbie Hayden, Polly and Greg Ikonen, Barbara Insley, Chris Kelly, Magdalena Kobayashi, Annette Kolodny, Mona Kreaden, Maithreyi Krishnaraj, the late Blue Lunden, Stephen and Joan Marks, Susan O'Malley, Elinor Polansky, Lynn Preston, Susie Rankine, Harilyn Rousso, Selma Rondon, Trudy Rudnick, Dalia Sachs, Dagmar Schultz, Deborah Sherman, Fran and the late Anselm Strauss, Rosella Talent, Joan Waitkevicz, Paula Webster, and Gene, Joe, and April Winograd.

With regard to the publication process, I am indebted to the NYU School of Education Research Challenge Fund for support in manuscript preparation; to Marilyn Coppinger for typing the earliest material; to Sonia Jaffe Robbins for her editorial expertise when I was seeking a publisher; to Jack Handler of the National Writers Union for sound advice; to Sarah Drury for photographing one of my classes in action; to Bettye Lane for her classic photos of feminist demonstrations; to Linda Nathan Marks for her lively cover art; to Jill Rothenberg for her heartwarming interest and valuable responses as acquiring editor; to Dean Birkencamp for his enthusiasm and experienced guidance as my editor; to Christine Gatliffe, Laura Larson, and Lynn Weber for their skillful professional assistance; and to Katie Gentile, who brought her own scholarly reflections to the hard job of decoding and typing my endless revisions.

— Introduction —

WHERE I COME FROM

I am leading a workshop on teaching for a group of feminist academics, and I begin by describing some of the tensions that arise in my women's studies classes. A student complains bitterly that the class feels unsafe. White students react with sullen resentment to writings by African American feminists. Some students insist that feminism itself is out-of-date. As I describe these classroom situations to the workshop participants, I struggle with the fear that they will see me as an incompetent teacher or a bad feminist. Yet, as others start to tell their own teaching stories, I feel less vulnerable. My fear turns to excitement. We are talking about issues that lie at the heart of our work. We are in this together.

Teaching in higher education is an odd profession because those of us who practice it can go for years without discussing with our colleagues what goes on in our classrooms. We talk about the subjects we teach and the research we pursue or about the papers we are grading and how pleased or disappointed we are with their quality. But we have relatively few serious discussions about the interactions involved in teaching or their meaning to us and the students.

In me, at least, this state of affairs has bred a sort of pedagogical loneliness to which this book is a partial response: a way of talking with others who have similar questions about their teaching. Over the decades, my own questions have changed. As a new instructor thirty-five years ago, I wanted to know how to construct a syllabus, make a presentation, and set reasonable course requirements. Beginning academic teachers today have a far wider range of resources on teaching than I did when I entered my first classroom with shaking knees.[1] Now, I have a different set of questions, although ones I consider equally relevant for both beginners and veterans. Why do I teach as I do, and how can I think about these practices? In particular, I want to understand what it means for me to teach social justice subjects such as gender, race, class, and sexual orientation.

Since most academics still have relatively little instruction in teaching and perform as teachers out of sight of colleagues, we risk humiliation and ostracism by going public with our work. Do others find us clumsy in our pedagogical approach or superficial in our knowledge? Such criticisms potentially increase when we teach social justice topics. Because I claim to teach as a feminist, I can be faulted either for being "too political" or for not meeting one or another feminist political/intellectual standards. Because I describe myself as doing antiracist feminist teaching, critics may judge my efforts paltry or politically defective. Given these possible responses, I have to choose between leading a pedagogically lonely life and taking the risk of sharing my concerns with others.

The story I tell at the beginning of this introduction conveys my belief that the risk is worth taking. This book is written in the same spirit. Through it, I seek to talk with teachers of social justice subjects who are wrestling with problems similar to mine. I expect that women's studies teachers will discover the largest number of parallels between their teaching and my own, but I sense that feminists in a wide variety of disciplines as well as teachers of many social justice subjects will recognize in this volume aspects of their work. I do not expect us to come to our teaching with the same questions or produce the same answers. Rather, I hope that through reflecting on our commonalities and differences we can help realize more fully the promise of democratic education.

For this is the larger context in which I am writing: the project of democratizing educational work to the end of developing a more just society. I do not take "democracy" for granted, however. The social movement protests of the 1960s and 1970s that persuaded colleges and universities in the United States to incorporate black studies, women's studies, and lesbian/gay, disability, and similar social justice issues into the curriculum also raised leading questions about what constitutes democratic society. These questions cannot get answered without cultivating viable forms of political discourse.[2]

For feminist activists and teachers, the problem of developing a discourse on gender justice has been especially knotty. Although we persist in doing so, the dominant culture still discourages women from speaking out politically. Women's speech is still stigmatized as mouselike or shrill or whining or hysterical or soft-spoken or sharp-tongued. Such stereotypes obscure the extent to which our expression of needs and desires has political meaning. In an academic context, this problem is magnified by the expectation that we will speak in an academically proper manner that often requires us to suppress those needs and desires. Such patterns render any discourse on gender justice, including the participation in such discourse by men, problematic. Feminist talk is dismissed as "women's talk," and the prospect of teachers and students pursuing a political discourse on gender justice remains dim.

In opposition to these denigrating images, this book treats women's talk about oppression as serious business. My argument centers on feminist pedagogy as *teaching through feminist discourse*. By this phrase I mean discussion aimed at understanding and resisting women's oppression. My approach here builds on an interpretation of feminist consciousness-raising that emphasizes a commitment to exploring connections between personal experiences and political issues, the expression of feelings, the development of analyses, and the evaluation of alternative actions. As I conceive it, this process promotes reflection and cultivates individual and collective judgments about what can be done about gender and related forms of injustice. Consciousness-raising offers no simple road map for feminist teaching, however. It presents numerous contradictions and confounds any casual attempt to incorporate its insights into an academic setting. This book traces my thinking through these contradictions and difficulties as they emerge in my day-to-day teaching.

In my teaching, I promote discussion in which the students and I try to come to grips with the different perspectives we variously bring to issues of gender justice. These issues have been posed by feminism as a social movement that interacts with other movements for social justice and by incidents of unfairness and violence we face in our daily lives. Feminist discourse requires us to address our different notions of gender justice and their implications for action. Thus, although such discourse may promote inquiry into the causes and consequences of women's and other forms of oppression, its overarching purpose is action rather than inquiry. Feminist classroom discourse aims at cultivating the individual and collective judgments that inform such political action. Inquiry plays a role. Both the students and I must discover and learn a lot as we talk through feminist issues. This process involves a great deal of effort. I call this effort *discourse work,* and much of this volume is devoted to exploring the forms it might take and the problems it generates.

The tradition of consciousness-raising as it developed during the feminist movement of the 1960s and 1970s provides a basic resource for pursuing such discourse work. The consciousness-raising emphasis on sharing experiences and feelings enriches and complicates the dominant image of democratic discourse as an exchange of ideas for the purpose of collective decision making. Feminist discourse entails drawing on experiences and feelings in a way that acknowledges and challenges the differing perspectives that participants bring to the discussion. Thus, this project involves figuring out how we can continue to communicate when conflicting points of view threaten to destroy the often insecure bonds that support our talk. It requires students to reflect on how much and what kind of discourse work they are willing and able to do and demands of me as a teacher that

I figure out my responsibilities in asking students to incorporate seemingly personal material into our political discussions.

I began to think more deeply about those responsibilities some fifteen years ago when several graduate students asked me to develop a course on feminist pedagogy. Creating such a course seemed a natural step for me. I had been teaching women's studies for seven or eight years, and I had published several pieces on feminist teaching. There was a growing literature that could provide the foundation for a course on this topic. Yet, as I began to teach this new course, I was struck by several facts. One was the hunger of so many graduate students who were themselves beginning teachers to understand what it meant to be a feminist teacher. Although the literature spoke to many of the issues that concerned all of us, it did not seem to sate this hunger. I also was struck by the fact that, although teaching the course helped me to articulate more of my own ideas about feminist teaching, I was not always sure what I was doing or why. Like many early writers on feminist pedagogy, I had tended to share with others those ideas and practices that worked in my teaching rather than analyzing those aspects that were problematic. I realized that the problems faced by beginning feminist teachers were not so different from my own, and that, if I looked at my own practice in more depth, I would discover many broad questions. The more I thought about these questions, the more I wanted to answer them.

In seeking answers, I found that I could not avoid paying closer attention to who I was as a teacher and how various parts of my life story shaped my theory and practice of teaching. I realized that at the core of my approach lay a passionate desire to understand what was going on around me and to respond to the hurt that I and others experienced through social injustice. But finding a way to talk about these things was very difficult for me. I was raised in a family that, despite taking for granted certain liberal values, did not encourage discussion or disagreement about how they were to be interpreted or implemented. It was a family system in which serious dissent might have threatened the fragile underpinnings of my parents' hard-won security.

My father, who had been forced at the age of fourteen to become the head of his widowed mother's household, was a self-made businessman and largely self-educated. He was the family intellectual, just as he was the head of our family. My mother, the eighth of nine children, was a skillful and creative homemaker. She talked easily about activities in her own sphere, but if she tried to voice opinions about something beyond it (which was rare), no one seemed to "hear" what she said. Having caught on to the dominant family ethos, I used to blush with embarrassment at her effort.

Early on, as I discovered that thinking could be my lifeline, I identified with my father. Emulating my father's intellectual style was not a simple matter. Both of my parents guarded gender boundaries with vigilance. My father struck out with cutting sarcasm when he thought I was becoming "too big for my britches." My mother reminded me that I was not as intelligent as my next-in-line brother. I learned to express my thoughts cautiously or keep them to myself. Yet, at the same time, my parents prized thinking and learning across gender lines. They were proud that my mother, born into a Jewish family in a small town in the Ukraine and raised partly on the Canadian frontier, was a college graduate. My father, who came from a German Jewish family, painfully gave up his nighttime college studies to give his mother and younger brother a better life. As Jews, my parents brought me up to believe that my mind was my greatest asset. If anti-Semitism required me to flee home and country, education would be the key to survival.

My parents carefully managed their middle-class resources so that their four children could have "good" educations. Because I kept getting sick and did not seem to be learning very much at the local public school, they decided to send me to the Laboratory School founded by John Dewey at the University of Chicago.[3] Throughout my elementary school years, I reveled in the activity-based, problem-solving education I got there. I loved developing projects about science and industry and exploring the links between our classroom and the world. In the morning, my father would leave for his business in the Chicago stockyards. In the afternoon, my school class might visit the stockyards to learn where the meat on our family tables came from. The fact that the slaughtering made me sick to my stomach and the working conditions made me wonder about what went into paying for my private education confirmed my belief that learning and thinking could help me answer questions about suffering and human relationships that I could never ask at home.

This unusual school also provided the first chance for me to discover and exercise a capacity for political talk. From the perspective of my childhood home, politics belonged to my father's masculine world. As World War II raged on, politics entered the sphere of women and children through daily activities, such as packing up clothes to send to our friends in Hull, England, who were living in underground shelters to protect them from German bombs, and through my parents' whispered exchanges about what was happening to European Jews. At school, on the other hand, a pubescent me was invited to do things like participate in a debate on socialized medicine, discuss the work of a great African American poet, and consider the role of business in the distribution of farm products. I was not always successful at this talk (an opponent of socialized medicine, the son of a doctor, made me feel like a fool in a classroom debate), but I came to know this process of political discourse and longed to make it part of my life.

In contrast to school, I could not imagine engaging in political argument at home. My mother never challenged my father on any topic in front of us children. My parents appeared to be unified in their liberal values, which strongly resembled those of Franklin and Eleanor Roosevelt. My mother had two quite self-defined sisters who, when they visited, clashed with my father on political issues. One of my aunts was a pioneer physician who had pronounced opinions on subjects such as birth control and Zionism. Both my parents seemed to avoid arguing with her on such questions. The other aunt, a social worker and a publicly vocal member of the Communist Party in Canada, challenged my father as an arch-capitalist. If my memories serve me, they both enjoyed these infrequent verbal battles. But my father clearly did not take either aunt's political opinions very seriously, and I could tell that these encounters made my mother anxious. Periodically, she let me know that despite their much admired accomplishments, these childless sisters had failed as women.

In the early 1950s, we moved to the suburbs. My lively elementary education gave way to a prestigious high school where my family's notions of how men and women should relate to each other were more fully reflected. Gender lines were back in force: boys were groomed to enter Ivy League colleges; girls were prepared for a smattering of higher education before marriage and children.[4] Through my family, I had acquired an ethic of hard work and seriousness in contrast to the values of "doing well" and creating the right appearance that prevailed in this suburban school. Although the conservative climate of the period made it hard to find an alternative, I eventually found one in the college created by Robert Hutchins at the University of Chicago.[5] Here, I discovered a world of young people like me who were eccentric, questioning, and eager to learn. I adored classes in which we explored together the meaning of classic texts. I plunged into all-night "bull sessions" about our conformist society and the cultural dissent of figures like Dylan Thomas, Henry Miller, and John Cage. I wore "bohemian" clothes, started sleeping with men, dealt with my first heartbreak, and ended up in psychotherapy. I felt very emancipated, but in some ways I did not feel very good.

Two things bothered me that I could not fully articulate at the time. The intellectual and sexual life I enjoyed led to an ambiguous sort of freedom. The keen social critique my college cronies and I developed provided us little hope for social change. We were specialists in skepticism, sharp at criticizing but cautious about staking out our own positions. Advocating social change was dangerous. In this period so dominated by the spirit of McCarthyism, I had classmates whose families had been harassed by the FBI and whose parents, I heard, were jailed under the anticommunist Smith Act. I went to left-wing meetings, where I was struck by the courage it took to talk about politically tabooed topics and to express open criticisms of class and racial injustice. Yet I was disturbed by the common assumption that politics required a single analysis and that political talk meant a competition among activists about whose analysis was correct. In about 1956, I made a brief attempt to join the tiny peace movement that was protesting the military buildup of the Cold War, but I became confused by the political atmosphere of suspicion (who in our group had what agenda?) that infected our discussions. All-night talks, in which my friends and I criticized other people's ideas, seemed safer. Yet a part of me longed for advocacy. I missed the spirit of Jane Addams, whose biography I had read as a child. She was my local hero, an intellectual, a reformer, and a public voice for women and children.

My love of ideas and my lack of clarity about taking action led me to pursue a master's degree in the University of Chicago's philosophy department. This study refined my ability to identify assumptions, probe concepts, and analyze arguments, but it drove a deeper wedge between my thinking and my understanding of what it meant to be a "woman." My intense desire to explore goodness, beauty, and truth came into quick collision with the cool cerebral style associated with professional philosophy. In 1958, the field was almost entirely male. I could not imagine going past the M.A. So, I took various research jobs while I tried to figure out how to follow my impulse to think and choose in a world where women like me were supposed to be taking a predetermined path to marriage and family.

This same world was changing, however, due in important part to the impact of the civil rights movement. As I tried to imagine a place for myself in this wave of social change, I wrote to my much older cousin, Anselm Strauss, who already had saved me from becoming a college dropout by supervising my bachelor's thesis. Since then, he had left to start a sociology program at the University of California at San Francisco. When I asked his advice, he suggested that I come to Berkeley where he had a friend on the education faculty. Education was a good field for reformers, he noted, and more friendly to women than the rest of academia. I jumped at the chance. I would get a doctorate, which would enable me to do an end run around the sexism I had encountered in the workplace. I would become some kind of credentialed reformer.

Berkeley in the early 1960s turned out to be an extraordinary place to explore my broad intellectual interests. I did independent reading and was privileged to take courses with a number of leading academic figures. In the end, I found myself studying with Anselm and following his current interest in applying sociological thinking to historical material. He taught me how to think in terms of social movements and people's affiliations with overlapping but sometimes conflicting social worlds.[6] I was fascinated by this work, but, as an unmarried woman in my late twenties, my life as a doctoral student was agonizingly lonely. Most graduate students in education were older, and I had little contact with students in liberal arts. By my second or third year of study, Berkeley had become the focus of intense student activism. As protests over free speech on campus and democratic education began to mount, I supported them through small gestures. I did not feel part of the rebellion, however. I was well into my doctoral degree and lacked any ties to the activist students. I saw the doctorate as my "ticket" out of a sexist work world. Graduate study had cost me years of isolation and a near-ulcer, and I was not willing to postpone or endanger my struggle for personal integrity and independence by increasing my involvement in protest. I would stand up for what I believed, give support, but save my greater political engagement until I found a place in the system. In 1965, I got my degree and started to work in higher education just as it was beginning to undergo tumultuous changes.

My first academic job, teaching educational sociology at the University of Wisconsin at Madison, brought together my life themes with dramatic force. I now had financial security (I was awarded tenure within a few years) and the independence that came with it. I was an intellectually "exceptional" and heterosexually adventurous woman in a world of academic men. I eagerly joined with other radical faculty members in supporting student protests and in organizing protests of our own. Still, however, a few cracks persisted in this picture. Being "exceptional" brought its own kind of loneliness. Political work raised problems about relating to men that I did not understand. My individual battle against sexism had left a strangely bitter taste in my mouth. Yet when in 1968 I followed the suggestion of a male colleague and attended a student-run consciousness-raising session, I could not see what this feminist talk about oppression had to offer me. The women were younger, I said to myself (I was now in my early thirties), and had not yet learned to resist domination. I did not see a connection between their search for an "analysis of patriarchy" and the fact that although my career was going very well, my life was not.

In an attempt to resolve the contradiction between my life and my work, I fled to a temporary appointment in New York City, where I hoped urban diversity would allow me to be less exceptional and more myself. During that year, I was able to obtain a tenured teaching position in educational philosophy at New York University. Political activism already had diminished on that campus, and I was relieved to step back from my confusion about political work to stay on the sidelines once again. Together with a college friend, Roberta Galler, who had been active for many years in the civil rights movement, I tried to make sense of the second wave of feminism that had been building since the 1960s. Roberta and I talked about our political involvements and the part that gender had played. We analyzed our relationships with men and the limits we had encountered. We discussed her disability (she had polio as a child), how it had affected her life and our friendship. Meanwhile, I read the work of Kate Millett, Charlotte Bunch, and Robin Morgan, and I tried to figure out how these ideas fit with my thinking and my experience.[7]

My first encounter with feminist writing had not changed my life. I had read *The Second Sex* in the late 1950s, and, aside from the chapter on lesbians, which I found unaccountably powerful and disturbing, I did not think that this book applied to me. I identified myself with Simone de Beauvoir, not with the women trapped in domesticity, just as in the mid-1960s I saw Betty Friedan's *The Feminine Mystique* as valuable for women who had not achieved my level of emancipation. As someone who had long identified as a socialist, I also thought that the ideals expressed in these groundbreaking books had little relation to the life chances for most poor and working-class women. It was not until I read the early writings of radical feminists that I began to take a long, hard look at myself as a woman and feminism as a collective political critique. By drawing my attention to the connections between my public and private lives, radical feminists helped me bridge the gap between my apparently successful career and my somewhat unhappy consciousness. What I had previously viewed as my individual problems—including my confusion about what it meant for me to make a home, to deal with attempted rape, and to affirm my value as a woman without children—now became part of my political thinking.

With my discovery of socialist feminism in the mid-1970s, I found my first ideological niche in the U.S. feminist movement. By bringing together issues of gender and class, socialist feminists helped me view feminism as a movement that intertwined with other movements for social justice.[8] As I became more involved, my feminism also became increasingly eclectic. Too many voices, images, and ideas were coming at me from different directions to contain my thinking in a single position. I was still deeply affected by radical feminist thinking, whatever my reservations about the tendency to overgeneralize. I was jolted and forced to think more deeply, as black feminists spelled out their criticisms of the predominantly white women's movement. I listened carefully to women in the trade unions and to lesbian indictments of heterosexism. I sometimes wondered what feminism meant for my work, but I did not see a simple answer. While I met with my socialist feminist group, joined protests, went on marches, wrote articles for a feminist newspaper, and attended conferences, little activism was evident in my academic life. For me, this picture changed entirely when I went to the first annual meeting of the National Women's Studies Association (NWSA) in 1978.

While I had been tentatively exploring and joining feminist activities outside my work life, hundreds of academic women had been struggling to develop and institute feminist ideas inside the ivy walls. They were creating feminist caucuses within their professional associations and challenging the misogynist assumptions on which academic organization, teaching, and research were based. Since the mid-1960s, teachers and students had been generating courses in what came to be called women's studies. Some pioneers in this field, such as Florence Howe, had participated in the civil rights movement and had gained firsthand experience of the power of social justice movements to generate consciousness and learning.[9] Others had joined consciousness-raising groups or had been inspired in myriad ways by the peace and justice movements of the 1960s and early 1970s to link their politics to their academic work. By 1977, when I learned that a national women's studies organization had just been founded, the field of women's studies had burgeoned on numerous campuses. When I dug through enough layers of my own internalized misogyny to realize what it might mean to combine these two apparently contradictory words, *women* and *studies*, I sensed that I might at last find for myself an academic home.

The first annual meeting of the NWSA in Lawrence, Kansas, brought together many of the values I had pursued in the disparate parts of my life. Presentations were intellectually thrilling, as feminist academics spelled out some of the pioneering theoretical work that had developed out of early 1970s political critiques. Both inside and outside formal sessions, talk concerned social change. What kind of movement should this be? How and where should we try to change society? What concrete steps needed to be taken? Some of these steps, like new approaches to women's health, were modeled at the meetings themselves. Our emotions, our bodies were fully part of the proceedings. We told our stories. We listened to poetry and music. We danced with each other for hours, and at least some of us felt the enormous sexual energy generated by so many deeply excited women. The outlaw feelings and thoughts I had been having for a number of years were coming together with the image of myself as a lesbian. My mind and my heart were alive.

I returned to the university fired up to do something about women's studies and soon joined with several colleagues in our school of education to initiate a women's studies group. Because we were based in a professional school, we could not start a degree program of the sort that was being built in liberal arts colleges and schools of arts and sciences.[10] On the other hand, we were faced with the interesting challenge of figuring out what kinds of courses best fit with our student body of mostly graduate women in women-predominant fields such as education, nursing, health, psychological services, and related arts professions. This mix of students has changed over the years, with a growing undergraduate population, more students of color, and increased preparation in arts and sciences. Yet then as now, students in general were highly committed to their school work, which was personally and financially costly and often purchased at considerable sacrifice. Some students represented the first generation in their family to graduate college. For many, finding and practicing a profession fulfilled a lifelong dream. Students wanted to get as much as they could out of their educations, especially but not exclusively an occupational credential. They were eager to relate their education to the world outside the academy.

This was a fertile field for women's studies. Our group developed and publicized courses to fit with our student body. I created both interdisciplinary women's studies courses geared to professional issues and courses that brought a feminist perspective to my teaching in the philosophy of education. Although we met a certain amount of resistance, our women's studies initiative quickly made an impact on the school. Students eagerly signed up for our classes. We sponsored conferences and symposia. We guided feminist doctoral dissertations. We created an ambiance that, whatever its limitations, captured for me some of the sense of integration I had discovered at the early NWSA meetings. Creating a women's studies presence in our school not only fulfilled some basic desires but pushed me to develop my thinking and politics and practice much further. I had to figure out my relation as a feminist to unionization drives within the institution. I had to reflect on my interactions with feminist and nonfeminist colleagues. I had to think about what being a feminist teacher meant for my relationships to students. I had to figure out what I meant by feminist teaching.

In becoming an academic teacher, I relied on what I had learned and observed as a student. I was particularly impressed by the teaching I encountered at the College at the University of Chicago in the mid-1950s. As conceptualized by Robert Hutchins and Mortimer Adler, this program aimed at cultivating the understanding and judgment needed by free citizens.[11] The role of teachers in our small classes was to lead discussions that would help us develop interpretations of classic texts. This pedagogy assumed that interpretations, by their very nature, were partial. Teachers taught us to test our understanding of a text through detailed analysis, to compare the partial truths entailed in these interpretations, and to explore the potential for developing wider perspectives that might embrace apparent contradictions. My (entirely white, male) teachers led these discussions with enthusiasm and subtlety, although I noticed that in following the college custom of calling us "Miss" or "Mr.," some of them pronounced these honorifics with a slightly ironic inflection.

This approach to pedagogy also pervaded the philosophy department, where Richard McKeon was the central figure.[12] McKeon, who had collaborated with Hutchins in developing the college curriculum, rejected the then dominant school of positivism and the growing enthusiasm for analytic philosophy, turned a critical eye on philosophical pragmatism and promoted, instead, a Socratic notion of philosophy as dialogue. Teachers expected students to treat all philosophical arguments with respect and, at the same time, to subject arguments to uncompromising criticism by delving into the meanings of the text. In contrast to the presentation of arguments for purposes of demonstration—that is, to defend and shore up one's own position—we were taught to analyze arguments for the purpose of communication. The teacher's work was to help us learn to distinguish among different kinds of arguments in terms of their organization, methods, and principles. Such analyses enabled us to compare and contrast arguments, to identify philosophical conflicts, and to discover areas of overlap and similarity. Although such scholarly activities were carefully distinguished from the process of addressing practical problems, this department (like the college) emphasized the importance of rigorous thinking and clear communication in all human endeavors. Still wet behind my theoretical ears, I shared this conviction, although I was somewhat disturbed by the contrast between the notion that we students could join in discussing the "great ideas" and my personal discomfort as a young woman and a Jew in a world of older, white, Christian, male philosophers.

My notion of good academic teaching underwent two transformations at the University of California. The first grew out of my relationship with Anselm Strauss. In contrast to my philosophy teachers, he nurtured me as an individual. He paid attention to the social context in which I was studying and gave me advice about how to handle the problems I faced as a doctoral student. Through his intellectual affiliation with the Chicago tradition of sociology and figures such as W. I. Thomas, Robert Park, and George Herbert Mead, Strauss also emphasized three values: a qualified belief in progress to which sociologists could contribute, a view of social movements as potentially progressive forces, and the importance of seeking communication among members of different social worlds.[13] Because his teaching style drew heavily on the pragmatic tradition, he encouraged me to follow my own interests, look carefully at the worlds to which I belonged, and ask how they related to others. Through his mentoring, I began to see the human face of theoretical arguments. I began to see teaching as an encounter of people from different social worlds who were variously affected by movements for change.

My idea of academic teaching acquired a further dimension because I started my doctoral work at a time of increasing social upheaval. By the early 1960s, student demonstrators against racism, militarism, imperialism, and authoritarianism in all forms were calling on faculty across the disciplines to respond to these evils. As a graduate student who was on the cusp of becoming an academic myself, I watched faculty members ignore, evade, embrace, or make their ambivalent ways through the sets of demands and criticisms voiced by demonstrators. The impact of power inequalities on political discourse became evident. I saw students silenced by faculty, administrators, and the police. I saw images and language manipulated to deflect leading questions. I caught the scent of participatory democracy as protesting students and dissident faculty were beginning to test out its meaning for academic teaching. I knew that this call to action would influence my own work as a teacher, although I did not yet know how.[14]

By the time I began to teach courses in the sociology of education at the University of Wisconsin, I had started to knit my own diverse experiences with teaching into what I might now describe as a *pedagogy of grounded dialogue*. In my classes, I tried to get students to compare arguments, clarify their own positions, and explore the meanings of these arguments in relation to social contexts. I encouraged students to bring in experiences and consider implications for action. This latter goal became increasingly easy to fulfill as political activism on the campus increased. I remember one protest in which our radical faculty group had decided that we should both hold our classes and support the dissident students. In one class in which we were discussing Emile Durkheim's social theory, students involved in the demonstration kept coming into and leaving the class, giving the rest of us reports about what was happening. As our discussion wove back and forth between the meaning of "anomie" and the demonstration taking place outside, both the students and I saw the strong connection between our talk and action, between the space the classroom provided to both protesters and nonprotesters to reflect on political activism and the activism itself. That day I knew, on some level, that I was becoming a different kind of teacher.

When I began teaching women's studies, my classroom practice forced me to think yet more deeply about what I was doing. In some ways, my approach did not change. My appointment in educational philosophy supported a focus on helping students to clarify and distinguish arguments. Since the feminist movement had generated an enormous number of arguments, I could continue to stress analysis for the purpose of communication. This perspective permeated my interdisciplinary women's studies classes as well, where I tried to help students identify the feminist arguments entailed in various disciplinary approaches, different schools of thought, and differing research strategies. The fact that students were drawn to their degree programs because of practical concerns about acquiring professional skills gave me a natural beginning point for talking about the meaning of ideas for practice. I could easily stress the importance of social context in discussing such ideas.

As a feminist teacher, however, I could not stop here. In my prefeminist teaching days, I did not tend to argue for the values that informed my courses. My socialist beliefs were reflected by including Marx or other radical thinkers in the readings, and I directed my political energies to getting students to engage with these unfamiliar and often frightening ideas. I rarely brought my own experiences into class and virtually never mentioned anything I would have considered "personal." My involvement with the feminist movement made me rethink these implicit assumptions. I was now not only a proponent of a way of thinking but an activist in a social movement. The strong line I had drawn between my professional and my private life (which had served to protect me against a good deal of discriminatory and hurtful behavior) had been rendered far more questionable through my feminist activism. The fact that my political involvement with women had developed into an erotic involvement complicated even further my earlier approach to teaching. Although I was fearful of coming out as a lesbian in my professional life, I also sensed the political and intellectual potential of this act. I could see how emotions could play a far greater role in my teaching—both the students' feelings and my own. My older approach of grounded classroom dialogue began to be transformed into the feminist classroom discourse that is the subject of this book.

The key to this transformation lay in my involvement with a movement for women's liberation that is intimately connected with other movements for social justice. The importance of these interweaving movements became clear to me in my first encounter with the question "What is feminist pedagogy?" at a 1978 celebration of the civil rights activist Ella Baker. There I found myself talking about women's studies with Susan O'Malley, an editor of the journal *Radical Teacher*. Susan asked me how I defined feminist pedagogy. To me, the answer seemed self-evident. Feminist pedagogy grew out of the work of Ella Baker, who emphasized bringing black community members together to talk about their experiences of oppression and think about how to challenge racial injustice.[15] Feminist pedagogy also drew on the feminist impulse toward consciousness-raising, women coming together to share their experiences and feelings of oppression and think about how to act in the face of gender injustice. Without hesitating or thinking myself too big for my relatively new, feminist britches, I told Susan I would write an essay, defining feminist pedagogy, for her journal. I called that piece "What Is Feminist Pedagogy?"[16]

Although this was a large question and I was just beginning to teach women's studies, I did not hesitate to propose my own answer because second-wave feminism opened up so many opportunities to develop innovative ideas and activities. Moreover, I never saw myself as a lone innovator but someone trying to capture the experience of a movement, to formulate a way of thinking that I believed was widespread. I was partly right. The notion that feminist pedagogy derived in some fashion from consciousness-raising was, as Barbara Scott Winkler has pointed out, quite common among feminist academics.[17] Unfortunately, feminist writing about teaching did little to explore this connection, and the backlash of the 1980s obscured it even further by branding consciousness-raising as outdated, silly, or pernicious.

Meanwhile, other notions about the relationship between feminism and teaching were gaining greater public and academic attention. Carol Gilligan's research on women's "different voice" took center stage in many discussions of feminism, and her argument for the values of caring and connection was quickly applied to feminist teaching. While Mary Belenky and her colleagues followed this line of thought in their much praised volume on *Women's Ways of Knowing*, few feminist academics seemed to notice that "feminist pedagogy" meant different things to different teachers.[18] Proponents often assumed that their particular thoughts and practices represented the whole of feminist teaching. Staunch critics of feminist pedagogy were quick to generalize from a few writings or examples, defining it in terms of the features they most disliked in what they believed to be the thinking or actions of certain feminist academics.

Two major streams of criticism developed in the late 1980s and early 1990s. One, exemplified by Daphne Patai and Noretta Koertge's *Professing Feminism*, pictured feminist pedagogy as intellectually irresponsible and politically biased teaching that rejected the time-tested academic standards of careful reasoning and objectivity.[19] Patai and Koertge's criticism was based heavily on the accounts of students who had been disappointed, angered, or hurt by what they encountered in women's studies classes. I did not doubt that some students were unhappy or even harmed by particular feminist teachers, but the authors' use of these examples to build a case against what they took to be "feminist pedagogy" itself reeked of political reaction and left little room to discuss the complex political and pedagogical questions that feminist as well as nonfeminist teachers often address.

I was far more concerned with feminist postmodern or poststructuralist criticisms of "feminist pedagogy" being launched in the late 1980s and early 1990s.[20] In part, the postmodern theory that inspired these criticisms grew directly out of second-wave thought, with its critique of Western rationality, narrowly materialist thinking, and male-centered notions of progress. In many ways, I felt kinship with feminist postmodern thinking, not only because of its connection to second-wave arguments but because the pragmatic dimension of my thought and practice had oriented me toward open-ended change, the symbolic element in human interaction, and the complexities of constructing selves and communities. I drew back, however, when I encountered other aspects of this academic trend. I bristled at postmodern hostility toward material reality. I considered any wholesale dismissal of experience as elitist. And I rejected the tendency to extol fluid and fragmented selves. My own self had changed and fragmented in many ways, but I had engaged in a lifelong struggle for coherence and integrity. Above all, I was highly distressed by skepticism toward the kind of activism in which people who suffered oppression joined together to work for social change.

The tone of contempt adopted by some postmodern feminists toward second-wave feminists, picturing us as authoritarian, naive, simplistic and romantic thinkers, shook me to my roots. I was accustomed to antifeminists of various kinds saying that feminists were out of touch with reality. "Whose reality?" I would counter. I was used to feminists, including academic feminists, telling, even shouting at, each other that their politics were dead wrong. "Politics involves conflict," I thought, "and since we are doing politics, of course we are disagreeing." However, I had not heard many feminist academics telling each other that they were intellectually inadequate. Although I acknowledged the authoritarian element in some feminist activism and readily granted the romanticism, I was cut to the core by the implied charge of being "stupid." I had struggled against this profoundly damaging claim my whole life. I grew up with the idea that women were stupid, could not engage in abstract thinking, and could not talk politics. At first, I did not believe that I was hearing this from other feminists. My writing slowed down and then stopped. I became deeply depressed and unsure about where I was going.

The feminist academic reaction to second-wave thinking came at a bad time for me. By the late 1980s, I had passed my fiftieth birthday and was struggling to grasp what it meant to be an aging woman in a society that devalued both aging and women. I was becoming an older academic in a research university world that gave little reward to experience, unless it was reflected in numerous and influential publications or large grants. The National Women's Studies Association, which had provided an anchor for my shifting academic identity, had entered a period of political and organizational crisis. I was losing people near and dear to me through sickness and death, and I was trying to sustain my political faith in a period of ever greater conservatism.

Continuing to work on this book in the face of such a sense of loss meant coming to grips in a new way with the profound disagreements that kept surfacing within feminism and among feminist academics. It also meant coming to grips with the rage I felt at being intellectually dismissed. The standard academic way to deal with rage at ideas we reject is aggression. My disciplinary training had given me tools that could be used as weapons, and at times I had used these weapons to attack competing feminist positions. I could expose irrelevances, assault arguments, explode contradictions. Using my mind in this way felt exhilarating, but it left me feeling rather ethically nauseous. The alternative seemed to be a "feminist process" of responding to others in a spirit of careful listening and support with an eye toward cooperation and collaboration. I was drawn to these values, but I could not apply them in anger. Moreover, I was often unsure how they applied to dealing with serious disagreements among feminists.[21]

In the end, I was able to regain my capacity to speak through my writing due to the faith that my lover and friends had in my capacity to do this work and through a great deal of introspection. Two insights helped reinvigorate my effort. One came from Barbara Deming, a Quaker-raised peace and civil rights activist, a feminist, and a lesbian. She had the simple but profound conviction that "we are all part of one another."[22] The other insight came from an early encounter with Gestalt psychotherapy and the opportunity to explore the deep fragmentations within myself and how they reflected contradictions in the external world. Through this awareness, I finally realized that the anger that animated my criticisms of competing feminist arguments often grew out of anger with my own conflicting feelings and actions.

I was a firm critic of liberal feminist thinking that focused on individualist values like "opportunity" and "choice." Yet without access to individual opportunity and choice, I probably never would have become an academic who spent her time criticizing the concepts of opportunity and choice. I tended to reject the work of feminists like Carol Gilligan on the grounds that a valorization of women's caring reinforced women's subordinate role as nurturer. But I also longed to be cared for myself and felt the profound connection that could result from nurturing others. I raged at postmodern feminist charges that second-wave thinking was "naive" and "romantic," but my skeptical self who came of age in the 1950s wondered whether my hopes for social change were not overblown. I was furious with academic feminists who attacked feminist pedagogy as insufficiently scholarly, but the voice of my rigorous academic training whispered that at least some feminist teaching did not make the grade.

I had to find a way to work through and write through these internal debates not simply for the individual therapeutic gain but for the contribution these conflicting voices made to my thinking. These voices did not get in the way of my thinking, I eventually realized. They *were* my thinking. They were parts of that thinking that both connected me to others and, at the same time, enabled me to discover where my ideas differed from theirs. They were parts of my thinking that connected me to conflicting experiences, to dilemmas of action, to the problems of practice.[23]

Practice has been basic to writing this book. My political activities outside academia and a host of other practices enhanced my notion of feminist teaching. My involvement in individual and group Gestalt psychotherapy has heightened my awareness of the role of internal conflict in individual expression and increased my sensitivity to the impact of groups on individuals and vice versa. Through classes and workshops I have taken in dance and movement improvisation, I have learned how to respect and follow my movement impulses and to improvise with others. I came to trust their spontaneous responses as well as my own, to create a collaborative movement piece out of our differences. I learned a similar lesson through years of working with a feminist theater ensemble and discovering how our different experiences could be brought together into a shared statement about the relation between our personal lives and our political convictions.[24]

In 1984, I went to France to study Augusto Boal's "theater of the oppressed" and adapted his techniques to my feminist teaching.[25] His forum theater provided a model for exploring the conflicts people encounter in trying to confront injustice. His image theater suggested how people can discover their responses to injustice through physical feelings and expression. This work prompted me to develop two multimedia workshops for women, experiments in feminist pedagogy outside the classroom that I offered through an independent feminist organization created by my life partner, Linda Nathan Marks.[26] Through this organization, the Crystal Quilt, I both presented and attended many workshops and discussions, where women from different backgrounds grappled with the issues we face in our lives.

The practice that most deeply affected the writing of this book was my teaching. Writing about teaching practice turned out to be far more difficult than I anticipated. Part of this difficulty stems from the continued bifurcation between theory and practice. Most writing about teaching (or other areas of feminist action) falls into one or the other of these categories. Work that seeks to bridge the gap reflects this strain. In his treatise on the "reflective practitioner," Donald Schön attributes this difficulty to the persistent assumption that theory should direct practice.[27] A great deal of experience suggests the problematic nature of this assumption. In an oft-cited piece, Elizabeth Ellsworth poignantly asks why the radical teaching approach she learned through the theoretical writings of critical educational theorists does not feel empowering.[28] Teacher educators have long known that teaching practice cannot be learned through theory alone.

After much thought, I decided to base my theory of feminist teaching on my own practice—in particular, what I have learned through participating in and observing classroom process. This approach has many limits. I do not deal in this book with questions of curriculum development or of teaching textual interpretation or writing. Although these elements play an important role in academic teaching, others have written about them in depth.[29] Focusing on my own practice means that I cannot generalize about the work of other feminist teachers. There are, however, an increasing number of studies about what feminist teachers are doing in their classrooms.[30]

The institutional context of my practice, the fact that I have had the privilege of teaching relatively small (usually with under thirty-five students) classes, my particular fields of teaching, as well as my own approach to feminist politics, will all limit greatly the possibility of other teachers directly applying my analysis to their own work.[31] But I am not really aiming at that kind of application. Rather, in the spirit of feminist discourse as I describe it at the beginning of this chapter, I hope that feminists and teachers committed to teaching social justice in a variety of forms and contexts will find within my work points of connection and challenge, ways of thinking freshly about or probing more deeply into the various assumptions we bring to our practices.

Writing about my practice also raises issues about my relationship to students. More than anyone else, students have forced me to think more deeply about my teaching. In writing about students in this book, however, I try not to speak for students. No matter how hard I listen to what students say, they would describe their experiences of the classroom differently. Rather, I have attempted to capture the way in which student voices enlarge my own concept of feminist teaching. I do this by presenting throughout the book a series of vignettes based on my classroom experiences. My depictions of individual students are fictional. These vignettes are not reports but mostly invented tales based on my years of teaching.[32] Although many of these stories are not literally true, I try to make them truthful. I want to convey the essence of a situation I have faced repeatedly. Each story includes some hard fact that has made me reconsider my assumptions, some contradiction that has given me a painful pinch, some ambiguity that has confused me. These stories do not prove the arguments and analyses I offer so much as give birth to them.

Although I use the term *story* because it reminds the reader that most of my vignettes are not literal descriptions, my way of dealing with them disrupts the usual sense of a storyline. At the beginning of each section of the book, I relate one or more stories that to me represent challenges I have encountered in my teaching. Often, then, I begin to explore what I see as the theoretical issues involved in these scenarios. Later in the same section, I usually return to each story, to continue and/or comment on it in the light of my analysis. Through this approach I have tried to convey my thinking process and encourage readers to consider the applicability of that thinking to their own classrooms.

Some of my stories include descriptions of teaching strategies that I have employed and that some readers may find useful. However, this is not a book about teaching strategies. The literature on feminist pedagogy, including the pages of *Feminist Teacher* and *Radical Teacher* and numerous anthologies on feminist teaching, are filled with interesting and provocative teaching ideas, including detailed descriptions of how feminist and other teachers of social justice subjects organize courses, conduct classes, and invent pedagogical strategies.[33] I consider this work of inestimable value, and I continue to learn from it. But my purpose here is different. It is not so much to supply solutions as to figure out what the problems are and to offer some ways of talking about them that are open to discussion, rejection, acceptance, and/or revision.

One final note concerning language. Although I recognize its dangers, I often use the word *we* to talk about feminist teachers or feminist academics or people who care about feminism, teaching, and social justice. I use *we* to evoke a sense of broadly shared concerns regarding feminism or scholarship or teaching, and not to erase the differences that divide us. I also have decided to use feminine pronouns to describe feminist teachers and students, because most teachers who identify as feminists are women and because most students I teach are women. I do not mean to diminish the importance of discussing what it means for men to do feminist teaching or the role of men as students in feminist classes, but, again, I defer to those with more experience in these areas.[34]

Finally, my most potentially problematic language involves the terms *feminist, women's movement, women's liberation, women's oppression,* and *gender justice* or *gender injustice*. The problem concerning these terms is twofold. They are the subject of endless debates among feminists. Who is a feminist? Are women's movements the same thing as feminist movements? What is the aim of women's liberation? Is there such a thing as women's oppression? Does employing gender distinctions simply reinscribe gender differences? What do feminists mean by "justice"?

The second problem concerns whether these terms, so closely associated with second-wave feminism, are now so dated as to have lost their meaning. Many feminists avoid singular forms and use expressions such as *feminisms* and *women's movements* to remind us, correctly, of the many routes taken by feminist thought and women's activism. Some avoid terms such as *liberation* or *oppression* because they seem too extreme, too vague. *Oppression* is often replaced by Michel Foucault's language of "discipline" or the notion that people are "policed" through discourses that produce our thought and actions. The concept of "gender" has been criticized for erasing transgender experiences, while the language of "justice" tends to be confined to the work of feminist political theorists and philosophers.

I have chosen my terms deliberately. I like the words *oppression* and *liberation* because their breadth invites discussion and discourages feminists from narrowing arguments and analyses to one dimension of injustice. Iris Young suggests that the phenomenon of oppression has "five faces": exploitation, marginalization, powerlessness, cultural imperialism (by which she means rendering invisible the perspectives held by members of a dominated group), and violence.[35] Keeping these "faces" in mind not only promotes inquiry into the multiple forms of oppression suffered by women but also draws our attention to the relations among oppression based on class, race, and other factors. The breadth of a concept like oppression suggests a comparable breadth for a concept like liberation. Women, by this expanded notion, cannot be "free" unless we are free from economic servitude as well as invisibility, unless we become personally and politically empowered as well as safe from erasure and abuse. Although the terms *women* and *gender* may to some extent trap feminist language within old and unacceptable limits, I think we need to hang onto these terms at the same time that we criticize them. Women's movements, let alone feminist movements, require the notion of "women." Unless women in considerable numbers consider gender relations in some sense unjust, it is hard to imagine why anyone would call herself a feminist.

In many places, claiming a feminist identity is still a dangerous act. My decision to employ expressions such as *women's oppression* and *liberation* has a certain element of defiance in it. Although I recognize that feminist gains give militant language a quaint ring in some quarters, I think the deeper reason for avoiding the language of women's oppression and liberation is fear of its persistently radical content. The call to end women's oppression and to foster women's liberation is one of the most frightening demands a society can face. It frightens not only men and children but women themselves, including feminists. It is a demand that requires us to question our most intimate relationships as well as the organization of local, national, and global life. It is a demand that does not imply a clear response or a simple vision or utopia on which many women, let alone men, can agree. It implies, as Juliet Mitchell once termed it, "the longest revolution"—a complex process of change that cannot be achieved overnight.[36] Feminists can, and I believe should, fight for many immediate ends. But I also find a great deal of comfort in the idea that feminist commitment means working toward changes that are slow and deep. It helps me see my struggles to teach as a feminist as part of a larger picture, although the picture itself keeps changing and must be painted by many hands.

— 1 —

WHAT IS FEMINIST PEDAGOGY?

*During a lunch break at the women's studies conference, I turn to Velma
and ask her what session she will go to next. "One on feminist pedagogy,"
she says with excitement. As a new instructor, she's hoping to learn some
techniques she can use in her classes. Across the table, Cassie raises an
eyebrow. "I've had it with that touchy-feely crap," she mutters. "My students are anti-intellectual enough, and my job is to teach them how to
think." Lucille bristles. She uses feminist pedagogy in her antiracist teaching, she says, "and there is nothing soft about that!" Edith makes a calm-
ing gesture and wonders whether we are "headed toward one of those
masculine debates about who is right rather than remembering the care
we owe each other and our students."*

What is feminist pedagogy? Do all feminist teachers employ a feminist
pedagogy? Should they? Are there different feminist pedagogies, and, if
so, what are they? Is one superior to the others? Is feminist pedagogy simply another name for "good teaching"? As my story suggests, these questions cannot be answered easily.

My colleagues and I have been drawn to this conference because of
common interests. We all see ourselves as feminists. We share a passion
for learning and teaching. This passion is reinforced by the tremendous
emphasis that the feminist movement in the United States has placed on
women's higher education. Yet the movement itself is complex and filled
with conflicting values. So are our ideas about feminist pedagogy.

Cassie's desire to teach her women's studies students how to think echoes Betty Friedan's insistence in her 1963 classic *The Feminine Mystique*
that women take higher education seriously. For Friedan, like Mary Wollstonecraft two centuries earlier, knowledge and intellectual skills offered
women a way out of economic dependence and the narrowness of domestic life. Although Friedan recognized that the academic disciplines contained sexist assumptions, she believed that women desperately needed to

acquire disciplined ways of thinking. Fulfilling the goal of equality demanded that women gain access to the best education currently available.[1]

Edith's insistence on bringing the value of caring into our discussion reflects the underside of this liberal faith in science and scholarship. Wollstonecraft and Friedan expected educated women to continue to care for others. A society based only on individual achievement would be cruel and destructive. It needs, as Carol Gilligan argues in her feminist best-seller of 1982, *In a Different Voice*, values of caring and connection to offset the consequences of rampant individualism.[2] For teachers like Edith, feminism pointed to a central role for caring in education.

Lucille's spirited entrance into the luncheon discussion indicates the great seriousness with which African Americans have viewed education as a means for social change. Despite limited material resources, segregated schools symbolized to many black citizens the possibility of progress toward social justice. The demand for teachers in these schools made it possible for numerous black women to pursue their own educations. In this respect, desegregation proved a mixed blessing: it called into question the role of black educators and, as bell hooks has pointed out, undermined the assumption that education should serve the black community as a whole. As integration proceeded, more and more African Americans found themselves studying and teaching in white-dominated institutions, creating what Patricia Hill Collins calls, in her landmark 1990 volume *Black Feminist Thought*, the dilemma of "outsiders on the inside." Black feminist academics would feel this tension, but it also would propel them toward a multifaceted vision of teaching.[3]

Given the differences in how feminist teachers view their work, it might have been helpful for me and my lunch companions at the conference to explain to each other what we meant by "feminism." Yet, as I think about this story, I realize that spelling out our various feminist positions would not be sufficient for us to understand our different approaches to teaching. Lived politics rarely falls into neat packages. I might have described myself to the group as a socialist feminist, but I know that this is not a simple, unified position and that I incorporate many other strands of feminism into my thinking and teaching. Moreover, I know that my feminist politics do not clearly direct me to one form of teaching, and this is true for my colleagues as well.

In spite of Cassie's attack on "touchy-feely" teaching, she often criticizes dominant notions of rationality. Yet she teaches in a small, conservative college where students show little interest in ideas or texts and a lot of resentment toward feminism. She emphasizes rationality because she is determined to break through their refusal to think. Lucille, in contrast, teaches in a school that prides itself on progressive teaching methods and at least formally supports her work. Although she pushes her mostly white students to pay serious attention to racial oppression, she recognizes their fears and responds to them in a caring manner. While Edith emphasizes care, she also is quite "academic" in her teaching style. She insists that undergraduates at her large research university write long, scholarly papers. She does not want them to think that her interest in the ethic of care implies an abandonment of disciplinary standards.

In describing these complexities, I do not mean to discredit any feminist teachers. All teachers face the task of realizing sometimes conflicting values within the limits of concrete situations. Often, our values remain only loosely tied to our practices. But, loose as they may be, these ties have a crucial function. While institutional pressures strain the relation between values and practices, our willingness to reflect on that tension prevents us from slipping into a shallow pragmatism in which we seek only methods that "work." As much as I empathize with Velma's eagerness to find help with the problems that arise in her women's studies teaching, I worry that discovering an effective technique might keep her from asking why she considers something "a problem" in the first place.

How feminist academics and other teachers define and respond to the problems that arise in teaching is shaped in great part through the conjunction of a teacher's political and educational values, the models of teaching and learning she has encountered and adopted, and the institutional and social conditions under which she teaches. Moreover, an individual teacher may subscribe to conflicting values or models of teaching and learning. She may be subject to contradictory institutional and social conditions. She may modify or abandon some of her values and acquire new models of teaching as she changes institutions or the institutional and social conditions change around her. Little wonder that answering the question "What is feminist pedagogy?" turns out to be such a difficult task.

The answer I propose in this book emphasizes *the value of social movements* to give voice to the needs and desires of oppressed people and to move society toward social justice.[4] Very simply, I see the United States as a society that has failed in significant ways to realize its democratic promise of freedom, equality, and justice. To realize this promise, we need to change social structures that disempower and marginalize certain groups of people and to radically question the meaning and application of basic democratic values. Social movements provide the main vehicle for this questioning because they bring suppressed needs and desires into public consciousness and have the potential to transform the process of political discussion and decision making. Of course, social movements do not always speak for democratic values. Fascism may begin as a social movement. Movements themselves can express contradictory aims. Yet, for people seeking social justice within a formally democratic order, social movements seem to me a fruitful source of social change. They can bring pressure against as well as permeate the dominant political, economic, and social structures. They can create new and more egalitarian relationships and institutions.

Feminism is such a movement, but one that is neither simple nor unified.[5] Feminists continuously divide along lines of political philosophy, class, race, sexual orientation, culture, nationality, and a host of other factors. Some feminists view these divisions as inherently destructive and fragmenting to what ought to be a united movement. Others believe such differentiations enable less privileged and powerful women or the feminists who speak for them to have a political voice. Still others, like me, consider this articulation of difference not only necessary but valuable. There is nothing self-evident about "liberation" or "justice." Even the most committed activists in movements for social justice can disagree on its meaning for specific contexts. Without the opportunity to delineate differences, no feminist political discourse is possible. Political action becomes limited to those positions on which feminists spontaneously agree or to which all can be persuaded. But given the wide range of differing situations and the differences of power and privilege, confining political efforts to actions on which feminists agree would greatly limit the movement. To be at all meaningful, the movement must, as Gloria Anzaldúa and other U.S. feminists of color have insisted, include many voices.[6]

Moreover, feminism as a social movement did not develop in a vacuum. Its very existence as well as its ability to attend to different feminist voices depends on its relationship to other movements for social justice. The reinvigoration of feminism in the 1960s owed a great deal to the movements for civil rights, economic justice, and peace. Feminism in the United States also has been profoundly shaped by movements for sexual liberation; the rights of people with disabilities, ethnic and religious minorities, and the aged; the protection of the environment; and the nurturance of children. Feminist activists often create bridges across such movements, through movements such as black feminism, ecofeminism, and lesbian feminism. This interweaving of individuals and movements does not run smoothly. It includes sometimes painful and destructive competition over values and limited resources. It involves deviousness and betrayals as a given movement provides opportunities for individual mobility or as its proponents struggle to survive reactionary responses. Yet this same interweaving of movements also gives feminism its durability and viability, its potential to change and grow.

The feminist movement that began in the United States in the 1960s and continued into the 1980s changed in numerous ways. Although grassroots activists created many of their own alternative organizations, activism also permeated governmental and other large institutions. As the number of women able and willing to do unpaid political work declined, movement energies became increasingly concentrated in large, formal organizations. This trend had mixed results. Diminished grassroots activity reduced the sense of urgency and the pressure on mainstream institutions to support feminist projects. The fact that some feminists had or were able to get jobs within such institutions made it possible for many of us to persist in our political efforts even when the country took a more conservative turn. Higher education offered one of the more hospitable sites for feminist activity. Women's studies and feminist teaching of many kinds became a vital location for movement work.

In this context, I see my feminist teaching through a double lens. It is part of a system of higher education that claims to help students succeed in society. At the same time, it is part of a social movement aimed at challenging and changing the current social order. In some sense, I as a teacher stand at the point at which the feminist movement interfaces with a non-movement world. The line between what is "inside" and "outside" the movement is not fixed, however. It can be firm or flexible, and students help construct it. At times, I firmly mark the boundary by saying, for instance, "Feminism requires us to look at certain topics that will make you uncomfortable." I also draw lines through my choice of readings or by the course organization. Students, in turn, may contest these boundaries by making suggestions or demands or by questioning what we are studying. They not only challenge me to negotiate the curriculum, to use Garth Boomer's expression, but to reconsider how I define "the movement" itself.[7]

My ideas about feminist teaching also are influenced by *educational values* associated with movements for social justice. Social movements require modes of communicating their purposes. Some modes are highly spontaneous, like the bread riots through which women historically have expressed their outrage at the difficulty of obtaining food to feed their families. To endure, however, social movements must develop ways to conceptualize and articulate their aims and to deal with the conflicting needs and desires that emerge as movements change. Activists and academics have long seen education as a vehicle for developing such thinking and communication.

John Dewey's progressive education grew out of the U.S. progressive reform movement of the late nineteenth and early twentieth centuries.[8] That movement fostered in him a vision of citizens as well as experts talking about how to solve the problems of poverty, mass immigration, and incipient class warfare. Antonio Gramsci's educational theory grew out of his communist party's attempt to organize poor and working-class Italians in the 1920s. He believed that education would develop in them a strong and unified voice that could challenge and change an oppressive economic system. Paulo Freire's pedagogy of the oppressed grew out of the socialist and liberation theology movements in Latin America. Through literacy education, he sought to engage the rural poor of Brazil in working for social change.

Freire's ideas, which developed at the same time as the 1960s wave of social justice movements of which feminism was a part, became particularly well known among U.S. activists because the values for which he argued mirrored many of theirs. He saw the experience of oppression as a source of knowledge. He was wary of teachers imposing their class-biased ideas on students. He exposed the dominant mode of teaching as "banking education" that treated students like empty containers into which knowledge could be poured. He proposed that students and teachers become "co-investigators" of the oppressive realities students faced, so that they could join the movement for social justice.

Although these and other political pedagogies remain rich resources for feminist teaching, they arose out of social movements that differed considerably from the "second-wave" feminism of the 1960s and 1970s.[9] Second-wave feminism placed a special emphasis on the relation between what in dominant terms are often labeled "personal" matters—including sexuality, reproduction, and caring—and the world of political talk and action. Feminism as a movement also has had to contend with the especially problematic character of the group it claims to represent. Women are divided from each other in so many ways that the very possibility of a movement focused on gender justice is continuously open to question. Finally, and stemming directly from these other two characteristics, a feminist movement requires a way of talking that can address both the political meaning of seemingly personal matters and the wide differences in how women experience and resist oppression. This need to develop a *political discourse adequate to feminism as a social movement* lies at the heart of how I conceive of feminist teaching.

The impulse to develop such a discourse emerged in the United States as part of an attempt to revitalize political discourse in general.[10] During the 1950s, talk about social justice had been stifled by McCarthyite persecutions. A national culture of conformity made it difficult to express dissident ideas. Revelations of Stalin's persecutions in the USSR created a crisis of confidence in political discussion among many leftists. Violent attacks on the civil rights and peace demonstrators of that decade sent the message that speaking out against injustice was a dangerous, even deadly, step to take.

Yet just as voicing dissent seemed a nearly hopeless endeavor, new movements were emerging once again to support discourse on social justice.[11] Ella Baker, a mostly unsung leader of the civil rights movement, encouraged community members to take leadership by sharing what they had learned through their experiences of racial oppression. New left activists, seeking to revive the socialist movement, incorporated personal issues into their notion of political discussion and tried to develop forms of self-criticism that would constrain autocratic speech. Peace activists, including those working within the Quaker tradition, stressed the process of patiently talking together until members of a group could reach consensus. Feminists involved in a grassroots women's movement sought a way of talking together about women's oppression that would overcome the silencing that many of them experienced in male-dominated activism.

This consciousness-raising approach to political discourse took identifiable shape among U.S. feminists in the late 1960s. Inspired by the civil rights and other social justice movements, including movements for national liberation, women came together in small groups to talk about their experiences of gender oppression.[12] These early gatherings had an electric quality for many of those who participated in them. For the first time, they talked in political groups about the shame, anger, and great frustration they experienced in their attempts to live full lives. Topics that had been considered strictly "personal," such as how a woman felt about her body, how sexual violence or sexual pleasure affected her, the consequences of marrying and having children, what it meant to become educated, how to deal with problems with work, at home or outside it, all became the focus of intense discussion. Many women who had been active in other social justice causes recognized that gender, too, was a site of oppression. Others, who had never been involved in activism, began to understand the need to oppose social injustice through examining their own lives.

The consciousness-raising of the late 1960s and early 1970s was not embraced by all feminist activists. Some felt that talking about oppression drained movement energy and undermined action by offering an outlet for anger and frustration and by keeping attention focused on individual problems. Other feminists, who considered a particular radical or feminist theory the foundation of political action, rejected the consciousness-raising emphasis on experience as antitheoretical and therefore antipolitical. Moreover, practitioners of consciousness-raising did not themselves espouse an agreed-on theory or follow one precise method. Some groups made more room for political debate. Others shied away from it. Some spent more time on individual problems. Others put more energy into analyzing structures of injustice. Some focused on areas such as politics or work or domestic life where members shared experiences—such as women who had been active in the peace movement or women who were artists or were married. Others ranged over a wide variety of topics. Some groups consisted of women who were deeply involved in activism. Others had members with little or no experience with politics. Like the emerging movement itself, groups that declared their purpose to be "consciousness-

raising" were predominantly white and middle class in their composition.[13] Yet, white women from working-class backgrounds joined such
groups, as did some women of color. In this period of heightened political
awareness, of course, women of color and working-class women also
talked about gender, race, and class issues in informal settings that were
not necessarily labeled consciousness-raising sessions.

Variation in formal consciousness-raising groups stemmed mainly from
the fact that the women's liberation movement in the United States was
highly decentralized. Although the National Organization for Women
(NOW) played an important role in defining a national movement, feminists hotly debated that role. Indeed, many feminists viewed any form of
centralized leadership as inimical to women's liberation. Having first expressed skepticism, NOW eventually adopted consciousness-raising as an
organizing tool. But no single feminist group had the power or authority to
establish standards for consciousness-raising.[14] In a period in which small
political groups produced a myriad of leaflets, pamphlets, and magazines
and a great deal of political information spread by word of mouth, ideas
about consciousness-raising were bound to vary.

Rather than representing one unambiguous method, then, consciousness-
raising might be seen as a general approach to talking about women's oppression and liberation. That approach was articulated by radical feminist
activists Kathie Sarachild and Pamela Allen, in distinct but overlapping
descriptions. In her 1968 statement "A Program for Feminist Consciousness-
Raising," Sarachild (who is credited with being the first to apply the term
consciousness-raising to this feminist process) stressed the importance of
women creating a type of "class consciousness" as the basis for their mass
movement.[15] Through consciousness-raising, women would pay close attention to their feelings as a way of understanding women's oppression.
They would testify to their experiences of oppression, discuss key issues,
and seek to find "common roots where women have opposite feelings and
experiences." They would have to confront what Sarachild and many of
her political sisters called "resistances to consciousness": the refusal of
some women to recognize that they were oppressed or the rationales that
others produced for not dealing with their oppression. Consciousness-
raising would help women understand how they sometimes employed such
resistances to survive. These discussions would also enable women to analyze their fears about talking with each other, as well as their fears about
acting in their own cause. They would discuss "possible methods of struggle" by looking at both historical precedents and current circumstances.
They would try to understand oppression in all its forms, including white
women's complicity in racial and other forms of oppression. They would
develop actions to promote consciousness among more and more women.

Pamela Allen's 1970 booklet *Free Space: A Perspective on the Small*

Group in Women's Liberation emphasized the importance of trust and group support in women's sharing experiences.[16] Allen stressed that members had to speak honestly and treat each other as equals. She argued that women needed to give each other "nonjudgmental space," so that each woman could express her feelings and "view of her life" without ridicule. According to Allen, consciousness-raising proceeded by a series of stages. In "opening up," women would begin to articulate their feelings to others. In "sharing," they would relate their experiences and begin to build "a collage of similar experiences from all women present" to "arrive at an understanding of all the social conditions of women by pooling descriptions of the forms oppression has taken in each individual's life." Then members would analyze their experiences, to gain a broader understanding of society. At this point, "books and other documentations become crucial" in helping women discover their own capacities to "think conceptually." Finally, in the stage of "abstracting," members of the group would strive for "a synthesis of the analysis" by which to establish priorities and a vision of what liberation might entail. No single group, however, could develop a program for women's liberation, Allen noted. This would require that "many organized groupings of women" articulate their needs. Any program for the movement would have to "be determined by poor women, and especially black and other non-white women" who, as Allen put it, were "the most oppressed of our sisters."

Both within and between these notions of consciousness-raising many strains emerged. Sometimes activists conveyed an image of consciousness-raising as a kind of scientific endeavor, in which women would gather data from their own experiences rather than relying on past theories. Sarachild compared the process to the seventeenth-century scientific revolution.[17] Yet this image was in tension with the acknowledgment that some theories and historical experience could be of great value. Moreover, the emphasis on collective empowerment did not always fit neatly with the need for individual women to become empowered. The assumption that members of the group would arrive at a common analysis of experiences and feelings conflicted with the recognition that women could disagree in their interpretations of such experiences and feelings. The commitment to discovering the common roots of women's oppression clashed with the acknowledgment that racial, class, and other forms of injustice might lead to great differences in how differently situated women defined oppression.

Other dimensions of consciousness-raising also persisted in uneasy relation. Many women experienced consciousness-raising like a bolt of lightning that completely transformed their view of the world. Yet, understanding the day-to-day workings of injustice and how to react to it effectively required more careful exploration. Some found the consciousness-raising process healing, because by being able to describe lifelong hurts, they were freed from shame and self-blame. However, individual healing did not necessarily motivate women to work for social change. Similarly, consciousness-raising often provoked anger with the injustices that were revealed and discussed, but anger alone could lead to self-destructive behavior. Finally, consciousness-raising often resulted in the development of strong and deep bonds among women that could support activism. But feelings of comfort and even love of other women could lead to an exclusive coziness that discouraged action or, in the case of heterosexual women who became uncomfortable with the intimacy, to homophobic panic.

These and other contradictions in the theory and practice of consciousness-raising might have taken decades to understand and unravel.[18] Yet, by the time I became involved in the movement in the mid-1970s, many of the activists I encountered thought that the consciousness-raising period was over. The movement was changing so rapidly that a 1969 or 1970 consciousness-raising group seemed part of a distant past. At the same time, the spirit of consciousness-raising still permeated many feminist activities. Feminist political talk often incorporated attention to feelings, experiences, analyses, and actions. The belief that feminist consciousness had to take into account the great differences among women was (at least in the circles in which I moved) regularly affirmed. Lesbians of color and white lesbians had embarked on their own consciousness-raising efforts to explore the intersections between gender, race, and sexual orientation. Feminists of all sexual orientations had attempted or were trying to start consciousness-raising groups with women from different classes and races. The notion of consciousness-raising as a kind of scientific investigation had faded into the background. Both activists and academics had raised serious questions about the standards of "science" and its political implications. As I became increasingly involved in the feminist movement, the political potential of consciousness-raising seemed to me to lie less in its capacity to generate a single scientific analysis on which action could be based than in providing women an opportunity to learn from and teach each other, collectively address problems of social injustice, and imagine and think through alternative responses.

As I began to put together an interpretation of consciousness-raising, the movement offered me only a rough form of guidance. I engaged in my own consciousness-raising by talking with other feminists about the relations between sexuality, work, and politics. I attended feminist meetings and workshops and conferences and tried to figure out what kind of consciousness-raising was taking place in these settings. I looked at what was happening in my own feminist classrooms, as I sought to engage students in discussing experiences, feelings, ideas, and actions concerning women's oppression. Over a number of years, I was able to identify those aspects of consciousness-raising that seemed most valuable for my teaching. I only slowly realized that my interpretation of consciousness-raising focused on its characteristics as a form of political discourse. I was not seeking to construct a general model of consciousness-raising but to understand what I, as a feminist teacher, was doing.

FROM CONSCIOUSNESS-RAISING TO TEACHING THROUGH FEMINIST DISCOURSE

I am at a conference, sitting with a group of Jewish feminists. For the first time in my life, I am discussing what it means to be a Jewish woman. I find myself speaking and listening to thoughts and feelings I long had kept to myself or for which I never had words. I am amazed to hear my sentiments echoed in the words of others and equally astonished to discover the great differences among us. Yet, we all have been affected in one way or another by the same set of conditions: anti-Semitism, the Holocaust, the fact that we are not only Jews but women.

My affinity group meets to plan its strategy for an upcoming women's anti-military protest at a large army depot. As we try to talk about how we will deal with confronting the military police, our discussion languishes. Finally, one woman admits her fear of being injured and says what it would mean to her to be struck by a club. Suddenly, others begin to talk about our experiences and feelings about harm to our bodies. Based on these stories, we are able to agree on who will take what physical risks and how we will support each other.

During a long workshop sponsored by a feminist organization on the topic of sexual orientation and friendship, anger starts to build. One after another, women tell stories of betrayal. A lesbian feels that her bisexual friend has deserted her by becoming involved with a man. A heterosexual woman feels rebuffed when her best friend comes out as a lesbian. A queer-identified woman believes that gay men make better friends than lesbians. As we talk about the ways in which misogyny and homophobia weave in and out of our relationships, we begin to see their impact on our political work. We recognize some of the reasons it is so hard to cooperate, to build coalitions, to sustain our efforts.

What do these stories say about consciousness-raising and what it can contribute to feminist teaching? Talking together in these feminist contexts, *women increase their awareness of relations between self and the world through sharing experiences, feelings, and ideas about the needs for and possibilities of liberatory actions.* This process has many features, some of which I will look at in subsequent chapters. Here, however, I want to look at consciousness-raising as an overall process and how I see it reflected in my own pedagogical practice.

The first and often most striking aspect of this process concerns a *shift in attention.*[19] This shift may be quite abrupt, when we suddenly pay attention to something that has been completely obscured or ignored. Some women who engaged in early consciousness-raising described their new awareness as an instantaneous "click" of recognition: a new view or interpretation of gender relations.[20] But the shift in attention also can be more gradual. In the story about my Jewish feminist consciousness-raising group, I begin a slow process of recognizing how being a Jewish woman affects my political identity and actions. I had not paid close attention to these aspects of my life because they involved contradictions that made me intensely uncomfortable (such as wanting to preserve my relations with non-Jewish feminists who sometimes made anti-Semitic assumptions) and that I could not see a way to resolve. As I become more aware, I also begin to think about what might be different.

Shifts in attention are usually provoked by changes in our relation to our environment. The kind of shift involved in feminist consciousness-raising may be triggered by reading a feminist text, being the object of an attempted rape, or seeing a news report about a factory that employs undocumented workers. In my feminist classes, I seek to shift student attention to questions that concern feminists and other social justice activists. The students may vary greatly in their familiarity with these questions. Some may find it shocking to pay close attention to the reality of women's economic exploitation; others may have been vaguely aware of it; still others may be quite familiar with this phenomenon. Although students frequently try to "change the subject" in the face of topics at which they do not want to look closely, part of my work is to see that their attention does not shift away too quickly.

The decision to keep the class gaze focused on a pattern or instance of oppression for a shorter or longer period of time is not easy or mechanical. Gaze can become fixated and static and reinforce rather than reduce a sense of powerlessness. Attention retains its vibrancy when it has the chance to vary. Thus, while insisting on the centrality of oppression to feminist discourse, my teaching may also direct attention away from immediate discomfort or pain and toward reflection on it, or away from guilt over other people's suffering to considering some of the very practical reforms that others have been able to effect. These shifts stimulate rather than deaden desire, by suggesting that political discourse can both speak to the hurts that stem from injustice and provide concrete visions of possible change.

A second aspect of the consciousness-raising process is its emphasis on relations, in particular *relations of unequal power*. If no systematic differences in power existed between women and men, there would be no reason to discuss gender injustice or women's liberation. If no power inequities persisted between heterosexual and lesbian or queer women, the workshop on friendship across sexual differences (in the story I tell at the beginning of this section) would not have had to address these differences as a political problem. To assert that there are systemic power differentials does not mean that participants in consciousness-raising can easily describe such a system. Indeed, one of the purposes of consciousness-raising is to develop and examine ideas about both the blatant and the subtle workings of power. All the elements of consciousness-raising—the sharing of experiences, reflecting on feelings, evaluating theories, and envisioning actions—promote this examination. So do the dynamics within the group itself. No group of people can talk very long without being affected by power differences. To talk about power in the world means, to some extent, to talk about power in the group.

Feminist teaching, too, concerns issues of power. To call myself a feminist teacher implies a claim that certain relations of power are unjust. It implies that I will use my power as a teacher to place certain topics and readings about injustice on the agenda for classroom discussion. Every time I say *feminist,* students know that they will have to address inequities of power. During the semester, some students object to the term. Indirectly, they challenge my power to make these issues central to the course. It is clear from what they say in discussions that they believe that gender-based power differences do not exist or, if they do, that paying attention to them "makes things even worse." But making things worse is, in a sense, one of the major features of consciousness-raising. That is, it requires participants to pay attention to incidents and patterns that may make us uncomfortable and, if faced alone, can lead to helpless rage or shame and a profound sense of powerlessness.

Paying attention to relations of unequal power involves making *connections among things that hitherto did not seem connected.* In the story I tell about the antimilitary affinity group, I do not begin by thinking about how military ideals of strength and courage might affect my willingness to engage in civil disobedience. I am not thinking about how my youthful experiences of boys picking on girls as they were developing breasts may have shaped my image of physical vulnerability. I only gradually make these connections. When women in the affinity group become willing to talk about our bodies and our feelings about them, it becomes possible for us to make connections between such experiences and our plans for political action.

Similarly, in teaching, when a student who is upset by receiving pornographic messages on her workplace computer is willing to talk about this in a classroom discussion, it becomes possible for the class to think about the connections between her experience and larger patterns. Several other women nod their heads or raise their hands to report that they, too, receive such messages. I urge the students to speculate about how these various incidents might relate to structures of domination. Our readings on occupational segregation, or the psychology of women, or sexual harassment may all suggest possible connections for us to explore. So may other experiences that students have had or readings in other classes on computer science or communications or ethics.

This discussion is fruitful, but it is also complicated by how we define and disagree about some of our basic terms, including *sexual harassment*. For the effort to describe the relations of unequal power also involves the issue of *naming experiences of oppression*. In the early years of second-wave feminism, Betty Friedan wrote about "the problem that has no name," and feminist activists continually generated terms such as *sexual harassment* to help women identify and reconceptualize relations for which they had no words.[21] Decades after second-wave activists began to name and describe women's experiences of gender injustice, feminist language has become rich and diverse. Terms such as *sexual harassment* seem less revelatory and more simply descriptive by pointing to a problem that many students in my classes recognize as requiring some attention.

Yet, as the classroom discussion of pornographic messages unfolds, the need for naming begins to surface once again. Although no one denies that some men try to sexually exploit or intimidate women workers, many of us still struggle to name experiences and thoughts for which adequate language still does not exist: words to describe situations that do not clearly fall under the rubric of sexual harassment yet in which something "feels wrong" or appears to involve an unfair use of power or a sexual violation. As we engage in this feminist discourse, our attempts to "name" shed light on incidents we have not stopped to think about before, on things that have seemed just part of the environment.

This discussion takes place because a student is willing to reveal something about her self. Thus, the consciousness-raising process is *self-reflective* in the sense that it requires women to pay attention to themselves. This feature has led to criticism that consciousness-raising is self-indulgent and selfish (charges that historically have been leveled at women who do not devote their energies to others). But the self-reflective quality in consciousness-raising is no more self-indulgent or selfish than responding to any deep need or desire. In some ways, it is impossible to respond individually or collectively to injustice without being sufficiently self-reflective. In the affinity group featured in my second story, we cannot figure out how to act during the peace protest until we pay serious attention to the meaning of the action for our physical and emotional selves. We each have to think about how we would feel if a military club struck different parts of our bodies and what the experience of arrest means to us. Such reflections require us to talk about the particular selves we bring to this political context, how we feel about those selves, whether we hope or fear they might change, and how they affect our prospects for political collaboration.

My feminist teaching encourages both the students and me to be self-reflective in ways that are both uncomfortable and liberating. For instance, the student who painfully describes how it feels to receive pornographic messages may not feel comfortable speaking this way. Despite the power inequities she faces as a low-paid woman employee, she may worry that her colleagues and the students in our class will see her as a "wimp," as sexually unsophisticated and not "cool" enough to take such messages in her stride. Yet being self-reflective may deepen the class discussion. In trying to describe her feelings, the student creates an opening for an exploration in which others can join. What might initially seem a problem only for her individual "self" is gradually transformed into a problem in which we can reflect on the relation between selves and others.

Consciousness-raising enables women to reveal a great deal about themselves because they see the process as *nonjudgmental*. Ideally, each person has a chance to describe her experiences, to share her feelings and thoughts without being silenced by standards concerning what speech is permitted, what not. Nonjudgmentalness enables those of us who attend the workshop on sexual orientation and friendship to say things that under other circumstances we might withhold for fear of being misunderstood, ignored, attacked, or humiliated. However, speaking out is also dependent on others listening to what we have to say and making some effort to understand what and why we are saying it. Thus, nonjudgmentalness is not simply a matter of withholding criticism or passively taking in the other's words. It requires active listening, to "get" both the familiar and unfamiliar elements in the other's speech. Nonjudgmental listening to women's words about gender injustice involves trying to understand the harm done by oppression and the responses women have made and can envision.[22]

Nonjudgmentalness needs to be distinguished from the equally important value of *cultivating political judgment*.[23] Cultivating political judgment requires participants in political discourse to both listen to and understand a variety of perspectives on a given problem and to look at the meaning and consequences of taking one rather than another political direction. Reason plays an important role in this process, but consciousness-raising suggests that narrowly construed reasoning may not provide an adequate guide in deciding how to act in the face of gender injustice. In each of the vignettes at the beginning of this section, participants in the discussions listen not only to the reasons others give but to the person herself—to her stories, to her feelings, to the actions she has taken or envisions. Political judgment requires that we understand the particulars that bear on our decisions, and it is through listening to many voices that we learn to appreciate these particulars. In supporting the decisions made by individuals or making more collective decisions, we need to recognize the meaning of such judgments for women leading different lives.

Nonjudgmentalness plays an important role in my feminist teaching. In part, this influence is expressed through my encouraging and trying to model an attitude of active listening to everyone and everything that is said in class. This approach cannot be simply a matter of teaching technique, because if I do not truly believe that each person potentially has something to contribute to the feminist discourse, I cannot sustain such listening for long. Sometimes I fail to do so, and sometimes students become impatient and angry with me or each other ("I didn't sign up for this course to listen to the stupid comments of other students!" or "Why didn't you stop her when she talked in a racist way?" or "I just can't stand it when she opens her mouth!"). Although such responses challenge the possibility of non-judgmentalness, they also raise valuable questions about the meaning of feminist political discourse which can be addressed by the class itself. Why should students listen to other students? Why do some ways of talking make us so angry that we are no longer willing to talk or listen? What responsibility, if any, do we have for how our talk affects others? Such questions do not constitute a distraction from developing good judgment about feminist political issues. They are part of what is required for any judgment to be considered a good one.

As this description implies, consciousness-raising is a *collective and cooperative* activity. People may become aware of oppression through a variety of means, but groups add an entirely different dimension to this process. Every aspect of collective consciousness-raising involves cooperation. Sharing experiences and feelings requires others to listen and in some fashion respond to them. Analysis demands an exchange of ideas through which different interpretations can be compared and assessed. Judgments about how to act in the face of oppression depend on such interactions to acquire a solid basis. Thus, consciousness-raising does not merely provide a platform for individuals to describe their experiences, feelings, and ideas. It provides a *collaborative process through which individuals are constituted and supported as political speakers and actors.*[24]

My encounter with the Jewish feminist consciousness-raising group enables me to grasp that what I say or fail to say as a Jew in the predominantly Christian, U.S. feminist movement has political meaning. That meaning gains depth and complexity through my listening to the experiences and feelings of others and voicing my own. As our group tries to trace the connections between gender and ethnicity or religion, I see how it is possible to engage in political talk with other Jewish feminists, non-feminist Jewish women, and non-Jewish feminists. Feminist discourse gives me a new basis on which to make political choices.

Most college and university courses do not begin as collective and cooperative projects. Students sign up for my feminist classes for all sorts of reasons, few of which entail the desire to work collectively. But, if they do not already know it, they soon learn that feminist talk involves collaboration. It involves listening to experiences and feelings about gender, racial, and other forms of oppression that may make students and me highly uncomfortable. It entails studying and developing analyses of oppression that may have very direct, and not necessarily welcome, implications for how we as class members are living our lives. Collaboration may pose problems that some of us have not previously considered and that require painful choices. Yet collaboration also can be filled with excitement. Learning how or strengthening the capacity to think and speak about oppression requires us to create an arena in which such thought and speech is supported. In this respect, when classrooms are informed by the spirit of consciousness-raising, everyone plays a role in making themselves and others into political speakers.

Thus, consciousness-raising *supports and generates women's political agency* because this process assumes that problems flowing from women's oppression are serious political issues and that women are capable of understanding, addressing, and responding to those issues. In feminist classroom discourse, both male students and nonfeminist women students can play a role in constructing women as political agents by taking gender injustice seriously and by seeing women as capable of working toward social change. Similarly, the notion that consciousness-raising supports and generates women's political agency requires an approach to classroom discourse that does not prejudge how variously situated women will relate to it. In this respect, teaching based on consciousness-raising is not a lockstep process that transforms students into feminists. It promotes awareness of gender injustice and cultivates women's capacity to make their own decisions about how to respond to that injustice, even when these decisions differ.

Consciousness-raising also entails *action*. Fundamentally, consciousness-raising gets its meaning from the possibility of action. This does not imply that consciousness-raising groups must be action groups. The workshop on sexual orientation and friendship in the third story I tell is not an action group, although many participants are activists. Some early proponents of consciousness-raising made a careful distinction between groups organized for consciousness-raising only and those organized for action. In other contexts, however, activists engaged in consciousness-raising also organized political projects. Kathie Sarachild's program includes the notion that consciousness-raising would lead to "zap" actions (quick, dramatic public demonstrations) that would themselves raise consciousness.[25]

Some second-wave activists devoted considerable energy to helping other women organize consciousness-raising groups. Others organized demonstrations or projects to serve women. Individuals also took actions that spoke directly to their "personal" situations. They left abusive husbands, had abortions, got or quit jobs, joined or left political action groups. Although for one woman finding a solution to her individual problem might end her involvement with feminist activism, for another being able to solve a pressing personal problem might make it possible to get involved in or continue such activism.

Feminist classroom discourse is also oriented toward action, although the kind of actions may vary greatly. In my classes, a small proportion of students come to class already engaged in clearly identified feminist political activities. Some come with questions about how feminism relates to their work in education or the human services. Others wonder how or whether feminist ideas bear on their personal relationships. Still others think about joining an activist group. Some are thinking about careers as feminist scholars and wonder about the personal and political implications. As discussion proceeds, the dominant distinction between the personal and political begins to blur. Students engaged in what is normally considered political action may discover the connections between their political actions and factors they considered personal or professional. An AIDS activist begins to see that her assumptions about women's sexuality have made it difficult for her to think of AIDS as a women's issue. A middle-class student serving an internship as a counselor starts to pay attention to the fact that most of her clients are poor women and thus can come for only a few of the many sessions they need. An abused woman may end up working in a project for battered women.

Consciousness-raising does not end with action, however. Rather, the process has an *ongoing* quality. This feature has been obscured by the notion of consciousness-raising as a personal transformation brought about by "clicks" through which individual women suddenly come to see the world and their situation in it from an entirely different perspective.[26] While such moments clearly occur both inside and outside consciousness-raising groups, they do not exhaust the meaning of this process and its full political implications. Although in the story I tell about my affinity group, individual members gain certain insights through our discussion, we have to continue talking to continue our political work. Although the workshop on sexual orientation and friendship helps those of us who participate in it to think and act differently, new social conditions and new social movements require our discourse to evolve. Indeed, in this very story the emergence of a bisexual movement requires us to talk differently about friendship and sexual orientation than we might have several years earlier. If consciousness-raising is seen as political discourse, it cannot end with a given insight, action, or moment of agreement.

In some respects, the notion of consciousness-raising as an ongoing process stands in stark contrast to the usual classroom format. Classes meet for a bureaucratically determined period of time that has little if anything to do with a process of cultivating political talk and judgment. Yet the classroom structure also resembles ordinary life, in the sense that most people have limited opportunities for political talk and it takes effort to sustain such discussions. The students and I are aware of the time frame in which we operate, both because it may become oppressive to any or all of us (too long, too short, too crowded between other activities) and because this arena of feminist discourse will be dissolved with the end of the semester. Yet to the extent that our discourse succeeds, both the students and I often feel reluctant to end it. We are left with the question of how we can pursue these issues in workplace, home, and religious, political, or other associations.

Finally, addressing questions of gender justice in the classroom or the worlds outside requires participants to attend to a feature of consciousness-raising that crosscuts many of the characteristics I have described: its concern with *the relations between personal and political life.* The importance of looking at these relations was first captured by Carol Hanisch's maxim "the personal is political."[27] This maxim has been open to numerous interpretations, including the belief that feminism calls for the abolition of all privacy or that all political matters are fundamentally questions of individual psychology. These interpretations make little sense in the larger context of feminist activism. The almost universal feminist demand for reproductive rights implies some notion of privacy. The feminist insistence that women's liberation requires a radical questioning of the division of labor implies an analysis that must go beyond individual needs. "The personal is political" suggests that women develop and sustain their agency by paying political attention to those needs and desires that emerge in the context of daily life.[28] These may include the need for more help with their children, the desire for sexual gratification, the need for water or firewood or a paying job to run a household, the desire to travel or paint a picture.

The story I tell about the workshop on sexual orientation taps into deeply personal impulses toward love and sexual fulfillment. As Nancy Fraser and others have pointed out, however, needs and desires are not self-evident.[29] Although some, such as the need for food, may be more immediately compelling, any attempt to define and assess the political implications of needs and desires requires discussion. Women engage in such discussion everyday, as part of making decisions about how to manage our lives. One woman talks to her friend about whether she should encourage her girl child to join an all-boys athletic team or to pursue a more traditionally female activity. Another woman talks to her coworker about whether they should risk losing their jobs by questioning the toxic materials they are handling or take the chance that their bodies will be injured.

The idea of the personal as political implies an expanded concept of "the political" that includes not only formal political structures and social movements such as women's liberation but cultural patterns (e.g., "myths"), economic organization (e.g., including women's unpaid work), and political discourse itself (e.g., consciousness-raising as a political act). A broadened idea of the "political" calls into question many taken-for-granted terms of democratic political discourse. What is the meaning of "equality" when women participating in a political discussion have to leave in the middle of it to tend to their aged mothers? What is the meaning of "citizen" for someone whose recent rape has deprived her of the capacity to speak about her life? What is the meaning of political "choice" for a woman who must choose between the low-paying job she needs to support her children and the risk of being fired by talking with others about forming a union?

By raising such questions, consciousness-raising promotes feminist discussion of the public/private distinction. White middle-class feminists of the second wave often targeted the public/private distinction for criticism because they experienced the private, domestic sphere as a trap or a prison where they were dependent on male economic support and subject to physical and psychological abuse. From this perspective, the public world of paid work and political activity promised liberation. But, as Aída Hurtado argues, this logic does not apply to all women. In the United States, she points out, poor women of color do not have privacy because of the continued invasion of the state into their "private" lives.[30] Unlike privileged women, their problem is not exclusion from the public world but how to survive in it. Survival requires women of color to develop political skills and strategies for dealing with oppression from their earliest years. In an important sense, as Hurtado suggests, racially and economically oppressed women do not need consciousness-raising to become political agents. They have no choice but to think and act.

Hurtado's analysis enriches the notion of consciousness-raising in several respects. First, feminist political discourse cannot take the public/private distinction for granted, either its advantages or its disadvantages for differently situated women. Joining the public world of work does offer a certain degree of liberation for many women and, at the same time, becomes a form of servitude for others. State intervention into private life may dehumanize some women, while for others it may prevent them from being beaten to death by their partners. To make matters more complex, the same woman who is being dehumanized by the state welfare system may welcome the intervention of the police if she is being beaten. The same woman who protests against state involvement in her reproductive choices may want the state to guarantee her equal right to employment. Thus, consciousness-raising requires exploration of the meaning of the public/private distinction rather than assuming that feminists already know its implications for our politics.

Hurtado's point about political agency also supports an interpretation of consciousness-raising that focuses less exclusively on the process of illuminating oppression and more on the relation between talk and action. Awareness of oppression does not automatically make people into political agents. Neither do many kinds of talk. Talk connects to action by way of desire. Consciousness-raising promotes action when it taps into desire for social justice and into a recognition that joining with others promotes that end. The "kitchen table" talk that poor women of color and neighborhood women of all colors traditionally use to support their survival and resistance to racial, gender, class, and other oppression demonstrates the importance of talking together about inequities of power.[31] Such talk can take the form of joking, advice giving, storytelling, or comforting, but it all affirms a shared desire and sense of entitlement to survive. This sense of entitlement is a political claim, and the talk that promotes it, as feminists of color have argued, is political discourse. Consciousness-raising is a kind of kitchen table talk in which the desire for justice fuels discussion, and the power of a social movement promises that action can go beyond survival to establishing more just social relations.

In my teaching, feminist classroom discourse sometimes takes on the flavor of kitchen table talk, although many factors, including my insistence that we address a series of formal texts and the heterogeneity of the students, keep this impulse within considerable limits. Yet our discussion continuously addresses needs and desires for gender and other forms of justice, both those needs and desires that the students express and those that are communicated through the course readings. One student feels a strong desire to nurture others and assumes that this inclination is a fundamental female or human impulse. Another views this desire as a result of patriarchal conditioning and cites the text to support her position. Our subsequent talk tries to make sense of these conflicting interpretations. In doing so, discussion flows back and forth between "personal" and "political" considerations. One student defends the need for privacy to support her desire to nurture. Another criticizes that idea of privacy as irrelevant to communities in which nurturing is shared. Still another indicates that she cannot talk about this topic because it touches on feelings that she considers too private. We discuss what it means to reveal private feelings and find that we must talk about the problems involved in talking together.

Because feminist classroom discourse inspired by consciousness-raising is itself problematic, any definition of feminist pedagogy built on such foundations has a contingent quality. Yet, at this point, I want to summarize my argument in the form of a rough definition. Feminist pedagogy, as I conceive and try to practice it, is *teaching that engages students in political discussion of gender injustice.*

- This discussion is a collective, collaborative, and ongoing process that pays special attention to women's experiences, feelings, ideas, and actions.
- It seeks to understand and challenge oppressive power relations.
- It supports and generates women's political agency by addressing women's "personal" concerns and taking them seriously.
- It questions the meaning for differently situated women of oppression and liberation.
- It proceeds nonjudgmentally but cultivates the political judgment needed to act in response to gender and interwoven forms of injustice.

This definition cannot stand alone, because it raises as many questions as it answers. These questions concern knowledge, authority, caring, safety, and the differences that emerge in feminist classrooms. One by one, I will try to address these issues in the following chapters. This definition also suggests how my notion of feminist teaching might relate to other feminist pedagogies. I want to turn to that question now.

FEMINIST PEDAGOGY IN THE PLURAL

Over a cup of tea, Ronnie seems very uncomfortable as I describe my work on feminist pedagogy. At last, she says with considerable hesitation, "I cannot teach that way." She does not want, she adds, to reveal very much about herself to her students. She considers her lectures "very feminist" and gives her students plenty of time to respond. She is ill at ease with talk about feminist pedagogy, she says, because she thinks it implies that she is not a good teacher.

Over the years, my interaction with Ronnie has been repeated with a number of feminist academics. I mention that I am trying to develop my ideas about feminist pedagogy, and a teacher responds as though I had challenged her teaching credentials. I recognize this response in myself. Both "feminist" and "professor" imply right and wrong ways of doing things. Yet, neither feminists nor professors have universally agreed-on standards by which to judge their activities. This ambiguity often leads to a teacher either rigidly insisting on her own standards or hiding her anxiety about whether her feminism or her professoring live up to what she imagines to be other peoples' standards. If "feminist professor" is not a contradiction in terms, it is at the very least an invitation to mental and emotional fatigue.

My desire to talk with Ronnie does not stem from an impulse to judge her work but a desire to understand what she is doing as a feminist teacher. In my own struggle to formulate how my feminist teaching relates to consciousness-raising and feminist discourse, I began to note differences in how feminist academics talked about and practiced their teaching. I also realized that different approaches to feminist pedagogy raised questions to me about my own conception. Ronnie's words make me think about whether there could be a place for lecturing in my own work. Another feminist teacher's insistence on "caring" as the core of feminist pedagogy makes me wonder about the role of caring in feminist discourse. In the end, confronting these differences has made an important contribution to my internal dialogue about my practice and to thinking about how I could discuss it with other teachers.

It is not easy to describe such differences. As I suggested earlier, feminist pedagogies do not divide neatly into distinct political and educational philosophies. The complications of political identity and the continuous interaction between educational theory and practice make it difficult and to some extent misleading to divide feminist teachers into clear-cut camps ("She's a radical feminist teacher" or "She's a Freire-type feminist teacher"). In the end, I have decided to deal with the distinctions that affect feminist academic teaching by identifying a series of *values* around which we seem to organize our work. Many of us draw on more than one of these values and often do so in contradictory ways. My own effort to develop a coherent notion of feminist pedagogy as teaching through feminist discourse involves dealing with such contradictions. Thus, in reviewing a range of values that inform feminist teaching, I will also suggest the challenges they pose to my own notion of feminist pedagogy.

The first of these values is *access*. My teaching depends heavily on *institutional access*, for both me and my students. I bring to my practice of feminist discourse a lifetime of access to relatively privileged educational institutions. The women students in my classes do not have trouble gaining entry to the institution on the basis of their gender (indeed, most of them are studying in women-predominant fields and could be seen as having greater access because of continued patterns of gender segregation in these areas). But some students have a hard time financially getting into and staying in school. Others are never able to enter at all.

In one graduate class composed mostly of white women with a scattering of African American and Asian American women, I ask the students to do a workshop exercise aimed at exploring the intersection of identities. (I think the level of trust and understanding is now high enough to do this work.) I ask everyone who is willing to do so to stand together according to whether they see themselves belonging or not belonging to a series of identity groupings. When we come to "Hispanic or non-Hispanic," all the participants stand on one side of the room and no one stands on the other. As we stare into the empty space, the impact of institutional access on our attempt to engage in feminist discourse becomes dramatically clear. So, too, does our need to address the meaning of absent voices and what we think might be done about it.

Early proponents of consciousness-raising often ignored the problem of access because they assumed that all women could participate in this process by joining or starting a group. Yet, to varying degrees, the belief in equal access was an illusion. Primarily middle-class women took for granted the higher and sometimes elite educations they brought into their consciousness-raising discussions, including academic skills in argumentation and a knowledge of various political theories and schools of thought. Many activists from working-class backgrounds could not take these skills or knowledge for granted. As long as the educational system perpetuates economic and social inequalities, the notion of equal access remains problematic.[32] As long as women from a particular class or social group dominate a consciousness-raising context, their cultural and class assumptions will limit access to that process.

Thus, feminist discourse is profoundly affected by *access to the discourse itself*. As many women who were hurt, angered, or disappointed by consciousness-raising have testified, the dominant assumptions, vocabulary, and expressive style of any discussion easily excludes those who do not share them. The same thing applies to classrooms. Elizabeth Johnson, who eventually became a professor herself, provides a sharp picture of what happened when she returned to school as an older, black, working-class woman.[33] Her teachers continually questioned and rejected the skills and knowledge she brought to the classroom. Despite my own teaching values, I, too, can find myself excluding rather than giving access to student voices. I may miss the ideas they introduce into the discussion. I may use terms that I neglect to explain. I may call on associations that some students do not make. I may employ an emotional vocabulary that is unfamiliar or embarrassing. Students as well may easily exclude each other from discourse through language, gestures, and periodic attacks that make others feel utterly unheard and unwanted in the group. As a part of teaching through feminist discourse, I struggle to remain alert to these breaks in our communication.

Academic skills are clearly relevant to access to feminist classroom discourse. If a discussion revolves around interpretation of a text and some of the students do not have the skills to read that text, they cannot enter the discussion. As a feminist teacher, I have a series of choices here. I can devote part of my class time to helping those students gain access to the text. I can change the reading assignment to a text that everyone can understand. I can encourage other modes of entrance into the discussion such as the narration of personal experience. But whichever route(s) I choose, that choice has implications not only for access to feminist discourse in this classroom but access to the activities and institutions feminist discourse aims to affect. Barbara Omolade has some wise words on this topic in an essay on black feminist pedagogy.[34] She recounts her long struggle to acknowledge the differences between herself as a teacher and the black rural-born women students with whom she identified and how she finally became willing to share not only her political understanding but her academic skills. She realized that her students needed these skills to take the roles in urban leadership that she hoped they would come to occupy. Honoring her students' experiences and knowledge was not inconsistent with recognizing the tools they needed for political empowerment.

The question of student needs relates directly to the second value that tends to be neglected in a consciousness-raising approach to feminist teaching and to which I have had to play far greater attention than I first imagined: *caring*. Like many feminists identified with a socialist or radical or lesbian feminist politics, I have tended toward a skeptical view of feminist theories that emphasize caring. Despite the great merit I could see in

Carol Gilligan's critique of a male-dominated developmental psychology (as privileging abstract standards of what is "right" and "just" over connection and responsibility to others), I often saw her emphasis on women's "different voice" as a threat rather than an opportunity for my own liberation. Having decided not to have children, I was especially wary of the version of this argument put forward by feminist philosopher Nel Noddings, in which motherhood provides the standard for caring and caring the standard for teaching.[35] Such an equation seemed to dismiss childless women and erase many of the pressing political and ethical problems feminist pedagogy needed to address: inequality of opportunity and resources, dominance, exploitation, and violence.

With all my reservations, however, I found myself unable to separate my feminist pedagogy from the value of caring. Over time, I realized that feminist discourse tapped into and generated intense and pressing needs in both myself and my students. These included not only needs developed in response to injustice but those arising from the classroom dynamics. Needs had to be met for students to participate in classroom work such as reading difficult texts. Needs arose in the process of discussion, such as the need to be listened to with compassion or to receive a response to one's ideas, feelings, experiences. Although I used to wince when students used maternal imagery to describe my teaching, I finally had to admit how issues of caring permeated the classroom. I directed a good deal of caring toward students, and they directed a lot of caring toward each other and me. I had to look more carefully at the unarticulated assumptions about caring that informed my interpretation of consciousness-raising and my notion of feminist political discourse.

The value of caring is also closely associated with the value of *community*, which has played an important role in the pedagogical thinking and practice of feminists who have retained a strong connection to their communities of origin or who have developed other strong community affiliations. I include not only feminists of color, such as Barbara Omolade and Patricia Hill Collins, but also exponents of working-class feminism, such as Terry Haywoode and Laura Scanlon.[36] Neighborhoods, sometimes reinforced by racial and class segregation, often play an important role in how education is defined. When teachers come from the same class and/or ethnic background as their students, they are less likely to have to spend long hours trying to figure out what things mean to them and students are more likely to "get" the teacher's intentions without extra effort. Feminists who are teaching within their own disadvantaged communities often share certain values with their students and take for granted the welfare of the community as a goal for feminist discourse.

The early advocates of consciousness-raising also took for granted the value of community, in particular, political community, to foster feminist discourse and action. My notion of a feminist pedagogy inspired by consciousness-raising includes commitment to encourage a type of temporary, political community. But the realities of a heterogeneous classroom as well as the realities of students' lives stand in considerable tension with this value. Some of the students have strong ties to their communities of origin. Others feel they lack community in any sense. Some seek or have already found community with other feminists. Others have found community with other social justice movements or in various political or social or religious or recovery groups. The meanings of "community" differ greatly despite the fact that the broad and persistent interest in community seems to reflect certain deep desires for belonging. Yet, there are often times at which a given class achieves a remarkable sense of shared purpose, of commitment to engage with each other in the work of feminist discourse. Given these contradictory patterns, community remains a value for my feminist pedagogy but also a complex problem.

Feminist teachers themselves, of course, belong to a series of overlapping and often conflicting communities, including communities of feminist academics. Such communities, like academic disciplines in general, support the pedagogical value of *transmission*. That is, teachers value the process of passing on the knowledge and disciplinary skills that lie at the center of our own academic identities. Few feminist academics speak or write at length about the value of transmission, perhaps because it is taken for granted in academia or perhaps because it has been the subject of so much pedagogical criticism. Following Freire's critique of "banking education," many progressive educational reformers and academics associate transmission with lecturing and lecturing with perpetuating domination. Feminist teachers like me often have joined this critical stream both because of our fear that transmission will make women students more passive and because teaching styles like lecturing seem to reinforce male dominance. Consciousness-raising emphasizes the criticism of received knowledge and the need to support women's thought and agency rather than the importance of teaching and learning what others have discovered.

For many years, I was both very prejudiced against lecturing in any form and unsure that I could do it. My most influential teachers in higher education, all men, had taught through discussion or some form of dialogue. Through them, I learned how to insert informative and interpretive remarks into an ongoing discussion rather than separating them out in the form of a lecture. To get up at a podium to lecture seemed to me to betray the intimate, passionate search in which two or more people engage as they try to understand something of importance to them. Yet, as I struggled with the problem of what to do with the accumulation of ideas, arguments, and research that came to comprise the subject matter of feminist scholarship, I began to make more "presentations" to students that linked their discussions to discussions among feminist academics. As I heard students over and over ask me to *share* with them, not *deposit* in them, what I had learned from my encounters with academic and nonacademic feminism, I found myself less sure that lecturing and other forms of direct transmission betrayed my fondest values.

For one thing, there is a difference between maintaining an environment for creative political discourse and ignoring the value of research or scholarship. For feminist academics who have themselves profited enormously from and often contributed to the fund of feminist research, bypassing this body of material makes no sense. Acknowledging its existence, though, does not tell us how to relate to it. In my conversation with Ronnie, I am so taken aback by her response that I fail to ask her how she lectures. Some lecturing styles may be fairly consistent with certain aspects of consciousness-raising. Feminist lecturers may bring in the experiences of many women; pay attention to feelings and their meaning; search out the relations among experiences, feelings, and feminist theories; and talk about possibilities for action. As many theorists have now pointed out, both listening and reading involve various degrees of construction by listeners and readers. For some students, at least, transmission might well support rather than prevent active learning.[37]

Even a teacher who uses the discussion method cannot avoid transmitting ideas, information and values through her practice. By selecting particular authors or topics for her course syllabus and arranging them in a certain manner, or by emphasizing certain parts of a text she asks the class to discuss, she asserts the importance of some ideas and minimizes or ignores others. By teaching in the way she does, she provides information about feminist teaching and the values that inform it. Her teaching style may emphasize her image of herself as an authoritative speaker. She may show students how to teach in a caring manner. She may demonstrate how to transgress institutional norms for what teachers should do or say. If she does not reflect on her practice, she may transmit what has been described as a hidden agenda (e.g., by continuing to favor male students in classroom interactions, she perpetuates the lesson of women's intellectual inferiority). At best, she consciously decides how she will teach and transmits a valuable example or model for her students to emulate.[38]

However, from the standpoint of feminist discourse, it is possible to place too much emphasis on how teaching is done and too little on what teaching is about. Feminist teaching has a purpose, which is to understand women's oppression and promote women's liberation. Employing liberatory learning methods may be crucial to working for gender justice, but it cannot represent the entire project. Feminist discourse requires us to wrestle with concrete instances of women's oppression, to figure out meanings and implications for action. This effort, in turn, is conducted not simply by individuals but in relation to a social movement—indeed, a series of overlapping and sometimes conflicting social movements aimed at greater justice. Classroom discussion divorced from such movements ends up serving the dominant educational goal of individual development. Whatever role transmission plays in feminist teaching, whether it focuses on content or method, it needs to go beyond individual change.

The fact that we as teachers transmit our philosophies in part through our actions is closely connected to the feminist pedagogical value of *performance*. As articulated by poststructural theorists such as Jane Gallop, the self-conscious use of performance entails criticism of the unified, authentic self and the "naive belief in bringing the authentic self into the institution."[39] Instead of assuming that the personal represents a coherent agent, teachers and students should be exploring the multiplicity of selves and/or voices through which they engage each other. This pedagogy has playful and serious aspects. It draws everyone into the pleasurable game confronting the ambiguities of "who" we are. It inspires us to investigate how these complex selves are shaped by linguistic and other forms of power. In this respect, pedagogical performance combines the process of enacting and trying on various selves with the intellectual project of discovering how and how much these selves are socially constructed.

In my efforts to make sense of performance in feminist teaching, I have found myself both violently rejecting and finding increased points of contact with this value. Although I do not measure my self or other selves against some eternal standard of selfhood, I think there is good reason for both teachers and students to try to bring their most authentic selves into feminist discourse. By this I mean being as honest as possible about what we think, feel, experience, and do. I see a tremendous need for more authenticity in academia because I think that many of the games we are pressured to play in these hierarchical organizations are neither pleasurable nor truthful.

Yet my own search for a feminist way of teaching does not assume a unified self. Like poststructural feminists, I seek to explore with students the structures that permeate our selves. I value the attempt to "get out of ourselves" to see ourselves as others see us and to understand how the world looks from the viewpoint of other selves. My improvisational theater work has helped me prize spontaneity in my relation to students and has served to remind me that neither they nor I can predict what "selves" may appear in our classroom. My emphasis on promoting women's agency through feminist discourse also argues for the concept of an open-ended self: a self who can form critical judgments and engage in actions that change personal and political realities.

The notion that our style of teaching itself conveys a lesson also bears on the final feminist teaching value that impacts on my own theory and practice: *critical thinking*. In adopting this term, feminists have adopted its ambiguities.[40] In one interpretation, critical thinking is identified with traditional skills in argumentation and analysis rooted in the Western tradition of logic and with the belief that good thinking involves conformity to a universal set of thinking rules. Everywhere, feminist and nonfeminist academics claim and are urged to cultivate such critical thinking. At the same time, other feminist academics excoriate any kind of disembodied rationality, pointing out the limits to abstract, objectivizing, and universalizing thought. In fact, all Western feminist thinkers draw on this tradition of critical thinking, even as we point to its limitations. We try to clarify our basic concepts. We look for consistency in argument. We count on others to be able to understand how we present our ideas.

The other leading interpretation of critical thinking involves a political and also often an ethical, aesthetic, or other critique of prevailing relationships, social structures, and/or symbol systems. Although this notion of critical thought owes a great debt to Marxism, it is reflected in a wide variety of theoretical projects, all of which seek to discover and reveal interests or forces or patterns behind, within or beyond the dominant ideas and structures that permeate our lives. Feminism, by definition, participates in this second meaning of critical thinking as well. Different versions of feminism seek to discover and reveal different interests, forces, or patterns that foster gender injustice. As these various versions of feminist politics combine with the academic disciplines, feminist academics find themselves teaching students how to think critically as, say, a Marxist feminist anthropologist or a postcolonial feminist literary critic or a lesbian feminist psychotherapist. From the standpoint of one approach, the others often seem insufficiently critical. How, one feminist academic asks, can really critical thinking leave out economic systems? How, asks another, can anyone ignore the role of the unconscious? From the standpoint of this second notion of critical thinking as discovering and revealing structures of domination, any claim to a universal set of thinking rules is suspect. From the viewpoint of the universalists, however, the second sort of critical thinking often appears "biased" and "political."

These rival interpretations of critical thinking both complement and conflict with the notion of feminist pedagogy for which I am arguing. Consciousness-raising assumes critical thinking in both senses. This process relies on the belief that it is possible to engage in clear and comprehensible discourse about gender and related forms of oppression and to make and evaluate arguments about its character and how it might be remedied. It relies on the belief that critical thinking can discover and reveal structures of domination that lead most men, as well as many women, to ignore or deny gender and interwoven patterns of injustice. Consciousness-raising is also in tension with the idea that universal rules of thinking transcend everyday experiences and emotional responses. It is in tension with the notion that one way of critical thinking takes automatic precedence over others, that the superiority of one style of feminist criticism can be established through thinking alone without exploring its connections to experiences, feelings, and actions.

Thus, the problem of articulating and developing a feminist pedagogy inspired by consciousness-raising involves figuring out the role of critical thought in this pedagogical process. As my discussion suggests, however, this is only part of the problem. Developing a feminist pedagogy includes making sense of the power and authority feminist teachers may exercise by virtue of their positions and knowledge of feminist research and scholarship. This project involves attention to the meaning of care in the classroom and to the areas in which teachers may fail to make feminist discourse seem sufficiently safe for classroom members to want to participate. A feminist pedagogy must take into account how the diversity of communities to which participants belong affects the dynamics of feminist discourse. Creating a feminist pedagogy requires sources of hope that this entire process is worth the effort and sources of support for maintaining it. Although these questions are tightly interwoven, I will take them up one by one.

— 2 —

IS WOMEN'S EXPERIENCE
THE BEST TEACHER?

Different Ways of Knowing

Eloise believes that feminism is out of date. She was raised by her parents to do what she chooses, and nothing has ever stopped her. If other women are smart, she says, they'll do the same. She is not interested in anything her classmates say in this undergraduate class, and when I introduce what I see as the still burning questions of gender justice, her mouth tightens into a hard line.

As the weeks roll by, Titania does little more than assert her feminist convictions. She learned feminism at her mother's knee, she tells us, and knows all about women's rights. She demands hers constantly. She does not respond to other students. Every time she speaks, the eyes of the others glaze over, and I become edgy. I do not know what she will do in the name of feminism or how she may hurt herself or others.

Beliefs remain suspect in academic work because, it is argued, they keep us from having the kind of open mind required by scholarly objectivity. Yet I encounter beliefs everywhere in my teaching. I call on my feminist beliefs to pump up my courage to meet with a new group of women's studies students. Eloise uses her beliefs to challenge mine. In another class, Titania displays her beliefs as part of her image of what it means to be a student in a feminist class. Although I, too, think that teachers and students need to open their minds to a wide range of ideas and realities, I do not see how we can do this by downplaying our beliefs. We are always, in one way or another, believers.[1]

In many fields of study, beliefs are pushed into the background. I find this impossible as a feminist teacher of feminist materials. The *-ism* in *feminism* connotes belief. This belief informs every part of my feminist teaching, from what I choose to put on the syllabus to how I conduct a discussion. Belief gives me a sense of direction. To the extent that I can articulate my beliefs to myself, I can explain to students why I think this or that topic is worth studying and why I teach it as I do. In effect, my beliefs about my feminist teaching operate to "hold" the class, to assure both the students and myself that we all can gain something from the work I want us to do together.[2] My beliefs are contingent rather than dogmatic. Thus, the holding function of feminist beliefs does not guarantee that the students will accept my beliefs or that I will be able to maintain them. My beliefs can be shaken. They depend heavily on the viability of feminism as a social movement, its ideas and actions, and the support of colleagues and comrades in that movement. Such beliefs also depend on the responsiveness of the students. If as a group they do not grant some credibility to a process of talking together about gender injustice, my own belief in the value of feminist discourse dims.

Eloise and Titania each jar my feminist beliefs. Eloise calls them into question by refusing to grant the legitimacy of such discourse. She does not believe that gender justice is a problem, so, she implies, there is nothing to talk about. In a class session devoted to gender and other forms of segregation in work, she says that anyone who tries hard can do anything she wants. Because most members of this undergraduate class belong to a generation that was born after the abolition of many discriminatory laws, I ask them to pay close attention to readings on informal and extralegal barriers to workplace integration. But Eloise dismisses this research. She still believes it is a matter of choice. As she passionately reiterates her beliefs, mine become more unsettled. What is it, I have to ask myself, that leads women like Eloise to reject feminism so violently? Is this rejection the product of a political backlash or a generation that can take feminist gains for granted? How can I maintain my notion of "women's oppression" in the face of her response? Just as the semester is ending, however, another student mentions her own fear of sexual assault. Eloise's expression of disdain changes. She quietly acknowledges that she, too, does not feel free to walk around the city at any hour. As we talk, she starts to consider that a person's opportunity to make choices may depend on certain advantages. The classroom discourse has begun to shake her beliefs, as they have shaken mine.

The beliefs I bring to my feminist teaching are both *substantive* and *procedural*. My substantive beliefs include the reality of women's needs and suffering and the importance of seeking greater justice and freedom for women. I believe that women's oppression constitutes a serious and widespread, if neither uniform nor universal, social wrong that calls out to be righted. My procedural beliefs include the value of a feminist discourse to the process of trying to right that wrong. I believe that such discourse involves not only the exchange of ideas but exploration of experiences, feelings, and actions. My procedural and substantive beliefs interweave with and shape each other. If women are not in any manner oppressed, as Eloise implies, there is little point in talking about gender injustice. If talk about gender injustice is not useful to feminists, as Titania's unwillingness to engage with the other students implies, it becomes impossible to understand and act on the belief that women are oppressed.

Even though substantive and procedural beliefs cannot be fully separated, my encounter with Titania helps me understand that I give priority to feminist political discourse over specific expressions of feminist beliefs.[3] Titania's pronouncements on the rights of women do not please me, even though she may be seeking my approval. They frighten me. I am afraid of people who are so committed to a cause that they cannot consider the meaning of their commitment for other people. Titania is not interested in what the other students think or say. She wants to separate feminist content from the feminist process in which I seek to engage her. She continually disrupts this process by citing her beliefs, and I become increasingly angry.

Titania's constant references to her mother as the source of her feminism fuel my anger. They seem to demean the intellectual stature of women's studies (who needs to go to school to study feminism when you can get it all from your mother?) and to undermine my authority as a teacher (which seems quite ineffectual compared to that of her mother). I feel competitive. When Titania starts to speak, I can hardly hear her. I do not want her mother intruding into my classroom. It takes many weeks before I can consider the possibility that Titania may be trying to join the discussion by bringing up something that is problematic for her and may be problematic for others as well: how our mothers' political values have affected our own. As I reflect on this possibility, I get an idea. I initiate a classroom go-around in which each person has a chance to say how she imagines her mother, living or dead, would respond if she were visiting the class. Several students note that their mothers would be frightened or appalled by the course content. Another says that her mother would be pleased. I remark that my mother would be uncomfortable. Titania says that her mother would think that she, her daughter, was "not feminist enough." We talk about how these imagined responses are affecting our participation in the class, and I lead the group into a discussion of how historic and generational changes might play into these patterns. Titania is very interested in the fact that both mothers and their daughters might have quite different interpretations of "feminism." This is the last class session in which she mentions her mother.

I do not stop thinking about Titania or my responses to her, however, because my anger at her bringing her mother into class is tinged with embarrassment. When I imagine my own mother visiting the course, I feel this embarrassment. Would she say "the wrong thing"? I am ashamed of having this response. As a feminist, I believe that it is very important to listen to what mothers, feminist or nonfeminist, have to say, because no feminist discourse can exist without the voices of mothers. Yet, as an academic, I am ill at ease. I am not at all sure what my mother could add to our class. Whatever my beliefs about my academic subject, they are supposed to be warranted by knowledge developed in my discipline. Disciplines, as Lynn Nelson and others have noted, are "epistemological communities" in which people share standards about what constitutes knowledge.[4] My mother would be an outsider to this feminist academic community, even more than the students who are being shown how they can participate in it. From an academic, even a feminist academic, viewpoint, my mother would not be a knower.

This conclusion pains me and clashes strongly with my desire to promote a discourse in which all women, in theory, can participate. Early proponents of consciousness-raising thought that women knew many things that their male comrades did not count as real knowledge or relevant to social change. Women activists, in effect, sought to create a women-centered epistemological community—a community that would produce feminist knowledge through a process of sharing experiences and feelings and considering ideas and actions. Consciousness-raising generated a great deal of feminist knowledge, which in turn laid the groundwork for much of second-wave academic feminist research and scholarship.[5] The inclusion of women's experiences, feelings, ideas, and actions in generating feminist knowledge broadened the means by which that knowledge was constructed.

But this notion of a women's epistemological community also contained serious problems. The distinction between women's ways of knowing and feminist ways of knowing became obscured. Proponents of consciousness-raising as the fundamental process for generating feminist knowledge, such as Catherine MacKinnon, often assumed that women shared a standpoint or particular perspective on their oppression. Consciousness-raising would provide women a method for reflecting on that standpoint until they arrived at a feminist analysis of it. In this interpretation, women's standpoint was essentially feminist, and through the appropriate sort of inquiry, that political and conceptual core would be discovered and developed.[6]

This logic was quickly challenged by many women and feminists and thoroughly criticized by feminist academics.[7] Sandra Harding and Elizabeth Minnich variously argued that any standpoint was partial and could not be the source of a complete truth. Patricia Hill Collins and Chandra Mohanty pointed out how racial and/or colonial oppression led black women and other women of color to standpoints that differed considerably from those of white women in dominant countries. Elizabeth Spelman and María Lugones showed how the notion of a women's standpoint that does not include racial and other perspectives both masks and reinforces the privileges that a white identity and other sources of power give some women over others. Judith Butler and Denise Riley critiqued the category "women" itself for assuming that people called women had any particular characteristics or concerns (let alone a standpoint on their oppression) in common.

As these and other arguments made evident, feminists cannot assume that either women or feminists share a similar and uniform standpoint on women's oppression. Yet here is a paradox. Feminism involves the belief that there is something generally wrong and unjust in gender relations. A feminist movement is grounded in the belief that women do or can recognize gender as a site of oppression and do or can oppose such oppression. Without these or similar beliefs, feminism makes little sense. Thus, there is a built-in tension between a belief in the reality of women's oppression and the need to explore the meanings oppression and liberation may or may not have for variously situated women.

This tension, in turn, has direct implications for feminist discourse and the teaching that seeks to promote it. Women's experiences may be a rich source of knowledge about daily encounters with oppression, but such experiences may not add up to a single, coherent standpoint. Strong feelings may supply important clues to the character of gender injustice, but participants in feminist discourse cannot assume a shared interpretation of those feelings. Ideas about women's oppression may be grounded in experience and feeling, yet such ideas may not coalesce into a unified feminist analysis. The actions that women take in response to oppression may help build a feminist movement, but they may not result in a unified program of resistance. Given the problematic character of its basic elements, then, *feminist discourse is not an ideal to be achieved but a process to be developed.* Experience, feelings, thinking, and action provide grounding for this process, but their place in it cannot be taken for granted.

Learning from Women's Experience

Several weeks after our discussion of sexual harassment, Olive asks to speak to me after class. A self-contained and studious woman from the Caribbean, she has always seemed sure of herself. In this conversation she hesitates. She tells me that for a long time she has been disturbed by her doctoral adviser's behavior. He is a much older white man who, although he has never actually touched or propositioned her, constantly stands uncomfortably close to her and seems to be making sexual advances. His behavior has been affecting her work, but she is afraid to tell him to stop or to bring a complaint. She isn't sure whether this is sexual harassment.

When our readings on race and gender lead to talk about childhood experiences, I suggest that everyone do some writing. Then, if they wish, they can share their writing with the class. Isabel reuds u description of growing up in her New York Puerto Rican neighborhood. I read a paragraph about my unreciprocated love for a black girl in my grade school. Another white woman, Clarissa, reads a passage describing her long ago failure to stop another white child from calling a black child in their schoolyard by a racist name. Marylou, who is also white, says that Clarissa's mode of constructing her narrative reinscribes the binary opposition white/nonwhite. I am jolted by Marylou's intervention and don't know what to do with this remark. I fill the remaining minutes with comments about next week's assignment. Clarissa looks very upset when she leaves.

As these stories attest, experience can be a powerful and problematic element in feminist classrooms. Consciousness-raising stresses the importance of paying attention to women's experiences. In the early years of the second wave, paying attention to certain experiences often required a special effort because they were not seen as appropriate to political discourse ("I can't imagine talking in a meeting about being raped") or because they seemed inevitable ("I know it's not much, but that's what they pay for taking care of kids") or because they could be ignored ("I just walk right by when they make those noises and call me a pussy") or because they could be explained away ("He doesn't mean to hit me; he's so insecure"). Women often did not, and still do not, want to pay attention to certain experiences because of the fear that doing so might worsen rather than improve their situation.

Paying attention to experience is not a simple matter. "Experience" involves the ongoing interactions that we, as human beings, have with our environments.[8] Both mind and body play a part in this interaction. The environment with which we interact may include not only external but internal elements like memories or imagination. Although living requires us to pay varying degrees of attention to these interactions, we become especially aware of our relationship to our environment when it becomes problematic. We think more about what is going on. Our feelings heighten. As Dewey argued, we see ourselves as "having an experience." Whether we view something as "an experience" or an experience worth communicating to others, and whether and how we communicate it, are strongly affected by the context.

As this argument suggests, *physical feelings* often play a key role in experience and how we define it. When Olive describes her discomfort with her adviser, she talks about bodily experience. Whatever she does to avoid him, he positions himself so closely that she can feel the heat and smell the odor of his body. She does not welcome these feelings. They are unpleasantly intrusive, in stark contrast with the physical reactions she has to her husband. Since she carefully monitors her interactions with other men and has always been able to keep her distance from white men, in particular, she has to struggle to describe her encounters with her adviser. She is not certain how to name them or what to do.

Olive's description of her problem taps into a second feature of experience implicit in the theory and practice of consciousness-raising: the emergence of *contradictions within experience*. One of the many things women involved in consciousness-raising noted was the disjunction among the many roles they played. The woman who spends the day running herself ragged to serve her children and husband might still be expected and perhaps even want to turn into the perfect and sexy hostess when he comes home from work. The woman whose own paid work requires her to behave in a compliant and subservient manner might be expected and even seek to become a tower of moral strength when she returns to her family at night. While these contradictions might run in many directions, some of the most powerful ones stem from what feminist sociologist Dorothy Smith has described as the "bifurcation" between dominant interpretations of women's lives and women's everyday experiences.[9] Olive not only has to exercise tremendous strength to deal with the racism and sexism she experiences in her daily life, but she has to contend with widespread stereotypes of black women as sexually available and superhumanly strong. These stereotypes are part of her external environment and to some extent shape her internal environment as well. Olive wonders out loud whether she has in any way invited this behavior and whether she should just ignore it and finish her degree.

Since some members of the class have initiated a group to discuss sexual harassment, I suggest that Olive join them. The group plans to review some basic literature in this area, look at the school's sexual harassment policy, and talk about their experiences. All the members of this group have had experiences relevant to discussing sexual harassment, but they differ considerably. Rima, a young white woman, has been overtly propositioned by her white male boss at her part-time job and worries that she might have to drop out of school if he fires her. Luisah, an African American woman, has already put a stop to what she considers sexually inappropriate behavior on the part of a teacher. Colette, a white woman, is about to marry a man who was her professor several years ago. Sharing stories allows the members of this group to engage in a collective process of comparing experiences to discover both similarities and differences among them.

Early proponents of consciousness-raising often expected that such comparison would reveal clear commonalities, which, in turn, would become the basis of making generalizations and developing a feminist analysis. The attempt to develop generalizations was not in itself a mistaken effort. As Susan Bordo and Susanne Bohmer each have argued, analysis requires the possibility of generalization, and without generalization feminist discourse cannot proceed.[10] Yet, even before an academic critique of what Elizabeth Minnich calls "false generalization" developed, feminist activists themselves were challenging generalizations that had begun to emerge through discussions of "women's experience."[11] Black, lesbian, working-class, and other feminist activists pointed out that generalizations based on the experience of white, heterosexual, and/or middle class women did not necessarily apply to them. Such challenges did not simply invalidate all generalizations, however. Rather, they required feminist discourse to develop more adequate and complex ones. Generalizations about women, as Pamela Allen had argued in her interpretation of consciousness-raising, had to be subject to broader comparisons than any single group of women could supply.

This process of comparing, however, has potentials other than generalization. By noticing not only commonalities but differences, students have the opportunity to examine how *context affects experience.* As a doctoral student, Olive is not only part of a distinct minority of students of color but also highly dependent on her adviser for his support and job recommendations. Luisah, a master's student, had courageously confronted her teacher, but she does not depend on him for anything significant and has a strong network of friends and colleagues who can help her with her career. Rima needs her job, but her dependence on her boss is not as complete as Olive's on her adviser. Colette found the sexual attentions of her former professor and soon-to-be husband both flattering and pleasing and interprets them as having enhanced her graduate education.

Colette's story suggests that comparison also promotes a broader understanding of gender injustice by drawing attention to the lack of experience that some women may have in contrast to others. Colette has never had to make a choice between her economic needs and career ambitions, on the one hand, and her sexual and social desires on the other. Much as she glories in the sexual attention of men, she has never had to deal with being seen as supersexual because of her race. As the four students compare their stories, I encourage them to consider how racial, class, or other privileges might shield some women from having to deal with certain oppressive social relations. I remark to the group that not only privilege but disempowerment can deprive people of certain experiences, and I recommend a piece by a feminist with a disability who discusses how much resistance women with disabilities encounter to their status as sexual beings.[12] As I leave the group to their discussion, they have started to consider how their different situations might affect their ability and willingness to act in this area.

The story I tell at the beginning of this section in which Marylou criticizes Clarissa's description of her experience (trying to stop another child from using racist language) suggests some additional issues. The encounter between Clarissa and Marylou makes a deep impression on me because it echoes an intense argument that is taking place among feminist theorists during the period in which this story is set. My suggestion that the students write about their childhood experiences with race draws support from both feminists of color and white feminists who argue that sharing experiences about race is crucial to feminist discussions of oppression.[13] Following my lead, Clarissa engages in the exercise and shares with the class what was for her an important experience. But the pedagogical turn to experience that I take in this story has been questioned by feminist theorists such as Joan Scott and Diane Fuss and is indirectly questioned in class by Marylou. From their perspective, experience constitutes less a resource for knowledge than a sign of potential ignorance.

Experience, Scott and Fuss argue, is neither simple nor innocent.[14] It involves assumptions that need to be analyzed, as Marylou tries to analyze Clarissa's assumptions. From this critical point of view, experience is *theory-laden*. Rather than assuming "the authority of experience," teachers and students should be interrogating experience for its hidden assumptions and limitations, for what Scott calls "the inner logic of experience." Scott herself opts for a mode of analysis that is historical and deconstructive, emphasizing how language constructs what we call experience. But this focus on analysis might take a psychoanalytic or Marxist or other form. Whatever theory such critics use, their arguments suggest that because of the suspect status of experience, we must give priority to analysis.

Social justice activists and academics have good reasons to treat claims to knowledge based solely on experience with suspicion. As Sherry Gorelick reminds us, the Marxist tradition, in particular, points to how dynamics underlying oppressive social relations may be hidden "behind the backs of the actors" who nevertheless feel their impact.[15] The immigrant worker who works for measly wages under health-destroying conditions does not learn from her life alone how international markets create or change her working conditions. Clarissa, as a child who was so concerned with schoolyard injustice, did not know how the real estate industry's policies of residential segregation prevented more than a handful of children of color from attending her school. Theories can offer powerful tools for interpretation, for discovering how and why we may hold false beliefs or where our viewpoint may need to be broadened.

But theories themselves can suffer from serious faults and limitations that can be located through *experiential criticism.* Such criticism constituted a major element in early consciousness-raising efforts. As Kathie Sarachild and others argued, women's experience controverts male-centered theories and misogynist stereotypes. In a similar way, feminist classroom discourse that builds on the comparison of experiences can serve to criticize both feminist and nonfeminist theories that rely on faulted or limited assumptions about women. Whether the theories are male centered or feminist, women's everyday lives can generate counterexamples that push us to reconsider or replace prevailing theoretical frameworks.[16]

Stories can play an even broader role in feminist discourse when we view sharing *experience as a form of argument.*[17] When Clarissa comes to talk with me after class, she tells me how her experience of trying to stop another white child from using racist language had haunted her. When she was a child, her father scolded her and her brother for using racist language, and her mother had urged her to be kindly and caring toward others who were weaker or less fortunate. To her, her failure in the schoolyard represented a failure to live up to her parents' liberal ideals. Although subsequently she joined a number of social justice projects, she always felt somewhat powerless in the face of injustice. She finally had the courage to bring this experience up in our class, she says, and was deeply hurt by not only Marylou's lack of appreciation but also my lack of support.

Clarissa's comments make me aware of what I have contributed to this classroom incident as well as why she has reacted as she has. By asking the students to write about their experiences in the context of reading articles on white women and racism, I have oriented them toward producing narratives that show what they themselves feel or think or have done in relation to this ongoing feminist concern. Clarissa responds by describing an experience that, in effect, argues, "It's not so easy for a white woman to oppose racism. I tried, and I'm afraid I may have failed. I think something may be wrong with how or why I am trying."

When I view Clarissa's experiences as argument, I can consider her reactions and the class dynamic in a new light. She is not someone who has simply misunderstood or failed to deal adequately with racism but someone who has struggled to do so and who enters our feminist discourse on racism with important questions. Were the liberal ideals conveyed to her by her parents adequate to dealing with racism? How are white women, in particular, expected to respond to social justice issues by their families and communities? How might others view those responses?

I think now about Isabel, who completed the same exercise by writing about her experience in a basically segregated Puerto Rican neighborhood. Her words can be seen as answering these questions with an experiential argument of her own. In her childhood, she says, Anglo children were quite distant, and she had been warned of the danger of getting too involved with them. Her experience argues that the dominant liberal ideal—of those with more power of being benevolent to those with less power—might need to be examined. As Clarissa leaves my office, I begin to think about how I might draw out both her and Isabel's experiential arguments and help the group explore them in relation to our readings.

While I am mulling over my ideas, Marylou comes in for an appointment that she, too, made with me. She tells me how puzzled and angered she was by the class. Recently, she says, she had taken a course that dealt with the concept of race from a deconstructionist point of view, by exploring the limits of "race" as a socially constructed category. Her other class had included some students of color, she notes, and everyone had joined in pursuing this powerful form of analysis. She was confused and disturbed by my suggestion that the students in our class write about their experiences with race. She saw this exercise as a rejection of theory and a way of reaffirming rather than criticizing racial categories. She was afraid that no matter what she wrote, she would be judged harshly by me and the students of color in the class.

Marylou's comments quickly get to the heart of another feminist criticism of the use of experience in teaching: that it promotes authoritarianism. Diane Fuss has argued that treating experience of oppression as a source of knowledge gives experience a kind of authority that places it beyond criticism.[18] Students who see themselves as oppressed expect to have the last word, and true inquiry is repressed, together with the teacher's own authority to promote it. From Marylou and Fuss's point of view, I was creating a situation in which Marylou's own knowledge would lack authority and she would be excluded from feminist discourse.

Without doubt, experience can be used to support or justify authoritarian and oppressive behavior. As I am working on this manuscript, I learn that two heterosexual men who have tortured and murdered a gay man cite their "experience" of his making a sexual pass at them to justify their actions. But experiences are no more intrinsically authoritarian than feelings or actions or reasoning. Logical arguments are often used to justify murderous and soul-destroying actions. As a resource for making judgments, any way of knowing is fallible and requires a critical assessment. Different ways of knowing often serve to criticize and correct each other, as when feeling alerts us to the fact that something is seriously wrong with our reasoning or our reasoning makes us reflect on our feelings. For a teacher seeking to promote feminist discourse, the task becomes one of how we can use our authority to bring these ways of knowing into a productive relation to each other. Thus, I believe our problem is less one of the "authority of experience" than of our experience with authority. After all, it is the teacher with whom the authority and power mostly lies, and her basic question is on what grounds she will use it.

In my classroom encounter with Clarissa and Marylou, I use my authority to try to get the students to include their experiences in their discussion about racism and feminism. Then, near the end of class meeting, I become unsure how to move. I seem to be faced with an impossible choice. Either I can ask Marylou to hold her response while the class further shares and compares experiences—and risk suppressing Marylou's critical comments—or I can lead the class toward discussing her critical comment—and risk the sense of objectification that Clarissa feels when her experiences suddenly become the object of criticism. The consciousness-raising emphasis on nonjudgmentalness suggests that I should give priority to listening to the participants' experiences, but the legitimate concern with suppressing criticism suggests that I should have given priority to Marylou's comment.

The difficulty with framing the problem in this way is that it preserves the split between theory and experience. While as Scott and others have argued, the way in which we define and describe an experience is theory-laden, it is tempting to ignore the extent to which theory is *experience-laden*.[19] That is one of the basic points that emerges through my office conversation with Marylou. She is willing to question not only the authority of Clarissa's experience but my authority in assigning an experiential exercise because she, Marylou, believes that we can talk about race in a more interesting and harmonious way. This theoretical stance, however, makes sense to her in part because it resonates deeply with her recent experience in the other class and because this other approach seems to rule out the racial polarization she fears she would have to confront in the class she is taking with me.

My emphasizing the extent to which social justice theories are experience-laden contains, of course, considerable dangers. The strategy of attending to the experiences that presumably inform a theory is often used to discredit and distort theoretical projects, as when students periodically try to discredit my feminist thinking on the grounds that my experience as a lesbian disqualifies me from understanding the virtues and pleasures of heterosexual life. But bringing out the experiential dimension of theory can make distinct contributions to feminist discourse. Had I been able to draw out the experiences that informed Marylou's argument, the class process might have taken a different turn. Clarissa and the rest of us could have understood the *meaning* of the criticism to Marylou, which would have helped us discuss its meaning for other members of the class. These discussions might have illuminated further the poststructuralist feminist readings on our syllabus. Attention to the experiential aspect of theory also might have helped us identify the *contexts* relevant to the theory.

Later in this course, Davida, a light-skinned woman with a African American father and Jewish mother, speaks quite persuasively about the problems and dangers of employing racial categories. Her own childhood problems in the schoolyard, she tells us, stemmed from the fact that she fit neither in the white world that Clarissa sought to reform nor fully in the community of color world that Isabel saw as a line of defense against racism. Davida, she says, avoids categories as best she can. Her experience not only gives greater meaning to certain feminist theories but pushes us as a class to look more closely at conditions under which categorization can be especially damaging.

I am not implying here that any given experience must produce a certain theory or that any given theory should be reduced to the experience that might inform it. Another woman of biracial heritage might place racial identity at the heart of her politics. Rather, I am arguing for the kind of teaching through feminist discourse that seeks to maintain and explore *the interplay between experience and theory* rather than asserting the priority of one over the other. This approach assumes that participants have valuable experiences and are able to think about them and that they can examine both the experiences and thinking. Such discourse seeks to avoid situations in which one person or group of people become objectified as the *bearers of experience* while another or others becomes *experiential analysts*—rather like the anthropologists described by Trinh Minh-ha who construct the experiences of the "natives" they study.[20] Making others into "natives," inside or outside the classroom, runs counter to the spirit of consciousness-raising and encourages people engaged in political discourse to separate thinking from feelings and action.

FEELING, THINKING, AND ACTING

After several meetings in which we discuss a classic feminist text, I ask each student to pick a passage that strikes her as particularly significant. Using a movement technique I learned through my work in political theater, I guide those students who are willing to participate through a relaxation exercise and ask them to shape their bodies in response to the passage. Later, Ida tells the class that she first stretched out her arms because a passage about women's liberation had made her feel so hopeful and free. Then, much to her surprise, she suddenly found herself cowering behind a chair and feeling very scared.

In a conference session on what it means to teach feminist theory, a commonplace battle breaks out between mostly older feminist academics who feel that their contributions to the field have been ignored or denigrated and their mostly younger colleagues who view their own theoretical activities as "cutting-edge." My sympathy flows toward my older comrades, but I am trying hard to get what the younger women are saying. At last one of the younger women cries out in rage and frustration: "Don't you see, your old theories don't mean anything to me! What I'm doing is so exciting!"

At the end of the semester, Zelda tells me that, although she loved the course, she remains troubled by conflicting feminist theories. "It's all so complicated," she says. "We can't know what to do until we have a more integrated theory." Then she asks me to wish her good luck. As soon as she graduates, she is going off to join an environmentalist project in a South American jungle.

Given my teaching conditions, I do not incorporate much movement work in my classes. I feel constrained by my own and others' discomfort with bodies and feelings in academic settings. Teachers and students can analyze bodies and feelings, but actually paying attention to them poses a problem for our work. This contradiction can become especially intense in feminist contexts where a connection between "personal" and "political" is emphasized. For instance, in an interview about herself and her work, a well-known feminist political theorist comments on how "unseemly" she considers the process of "spilling one's guts." Yet in a moving part of the interview she also talks about the impact of her disability caused by childhood polio on her life. To evoke strong feelings, as our life stories often do, and at the same time to condemn the expression of feelings create both emotional and epistemological confusion.[21]

Feelings are intrinsic to a pedagogy based in experience because, as Dewey argued, feelings give coherence to experience.[22] Stories told without feeling have an irritating, confusing, or comic effect. Yet feelings do not have self-evident meanings. Unless we understand the feelings expressed in a given story, the story remains incomprehensible. Numerous feminist projects have floundered because some participants do not "get" the feelings of others and how these feelings are linked to certain interactions or events.

As troublesome as feelings have been in activist and academic contexts, the pioneers of consciousness-raising gave them special prominence. "We assume our feelings are telling us something from which we can learn," wrote Kathie Sarachild.[23] Such early advocates insisted that political inquiry into feelings did not amount to "therapy." While their feminist and nonfeminist critics accused them of individualism and self-indulgence, proponents of consciousness-raising stressed the collective and cognitive gains reaped from careful attention to feelings. Giving voice to feelings, their writings suggest, served three functions: to break through the dominant definitions of reality, to promote bonding among women, and to foster action. Each of these functions suggests a place for feelings in feminist discourse.

Feelings may break through the dominant definitions of reality in two respects. Like the experiences to which feelings are linked, they can challenge what Arlie Hochschild calls the prevailing "feeling rules."[24] Feeling rules are developed to control and shape the feelings that people display in certain situations. When disempowered people express what Alison Jaggar has named "outlaw feelings," they not only vent reactions that feeling rules bid them to repress (the white middle-class woman taught never to offend others shouts out in delighted rage, "No more nice girls!") but invite discussion of both feeling rules and the feelings we have despite them. When as a feminist teacher I find myself having feelings that seem to be inappropriate to my role as a professor—for instance, I become ashamed of something I have said or done in class—I may either repress those outlaw feelings or take them as the beginning point for reflection on my practice. Similarly, when Ida (who features in my first story) expresses her fears of women's liberation, she raises to me and the class the question of whether it is acceptable for a feminist to have "disagreeable feelings" about feminist values.

Feelings are directed toward both external objects and internal objects such as memories. We are not simply angry but angry at something, not simply sad but sad about something. Thus, as Morwenna Griffiths argues, feelings involve perceptions and judgments.[25] These perceptions and judgments are not infallible or, I would add, necessarily consistent. Paying attention to feelings in the context of feminist inquiry involves paying attention to the sometimes conflicting perceptions and judgments implied by them. Ida's expression of hope in the movement exercise challenges the dominant feeling rules for a white middle-class woman like herself because, as she later explains, her family expected her to put her maternal feelings and desire to have children ahead of her longing to become a professional dancer. The fear her movement expresses directs our attention to the price women might pay for following their hearts' desires. These feelings involve perceptions and judgments that the class can discuss. What is the price, I ask the class, that variously situated women pay for breaking the feeling rules that govern our worlds? How should we evaluate the hopes women like Ida have about choosing a path of which their families disapprove? What does it mean to choose an "unrealistic" career path? What is realistic? When do our hopes or fears simply reproduce or question the range of choices imposed on us? The feminist text we have just read provides a set of answers against which we can test and shape our own.[26]

As Sue Campbell points out, however, our feelings do not always fit neatly into the dominant vocabulary of feelings.[27] When our feelings go beyond established categories, we need to communicate them to others to discover how they can be satisfactorily described. In a women's studies class, where students may hold strong beliefs about which feelings are acceptable ("Will the teacher punish me for expressing this? Will other students find my feelings disgusting? What if it is hard for me to say what I feel?"), teachers need to be especially aware of how difficult it is to convey outlaw feelings. In the case of Ida, she courageously struggles to describe the kind of fear that sent her cowering behind a chair. It was fear, she says, but of a special kind: linked to the possibility that your family might exclude you. This was not a feeling, Ida noted, that was easy to describe, particularly in a women's studies class.

Early descriptions of consciousness-raising also refer to the *bonding* that emerges as women share feelings about oppression and liberation. This bonding has implications for both thinking and acting. Talking about gender injustice requires openness to ideas, experiences and feelings and patience in tracing through their relations and implications. Emotional bonding, including the sense of connection, the desire to continue relationship, and the feelings that accompany connection, plays an important role in sustaining such discussion. It plays an especially valuable role in feminist discourse that invites emotional forthrightness. I seriously doubt that Ida would have allowed herself to express her hopes and fears if she had not felt a certain degree of bonding with me and others in the class. For this reason, I waited until I thought that enough bonding had developed to try such an exercise, and I checked with the students about how they felt about participating.

Bonding, however, is emotionally and epistemologically complex. People bond not only through love and affection but through anger and competition. In her essays on black women and emotions, Audre Lorde argues with respect to anger that feelings can connect or separate women, depending on many factors.[28] As Lorde's thinking suggests, students sometimes use anger to break through what they see as resistance on the part of other students or the teacher to making a real connection. Both Clarissa and Marylou (of the story in the previous section) direct anger toward me to make a connection and expand their participation in the class. They want their own experiences and thoughts to be more fully a part of our discussion. By acting out her fears in the movement exercise, Ida indicates that feminism has problematic consequences for her that could lead to separation from or greater bonding with other women.

Proponents of consciousness-raising often assumed that women's anger generated through discovering and discussing oppression would fuel feminist activism. This simple cause-and-effect relationship could hold only if consciousness-raising evokes predictable emotions. If feelings have more than one meaning and if contradictory feelings can arise in response to a given experience or perceived pattern of injustice, *particular emotions do not lead to a predetermined course of action.* For some women, discussion of oppression leads to fear and shame rather than anger. For some, anger is more easily directed at mothers or sisters or at less or more privileged women than at male domination.

Nevertheless, feelings do have deep connections to action, and exploring these connections can make a valuable contribution to feminist discourse. If Titania (the student who constantly claimed to be a feminist but kept her distance from the class) was actually angry with her mother for insisting that her daughter live up to some particular ideal of feminist behavior, my asking the class to reflect on our feelings about our mothers might help us all understand the frequent disjunction between feminist beliefs and feminist actions. If Ida, whose hopes and fears seemed to be opposite sides of the same feminist coin, could talk about what frightened her, the class might be able to explore how women could support each other in areas where some of us are more frightened than others to undertake risky actions. *Shared feelings are not required for shared action* and sometimes even get in the way of it. In another class, a student describes a meeting of mostly women graduate student instructors in which everyone talked about how frightened they were to try to organize as workers. She tells us how she longed to hear someone speak up who was not frightened, who might share with them her hopefulness and excitement about the changes their collective actions might effect.

Thus, there is nothing self-evident about the role of feelings in feminist discourse, either what they mean or how they should function. What is evident in the viewpoint I am developing is that attention to feelings broadens the opportunities for reflection. This type of reflection has a friendly quality, in the sense that it does not objectify a given feeling response as though it were an alien or dangerous specimen to be examined under a microscope. Rather, such reflection recognizes the kinship as well as the differences between thinking and feeling. Both involve ideas. Both presume and contribute to judgments. And both remain important elements of feminist discourse.

のﾝ

Thinking can have a friendly relation to feeling and the other elements of feminist discourse without being imprecise. In fact, to play its part in feminist discourse, thinking needs to be conducted with great care. The call to consciousness-raising was not a call to fuzzy thinking. Quite the reverse. Early proponents claimed with good reason that women needed to think carefully and thoroughly about gender injustice. The drive to develop a feminist analysis that permeated a good deal of early consciousness-raising had at least two qualities. It emphasized the interactions between subject and object, and it was oriented toward action. Both of these qualities involve complications that make thinking a problematic element in feminist discourse.

When experience and feelings are both seen as ways of knowing, subject and object cannot be permanently separated. Knowing involves a relation between the knower and the known, and claims to knowledge must include an understanding of that relation.[29] This does not imply that feminist discourse precludes us from separating ourselves temporarily and contingently from the objects we seek to know. We periodically can and should "step back" from our experiences, feelings, thinking, and actions. The problem is less whether we can or should seek to make such distances than under what conditions we might attempt to do so and how.

The story about Marylou and Clarissa that I tell in the previous section is also a story about making distances between the knower and the known. When Marylou makes her critical remark about Clarissa's writing, I need to decide whether to increase or decrease our distance as a class from the object of discussion—that is, our experiences with race. The problem is that some students feel that they are very close to these experiences through memories, sensory impressions, and feelings that are strong and alive, and other students stand at a considerable distance from them. To avoid making some students into "natives" while others become the scientists who study them, I must see whether I can bring all of us within roughly the same distance from the experiences we are trying to understand. The distance may vary as our discourse proceeds. This does not mean that we must have the same relationship to the objects of our discussion. Marylou will never be in the same relation to Clarissa's experiences of race as Clarissa herself. But considerable points of connection may emerge. As white women, they both may have acquired ideas that are relevant to their experiences of racial difference, and they could look at these ideas together.

My story about the conference, in which younger academics reject the theories espoused by older academics, brings out another aspect of the subject–object relation: the role of feelings. As Lorde notes, feelings can make connections where other factors, such as racism or homophobia, create distance. In the conference story, feelings run high. The older academics feel pride at having developed groundbreaking feminist theories and anger at the lack of recognition for their work. Their younger colleagues are deeply excited about the theories they themselves are developing. Yet none of the participants talks about the source and meaning of their pride or anger or excitement. They assert the value of their theories without making it possible for others to come closer to these exciting ideas. According to Lorraine Code, our understanding of the subject–object relation might benefit by using the vocabularies of touch and hearing.[30] Feelings in this sense can provide a kind of invitation into the thinking of others and a clue to understanding what that thinking means. "This idea intrigues me," we could say. "Come with me close enough to touch it, to hear its subtle nuances."

Thinking is also directional. It flows in one direction or another. That flow, however, is continually shaped by what Elizabeth Young-Bruehl characterizes as the conversational or, I would say, discourse-like quality of thinking.[31] To varying degrees, thinking may incorporate the divergent points of view we encounter in the world around us. This quality is especially important to feminist classroom discourse through which individuals with different experiences and ideas can evolve into a group of people who self-consciously incorporate elements of each others' thinking into their internal discourse. Self-consciousness is important here. Consciousness-raising demands that women become more self-conscious about the points of view that they incorporate into their thinking about gender relations: where they adopt sexist assumptions and where they challenge them. As a feminist teacher, I am constantly asking students to become more self-conscious about what points of view they are accepting or rejecting as part of their own thinking processes. No matter how ardently they advocate or reject feminism, I do not believe they can think well about feminist issues without looking at them from more than one point of view.

Thinking as external and internal discourse can go on endlessly or at least until the question being addressed is in some way resolved. In one respect, this image of ongoing thinking fits with an early image of consciousness-raising as a kind of political talk that would continue as long as women were oppressed. In another sense, however, ongoing feminist discourse exists in tension with two other aspects of the consciousness-raising process: the attempt to develop a theory of women's oppression and the need to interrupt talk by engaging in actions that challenge the order of things outside the consciousness-raising group.

The prospect of developing a unified theory of women's oppression has been open to question from the beginning of second-wave activism. Ellen

Willis remarks that women activists often brought radical but also divergent theories of social change into their consciousness-raising discussions.[32] Pamela Allen's notion that groups of differently situated women would have to come together to discuss their different ideas suggests that a unified theory could only be developed through a far more extensive process of political talk than has yet taken place. While this discourse proceeds, increasing numbers of feminist academics propose their own theories of oppression or of the oppression of particular groups of women. The problem posed for feminist classroom discourse thus becomes twofold: how to view this multiplicity of theories and how to support the process of theory building.

Theorizing, of course, is never pursued in an intellectual vacuum. At the same time that Kathie Sarachild envisioned consciousness-raising as breaking entirely new ground, she pointed to the tremendous contributions that Simone de Beauvoir's analysis had made to women's liberation. Yet previous theory in no way erases the importance of continued theory building.[33] As long as groups of women newly engage with each other to talk about their particular experiences of oppression, the definition of gender injustice remains open to differentiation and change. In the context of feminist discourse, the first question is not how to determine which of these theories is superior to all the rest but, as Marilyn Frye has suggested, how we can understand the relationships among emerging theories.[34] Assuming that each theory articulated within the context of a feminist movement corresponds to some systemic problem in gender relations, the effort to grasp relationships among theories is also an attempt to understand the connections among the different ways in which women experience oppression.

This sort of feminist discourse requires not only the continued generation of new theories but a willingness to question again and again what constitutes "a theory." When an unfamiliar voice enters a given arena of feminist discussion, it is tempting to those who have been talking together to dismiss the newcomer's words as irrelevant, anecdotal, or "atheoretical." In feminist classrooms, where the teacher and sometimes students have considerable knowledge of one or more feminist theories, it is easy to assume that newcomers to this feminist discourse have nothing theoretical to contribute.

Yet I find theory building often taking place in my feminist classes through both *spontaneity* and *intentionality*. Theory building may begin spontaneously when students are reflecting on or comparing experiences. For instance, Dominic is struck by the difference between the tough stance he took as a member of a gang of Italian American boys who fought many turf wars with a neighboring African American gang and Clarissa's childhood belief that she should prevent harm to a black child in her schoolyard. Dominic has been drawn to discussions of masculinity and wonders how the particular Italian American version of masculinity he learned as a child may have supported or contradicted the racism and sexism that permeated his teenage culture. I, in turn, identify Dominic's thinking as a theory in the making. I suggest to him that he do more reading as well as see whether others in the class would be willing to work on this topic as part of a final project.

Although spontaneity can spark the process of theorizing, theory building also requires focus. It demands time out from the ongoing flow of thinking. Ellen Shumsky recounts how her lesbian feminist consciousness-raising group eventually created a subgroup to develop more fully the theoretical ideas that had been emerging in the original group's discussions. Barbara Christian's image of theory as "fixing a constellation of ideas for a time at least" nicely captures both the sense of flow in thinking and the fact that "fixing" takes concentrated effort.[35]

Dominic, who has been thinking about masculinity, finds two other class members to join him in talking about race, ethnicity and gender in the lives of young people: Perry, an African American man who was part of the sort of gang with which Dominic fought, and Doris, who is teaching in a school in which the girls have begun to form gangs of their own. Dominic and his partners spend a number of weeks both reading and talking about developing a theoretical approach adequate to this topic. As their teacher, I do not know how far they can take their project, but I am certain that their work will make a considerable contribution to our ongoing discourse and play a role in the way they or other class members approach questions of action.

No matter how successful this group is in developing a shared analysis of these issues, their effort to relate theory to action cannot rely on theory alone. *Theory rarely leads in a straight line to action.* It usually encounters both theoretical and practical contradictions that indicate the need for taking new points of view into consideration. This kind of interaction among theories and practices takes place constantly in political decision making. For example, a group of white feminists makes an action plan informed by their theory of change. In trying to carry out their plan, they discover that substantial numbers of women of color object to it. At this point, the predominantly white group must either ignore the contradiction between their theory and the possibility of a multiracial practice or open up their discourse to other theories and the likelihood of having to modify or abandon their project. Thinking does not stop because a group has developed or adopted a theory. Both theories and thinking contribute to political judgments and actions. If Doris attempts to apply her classroom-developed theory to the girl gangs in her school, she will probably encounter practical impediments and points of view that have to be taken into account for her work to succeed. She may not like the positions taken by other teachers, administrators, or even girl gang members, but she will have to think about and come to grips with them.

This very multiplicity of viewpoints deeply disturbs Zelda, the student who comes up to me after class to complain that conflicting feminist theories do not direct her toward one clear action. In part, Zelda's distress stems from her notion of "action." At the time Zelda is taking my course, there are virtually no mass feminist actions. She is attracted to the environmental movement (and apparently not interested in exploring its connections to feminism) because it represents to her an area in which she believes she can "do something."

Action was a problematic word for second-wave feminists as well. From the early years of this resurging movement, feminists employed this term in conflicting ways. Action could be individual or collective. It could be generated by grassroots organizing or through governmental or other formal political structures. It could mean making political demands for services for women or creating alternative institutions to serve them. Although activists fought bitter battles over the priority of one or another form of action, they also acknowledged connections among these modes (e.g., in rejecting her role as a battered wife a woman might join with others in trying to stop patterns of such abuse). And, as Nancy Whittier points out, feminists themselves might move between different forms of action, in particular, from grassroots activism to more institutionalized forms, as the movement itself became more institutionalized.[36]

Such shifts in the focus of activism reflect the fact that political judgments are not made in the abstract: they depend on our *values*, the *contexts of action*, and our *options as actors*.[37] Any of these elements may change, of course, but the greater our awareness of them, the more vigorous our political agency. This applies to situations inside as well as outside the classroom. When Zelda tells me about her plans to join an environmental project, I cannot help smiling at her innocence: she does not realize that the theories associated with environmental activism conflict with each other just as much as do feminist theories. Yet, on a deeper level, I am disappointed with Zelda's announcement. She is drawn to an area of action that she sees as dramatic, even dangerous, and effective. She does not find feminism exciting. She is young and strong and lacking attachments and obligations that might keep her here. Even though her activist experiences may give her a chance to think more deeply about the relevance of feminist theories, she does not need to call on them now. Her choice makes me a bit sad and slightly envious, but I am not sorry about my own, my somewhat domesticated but persistent passion for feminism, my decision to continue working in an institutional context, my deep and complex involvement with others that would make it difficult for me to make a comparable choice.

Although some early proponents of consciousness-raising hoped to create a unified theory of women's oppression to direct political decisions, they also expected action to inform theory as much as theory informed action. This image of interaction between theory and action assumes that theoretical differences must be discussed in terms of their relation to action—the different practical meanings and consequences they entail. In a second-wave essay that argues for the importance of developing distinctly feminist theory, Charlotte Bunch points out that asking students to address questions of action from a multiplicity of feminist theoretical viewpoints supports creative and practical thinking.[38]

In Zelda's class, several students explore this theory–practice interaction. A small group develops a critique of several major feminist theorists we have read during the semester and spells out the implications of this criticism for their own practice as school counselors. Another class member draws on the readings to develop a plan for introducing a discussion of racism into the women's organization to which she belongs. Two students analyze different arguments about sexual harassment as part of developing a staff workshop for a hospital where they work. In this latter case, the students report to the class, and we talk about where the event succeeded or failed and why different class members think this was the case. These projects, of course, reflect the student population I teach, as well as a time period in which very little feminist activism is taking place in the streets. Had this been a period of more dramatic activism, perhaps Zelda would have joined a battle closer to home, despite the conflicts she found among feminist theories.

As a feminist teacher who advocates action, I am cautious about substituting my own for the students' political judgment. In the end, they do and must decide what actions they will take, or continue, or cease. I can require them to learn about how other people have acted or are currently acting in response to social injustice. I can urge them to try out (in or outside school) those forms of activism they deem valuable and effective. I believe that by engaging fully with experiences, feelings, and ideas about gender and other forms of injustice, students will become more reflective about their ongoing actions and/or will embark on others. Many of these actions will begin with their personal situations. In the last weeks of the semester, Lindsey tells me that she plans to leave her abusive husband. After the end of another semester, I hear from Kitty that she has decided to come out as a lesbian on her job. Such individual steps can lead to more collective actions. Lindsey cannot engage in any collective efforts as long as so much of her anger and fear is tied up in her relationship with her husband. If she leaves, feminist activism becomes an option. Kitty's decision owes a great deal to her growing interest in the movement of Asian American feminists. She already has put in a call to an organization of Asian American lesbians like herself that was listed at the end of one of our readings. She is ready to explore acting in a more collaborative way.

In figuring out the best role for action in my teaching, I also try to keep in mind the fact that *political actions involve differential risks*. As Mitsuye Yamada notes, white women often underestimate the risk to women of color in taking a feminist stance.[39] Feminist discourse, however, can clarify these differential risks. In a discussion of discrimination in promotions, for instance, we end up talking about both the different courses of action the individual who faces discrimination might take (an informal discussion with the boss, filing a grievance, organizing other employees to protest, etc.) and how each course of action might affect differently situated people (a woman of color with a white male boss, a poor woman who might lose the only job she has held in years, the lone out lesbian in a workplace). This discussion does not mandate decisions. Some students might want to take certain actions despite the high risk, and some might not want to act at all despite very low risk. Rather, the discussion illuminates decisions, not only their possible consequences for the actors and others but their meaning for those who consider taking them.

Although participants in such discussions do not necessarily arrive at the same judgments, this kind of interchange helps them become accountable to each other for the judgments they do make. The process of feminist classroom discourse encourages them to take into account each others' perspectives, their thoughts, experiences, and feelings in supporting or committing to one action rather than another. In this respect, although students may or may not engage in shared actions outside the classroom, they practice in their feminist discourse what Patrocinio Schweickart has described as "coordinating individual agency in a collective enterprise."[40] At its best, feminist discourse not only orients its participants toward action but (as the early proponents of consciousness-raising said about that process) is itself a form of action. If people who care about gender injustice cannot talk about action, it is unlikely that they will be able to act together.

Second-wave activists displayed a good deal of optimism about how individual agency could be coordinated. Many women were drawn together by their desires to change their lives and the prospect of changing a social system that disadvantaged women. In the spirit of this new freedom, women could self-organize into groups and projects of many kinds. Joining a social movement was an act of faith in the future, not a way of accommodating to an unfree present. No hierarchy seemed necessary to coordinate feminist activities. Movement values suggested that as equals women together would decide how their energies could be organized. But these assumptions about freedom and equality quickly ran into difficulties. Whether activists liked it or not, distinctions of power and authority too often emerged in their ranks. This was as true of consciousness-raising as other activities in which feminists engaged. It was even truer for feminist classrooms, where compulsion and inequality were built into the educational system. As feminist teachers tried to incorporate the insights of consciousness-raising into their classrooms, the problems of authority became daunting.

— 3 —

THE ROCKY ROAD TO
FEMINIST EMPOWERMENT

Questioning Authority

Although I usually sit in a circle with the students and make some opening remarks from there, the large size of this women's studies class and the poor acoustics tempt me to use the podium set up for the instructor who teaches the class before mine. As I stand behind the podium and place the notes for my brief presentation on its surface, I find my back straightening, my shoulders widening, and my head lifting in a gesture of authority. I remember what it feels like to stand in front of large classes. Yes, I think, this is what it takes to be a "professor."

Kip sits in my office talking about the possibility of coming out in class. I acknowledge that this act always involves risks, but I assure her that if she wants to take them, she will have my support. We talk about the invisibility of lesbians in our school and how she might deal with homophobic reactions from the class. I suspect that some members of this apparently heterosexual group might direct toward Kip the fear and anger that they have hesitated to direct toward me. I am not sure how much I can trust the students to respond to Kip in the spirit of feminist discourse. I am not sure how much the students will trust me.

Two of the strongest charges against feminist teachers in higher education involve the misuse of authority. According to some accounts, we corrupt the meaning of professorial authority by brainwashing our students, by directly or indirectly forcing upon them our own political values. According to others, we fail in the proper exercise of authority by not passing on to our students the fruits of feminist scholarship, by substituting "touchy-feely exercises" for "real teaching." Feminist teachers often have difficulty responding to these criticisms because we are still struggling ourselves to articulate the meaning of authority in our work. For those of us drawing on the legacy of consciousness-raising, this struggle is compounded by the contradictions we have inherited from that practice.

Consciousness-raising arose during a period of growing suspicion toward authority as an expression of power.[1] Grassroots activists, in particular, commonly assumed that individual claims to authority masked oppressive power structures. In the historical context of second-wave activism, an army general's authority represented the interests of the military, a boss's authority expressed the interests of capital, and a doctor's authority mirrored the interests of organized medicine. By virtue of their locations in powerful and interrelated groups, such individuals could deploy various political, legal, economic, social, and cultural resources. Because of the great constraints society imposed on oppressed groups, people in authority expected their commands or even their mere suggestions to be followed. According to the activist critique, this merging of power with authority was not necessarily conscious. A doctor might believe that his orders to his patient were "for her own good" although, in fact, he was serving his own group interests. Questioning authority, most grassroots activists would have argued, involved questioning the oppressive power that permeated it.

The pioneers of consciousness-raising set out to question authority that oppressed women and to uncover the power structures that supported such authority. By talking about their experiences and feelings, women could explore why they sometimes complied with oppressive authority and sometimes were able to challenge oppressive commands or expectations. Thus, consciousness-raising would help women *reconfigure both authority and power*, by developing more self-conscious and effective responses to gender injustice and by building the mutual understanding and trust required to support both individual and collective action. Questioning oppressive authority was a key element in nurturing women's political agency.

One of the great strengths of this approach lay in the belief that no matter how powerless women felt in their daily lives, they could become empowered through political discourse embedded in a feminist movement. One of the great weaknesses lay in the fact that by joining such groups women did not necessarily or even typically sever their ties to the structures of power in which they were enmeshed. A heterosexual member of a consciousness-raising group still benefited from her relationships with heterosexual men; a white woman, from the everyday privileges automatically granted to her on the basis of her skin color; a middle-class woman, from her economic resources. Women in the same occupations, such as academics or artists, noticed that relationships with powerfully situated men or women outside the group (someone's husband was a tenured professor, another's lover an art critic) might result in some women's words being given more weight and other women hesitating to say what they thought. Working-class feminists and feminists of color noted how the upbringing and education of white middle-class women led the latter to identify their own way of talking with authority. And, as Jo Freeman early pointed out, the friendships some members developed with each other outside their consciousness-raising group gave them special authority when they spoke within it.[2]

In trying to avoid inequities among participants, many proponents of consciousness-raising emphasized equality of participation. But the underlying problem could not be easily addressed. A consciousness-raising group was not the world: power stemming from individual women's connections outside the group still affected their authority relations with each other. If this was true for consciousness-raising, it was even truer for a feminist classroom. Located in hierarchical institutions, teachers and students could not avoid having different relationships to structures of power. In various ways, these were compounded by varying combinations of racial, class, heterosexual, and other privileges. A white, tenured, female faculty member might easily exercise authority over a nervous, white, female undergraduate. But the authority dynamics would be far less straightforward for an Asian American adjunct teacher, all of whose students were white, or for a young, white, working-class woman professor facing a room of rather jaded, middle-class graduate students.

The story about my stepping up to the podium to make a presentation to a class with whom I usually sit in a circle suggests how complex the problem of authority may become in teaching through feminist discourse. To some extent, as we pursue our often heartfelt and intellectually intense discussions, the students and I downplay our different relationships to structures of power outside the classroom. Most of us are excited by how we talk together. When I step up to the podium, we all are suddenly reminded of what at least some of us have momentarily forgotten. The podium is intended for me, rather than the students. It has been placed there by the university so that I can deliver to them the knowledge I have been professionally and institutionally authorized to convey. The notes I place on the podium have an entirely different status than the notes the students are now energetically taking. Despite how much I enjoy the circle discussions, I now notice how much I like the feeling of standing behind this podium. It is made out of real wood, smooth and warm, rather than the cold plastic and steel chairs on which the students are sitting. I can lean on the podium for support, just as I depend on the university to support me with its monthly checks. My sense of authority, like my posture, expands with my awareness of the resources to which I have access because of my institutional and professional location.

Moreover, I feel proud of being able to stand here. As a girl child, I found it hard to imagine myself exercising authority in relation to anything outside a household. I want the students to understand what it takes for me to claim authority in a classroom, not only to grasp that a woman can speak with authority but to appreciate the kind of serious work that shapes my authority as a feminist professor. My pleasure in this moment is mixed with wariness, however. The podium symbolizes a trap into which I can easily fall. It is the trap of taking for granted the structures of power to which I have access, of assuming that I can draw on the resources they afford me without paying attention to how my participation in the institution may maintain my own oppression and/or the oppression of others.

More than a decade before the first rumblings of second-wave feminism, Simone de Beauvoir identified this problem as one of *women's complicity* in gender oppression. By accepting dependency on men, women exchanged their freedom for the security and self-satisfaction of domestic life.[3] As the second wave rolled into academic settings, white feminists such as Madeleine Grumet and Jo Anne Pagano argued that women teachers who serve and depend on patriarchal educational institutions make a similar trade-off when they exert their professional authority over female students or mothers who are not professionals. In a similar vein, feminists of color such as Linda Carty pointed out how white women's complicity in racism was manifest in our ignoring the ways in which racial privilege contributed to our academic authority. In the days that follow my spontaneous decision to use the podium to make my presentation, I am still wondering how much the authority I exercise in teaching through feminist discourse involves me in complicity.

Both feminist and nonfeminist teachers who want to avoid the trap of complicity turn to the notion of sharing power and authority with the students. This ideal fits well with the spirit of consciousness-raising and the attempt to infuse it into feminist classroom discourse. Like many teachers, I use various techniques to accomplish this end. I ask students to meet in small group discussions, to develop their own projects, to take a hand in their own assessment, to make their own presentations from the podium. But employing such techniques does not fully clarify what it means to "share authority." To understand this, we need to take a closer look at what we think we are sharing.

My teaching position gives me a form of *authority as the capacity to issue commands* backed by sanctions. Whatever rationale I give, the students know that they have to do what I say to pass the course. That authority is not absolute. It is relative to how I interact with a predominantly white, male, middle- and upper-class, and heterosexually structured world that can support my authority. It is also relative to the opposition it encounters. Any structures of power can be challenged by those with less power "acting in concert," to use Hannah Arendt's well-known phrase.[4] Students or teachers or other employees can organize, protest, garner inside and outside resources to contest the relationships that prevail within their school. A feminist teacher's authority might rapidly soar or completely collapse, depending on movements to realign power both within and outside the institution. Over a given semester, I may encounter numerous small-scale versions of this pattern, as students get together inside or outside class to talk about their concerns and to present to me complaints or demands. Under these conditions, my ability to command can be seriously reduced. Even if I were not inclined to listen to what students have to say, I would feel pressured to share my authority by negotiating with the students.

For many teachers trying to avoid the trap of complicity with oppressive structures, the possibility of negotiating with students about the content and form of a class seems to offer a just alternative. In this approach, a teacher relies less on her ability to command and threaten ("if you don't write that paper, I'll give you an F for the course") than on the *authority of agreement*. Indeed, the very notion of authority, as opposed to direct force, implies some degree of agreement to comply with those in authority. (The student being threatened with an F could in theory agree to take that grade, even though the results might be quite harmful to her.) The argument that teachers can and should negotiate with students, however, assumes that teachers will broaden the range of choices so that students can find options that they consider genuinely agreeable. These options might include selecting a paper topic that is of special interest or working with other students who have similar interests. A teacher might negotiate with the students and finally agree to a project that fits within the framework of the course. Or she might be willing to stretch that framework to include a topic that at first did not seem relevant to her plan.

From the standpoint of feminist discourse, the notion of sharing authority through agreement has a great deal of appeal. It permits a teacher to share at least some of the power the institution affords her. It supports the agency of both women and men students. It encourages students to bring into the classroom experiences, feelings, ideas, and proposed or previous actions that they might see as relevant to the course and of which the teacher might not have been aware. But the idea of authority as agreement (sometimes expressed literally through a student–teacher contract) has serious limits in its applications to teaching through feminist discourse. To begin with, in the absence of a student or other movement to truly call into question the authority of educational structures, such negotiations still take place at the sufferance of the teacher. Moreover, it is far from clear that a feminist teacher should consider every aspect of her work negotiable. This is particularly evident to me when students want me to drop the term *feminist* or complain about my including readings on race or sexual orientation in the syllabus because "they are not about women." I do not consider these issues negotiable because of how I view feminism and related social justice movements.

For my authority as a feminist teacher stems not only from my institutional and professional position but from the power and authority of a feminist movement. The power of the movement grows out of feminists acting together to address gender injustice and all the other forms of injustice with which it is intertwined. The authority of the movement stems from the ways it uses power as well as the extent to which both women and men consent to its initiatives. Since the movement is not monolithic, its power and authority take complex and contradictory forms. Yet without such a movement, the meaning of my authority as a feminist teacher would become highly problematic.

Another serious limit grows out of the fact that reaching agreements requires a fairly high level of predictability. Feminist discourse as I conceive it does not allow for a high level of prediction and control. I can say to students at the beginning of the semester that this course will invite strong feelings and touch on important experiences. I can describe the class process and assure students that I will monitor that process carefully. Yet they do not know what actually to expect, and neither, to a certain extent, do I. Under these conditions, a contract model of authority might well lead both students and me into situations we find intolerable, in which we do not want to keep our words.[5]

This lack of predictability and control, however, provides the soil in which other forms of authority can flourish. A lack of predictability and control supports *creative authority*—that is, the authority that develops through the use of the imagination, by showing others that a situation can be viewed differently. Because feminist discourse combines elements that often remain separated and alienated, such as feelings and ideas, it requires a high degree of creativity to bring these elements into a constructive relation. What is more, the lack of predictability and control implies that to some extent *authority must be rooted in trust*. As Annette Baier points out, even the most rigorous contract requires a degree of trust.[6] Where a feminist teacher is asking students to share experiences and feelings, authority requires considerable trust.

In the story about Kip wanting to come out as a lesbian in class, trust emerges as integral to the exercise of authority in a feminist classroom. As a teacher, I am trying to get this class to consider more seriously the meaning of sexual diversity for questions of gender injustice. I can see that many of the students (none of whom have identified themselves in the class as lesbian, bisexual, transgender, or gay) have a lot of discomfort with this topic. Authority-as-command does not get me very far in this situation. I cannot command students to open their minds and hearts to these questions. Nor does authority-as-agreement take me very far, when students would just as soon avoid the topic. To exercise my authority, I need to be more creative, and the students and I need to develop a higher level of trust.

Kip's desire to come out in class promotes creativity in the use of my authority. Since I cannot be certain how class members will react and how Kip, in turn, will respond to them, I know I will have to be alert to many possibilities. I know, too, that I do not want the situation to turn into one that hurts Kip and reinforces homophobia. I talk to Kip about whether she would like me to lay some more ground for her, perhaps using a visualization in which students have to pay attention to the heterosexist assumptions around which so much academic activity is organized. She says no but hopes I will step in if the reactions become too aggressive. I realize how much trust is involved here. Kip has entrusted me by telling me about her sexual orientation. I am testing out how much I trust the class, not simply to treat Kip with respect but to continue the work of feminist discourse. I also hope that they will trust me to lead them toward exploring more fully how sexual orientation affects gender injustice and what might be done to combat it.

Thus, over and above the power granted to me by the institution, the students' trust enables me to take and sustain a kind of leadership in the class. I set and maintain a direction, even though the actual destination remains less than fully known. Most students do grow in their trust of me, just as I grow to trust them and they to trust each other. This relationship is not vague or general. Such trust is specific to the situation in which the students and I encounter each other and the end to which I exercise authority. Given the variation in our different social locations and our relationships with each other (Kip's to me will be different from that of the heterosexual students), this trust will always be *contingent* rather than complete. Contingent trust, however, is very common in our lives, particularly our lives in formal institutions, so that this qualification need not prevent us from doing our work together.

∾

My ability to share authority also depends on the extent to which students themselves are willing and able to take leadership in the feminist classroom discourse. When Kip comes out in class, I am in for a surprise. When one of the students makes a subtly denigrating comment, Zillah, who is a tall, muscular heterosexual woman, begins to describe what it is like for her to be taken for a lesbian. She notes the comments men make and how she has been treated in workplaces. She talks about how she engenders fear in some heterosexual women and how she herself used to be afraid when lesbians made overtures to her. She also notes her complex response to a lesbian feminist reading assigned for this session, because of the contrast between her experiences of being taken for a man or a lesbian and her sexual self-definition. With this comment, she directs both me and the rest of the class to a closer analysis of the reading and to consider what it means for the choices and actions open to us. As I ask her to begin with her interpretation of the text, I feel pleasure and pride in the authority she has assumed.

This notion of sharing authority is not based on asserting a feminist identity or arguing for a particular feminist point of view. Often a student who is unsure of her relation to the movement or even doubts its necessity can take leadership in a given discussion. She might do this by exploring the conflict between some feminist claim to knowledge and knowledge she brings from other sources, by contrasting her commitment to another personal or social cause with the passion that feminists express, or by insisting that the group look at some underlying tension between the classroom process and the institution in which she and her classmates are trying to make their ways. Conversely, students who come to class as self-identified feminists or who in the classroom context eagerly embrace a feminist identity may or may not assume leadership in feminist classroom discourse. Such authority requires an understanding of that discourse as a collective enterprise, which leaders can direct but not determine. It requires respect for experience and feelings as well as for ideas and options for action.

Why, in a feminist classroom, should students or teachers acknowledge such leadership? In the remainder of this chapter, I will approach this question by exploring three particular dimensions of authority in feminist classrooms. These are *authority as knowledge, authority as passion*, and *authority as position*. In its exercise, each type of authority involves both power and trust. Each includes the temptation toward complicity and the potential for creativity. Each requires leadership of a teacher and encourages the leadership of students. These meanings are not exclusive or exhaustive. In the next chapter, I will address a fourth and very important dimension of authority in feminist teaching: caring. For now, I want to concentrate on these first three and the manner in which they serve or impede feminist discourse.

AUTHORITY AS KNOWLEDGE

Agnes comes up to me after an especially exciting discussion and says she is dying to hear about what I have to say on the topic. She loves the discussions and the readings, but she is sure that given my years of involvement in the movement and my feminist research and writing I have something special to say.

As far as Simon (a heterosexual, white man in his midtwenties) is concerned, I cannot do anything right. If I introduce a topic, he says I am avoiding another issue. If I suggest an exercise, he points out that it ignores certain factors. I listen carefully to his criticisms, and I modify or eliminate some activities as the result of his remarks. But I know something else is going on here. There is a power struggle between us, a struggle over my teaching authority.

After the class in which Agnes makes her remark, I spend a long time thinking about its meaning. Later this same week, another student, an undergraduate named Shari, complains in another women's studies course that I am not lecturing. Her parents have paid good money, she says, so that she can learn from her teachers and not listen to a bunch of ignorant students. Shari hints that she might take her dissatisfaction to the dean. I feel a lot of pressure from students to live up to a traditional, professorial image of authority. Yet I see a world of difference between Shari's complaint and Agnes's request. Shari acts like a dissatisfied customer. Agnes wants me to bring more of myself into the class: what I have experienced, what I know, what I make of the perplexing problems we discuss.

I do not change the format of Shari's class, although I spend considerable time trying to explain to her why I teach the way I teach. The next week, however, instead of beginning Agnes's class with a discussion of readings on mothering as I had planned, I start with a lecture. I talk some about mothering as a global phenomenon, reading excerpts from autobiographical accounts of mothers from different classes and cultures. I point out some of the different ways in which feminists have conceived of mothering, the conflicts among feminists and between feminists and nonfeminists about what theories account for mothering and what actions might be taken in relation to it. I describe activist conflicts I have encountered about how to frame issues concerning motherhood. I bring in my choice not to have children, and I mention the tension that this choice created with my own mother, how difficult it was for us to understand each others' point of view. I note that the assigned reading has brought up mixed feelings in me, and I ask the students to do some free writing on the term *motherhood* before we begin our discussion.

After class, Agnes comes up to me again, this time with tears in her eyes. She tells me that she has been trying for several years without success to have a child and that this effort not only has put tremendous strain on her relationship with her husband but has stood in the way of joining a feminist organization in her community. She has been afraid that her intense wish to have a child is too "traditional," not sufficiently "feminist." My presentation has helped her see that there is room for her thinking in the complex feminist discourse on motherhood. In her discussion group, she has discovered that one of the other students, another white, middle-class mother who lives in Agnes's community, is very angry about the lack of attention to the impact of poverty on mothering (in both a text we are reading and in the country as a whole). They have decided, Agnes says, to join a feminist organization together, to see what they can do.

In this story, Agnes's request allows me to display and share my knowledge of feminist literature through a creative interweaving of my thoughts, experiences, feelings, and actions. To make such a presentation, I draw on the *authority of expertise*. I know a great deal more about the feminist writing on this topic than the students do. Although I can encourage and help them learn to do so, I can far more easily give overviews, characterize positions, and point to alternative ways of thinking that are being explored. This knowledge and these skills provide material for the creativity I demonstrate in class. However, since the early years of second-wave activism, feminists have had an uneasy relationship to expertise. They have clashed with experts, most notably in the area of women's health, because when male-centered expertise has been combined with male-dominated systems of power, experts harm women. In classrooms, expertise that undermines the agency of women has made us feel intellectually inferior. In this story, while I feel the pleasure of having delivered an engaging and informative lecture, I run the risk of undermining the students' own agency in the process.

This story also suggests how authority based on expertise interweaves with the common struggle over the classroom division of labor: who will do what kind of work and why. Both the students and I bring to the classroom desires to engage in or avoid certain kinds of work. Despite the pleasure I can feel in displaying to students my intellectual creativity, I do not want to do a lot of lecturing. I find discussions far more exciting. Despite their desire to participate in the class, many students do not want to take the initiative in shaping the direction of the course. They want me to do it. Throughout the semester, we engage in implicit and explicit negotiations about who will take what kind of responsibility. During these negotiations, they may make claims on me as an expert ("You know—you tell us") or attempt to evade my expertise ("I'd rather do readings outside the syllabus"). I, in turn, may assert that my expertise especially qualifies me to do certain kinds of work ("I include this topic because of its importance in current feminist debates") or that they should do certain kinds of work because they are more qualified than I am ("I cannot choose a topic for your paper because you know what issues you face").

To conduct such negotiations, however, I must have a strong sense of what my expertise means in this context. One way of seeing expert authority is suggested by Anne Seller in her analysis of *authority as legitimated through problem solving.*[7] We consider people as authorities, she notes, when we believe they can solve our problems or when we believe that they can "share their view of things with us" so that we can solve our own problems. I see both versions of authority being played out in my feminist classrooms. Sometimes students see me as an expert who can solve what they take to be gender-based problems with husbands or advisers or employers. In these instances, students, in effect, ask me to substitute my judgment for theirs. More frequently, students see me as an expert authority in the second sense, as someone who by sharing her view of things, as Agnes asked me to, can help them think through and arrive at their own answers and judgments. While I shy away from the role of expert in the first sense, the second meaning of expertise seems quite consistent with teaching through feminist discourse.

Yet, as Seller herself acknowledges, these two versions of expertise do not fully speak to the difficulties women have encountered in dealing with experts or to the harm that can be done by those to whom not only consent but trust is given. Naomi Scheman addresses this issue when she links authority to accountability.[8] When academics look to their training in and contribution to certain disciplines as the source of their authority, we assume accountability to our disciplinary colleagues. Our teaching and research will be constrained by certain disciplinary norms, or at least one or another version of those norms. Although accountability to a discipline may be of great value, this outlook, as Scheman points out, pays no attention to a teacher's accountability to her students to take seriously the responses they make and the questions they pose to the view she is sharing. Teaching through feminist discourse, I would add, needs a concept of *expanded accountability* to embrace not only students but others in the discourse process.

Expanded accountability plays an important role in teaching that emphasizes experience and action. As a teacher, I see myself as accountable not only to a series of interweaving feminist disciplines and to the students in my classes but to feminist movements and the women for whom they claim to speak. By being accountable to these various groups, I mean that

I am prepared to render to them an account of why I frame my approach in the way I do. I am ready to show them that I have, among other things, taken them and their view of things into account. To take their view into account does not mean that I must engage in a direct dialogue with them or necessarily agree with them but that I have considered the facts, analyses, experiences, feelings, and values they bring to problems of social injustice and the situations in which they encounter such injustice. Thus, my exercise of authority involves acknowledging theirs. As participants in ongoing feminist discourse they can potentially *call me to account* for my views and judgments.

For example, I am teaching a unit on affirmative action in which feelings run high. My authority as a feminist teacher rests in part on my expertise concerning research and different arguments that bear on this topic, in particular, but not exclusively feminist research and arguments. I draw as well on the authority of my own experience by describing to the students both the disadvantages and advantages I myself had in the process of becoming a university teacher. My authority in addressing affirmative action also rests on my attending to what this question means for people both outside and inside the academy: the community organizer I heard speak at a recent conference, the child care worker quoted in a newspaper article, the graduating students of different races and genders who describe to me their difficulties getting jobs. In the same spirit, my authority rests in part on my capacity to take in what students are saying, to consider seriously how their "view of things" relates to the problem we are addressing.

This analysis suggests that, as Patrocinio Schweickart has persuasively argued, listening is as important as speaking in the conduct of feminist discourse.[9] I cannot take into account the experience or ideas of a student or a feminist theorist or a community organizer unless I am able to really hear what they are saying. Listening, of course, always involves interpretation, but that well-known fact simply enjoins me to take responsibility by making sure that I understand the speaker or the text as best I can. Both speech and written texts are open to endless interpretation. What I am seeking in the context of a given classroom discourse is sufficiently responsible accounts (always open to later correction) in which to ground my own and the students' authority.[10]

As students are able to share their view of things, locate it in the context of other views, and render an account of their position to others to whom they are accountable, their authority increases. So does mine. Too often authority is seen as a zero-sum game in which the teacher must rid herself of authority in order to give over authority to her students. Yet, *the more fully students can render their own accounts, the more fully I can render mine.* As I pursue my discussion with them, I enrich my understanding of the topic and better communicate its complexities and contradictions.

Several questions arise from this view of feminist teaching authority that stresses accountability. One involves what it means to "render an account." By the standards of most academic teaching, rendering an account means offering a reasonable and informed argument. In a feminist classroom where feelings, experiences, and actions play important roles, these elements of discourse also are relevant to any account that is rendered. An account that includes them gains rather than loses authority. It is more dense, more meaningful, more creative. By this definition of rendering an account, the student who challenges a teacher's authority because what she says "feels wrong" puts the teacher on notice as effectively as another student who offers a brilliant counterargument. When Dimitri, who has recently immigrated from Russia, says that something "feels wrong" about an article we are reading in favor of affirmative action, his comment signals to me that we need further discussion. Although at first he has difficulty describing his feelings, he gradually relates his experiences with economic deprivation and survival: how he and his mother came to the United States with nothing and how hard it has been for them to make their way. As he tells his story, he provokes further discussion about how social structure affects our opportunities and choices. Neither the uncomfortable feeling nor the brilliant argument can stand alone. We all need to keep looking for how these responses relate to each other.

Another question concerns the role of persuasion. The notion of a feminist teacher's accountability implies a definite restraint in how she employs her authority. Knowing that I am accountable to others prevents me from using my authority to try to simply persuade others to my point of view. Yet, few teachers do their work without employing some form of *persuasive authority*. The language of persuasion, especially in connection with education, makes many people uncomfortable. Leading political theorists such as Max Weber and Hannah Arendt have insisted that a clear line be drawn between education as the cultivation of reason and politics as the realm of persuasion.[11] In practice, this distinction cannot be so easily maintained. Direct commands yield only limited compliance. Every aspect of teaching involves some element of persuasion, including the effort to persuade students that the subject of the course is worth studying. Persuasion permeates classroom process, whether in the form of convincing white students that a topic like race belongs in a women's studies class or of getting students to participate in a discussion. To foster fuller involvement, teachers often end up not only persuading but enticing and coaxing students to do the readings, to write papers, to take seriously both an intellectual tradition and the process of creatively engaging with it.

Persuading, enticing and coaxing take different forms, some of which may do real harm to individuals, to the class as a group and/or to the project of fostering feminist discourse. The kind of trust I see as intrinsic to feminist discourse involves risks to the self. Students and teachers risk hurt and humiliation when they talk about experiences, feelings, ideas, and activities through which their selves are revealed. Persuasion, enticement, or coaxing can result in students decreasing their degree of trust and blocking out vulnerable parts of the self to conform to what the teacher expects. So, a student can be "persuaded" to adopt a feminist position at the cost of denying her deep reservations about feminist critiques of the family, or "enticed" into developing a liberatory analysis of sexuality even though she is actually terrified in sexual encounters, or "coaxed" into joining a classroom exercise in which she feels humiliated.

The main problem with employing persuasion and its less reason-associated sisters as forms of feminist pedagogical authority stems from the ways in which we as academic teachers are tempted to deceive ourselves. As experts, it is easy for us to assume that students are swayed by the power of our rational arguments or follow our lead because of how attractively we present our requests rather than because they are scared to question or defy us. Thus, learning how to use persuasion, enticement, or coaxing involves becoming familiar with fear—with our own fears as well as those of our students.

Through acknowledging the fears that arise in me in response to various feminist critiques of the family, I can remain attuned to the fears of a student who does not want to be persuaded to adopt such a critical position. Through recognizing that I have fears around sexuality or about being excluded from a group whose activities make me uncomfortable, I can more easily determine whether and what degree or kind of persuasion is right for the classroom situation. At the same time, I must be careful not to assume that my fears necessarily mirror those of students. Student "resistance" to my persuasive efforts are a far more accurate indicator that I have touched on something that, for one reason or another, students consider damaging to themselves. No matter how valuable I think an exercise or assignment, their resistance serves as a warning to me that I need to reflect on my exercise of authority, to talk to students, colleagues, and others about the consequences of my trying to convince the class to do what I think is good for them.

Another element of persuasion is especially relevant to the story I tell at the beginning of this section about Simon, who challenges virtually everything I say or ask the students to do. On one level, Simon grants my authority in the sense that he meets the course requirements in a reasonable fashion. His criticisms of my thinking and actions fall within the framework of the class. His comments are appropriate to the subject matter and class process, in contrast to someone who disrupts by constantly talking about matters not connected to the course. Some of his individual points make me revise my thinking or modify the direction in which I am leading the class. But, on another level, Simon does not grant me authority. He does not seem to trust me as a teacher. Through his pattern of constant criticism, he conveys the notion that the other students should not consider me trustworthy, either.

Although I make several attempts to talk with Simon outside class, he only continues to tell me what is wrong with my teaching. Our relationship reaches a crisis of sorts when I try to lead the class in a dramaturgical dialogue on the relation between family and work. I decide to try such an exercise because the students have reached an impasse in talking about an article on men's roles in homemaking. I sense that the students in this undergraduate class have thoughts that they hesitate to share or are having trouble articulating and that trying another expressive vocabulary will help them communicate their thinking.

So, I ask the students to break up into a series of groups to represent the "roles" (e.g., househusband, divorced husband, etc.) that are being discussed in the article and then to use the text to help create a "voice" for the particular men they are representing. The students address the text with renewed energy, but when I try to get group representatives to engage in a dialogue in front of the class, the students balk. Some of them do not want to move their chairs. Some do not want to stand up. Some do not want to speak. I try to persuade them by telling them that this kind of dialogue has worked very well in past classes. I entice them by saying how much fun it involves. I coax them by telling them how much better they will be at this exercise than they imagine. I promise them that no one will have to speak who does not want to. I tell them that I, too, am taking a role and show them that I can do so without looking foolish. Finally, I propose a variation of the exercise in which a whole group gets up to support each other. This activity appeals to them a lot. The small groups articulate each position, with some members speaking and some supporting. The resulting dialogue is rich and fascinating.

Meanwhile, however, at the beginning of the exercise, Simon comes up to me to object to what I am doing. He argues that a "regular" discussion would be better because everyone would have a "fairer" chance to talk. When I point out how little talk had been taking place before and how lively the small groups have become, he starts to complain about what I had done in another class. I tell him I do not have the time for this discussion now and that if he does not want to join a group, he can spend the time reading additional material or working on the proposal for his paper. I assure him that he is welcome to rejoin the class when we reassemble for a whole-group discussion following the dialogue, which is what he chooses to do.

As I leave the class that day, I feel that my exercise of authority has both succeeded and failed. I have commanded the students to read a text that I consider of value. I have both persuaded and negotiated with them about how we should approach that text and created new options for pursuing discourse. They have taken risks, and so have I. Foremost among them, I have risked the trust students have placed in me to know what I am doing. Students have many ways of showing that they do not trust me, but, in this class, the general level of trust seems high. The students engage deeply in discussion with each other and clearly learn from it. My persuasive authority worked because it touched their desires to go into what they consider stigmatized or frightening territory: a world in which men act "like women" and women go it alone.

Because I never get to know Simon better, I do not know why he systematically refuses to follow my lead. I suspect that he has deep fears about what feminism means for him as a man. He may simply resent me as a woman being in a position to give him orders. But I also wonder whether he wants something from me, something I cannot identify and that he cannot or will not articulate. That something might concern the passion that fuels my authority and the passion that leads him to challenge it.

AUTHORITY AS PASSION

Reading the paper one morning, I come across a piece about the city's failure for many weeks to pay a number of the workers employed in public child care centers. A spokesperson for the administration explains that a bureaucratic snafu merely has delayed the checks, but this reasoning does little to quell my rising anger. I make one after another phone call to city officials or their assistants, barely containing my impulse to scream. Then I go to class to lead a discussion about women and work.

Cornelia's words are filled with hurt as she describes to me the comments made in her small-group discussion of race and gender in which she was the only woman of color. She had a lot of reservations about taking this class, she says. Feminism always seemed to her a white woman's thing. She had started to believe that this class would be different, that it would not reflect the racism that pervaded so many other classes. She is clearly disappointed not only with the course but with me.

My authority as a feminist teacher derives in part from my relationship to a movement for social justice, and such movements, by definition, involve the passions that move us. After the incident with the newspaper article and the phone calls, my teaching is fueled by anger. I want to find an alternative to this terrible system. I want the students to care about finding one.

My authority does not stem from my knowledge alone, although I can describe to the students some recent research on the poverty of many working women. The authority I exercise also comes from the passion I bring to this issue and how I, therefore, lead the discussion.

In social movements, leaders often reflect and embody the passion of those who identify with the movement.[12] In this respect, my passion as a feminist teacher provides a ground for authority to the extent that it reflects the passions of the students themselves. In the class during which I express so much anger about the child care workers, my passionate response finds some counterpart in the reactions of a number of the students. Yet the concept of leadership based in mutually reflecting passions is not a simple one. Many second-wave activists remained deeply suspicious of leaders or media-designated "stars" who seemed to draw passion away from the collective movement for women's liberation and toward themselves. Even in small groups and projects, activists often viewed individual leadership as competing with collective passion. Many activists believed that the desire of leaders for distinction, reward, and privilege would lead to political betrayal. Although feminist and other grassroots activists have continued to experiment with many forms of collaborative and democratic leadership, the suspicion of leaders remains.

Despite such ongoing criticisms, the feminist movement and the media have produced not just public leaders but leadership of a more personal sort: role models. Role models have a curious sort of social authority.[13] For many women, they become symbols of hope, repositories of moral faith that their own lives can change. A woman might think, "If she can do this" (whether she is Amelia Earhart or Ella Baker or an older cousin), "so can I." In some ways, role models, like media-designated stars, also seem to draw passion away from the movement and into individual achievement. But many activists rely on role models, like Ella Baker, to fuel their own activism. Thus, the emphasis on individual achievement also can result in supporting collective action.

For feminist teaching, the confluence of individual and collective passion seems especially important to the exercise of authority. I see this occurring in two particular forms in my own teaching: in the power of passion for *initiating* activity and in the tendency of passion to lead to *idealizing* others and ourselves. Both formally recognized leaders and privately cherished role models can represent a longing for something new, the desire to innovate, create, and imagine. Some students sign up for my feminist classes because they want to find a new way to pursue their lives and cannot quite imagine it. Leaders and models also represent the longing of individuals and groups of people for something better. Other students bring their own ideals to class and hope to find fulfillment. Each kind of longing can inspire efforts toward individual and collective change. Each kind can lead to disappointment. The new order becomes as unjust as the old. The idealized other turns out to have clay feet. Feminist teachers whose authority rests in part on passion can spark innovation or embody possibility. They can also end up reproducing injustice or courting failure and shame.

My fury over the unpaid child care workers leads to my initiating a number of activities. I tear the article out of the paper and quickly reproduce it for the class. Instead of beginning the class with an overview of the reading on women's relation to the economy, I start with the situation of the child care workers. I ask the students to think about their relation to female and male workers of different racial/ethnic groups, in different occupational categories. I ask them to bring in their own experiences in the job market and the theories about occupational segregation we have been studying. I might have initiated any of these activities on another day, but my sense of accountability to the child care workers, the passion this injustice has called out in me this morning, gives my teaching a special energy and impact.

This same passion, however, can undermine my commitment to sharing authority. If I present myself as a kind of role model who requires imitation, I risk making the students feel that their own passions are by definition inadequate.[14] My outrage can take up so much space that students find it difficult to express feelings that do not match mine. What if they do not feel the same kind of anger? What if my anger obscures the expression of their own passions as a way of initiating or redirecting discussion? Conversely, students may resonate so deeply with my passion (mine mirrors theirs, theirs mirrors mine) that the possibility of our diverging in our thinking or judgment becomes problematic. To counter temptation to overwhelm students' passions with my own or to allow my passions to merge too easily with theirs, I need to acknowledge how contradictory passions mark participation in feminist discourse and how our interpretations of passion may differ.

The passion that drives my feminist teaching is marked by contradiction. Telling my story, as I invite students to tell theirs, can make those contradictions visible. Thus, in teaching the class about the child care workers, I not only express my anger at gender injustice but acknowledge how hard it is to take on the responsibilities of feminist agency. I am tempted by and in many ways take advantage of the privileges associated with my social position. My desire for justice often collides with my desire for an easier life. Such contradictory passions may be conveyed by a simple anecdote, say, in which I talk about how it feels for me as a well-paid professional to go to a demonstration of low-paid clerical workers and depict my effort to understand who I am in this situation and what it means to align myself with someone else's cause.

As I describe my conflicting passions, I also help create a context for their interpretation. Simply declaring my desire for social justice does not convey a clear meaning. For example, I can say to students that I am dedicated to gender justice. But they still may wonder whether my feminism is animated by hatred of men or why I am deeply devoted to certain values and implacably opposed to others. By revealing the complexity of my feelings, I help clarify their meanings and signal to students that acknowledging conflicting passions may enhance one's authority in our discussions.

After I relate my anecdote about attending the demonstration, Frieda begins to talk about her own experiences as a child care worker and how they led her to pursue a degree in early childhood education. She wants to support the workers, she says, but she also hopes they will get more education, as she did. Henry brings in a theory of occupational segregation we have studied as one possible explanation for the low wages, but he wonders about his own responsibility for the wages paid at the child care center where he takes his own child. Marita describes how she hated her work for a city agency but stresses how she and her colleagues organized to challenge government procedures. I point out that the discussion has started to address efforts for social change: who desires it, how individual solutions relate to collective efforts, what efforts toward social justice might be effective. I am leading the discussion, but I am also being guided by it.

By keeping desire in the foreground, its initiatory power remains part of the pedagogical consciousness, and the exercise of authority tends to draw more on initiation and less on obedience.[15] For instance, about halfway through the semester, I find the energy of a particular class lagging. Though I am eager to talk about this troubling topic, the meaning of "masculinity," leading the discussion is like pulling teeth. I am irritated and impatient. I say, "I am tired of doing all the work. Break up into small groups, and figure out what you want to discuss." The students start to talk about what they feel is missing from the course. Many express concern that the values of "traditional homemaking" have been ignored and denigrated. This response enables me to describe the mixed messages that feminist scholarship sends out about women as homemakers and the extent to which homemaking can be a genuine choice for women. Now the students begin to explore their own mixed feelings. The class has come alive.

Part of the power of passion to initiate pedagogical activity stems from the excitement it introduces, which, as bell hooks notes, is often seen as antithetical to academic work.[16] Such excitement, I believe, gains a special intensity from the experiences of revealing what is hidden, of exposing what is normally not presented in public. When I reveal my desire not to carry the burden of a low-energy class, when the students discuss their hidden responses to the class, when I suggest that what is hidden in their responses can be a source of learning, the classroom becomes filled with energy.

This same excitement, however, can feed the tendency to idealize those in authority, reinforcing and laying traps for feminist teachers. As a feminist and lesbian teacher, I know that I may be idealized, that I can become the repository of students' hopes for themselves and for social change. This pattern can make me very uncomfortable. I wonder, "How can I possibly live up to such expectations?" Yet, I also see the ways in which idealization mirrors and supports my own passion. I, too, yearn to realize ideals; to the extent that I succeed, students may identify and applaud how those ideals are embodied in my words and actions. Idealization involves many pitfalls, however, including the fact that it sets us up for disappointment. Our idealization of particular individuals (whether they are public leaders or role models) grows out of our longing for fulfillment in a given situation. Longings change, conditions change, ideals are tested and often fail to live up to reality.

The story I tell at the beginning of this section, about the racism Cornelia encounters in class and the hurt she feels, suggests the deep disappointment that can accompany idealization. Cornelia's idealized image of what I can accomplish (and of how the students will behave in such a class) is not made up of whole cloth. She correctly perceives my desire for social justice. My leadership of the class, the texts I choose, the ways in which I encourage students to focus discussion, the projects and papers I encourage them to write, all express my passion and support that ideal. To some degree I approximate it. But, when I fail to do so, the disappointment can be grave. In this story, I fail not only Cornelia but myself. My failure lies not in the fact that some students continue to hold racist assumptions but in not creating conditions that enable her and other students to challenge those assumptions. I sense that I have given the small groups too much authority, and they lack the ability to exercise it. The discussions have been unfocused, leaving a lot of room for students to make casual comments without having to explain or discuss them. At this stage of the course, neither Cornelia nor many other students can use their passion to initiate a feminist discourse on difference in our classroom. Understandably, Cornelia does not trust the others enough to express her feelings to them.

As a feminist teacher who voices her passion for social justice, I often become the repository of the students' political hopes that my classes will become a safe harbor from misogyny, that they will not perpetuate racism, that I will have the power to create a harmonious community. As an out lesbian, I unwittingly invite an idealized image of myself in which I courageously stand up to homophobia in any form. In many small ways and occasionally in very large ones, I disappoint these hopes. In one class, I fail to deal firmly with a particularly hostile male student. In another class, I miss what in retrospect I realize was a clearly racist remark. Yet another time, I fail to realize that a student is trying to tell me that she is a lesbian and wants help engaging with the class or surviving within the institution.

Idealization opens the door to feelings of shame—an emotion that many second-wave feminists vowed to purge from women's emotional palettes. Sometimes, I am deeply ashamed that I have not lived up to student hopes. They, in turn, can feel ashamed because they believe they have not lived up to what they imagine I expect of them. For instance, sometimes students express fears that I may not find it acceptable that they have male partners or children. Since shame stems from the sense that one has failed to live up to an ideal and idealization may be an unavoidable part of a feminist teacher's authority, the potential for feeling shame may be intrinsic to our exercise of authority.[17]

Yet, as I argued in the previous chapter, feelings can prompt deeper reflection. One important feature of shame is that it carries with it the sense that we do *have* values. We may fail to live up to them, but we may also prize, reject, reevaluate, or allow them to fade. The shame of not living up to values unwillingly imposed on us and internalized in destructive ways (such as the shame of not being thin enough, light-skinned enough, "feminine" enough) assumes values that feminists analyze and properly reject. Yet shame may also refer to values feminists claim and articulate through the process of feminist discourse. My shame at failing to confront the hostile male student, to catch the racist remark, to recognize the struggle with homophobia, is appropriate—not because I fall short of some imaginary state of political perfection but because the voice of shame reminds me of my political passion. "Remember," it might say, "you really do believe in racial justice even though you failed to practice it here." If I accept the uncertainties of feminist discourse and my fallibilities as a teacher, I know that at times I will fail to fulfill my own or the students' hopes. Shame not only reminds but animates me to keep creating a teaching practice that gives my ideals concrete form.

In the struggle to develop that practice, I also tend to idealize students. The passions they bring to class not only lend their participation authority but promote such idealization. When students express passion, I want to support in them the most courageous facets of themselves, the parts that dare to think dangerous thoughts and imagine new actions. But, just as the students' idealization of me may lead to disappointment or anger, so my idealization of them may be pedagogically harmful. I can set standards at which students are bound to fail, push them in political directions they cannot follow. When they are truly engaged, students themselves may articulate the limits to my idealized image of them as participants in feminist discourse. Nilda notes, "I could introduce this idea to my family, but I would not call it feminist." Geraldine says, "I could never say this to my husband." Isaac worries, "If I said this at the gym, they would think I was gay." We can, as a class, then talk about the power and limitations of feminist discourse, how and when and where it can be initiated, changed, sustained.

My idealization of students takes a somewhat different turn when it collides with the institution itself. I can idealize the students' capacity to develop authority based in knowledge and thus inspire them to do so. I can idealize their interests in exploring feminism and thus bring out passions that support their authority as participants in the class. But no matter how much I encourage students' potential for leadership, I cannot share with them my position as a professor—and this position is one important meaning of my authority. They know it. I know it. The others connected to this institution know it. This meaning of authority does not erase the others, but it remains a constant and sometimes embarrassing presence.

AUTHORITY AS POSITION

From the first meeting of the class, Keith's behavior is strange. Sometimes he looks at me with malevolence. Sometimes he looks at me slyly, as though we were joined in a conspiracy. I suspect he sees conspiracies everywhere. Other students avoid sitting near him, and I find it very difficult to get a discussion going. I also become increasingly afraid, which undermines my capacity to lead the class. Because Keith's behavior is so unfamiliar to me, I am not sure what he will do next. I want to feel more in control, but I don't know how to handle the situation. The class stumbles on.

Joy sits in my office crying. She cannot believe that I gave her a B + for the course. She has done everything I asked the students to do, and she has tried very hard. Her entire school career hangs on this grade, she says. Without an A, she will be rejected by the professional program she hopes to enter. Her immigrant parents have invested so much in her schooling, and they expect her to succeed. She thought she knew me. How could I do this to her?

The story about Keith brings out the complexities that permeate my position and authority as a feminist teacher. I cannot simply command Keith to drop the course, and I do not feel that I can ask him to leave a specific class meeting since his behavior is only minimally disruptive in the usual sense. Although I talk with him outside class, nothing changes. I have great reservations about bringing this problem to the administration. I am reading Kate Millett's book, *The Loony-Bin Trip*, about what it means to be "crazy" in our society. She raises my consciousness about how difficult it is to pursue a life that conflicts with dominant expectations of emotional self-control. As I face Keith, my own internal voices remind me of the oppression suffered by people who are categorized as mentally ill. Imagining an appeal to administrators, I feel that I would be a little like the mother who tries to get her child to comply by threatening, "Wait until Daddy comes home!" The institution, "Daddy," will do my disciplining for me.

In the historical context of second-wave activism, bureaucratic authority had contradictory meanings. By using their positions in government, many highly placed women were able to promote significant advances in women's civil rights.[18] Grassroots feminists, in contrast, tended to make what Kathy Ferguson calls "the feminist case against bureaucracy." They saw bureaucratic authority as intrinsically oppressive, leading not to the rationality and efficiency described by Max Weber but to patriarchal domination. Such domination expressed itself through subtle and not so subtle pressures toward conformity. People at each level of the institution were required, like women in relation to men, to play roles that served those above them. Everyone—from the workers, clients, or consumers to the middle-level bureaucrats to the institutional elites—had to act or at least create the appearance of acting in the interest of the institution in its articulation with other social institutions. Ferguson, like many other radical critics of bureaucracy, held relatively little hope for this form of social organization. The only true alternative to dehumanizing dynamics of bureaucracy, which Hannah Arendt labeled the rule of Nobody, lay in self-organized groups such as consciousness-raising and other small feminist projects.[19]

The problem with this alternative, as Jo Freeman and Ellen Messer-Davidow have both argued, is that small groups committed to social justice have to articulate with broader institutions to make a real impact.[20] Freeman and Messer-Davidow each suggest that feminists need to build national institutions and appropriate political resources, including electoral strategies and the use of the media. Otherwise, they claim, small groups like those devoted to consciousness-raising have little or even negative effect. From this viewpoint, institutional resources of any kind are viewed in terms of their potential for extending the impact of the social movement rather than in terms of their presumed intrinsic virtue (the small group) or intrinsic immorality (the bureaucracy).

Because I continue to work in a hierarchically structured institution, my very presence in class signals to students that I consider bureaucracy a form of social organization in which I am willing to try to do my feminist work. No matter how much criticism of hierarchy I might voice or support students in expressing, I remain, as Jane Rinehart puts it with respect to teaching women's studies, a reformer with "revolutionary aspirations."[21] Thus, the very act of my teaching as a feminist implies a set of questions about what it means for feminists to work within bureaucratic contexts.

Feminist classroom discourse encourages students and teachers to reflect on and judge under what circumstances bureaucratic or any other institutional structures serve or undermine social justice. In class we may discuss whether affirmative action laws reduce or increase discrimination, whether the current organization of health care can meet women's needs, and whether educational bureaucracies only perpetuate or can be used to correct social inequities. At best, such discussions are both rooted in knowledge of concrete contexts (provided by research and student experience) and oriented toward current or future actions that a student might take as an employee, unionist, professional, family member, citizen, or political activist. Since contexts change with historical circumstances, so might judgments about the value of working within a given institutional setting.

Even Kathy Ferguson's indictment of bureaucracy leaves room for this kind of contextualized analysis and judgment when she notes that bureaucratic discipline is not equally tight or direct in all organizations: educational institutions tend to grant teachers more "organizational slack" than many other kinds of bureaucracies.[22] This, she suggests, results from the fact that schools (and I think this may apply to higher education in particular) have a far greater interest in how they articulate with other institutions than in what goes on within a particular classroom. I would add that in higher education, the tradition of academic freedom plus an institutional commitment to generally liberal values can (although it does not necessarily) lead to tolerating a wide variety of activities. Thus, to differing degrees, many educational institutions leave room for teachers, students, and others to create enclaves in which to pursue activities that may challenge or stretch the purposes of the given institution.

While such enclaves can reproduce the problem by remaining isolated groups that do not affect the larger system, they also can serve as a means for placing social justice issues on the institutional and larger agenda. They do this in part by *transforming bureaucratic authority into political discourse*. That is, instead of responding to bureaucratic orders through compliance, manipulation, or refusal, they proceed to treat rules and commands that do not serve social justice as open to discussion. In this spirit,

Annette Kolodny argues for democratizing authority in higher education institutions through genuine policy discussions among those affected by administrative decision making.[23] Such an approach distributes authority and incorporates different experiences, ideas, and plans for action into institutional decision making on all levels.

Teachers committed to fostering feminist political discourse have a special interest in this sort of transformation, as the story about Keith suggests. In this vignette, I am faced with a student whose unusual behavior is disturbing both class members and me. Unlike a strongly antifeminist student who holds opinions with which I and many of the students disagree, Keith's behavior cannot easily be incorporated into our feminist discourse. Rather, his behavior suggests an inability to participate in such discourse and has a chilling effect on the participation of other students. Viewed in this light, I might say to myself, "My job here is to direct feminist discourse, and someone who interferes with this work should be removed from the class. If I do not have the power to do so, then to facilitate my work the administration should do this for me."

This logic, however, quickly rings false. Here is a class in which I am trying to get the students to engage in a deeper way with questions of difference. Many class sessions are devoted to understanding how and why various groups of people are viewed as different and what this means for questions of social justice. Keith's "difference" clearly disturbs many of us, but differences in sexual orientation also disturb many of the students. That a participant in feminist discourse makes others uncomfortable hardly supplies a reason for their exclusion. I am not sure that Keith qualifies as a "participant," but I suspect that excluding him on the basis of discomfort alone is a questionable solution.

Another element of this situation concerns agency: I hope for and expect feminist discourse to enhance both the students' agency and my own. Some of us might be relieved if an administrator removed Keith from the class, but this action could diminish my own agency (in line with the notion that the institution is protecting me) and would certainly do little for the agency of the students. However, the story so far takes for granted bureaucratic authority as the power to command. If, as the teacher, I am able to reconceptualize my authority as part of a collective project of transforming bureaucratic authority into political discourse, I might have another option. In the context of this story, I do not have a chance to exercise that option because Keith suddenly disappears from the class. Before he disappears, however, I begin to think about the kind of discourse this situation calls for.

I realize that I should be talking with feminist colleagues about what it means to have students who might be described as mentally ill in our classes. Does it make any difference whether the student is male or female? Whose interests do we serve by trying to eject such a student? Are there features of our feminist classes such as talking about feelings and experiences that attract such students and/or make their presence particularly problematic? What are our obligations to students who might be labeled mentally ill in the light of the relationships among institutions (educational institutions, psychiatric institutions, and families or communities)? What messages are we sending about "difference" through our responses to such students in classes devoted in important part to a critical examination of difference? I need this kind of feminist discourse to fully draw on the authority inscribed in my position, to use it well in relation to both students and the institution. I need to think and talk with others to decide how to act myself.

In the process of talking with colleagues, we might also decide that we need to take action beyond our individual classrooms. We might envision changes in institutional policies. In the spirit of Kolodny's argument for more democratic governance, we might engage sympathetic counselors and administrators in discussion of mental illness from their particular professional perspectives. We might talk with members of student groups who are working on disability issues within our school. We might, in short, see what kinds of broader bureaucratic changes we might initiate by taking our own discourse seriously.

The story about Joy, who begs me to change her grade, brings out yet another dimension of bureaucratic authority. This point involves the relation between the personal lives of the individuals involved in bureaucratic contexts and their professional roles. Weber's classic argument about the advantages of bureaucratic organization stressed the importance of separating personal considerations from decision making. He believed that bureaucrats could not function in the interests of rationality if they had to take everyone's individual circumstances, feelings, and needs into account. Weber, as Roslyn Bologh points out, also wanted to preserve a realm of freedom outside bureaucracy.[24] But this distinction between bureaucratic discipline and extrabureaucratic freedom makes little sense for most women. Domestic responsibilities usually make it impossible for us to separate our encounters with bureaucracies from the rest of our lives. Moreover, many feminists do not want to trade bureaucratic efficiency for a kind of freedom modeled on the ideal of the autonomous man.

Joy's tears wash away any illusions I might have about using my authority in a way that separates the person from the office. My feminist philosophy of teaching leads me to reveal many things about myself as a person in her class. This approach encourages Joy to talk honestly about her own thoughts and experiences. As her pained words reveal, she believes that she and I have developed a personal relationship: since I now understand her as a person, how can I not be her friend and ally in her effort to make her way through this bureaucratic structure?

She has a point. After a semester of interaction, I cannot simply ignore her as a person and quote the rules. The class has rules, of course. At the beginning of the semester, I outline my expectations, including my standards for grading. I try to articulate a grading process that reflects my feminist teaching values. I seek to express a balance between the traditional requirements of reading and writing and the less familiar ones of participating in discussion and reflecting on experiences, feelings, and actions. I invite the students to write self-evaluations and join in discussion of their own grading values. Joy has had a chance to help shape these standards, but she, like many other students in this undergraduate class, has been reluctant to participate in such a discussion. She wants it both ways: for me to set and apply the standards without involving her and, at the same time, for me to understand her needs as an individual in making my grading judgments.[25]

I want it both ways, too. I want to create a set of standards and apply them in a way that fits sufficiently with the demands of the bureaucracy and does not call into question either the legitimacy of the course or my own teaching competency. At the same time, I want to question the system of which I am a part, including the split it fosters between our academic roles and our lives. As this anguished discussion with Joy continues, I think about how much I loathe grading. No matter how clearly I articulate my standards, no matter how fully I involve students in setting them, I am forced to fit the thoughts and actions of a vibrant, changing human being into a set of ranked categories. I imagine throwing up my hands and saying that I have had enough of this.

At this moment my memory brings up an image. It is the late 1960s, and I am talking with members of my radical faculty group about how we can protest the use of college grades by draft boards in their decisions about who will be sent to serve in the Vietnam War. We want to end our complicity in this system. We talk about a protest in which we refuse to submit grades as long as they are used to sacrifice our students to this unjust cause. I think about whether I am willing to lose my job over this issue and tell myself that I am. But I am never tested. We are assured by the administration that grades will not be released to the draft board, and I go back to my usual procedures.

This image from the past provides me with a touchstone. It reminds me that I do have a choice. It also reminds me that choices are always relevant to the larger context. My anti–Vietnam War decision not to grade grew out of political discourse aimed at collective decision making. The discourse itself emerged out of an antiwar movement that, in conjunction with a group of overlapping social justice movements, promised alternatives to the dominant system. As a young faculty member, I did not want to give up the professional role I had worked so long and hard to achieve, but as someone who had become connected to collective struggles for social justice, I felt more confident that I could work for these causes elsewhere. The economy was expanding, and there were still jobs to be had in both mainstream and alternative institutions. I could afford to be less complicit.

As I face Joy, however, my question is less whether I am willing to reduce my complicity in a bureaucratic institution than how I can do so. In the late 1960s, students were trying to get out of the dominant system, and whatever the moral ambiguities of my position then (including the fact that I was helping middle-class men avoid the draft while poor and working-class men were sent to fight), I supported the draft resisters' aims. Joy, on the other hand is trying to get into the system to which I both belong and which I am trying to change. My notions of grading reflect the tension between belonging and changing. I am, in effect, requiring Joy to live with those tensions as long as she is a student in my class. I am asking her both to conform to some traditional ideas of academic achievement and to broaden her thinking about what it takes to be a good student. This demand on my part increases her burden, which is already heavy enough. If I am going to ask her to make this kind of effort, I also owe her something.

In response to her distress, I do not simply reiterate the rules. I spend a long time with her, going over her course materials, talking about the grading standards, and discussing her participation. I point out how much her work has improved (she had gotten a B − on her midterm essay) and ask her to consider what she had gained from the course. In the end, she acknowledges that the grade is fair but cries through a fresh torrent of tears that it is ruining her life. No matter how much I point out to her that this grade constitutes only a fraction of her total average, I sense that in some way she is right. She keeps calling my attention to the fact that I cannot view the class I teach and her participation in it as separate from the rest of her life. Although I might hope that feminist discourse affects that life, the grading will, too. In particular, she reminds me of the institutional consequences of my actions and thus my agency within that context.

In fact, Joy's pain makes me look at how my course fits with the requirements of the program she hopes to enter. It leads me to initiate conversations with faculty in that program and question the relationship between their requirements and my course. It leads me to discuss how standards are being set and what this means for students like Joy, whose educational background might not make her a prime candidate under the current standards but who might make a top-notch professional nevertheless. As a result of these conversations, I discover faculty in that program who themselves question the prevailing admissions system, and I offer my support for any effort they might make to challenge it.

My talk with Joy also reminds me of how important it is to keep raising the question of grading with the students themselves as an intrinsic part of teaching through feminist discourse. My attempts to talk about grading are not always successful, but I do not give up trying. Since so many students like Joy shy away from classroom discussion of grading, I sometimes ask for volunteers to form a small group to talk about the topic and report to the class. Whether in a small group or the class as a whole, we can discuss how various feminist theories might give us insight into the dangers and benefits of grading. At best, we can look together at the tension between institutional requirements and the students' attempts to lead fulfilling lives. Our discussions enrich my own judgments, about both individual students' accomplishments and grading as a bureaucratic imperative.

Difficult as it is, my discussion with Joy also reminds me that connection and context are important aspects of my authority as a feminist teacher. The conflict with Joy develops in part because I have promoted connection in this course and because of tensions between the classroom and larger context. Attention to context and connection is a major feature of feminist discussion about caring. The encounter with Joy makes me wonder whether my bureaucratic position has turned me into an uncaring human being. What does authority have to do with caring? Because the meaning of caring has become such a central question for feminists, I devote the following chapter to exploring its implications for my notion of feminist pedagogy.

— 4 —

NO ANGEL IN THE CLASSROOM

Exploring the Ethic of Care

Rickie seems distracted throughout the discussion on rape. Later, I learn from her journal that she was raped and severely beaten several years ago. This class, she writes, has given her the first opportunity to really describe what happened. I cry as I read her journal.

Almost eighty students register for my women's studies class, more than twice the size I anticipated. I am not sure how I will manage. The night after the first meeting, I lie in bed worrying. Suddenly, I imagine myself surrounded by fish. Like the fish in my aquarium, they rush toward me to be fed. Everywhere I turn there are open mouths, hungry, waiting.

Celia explains that she missed the last class because of a cold she got from our overly air-conditioned room. I tell her I am trying to get the air conditioning lowered or the room changed, but I do not describe the endless discussions I have been having with the building manager and the room assignments office. Celia sits down with a deep cough. I am beginning to sniffle myself.

Do feminist teachers gain a certain kind of authority through caring for our students? Even if we do, is it a good idea to emphasize the caring aspects of our teaching? Does a commitment to caring lead feminist teachers into dangerous or muddy waters such as having to respond to the kind of trauma that Rickie endured or worrying too much about whether we can meet students' needs or spending our time doing work that ought to be done by others?

Answering such questions is especially difficult because feminists are deeply divided about how "needs" are defined and whether women have a special obligation to meet them.[1] One debate centers on the issue of universal needs. Some feminists insist that women should be viewed as having the same needs as men, while others believe that legal and other norms should take into account women's special needs. Still others contend that the claim that women share common needs is misleading and that differently situated women have distinct needs. Meanwhile, feminists also point out that more powerful groups are in a position to define the needs of the less powerful, so that we cannot take the interpretation of needs for granted. Finally, some feminists see the traditional role of women in caring for the needs of others as a source of political strength through which women can bring caring values to the wider society. In contrast, others argue that the association between women and caring is fundamentally conservative because it reproduces the old, middle-class ideal of the woman as an angel in the house who sacrifices her own needs to the well-being of her husband and children.[2]

These political differences cannot be easily resolved because to a considerable degree they reflect the different contexts in which women face the problem of caring. An able-bodied woman who applies for a job as a construction worker does not want to be told that she is not fit for the work because her needs differ from those of men. A woman with a disability that limits her movement and who is scheduling a gynecological appointment wants her health facility to have an examination table that can accommodate her particular needs. A woman receiving welfare benefits wants to be able to define her own family's needs for nourishing food, while a woman whose baby was born with a defective heart hopes that the doctors know what kind of surgery is needed by the infant. A woman from a poor, working-class, and/or community of color may value her caring role as the key to her children's survival, while a woman from a less endangered community may see the obligation to care as threatening her own survival. Because the conditions of caring differ so greatly, we may have to develop more than one argument about caring and needs.

To make sense of caring in her work, a teacher clearly has to pay attention to the particular classroom context in which issues of caring arise. Some features of this context are not of our making, yet they create caring needs in the students and place caring demands on us as teachers. Large classes provide standard examples of this situation, by generating student needs ("I'm confused about this course, and I can't get an appointment with the teacher") and teacher uncertainty about how to meet them ("I don't know who I'm talking to. It's just a sea of faces out there"). Other features of our teaching contexts, however, stem from decisions that we ourselves make about how the course should proceed.

Teaching through feminist discourse creates a context in which the interplay among experience, feelings, thinking, and action evokes certain needs. If I encourage students to talk or write about their experiences, they may end up needing comfort or help in clarifying the meaning of those experiences. If I prompt the expression of feelings in class, I may foster needs to validate those feelings or respond to them in particular ways. If I urge students to articulate ideas they consider dangerous, I may call out new and pressing needs for support and action. I am not responsible for the students' reactions, but I am responsible for choosing a certain mode of teaching and for the fact that feminist discourse stimulates and shapes the needs of participants. As someone committed to a pedagogy revolving around feminist discourse, I cannot avoid asking whether, when, where, or how these needs should be met and what, in this context, is the role of caring.

Bending over Rickie's journal, in which she describes being raped, I begin to think about her needs. Her responses to this violation predate the class, and she already has taken some steps toward healing. Yet, the readings, writing, and discussions reopen the wound and bring to light additional needs for recognition and response. The journal format virtually guarantees some degree of response because I become a witness to the violence and pain she has suffered. Her journal continues the classroom discourse through a separate conversation with me. I understand why she may want such a "private" conversation, but I also have to consider whether bringing her experiences back into the class would serve both her and the developing discussion.[3]

I try to answer this question first by consulting Rickie, who says that she is not sure she can talk about the experience in class, but that she might. At the next meeting I return to the topic of rape and note how many deep feelings it aroused in me and may have aroused in others. My remark makes it possible for several other students to mention near-rapes or rapes of friends and how difficult the topic has been for them. Although Rickie does not tell her story in class, she listens closely to other students and nods slightly as they speak. When I direct discussion to proposed political and educational solutions to the problem of rape, she has a great deal to say. The discussion itself begins to fill needs for both fuller expression and understanding. My authority in this classroom is intricately interwoven with my caring. In Rayna Green's words, "Power is given to those who give."[4]

Caring involves authority because human needs render us dependent on each other. We follow the commands or leadership of certain people not merely because they know more than we do, not simply because their passion inspires us or their position in relation to us requires our compliance, but because our needs compel or strongly argue for choosing the path they indicate. We want them to take care of us or show us how we can take care of ourselves. When we engage in caretaking or help others take care of themselves, we exercise a form of leadership that Kathleen Jones has named "compassionate authority."[5]

Compassionate authority, Jones argues, contrasts with Max Weber's classic notion of authority as the exercise of rule-governed, impersonal judgment. Unlike the bureaucratic model, caring authority does not remove itself from the immediate context but attends to its details, "personal" as they may be. Yet, the kinds of caring appropriate to any given context, Jones cautions, are not self-evident. Discerning them requires communication and dialogue. It involves the ability to take the perspective of the other—the one who is being cared for, the one who needs or asks for care. Grasping and responding to the needs of another in a given situation requires that the carer not only comes to understand those needs through as much interchange as possible but knows who she, the caring authority, is in that situation.

Jones's analysis aims at displacing bureaucratic by compassionate authority. However, as long as feminist teaching takes place in hierarchical institutions, we as teachers face the problem of how to reconcile the values of caring with this institutional context and the needs it generates. This dilemma does not mean that caring values should give way to bureaucratic ones, but it suggests that judgments about caring must take into account the needs created and shaped by the institution and not simply posit a world free of its limitations.

As I lie in bed envisioning my feminist class as a swarm of hungry fish, I can easily imagine an ideal caring situation. This pedagogical paradise contains a class of ten carefully selected students, each self-aware and eager to learn. We have an endless amount of time and energy to talk with individuals about their needs and endless amounts of time and energy to devote to the class process.

In the real world, however, I must figure out how to deal with all these hungry students without being consumed by them. I get an idea. I develop a system of "course partners" to provide a first line of help for students whose needs arise immediately out of the class situation and who might have to wait for a day or two to talk with me if I were their only resource. The course partner system is not perfect (I keep working out its problems and refining it for different classes), but it goes some distance in meeting the students' needs and my own.[6]

As the story about the overly air-conditioned class also suggests, many structural arrangements impact on the potentials for caring and being cared for. One of the great weaknesses of the nineteenth-century ideal of a woman as an angel in the house lay in its middle-class assumption that women could concentrate on the moral and emotional aspects of domestic work because capitalist husbands would support them and servants would do the more menial chores.[7] But most teachers, including women teachers and feminist teachers, do not have the option of concentrating our caring solely on its ethical and psychological aspects. Our institutional "husbands" do not always support us in the manner we expect or want, and there are often few institutional "servants" to do our bidding. Nor, for many feminist teachers, is this privileged model of caring an appealing or appropriate one. Rather than assuming a world that supports our caring activities, we have to look at how caring is organized, not only within our classrooms but within the institution and wider world.

My story about the excessive air conditioning provides a mundane example. This particular class proceeds for many weeks without my paying any attention to the physical conditions. Since the classroom suits our needs (I am comfortable, and none of the students has complained), I do not think about the maintenance workers and administrators who provide conditions that enable me to attend to other caring needs. Suddenly, with the first blast of cold air, I am made conscious of these conditions. The students look to me, or someone, to respond to their needs, and I, too, see this as a caring issue. As I am trying to get the room changed, I keep talking to the building manager about how the cold air is making the students sick and interfering with their learning.

Finally, the air conditioning is turned off. However, while it is still not clear whether I will succeed in improving the situation, I keep thinking about how far and with whom I should extend my caring activities. As a feminist teacher, I do not consider the students' health or my own a small matter. I hope that one of the effects of feminist discourse is to encourage women students to take their own bodies seriously, to reflect on and discuss what is entailed in such an effort. So, in deciding how to respond to the air conditioning, I am also adding my actions to this discourse. Should I simply wear a heavy jacket to class, signaling to students that each of us should take care of ourselves? Should I continue to negotiate with institutional representatives, as a way of taking care of the students' and my needs? Should I engage the students in solving the problem and ask them what they think we should do? Should I encourage students to form a delegation, to make demands on (and therefore also themselves learn about) the institution that in so many ways shapes their classroom experiences? These questions are not abstract or frivolous but tap into basic contradictions in the caring process.

Each of the stories at the start of this chapter raises a question about caring. What does caring mean in relation to classroom discourse? How can feminist teachers deal with the potential conflict between meeting our own needs and meeting the needs of students? How do conditions of caring affect our classrooms, and what responsibility, if any, do we have to change those conditions? In the following pages, I will explore some possible answers.

TEACHING AS A CARING RELATIONSHIP

At a reception following the graduation ceremony, I join Barrie and a group of doctoral students with whom I have worked over a long time. Flushed with the pleasure of earning her doctorate after so many years of effort, Barrie turns to thank me from her heart. "I could not have done it without you," she says. "You are the mother of us all." I become intensely uncomfortable.

Francesca approaches me after class brimming with anger and hurt. How, she wants to know, could I fail to understand the point she made in our discussion of the ethic of care? What did I know about what it meant to raise three children and deal with an aging mother who is in and out of the hospital? She, Francesca, thought feminist teachers were supposed to be caring. Either feminism is a fraud, she implies, or I am a total fake.

I have never been a mother, and I have often reacted negatively to feminist theories that make motherhood the model for caring or that posit women as more "relational" than men. To some extent, my own academic career represents to me an escape from the angel in the house ideal, a way, in Simone de Beauvoir's language, to "transcend" the dailiness of caring obligations. I am thrown off balance by the kind of praise Barrie gives me after her graduation. My first reaction to her gratitude is to fear she wants to squeeze me back into the angel role, to diminish my "real" work as a teacher and scholar.

Despite the momentary panic I experience in this story, however, I have a complex and contradictory response to caring. As a feminist teacher, I find myself described as "caring." Moreover, I recognize that I want to be seen as caring, that I have an internal image of myself in which caringness plays a central part. I am shamed in the story about Francesca because she appeals to a caring ideal that she believes I have failed to realize. I am, I discover, at war inside: the me who has escaped the trap of caring confronts the me who wants to care and be cared for. Despite my intellectual and political reservations, I turn to the work of feminists who have written about the ethic of care, especially those who describe this ethic as related to women's "different voice."

The contemporary feminist notion that women have "a different voice" owes a great deal to Carol Gilligan's now classic work on women's moral development and to the argument that women's relational thinking should be more fully appreciated and valued in Western society. Pursuing a feminist ethic of care in this spirit, philosophers such as Sara Ruddick and Nel Noddings also have examined the meaning of mothering and caring. Such theorists do not produce identical analyses. Yet, taken together, their writings suggest an ethic of care for feminist classroom discourse.[8]

Different voice theorists have made two general and related contributions to understanding the role of care in feminist teaching. The first is their insistence that mothering and caring in general remain a primary item on the feminist agenda. I see this insistence as especially important for feminist college and university teachers. As I look into the often haggard faces of my women doctoral students, pushing themselves into the homestretch of finishing their dissertations, I think about the self-care that is sacrificed in this effort. For many of these women, reducing and postponing caring responsibilities toward others (in particular, family members) makes their sacrifice seem even more personally and ethically costly. I am reminded that the institutions in which we work are not structured to take these caring costs into account, either at this stage or during any later part of students' careers.

Moreover, the institutionalized split between intellectual and caring work often erases "caring" as an intellectual concern. As Joan Tronto shows, modern Western thought has tended to banish caring to the privatized (female) realm.[9] In the United States, critiques based on the experiences of people of color, white women, working-class people, and people with disabilities that might bring caring to the foreground have had only limited impact on the intellectual mainstream. The stigmatizing and erasure of the socialist tradition have made it especially difficult to look at caring as a matter of broad social responsibility rather than as a burden to be borne by individual women and their families.

The other major contribution of different voice theorists lies in their attempts to develop a vocabulary of caring. Although no one vocabulary may be adequate, a lot can be learned from looking at actual experiences with doing, feeling, and thinking about caring. Though mothering need not be the only model for caring, it nevertheless constitutes an enormously important arena of women's caring work. If theories of caring that focus on individual relationships tend to downplay the impact of power structures and cultural norms on caring, such theories nevertheless require us to include women's perceptions about their caring relations in our ethical and political arguments. Whatever the limitations, I think that different voice theorists draw our attention to a number of properties of caring around which feminist teachers can develop an ethic of care.

The first property grows out of the fact that human connection precedes action and involves *asymmetrical, mutual dependency*. Most people are born into caring relationships, connected to their mothers, other family members, communities, and other groups to which they automatically belong. For many different voice theorists, the mother–child relation exemplifies and symbolizes this original connectedness, its virtues and dangers as well as its absolute necessity. In this relationship, both parties need each other but in different ways. The relationship may vary in the length of time it lasts. It may cover a greater or narrower range of needs, but it is not dispensable. The infant needs the relationship to survive, the mother to mother. Even as adults we cannot totally abandon relations of asymmetrical but mutual dependency. If I have the flu, I depend on my partner to shop and prepare food for me. Both of us assume I will do the same for her if necessary. We need each other as carer and cared for, in the course of a day or a lifetime.

The notion of a prior connection between human beings that involves ongoing relations of dependency cannot be applied simply to teaching, let alone to feminist pedagogy. In what sense can we say that teachers and students, who so often meet each other as somewhat suspicious strangers in college and university settings, have a fundamental and prior connection? In her work on caring, Nel Noddings answers this question in an interesting way. She suggests that teachers have a prior connection to their students because of "formal" links to the students previously cared for. The chains of caring that tie a teacher to her past students mean she is "prepared to care" for the next student she encounters.[10]

Although Noddings eschews the language of "role" as inappropriately instrumental, I think we could translate the connection she describes into the fact that students and teachers meet each other already immersed in a world of experience and expectation about teaching and studenting. These layers of experience and expectation tie us together even before we can test out or try to transform the past we bring with us. Until we are sure we will be teachers and students to each other, however we interpret these roles, we operate in a kind of limbo. At the beginning of the semester, both the students and I go through an anxious period in which I do not know precisely who is in the class. Students are registering late and adding and dropping. I do not know who will be "my" students. Some students do not know whether I will be "their" teacher. Occasionally, this ambiguity extends well into the semester, when a student's attendance is uneven. But for the rest, we settle down in one fashion or another to live out a connection that precedes us. The students need me to complete the course successfully, and I need them to succeed at being a teacher.

In my feminist classes, the prior connection between me and my students takes a special form. Although each of us comes with a series of overlapping experiences and expectations about what it means to be a teacher or student (in higher education, in this particular institution, in graduate or undergraduate classes), we often expect the educational process of this class to go beyond those predefined "roles." After all, this is a class in which the teacher is a feminist and the students know they will be interacting with someone who has taken a critical posture toward certain fundamental aspects of the social order. If teachers are supposed to be fair, can a feminist teacher be fair to male students? If teachers are supposed to keep a certain distance from their students, will she be more intimate? Will a feminist teacher be, as Francesca clearly expects in the story about her anger and disappointment with me, more caring?

As such questions suggest, feminist teachers cannot simply presume connection to their students, yet certain general cultural connections tie a teacher and her students together. All of us bring to the classroom experiences and expectations concerning gender and most, if not all, experiences and expectations concerning feminism. To the extent that we inhabit a "common world," we are connected through both the existence of and the disagreements about the meanings of gender in our lives. Part of the burden of the course, and in particular of the teacher, is to make those connections and the contradictions they involve more explicit. Both the students and I anxiously, excitedly, or defensively wait to see how this will be done. In such a setting, the relation of asymmetrical but mutual dependency is conducted in the context of a great deal of uncertainty. Disappointments of the kind that Francesca and I experience, she with me and I with myself, seem inevitable.

The asymmetrical meeting of needs includes dependencies students may develop in relation to each other or that I as their teacher may develop in relation to the students. If feminist discourse involves sharing experiences, feelings, ideas, and actions, the individual who communicates them becomes in some respect dependent on others for a response. Such a response does not necessarily confirm the truth of what the speaker has said but it must be a response that confirms the agency of the speaker. A speaker depends on other group members to validate her as a full citizen in the discourse. Such validation may be relatively silent, conveyed through a small gesture or a look, or it may be quite lively, as it is conveyed through a passionate counterargument. The more risky a particular expression, the more the speaker may fear its negative consequences for herself and others and the greater this dependency on the validation of others becomes.

Such dependency is closely tied to a second property of caring: *attention*. Attention is crucial to caring because, as Joan Tronto and I have argued, it constitutes a prior condition for every other aspect of caring.[11] Paying attention does not always require us to take responsibility or give care, but without attention no caring can take place.

Attention, of course, is a central quality of consciousness-raising. Awareness of injustice requires the ability and willingness to maintain sustained attention. In a class on women and work, I read a description of the life and working conditions of a Southeast Asian woman who works in an American-owned clothing factory. In the following discussion of gender in the global division of labor, Elsa says nothing. At the next class meeting, however, she talks about the shock she experienced when she noticed the label on a blouse she was putting on to go to school. Her blouse, which she dearly loves and was "such a great buy," might have been made by this very woman whose life had been described in the previous class. At that moment, Elsa tells us, she suddenly started to pay attention to many things she had virtually never seen. She now notices the picket line in front of a clothing store at which she often shops. She looks at labels she used to ignore. She is "prepared to care," to use Noddings's phrase, in ways she never was before.

People are prepared to care for others because every society has established patterns of caring. These habits of care have enormous advantages for the effort to meet human needs. It would be disastrous to our survival if we had to reinvent care in response to every need. Yet habitual caring activities often fail to provide an adequate response to those needing care. An experienced mother may still misread the needs of her new infant, who is significantly different from the others. An experienced teacher may find that a teaching strategy she has used with great success in the past hurts and confuses a new group of students. Different voice theorists often speak to this problem by emphasizing the *receptivity of the carer*. Caring requires patience and the carer's willingness to project herself into the world of the one cared for. A student like Elsa who now cares about the fate of exploited Southeast Asian women workers may still fail to care in a way that truly helps them (e.g., by thoughtlessly contributing to the first international charity that approaches her). If she wants to be truly caring, I say to her, she needs to move out of her world and understand the world of Southeast Asian women workers more fully. I suggest she read more on this topic and perhaps make the strike she observed the focus of her term project.

Cultivating patience and a willingness to enter the world of others are closely related to the nonjudgmentalness stressed by many proponents of consciousness-raising. As Ann Diller argues, the process of students and teachers "coexploring" a given subject matter requires a kind of mutual attentiveness and reciprocity.[12] To some extent, I model such attention as I listen to student stories, thoughts, or feelings. Students also model attention to each other and to me. Coexploring, however, does not rule out disagreement. At best, caring orients both the students and me toward moving back and forth between differing perspectives. It shores up our patience for dealing with the external and internal tensions that develop as we try to make sense of another's viewpoint in its relation to our own.

A third property of caring that is discussed by different voice theorists and that I see as especially valuable in developing feminist discourse is *protection*. The question of safety in feminist classrooms will be dealt with in the next chapter, but certain features of protection spelled out or implied in the work of different voice theorists seem particularly relevant to the relation between caring and feminist pedagogy.

In describing how protection relates to caring, different voice theorists often begin with mothering. Protection of infants, or what Sara Ruddick calls "preservative love," is an absolute requirement of growth. All children need a certain amount of "holding," which in psychoanalytic terms refers not only to the original physical holding of a child but to the process of creating a set of emotional conditions under which the child can survive and develop. Holding leads to trust and to the possibility of a child suspending fear long enough to take the risks needed to learn.[13]

The educational version of "holding" provides protective conditions of physical, intellectual, and emotional safety so that students can take the many risks needed for learning. Classroom rules play a part in establishing such conditions because they alert everyone to what kinds of behavior are and are not permitted and therefore what kinds of actions are safe, what kinds risky, within a given institutional context. Although different voice theorists have tended to reject rule-governed ethics as overly abstract and universal, clear rules may be an especially important feature of creating a holding environment for feminist classrooms. The farther the teacher departs from expectations of what it means for the students to be "students" and for her to be a "teacher," the more important rules and the clarity and consistency they symbolize may become. If I invite students to talk about sensitive feelings and controversial ideas, we all need rules about respect. If I include physical activity such as dramatization or body awareness techniques in class, I must convey a clear set of standards about how these things can be done safely, including how students can indicate that they do not want to participate. Such rules to promote caring can be negotiated and changed, but students need to know what to expect, and I need to remain aware of how anxiety and fear can prevent both the students and me from trying out wings.[14]

Holding as an aspect of caring seems indispensable in classrooms in which students are asked to weave experiences, feelings, and potentials for action into their effort to understand and assess ideas about gender and interwoven forms of oppression. Yet the teacher–student relationship cannot be the sole source of protection. To conduct relations of any kind, certain conditions must be met. Teachers have direct control over some of these conditions and little control over others. As public school reformers have long known, students cannot learn if they are too hungry, cold, or afraid for their lives. Even in my relatively privileged classroom, students fall asleep because they work full-time jobs and/or care for others. Students' attention sometimes wanders because they are hungry and do not have time to eat or because the classroom is too hot, too cold, or too noisy. Where possible, I encourage them to acknowledge these conditions. At the beginning of the semester, I say something like "I believe that our capacity to think and talk together is seriously affected by the state of our bodies. If you are hungry, bring food to class. If you need to go to the bathroom, feel free to leave. If you are cold or hot, say something. When I teach, I often lose track of the physical conditions, but I know they are affecting all of us. Please help us to remain aware."

Creating conditions under which any kind of learning can take place requires teachers and others who support their work to engage in a wide range of holding activities that might well be called *educational housekeeping*. For me, these include arguing with the building manager's office about the air conditioning, standing at the copying machine to make copies of class materials, making sure there are enough chairs in the room, and tracking down hard-to-find books or articles. Teachers in more privileged educational environments can delegate a lot of the educational housekeeping to others. Those in poorer institutions have to do a great deal more of it than I do.

The effort to promote feminist discourse often creates even more such housekeeping tasks. For example, I realize in one women's studies class that students enter the discussion more easily by using certain phrases, which I later call "entering phrases." I can see that more students want to talk but do not know how. Thinking about this pattern afterward, I imagine a series of giant flash cards containing such phrases as "Wait—I want to make a point!" The night before the next meeting, I find myself on the floor of my living room with a Magic Marker and large strips of cardboard making these giant flash cards. Down on my knees, I have mixed feelings. The me who sees myself as a university professor views these activities with a certain contempt: "This is certainly not *higher* education," I think. The me who at one point had wanted to be a kindergarten teacher, precisely because it combines intellectual, emotional, and physical nurturing activities, feels a certain pleasure. It is the same pleasure I feel sometimes doing domestic housekeeping, doing the direct work of keeping myself, my loved ones, and my world going.

The giant flash cards are only partly effective. They help some students become more fully involved in class but do not help others. As some different voice theorists stress, no matter how loving or thoughtful or skilled our attempts at meeting needs, caring is intrinsically imperfectible. The *imperfectibility of caring* stems from the fact that it is very difficult to fully meet the needs of others. Needs fluctuate and vary with the context. Many factors limit and constrain even the most devoted carer's efforts to do her job: the amount of work she has to do, the resources at her disposal, and her opportunities for self-care, such as getting enough sleep.

Recognizing the imperfectibility of caring offers solace to teachers who are frustrated with their limited ability to respond to student needs or blame themselves for not being sufficiently "caring." Given the conditions under which many teachers work, what is remarkable is not that they fail to live up to what Noddings would call an "ethical ideal," but that they continue to care at all. Many do not. The pressure and temptations to withdraw from pedagogical caring are enormous in many situations. The rewards, as different voice theorists suggest, mostly stem from the gratification of doing the job well rather than from institutional or social validation. Caring work tends to become visible only when it fails. Otherwise it remains taken for granted, like the ground on which we walk.

Acknowledging the imperfectibility of caring also makes room for what I like to think of as *repair work*. Since as a teacher I sometimes will fail to be sufficiently receptive to the signals sent by students, I need to remind myself that teaching through feminist discourse is an ongoing process and that I often can repair the damage I have done to it. After class, I may realize or learn from a student that I have misread her feelings. Reviewing a text, I may recognize that the interpretation offered by a class member was far more cogent than I had assumed. Knowing that there is another class in which I can make a better pedagogical response orients me toward thinking about what that response might be, rather than endlessly blaming myself for what I did "wrong." At times, of course, a failure to give adequate attention or to respond in a sufficiently caring way cannot be repaired in the particular context. Francesca never forgives me for my lack of attention to her experience of trying to give care to her family. She remains distant and untrusting for the rest of the semester. But, in the spirit of Noddings's notion of caring as a series of ongoing connections, the next time I teach this class, I keep my eye peeled for other "Francescas" and caring needs I might previously have ignored.

Keeping in mind the imperfectibility of caring is particularly important in the kind of feminist pedagogy I am describing because it taps into so many unpredictable and unfulfillable needs. If a teacher believes that she herself must understand and respond to all these needs, she is destined for massive burnout—the kind of burnout often reported in the early years of women's studies in which many teachers found themselves reeling from a tidal wave of student anger and pain. If she sees caring as a continuous series of achievements rather than a test she is failing, she is more likely to continue teaching in a caring way and find methods to improve the caring component of her work. To make some of these improvements, she may have to go beyond a framework that emphasizes caring for others. She may have to give more serious attention to her own needs for self-care. She may have to engage more fully with the structural conditions that shape her caring activities and consider her own responsibility for changing those conditions.

LIMITS TO CARING

Wanda wants something from me that I cannot give her. She brings draft after draft of her final paper to my office, and I spend many more hours with her than anyone else in the class. I appreciate her eagerness (is it desperation?) to write a fine paper, but my attempts to help her are relatively fruitless. No matter what I suggest, she returns to her narrow formulation. My patience is exhausted. She drains energy I need for other projects.

The staff workers are gearing up for a strike, and I am filled with ambivalence. I think their cause is just, and I want to support them as fully as possible. However, doing so will disrupt my world in major ways. I will have to reorient my teaching, stop working on a paper, and spend time organizing faculty and dealing with the tensions that arise from that. I believe that caring should be a collective responsibility, but I find this ideal hard to realize.

Feminist criticisms of different voice theories stress two basic points. First, critics contend that by focusing on meeting the needs of others, such theories perpetuate the norm of women's self-sacrifice and undermines their liberation. Second, critics claim that, by emphasizing individual relationships, the ethic of care distracts feminists from dealing with broader issues of gender and other forms of social justice. Both of these criticisms come alive in the contradictions that pervade feminist teaching. When Wanda first comes into my office, I want to meet her needs. She seems intent on thinking through a question raised by the course, and she wants my help in doing so. I imagine both of us profiting from this interchange. I will help her develop her analysis and argument; she will reciprocate with her insights, excitement, and pleasure at making sense of her question. I expect to learn about her and from her. But this caring dream never materializes. I cannot meet her needs because I have not been able to understand why she pulls back from following out the implications of her own line of thought. I cannot meet my own needs because she does not reciprocate and because spending this time with her conflicts with meeting my needs in other ways. I do not want to "care" any longer. I want to throw her out of the office. I restrain myself and simply say that this is all the time I can give her.

A number of lesbian feminist theorists such as Sarah Hoagland, Janice Raymond, and Jeffner Allen have criticized the feminist focus on caring in especially sharp terms.[15] These feminist philosophers argue that an ethical ideal based on women's caring role tends to reinforce a patriarchal ethic of domination. The mothering model, in particular, valorizes asymmetrical social relations. It downplays the anger and resentment that so often accompanies acts of "caring," and it supports heterosexual institutions that are organized around male power. What the ethic of care takes to be reciprocity (the baby's smile, the student's moment of understanding) is not true reciprocity. In contrast to egalitarian relationships such as friendship, "caring" interactions do not include the carer's needs in the picture. They do not require the cared-for to see the person who is attending to her from the latter's point of view. As a result, the carer is solely responsible for her own care, which others value only to the extent that it serves them. Caring, at base, becomes a default activity to compensate for the damage done by a world in which care is unevenly distributed. Those in power demand it but do not give it, and those with less power must give it but cannot demand it. Under such circumstances, as Hoagland argues, it is appropriate for women to refuse to care, to withdraw from relationships in which they cannot realize their own ethical values and develop their own moral agency.

From this viewpoint, nursing, social work, teaching, and any of the women-predominant professions become highly suspect career choices for women, and any feminist claim that women should organize their professional practice around an ethic of care becomes a dubious one at best. A caring teacher may consciously or unconsciously perpetuate both her own oppression and the oppression of her female students by subjugating her own needs to theirs and making them conform to "good girl" expectations that subordinate all women. To be truly feminist, a teacher might have to place her own needs and development ahead of those of her students and insist that the students recognize and claim their own moral agency. Both teacher and students, this argument suggests, owe it to themselves as women to take care of themselves. Only under conditions of genuine self-care—that is, freedom—can they truly give care to each other.

This notion of grounding agency in self-care has direct application to feminist discourse and presents a powerful lens through which to view my work. As a teacher, I cannot presume that I know what students need to participate in such discourse. I cannot assume that, in their own needs interpretation, students need such discourse at all. I can only follow my own light and hope that, if a critical mass of students choose to devote themselves to the same project, we will together create a viable way of talking about and responding to women's oppression. To the extent that I am able to maintain this posture, I avoid forcing students into the role of dependents. I make room for everyone in the class to attend to each other's needs without assuming that these needs should be met by any individual or in any particular way. From this perspective, my basic misstep with Wanda is to assume that I understand her need to write a good paper and can help her meet it. I bring to our relationship a notion of caring that may have nothing whatever to do with what she needs.

In this lesbian feminist approach, needs get met as the result of individuals exercising their capacity as self-aware choice makers. The development of moral agency parallels the process of building community. Community in this sense supports choice making in which individuals are able to attend both to themselves and to the other moral agents with whom they have a relationship. In these terms, too, I may be reducing Wanda's capacity for choice making by separating our relationship from the class context. By spending so much time giving her individual help, I become the only person to attend to her needs, and my model of caring becomes the only model. I might foster everyone's agency by bringing the problem back to the class and discussing with them collectively what sorts of problems people were having with their papers and to what extent these problems lay in the way I have framed the assignment. Then, perhaps, Wanda could make better choices about what kind of term paper she would write, and other students might be of more help to her than I have been.

This solution, however, ignores the fact that feminist discourse may stimulate needs in both students and teachers that cannot be met within the limits of the classroom. Unlike lesbian feminist communities that provide the reference point for Hoagland's and similar analyses, most classrooms do not create ongoing, close relationships. Even if they could, the diversity of needs requires that participants go outside the classroom to meet many of them. In terms of self-care, teachers often need time for specialized or wide-ranging reading, careful reflection, the opportunity to talk to colleagues, or the chance to write. Except for especially privileged feminist teachers who work in certain elite institutions, such self-care activities remain in tension with the caring needs of students. In the United States at least, most college and university teachers find themselves competing with students for caring time. This situation is most severe where the prospects of building classroom community are slight, where the teacher cannot count on students to pay attention to each others' needs or honor hers.

Feminist teachers of color, working-class teachers, and lesbian teachers whose lives and values may differ radically from those of their students often face this situation in an extreme form. Implacably hostile or self-righteous students or a bigoted administration may virtually force such a feminist teacher to give priority to her self-care. If she cannot survive intellectually, emotionally, and politically, she cannot engage in any kind of teaching, let alone teaching through feminist discourse. When students, as Indira Karamcheti describes, persist in seeing "minority" teachers like her as exotic storytellers whose experiences merely confirm the assumption that people from "third world" countries cannot think theoretically, then such a teacher's self-care (as well as the education of her students) may demand that she withhold these experiences.[16] When students show strong racial prejudice, the self-care for a teacher of color may require her to hold in check feelings that render her more vulnerable and limit student expression of feelings that increases her vulnerability. If a feminist teaches at an institution that might fire her for being a lesbian, self-care may involve the decision not to come out or not to encourage discussion of sexual orientation in her classes.

Because self-care is as complex as caring for others, any decision to avoid or modify feminist discourse in the interests of self-care is likely to involve many considerations. The lesbian teacher who is supporting two children might include them in her definition of self-care, while a single lesbian who has community support elsewhere might say "to hell with it" and come out with a vengeance. In either case, as Hoagland's argument suggests, a teacher who makes herself vulnerable by exposing her caring needs in a situation in which she lacks such support may do more harm to herself and others. Lacking such community, she may need to keep her distance from people who would undermine her agency.[17]

This emphasis on the importance of community to caring tends to be shared by black feminists and socialist feminists who look at caring as a collective issue.[18] To think of caring as a one-to-one phenomenon, they imply, puts an unbearable burden on individual carers. The attempt to care is often systematically distorted and fragmented by the effects of racism, sexism, economic exploitation, and bureaucratic domination. Feminists, such critics suggest, need to place caring in "the big picture" and make demands for better conditions of caring.

Patricia Hill Collins, Bonnie Thornton Dill, Carol Stack, and others suggest that caring can be both a key to community survival and the site of harsh exploitation.[19] Within African American communities, caring is often viewed as a shared responsibility. Not only biological mothers but numerous "othermothers" give care to the community's children. Caring is not merely unpaid work, to be separated off and marginalized in relation to "real work," but a crucial component of the interdependence required to meet survival needs. Outside the community, where many women of color exchange their caring work for wages, caring is often shaped by exploitation and domination. Caring becomes divided, with richer white women controlling its direction and poorer women of color carrying out their orders. Class and race inequities, rather than the community's experience and wisdom, define what constitutes "care."

In the educational realm, as Michele Foster points out, African American women teachers can serve as othermothers, claiming the caring prerogatives of the domestic sphere.[20] Although this appropriation of caring roles may apply most readily to teaching small children ("Long as you're here with me," Foster quotes one elementary school teacher as saying, "I'm your mama . . ."), the logic of pedagogical caring extends past the lower schools. Teachers more easily view themselves and are viewed as appropriate carers when they know and are known to members of a community. Teachers who know their individual students' histories as well as the histories of their families have a rich background through which to develop judgments about what caring is needed. Both beliefs about the teacher's ability to care and her own caring judgments assume that she and other community members share a common set of caring values.

The possibility of community members claiming and exercising caring actions is limited by constraints internal and external to the community, however. Internal limits stem from divisions within the community such as class differences that may greatly strain community bonds. Class distinctions, as Foster notes, may crosscut the familial imagery that informs community-based teaching, rendering teachers, students, and their families less willing to assume shared values. Moreover, when someone leaves the community to teach or study in white-dominated institutions, racism quickly can turn pedagogical caring into a site of exploitation and domination. A black feminist teacher who might call on traditions of mothering within her own community has good reason to suspect that any attempt to act as an othermother to white students would result in her being seen as their "mammy."

☙

I experienced a diminished version of the community caring patterns that Collins and others describe, as a Jewish child raised in large urban settings where Jews were geographically dispersed. In religious school, the teachers knew my parents, who were active members of the congregation, and my parents knew something about the teachers. This sense of being known as a member of a community did not last as I became more fully involved in the secular world. Nor did I easily find a replacement for that community as I became aware of the deep divisions among Jews.[21]

Thus, as a feminist teacher, I am not inclined to think of myself as an othermother to Jewish students. In one course, Marta, a Jewish student from Mexico, comes from an upper-class background. Another student, Lila, comes from a poor Jewish family and was raised on the Lower East Side of New York. One student may define herself as a religious Jew, another in cultural terms. Although I myself inherited a set of Jewish caring values that stress the importance of social justice, I do not know whether these diverse students interpret the tradition in the same way.

Batya makes me think more about this relationship, however. She comes from a tight-knit orthodox Jewish community, and at the beginning of the semester she announces that she has no use for feminism. Her stance recalls in me all the prejudices against orthodoxy as irrational and narrowminded Judaism with which I was raised. Despite the fact that Batya sees herself on foreign turf, she is eager to talk about her life. Through it, we learn her definition of caring, which at its core involves meeting a series of needs that emerge in the daily life of her community. But Batya, her classmates, and I also are beginning to share a kind of daily life. As the semester proceeds, I can see more of the caring she exercises in her community life reflected in her interactions with other class members and with me. She listens keenly to experiences of her Christian classmates and responds in an appreciative manner. She explains her religious needs and obligations (how she will miss class due to a series of Jewish holidays) in a way that increases the class's and my own understanding about how caring is constituted in her world. She warmly tells me at the end of the semester that she understands feminism much better and that some parts of it make a lot of sense to her.

Although I do not see myself as Batya's othermother, it flashes through my mind that I have developed the kind of caring posture toward her that I might have toward a distant relative, for whom I am prepared to care a little just because she is a relative and who, in the light of the Jewish Diaspora, Batya may actually be. Perhaps, I muse, it is precisely because we are not members of the same local community that Batya and I can have such an interchange. She can bring her vision of caring to me without threatening my way of life or kind of teaching, and I can bring my vision to her precisely because of my outsider status. I am an outsider to how she and her community define Judaism, and I am a Jewish outsider in an academic setting organized around the Christian calendar.

I become acutely aware of this latter status at the beginning of the fall semester, when I must choose between being a feminist teacher committed to promoting feminist classroom discourse and a Jewish woman trying to prepare for and observe the most sacred holidays in my own cultural and religious year. The caring dimension of feminist classroom discourse requires continuity. If I am absent for several classes at the beginning of the semester, the development of caring responses is retarded or even undermined. Yet I also need to play a caring role in my Jewish feminist community and my own self-care as a Jew demands that I miss classes. I manage, but I am angry. I meet for extra sessions with several orthodox Jewish students whose stricter pattern of religious observance requires them to miss more classes than I do. As we sit crowded into my small office, I see us in the tradition of Marranos, Spanish Jews who followed their religious practices in secret and maintained the posture of Christian converts in their daily lives. We are not keeping our identities secret, of course, but are taking care of ourselves in the shadow of the institution that to some extent erases our lives. Maybe, I muse again, I am an othermother after all.

Like bureaucracy, the state and marketplace also affect patterns of caring within educational contexts. When budget cuts for education lead to larger classes and fewer counselors, teachers find it is harder to pay attention to individual students' needs. When the costs of books go up, students who cannot afford them remain educationally needy. When bureaucracy fragments caring by giving teachers more responsibility than power and rendering students' caring needs invisible, the attempt to practice feminist teaching with care becomes increasingly problematic. As Joan Tronto and I have argued, the capitalist market and bureaucratic organization virtually guarantee that caring will be imperfect.[22]

Nancy Fraser points to the fact that government and professional groups have far greater power to define the needs of poor women than poor women themselves.[23] Yet, to move toward greater social justice, disempowered groups must be able to discuss and define their own needs. The same logic applies to the relation between the hierarchies within which most teaching takes place and the possibility of those with less power defining their own needs. To the extent that a feminist teacher seeks to be caring, she has to confront conflicting interpretations of need within her institution.

This point emerges dramatically in the story about the staff strike I tell at the beginning of this section. The organizing efforts of the staff local, representing a workforce that is predominantly women of color, convince me that these workers have good reason to put their needs ahead of giving care to anyone else in the university community. In fact, by making their needs central, the union is for a short period able to counter bureaucratic fragmentation and inspire at least some staff, faculty, students, and even, unofficially, administrators to discuss a more equitable distribution of caring.

As I begin with some colleagues to organize a faculty support group for the strikers, I notice how this discourse on needs unfolds. The local lays out the workers' needs in the form of a series of demands. Workers talk with each other and their supporters about these and other needs that they have not yet gotten on the union agenda. Many faculty, administrators, and students charge that the union and its supporters are ignoring the needs of the students because the strikers and their faculty sympathizers do not care. I care about the students, but I want them also to care about the staff. Together with other faculty supporters and according to the strategy agreed on with the union, I move my classes off campus. Now the discourse on needs interpretation becomes an issue in my teaching. Some students complain about the inconvenience of holding class off campus, but whatever their posture toward the strikers, students in my women's studies classes do not challenge the relevance of this strike for our discussions.

In one graduate class of mostly white women, we happen to be reading Friedrich Engels's theory of women's oppression. Discussion of his analysis quickly interweaves with discussion of the strike. Talk focuses on how economic inequities pervade the university and what these mean for students, staff, faculty, and administrators. Special attention is paid to the contradictory position of teaching assistants, adjuncts, and lower-status administrators because a number of the students work in these roles. We talk about how their current needs to retain their insecure and low-paying jobs conflict with full support of the strike. We consider how these needs are linked to their hoped-for mobility as professionals, whereas the needs of most of the staff involve the survival of their families and communities.

Like all feminist discourse, these discussions are linked to judgment—in this case, to decisions we have to make individually and collectively about the immediate situation. I have to decide how much of my self-care to sacrifice (it is easier for me to let go of writing a paper than to give up sleep). Students have to decide whether to miss classes that require them to cross picket lines. Student employees have to decide whether and how they want to support the union.

The bonds that are created in the process of these discussions play a role in this decision making. A group of students who are also low-status administrators may figure out together how they can offer aid to the strikers while giving each other a certain degree of protection against losing their own jobs. Another group of students may get together to draft a letter to the administration which none of them might be willing to write individually. In the course of these conversations and actions, needs are assessed and reassessed. The meaning of women's oppression is discussed and reevaluated in relation to racial, class, and other forms of injustice. This is not a simple or smooth process. We risk the possibility of developing political splits among class members that cannot be mended. Yet the connections we have developed through our project of talking together hold. Our feminist discourse is alive, clear, and compelling.

CARING IN CONTEXT

It is late in the semester, and a graduate class of about thirty students is reading Trinh T. Minh-ha's provocative book Women, Native, Other. *The author begins with the image of a village in which people have gathered to discuss matters of importance to them. Their discussion proceeds without the kind of order demanded in Western political discourse. "A mother," writes Trinh, "continues to bathe her child . . . two men go on playing a game . . . a woman finishes braiding another woman's hair."[24] Although I am wary of Westerners imitating Eastern traditions, I am inspired by her description. I suggest at the beginning of class that we see what would happen if everyone just responded first to their own physical, emotional, and intellectual needs. The class breaks up into a shifting configuration of individuals, pairs, small and large groups. Some go to the bathroom; others rest with their heads down on the note-taking arms of their chairs. Individuals read or write. Someone shares cookies she had baked for a holiday party. Two women talk about the tension that had arisen between them during the semester. Now and then, students wander over to talk with me, about the reading or other course matters. Most members of the class eventually end up in small or larger groups, talking about the text. I join one group and listen to their intense discussion.*

Feminist theories of caring do not and cannot fit together neatly into a feminist teaching practice. Some notions of caring make far more sense in certain contexts than in others. Different voice theories work best in one-to-one relationships characterized by a high degree of unavoidable dependence. These include situations in which mothers must care for children and in which teachers must give students a great deal of help for them to meet their minimal needs for survival in the institution (such as being able to do the reading or writing required to pass the course). Theories that stress women's moral agency work best in relationships among people that come together as relative equals, not only friends who can give and receive care from each other without compromising their integrity but teachers

NO ANGEL IN THE CLASSROOM

and students who meet in small seminar settings in which their relationship approaches that of colleagues. Social structural analyses of caring apply to every teaching situation, but they cannot be put into practice unless teachers and students are able and willing to move beyond the boundaries of the classroom to engage with those in the institution, marketplace, or state who effect the conditions of caring.

Despite the tensions among these approaches to caring, I think it is possible to identify certain overarching concepts that can help teachers committed to fostering feminist discourse think about the relation of caring to our work. I want to suggest three such concepts that are implied in my earlier discussion. The first is *attention as a refocusing lens*. By this I mean that although attention is central to caring, it must shift and refocus as conditions of care change. Although a new mother may devote virtually all her attention to a first infant, exclusive attention becomes increasingly impossible when a second or third or fourth child is born. Now her attention constantly refocuses, from the immediate needs of one (the baby is screaming to be changed or fed) to the more distant but equally important needs of another (the ten-year-old is unusually late in getting home from school). Teachers with many students know very well what it means to constantly refocus attention.

The capacity to refocus attention may be a liability as well as an advantage. At worst, it becomes a source of continual distraction so that in focusing on everything, the carer focuses on nothing. But the capacity to refocus attention has several important advantages for teachers attempting to practice a feminist ethic of care. It reminds us of the fact that we operate simultaneously in a series of contexts and that what is happening with a given student or even in a particular classroom is not the whole picture. The student who is falling asleep in my class may be doing so because the topic angers her and she is closing down emotionally, because the room is overheated and she cannot keep her eyes open, because she is working full-time and has not gotten enough sleep, and/or because her adviser has allowed her to sign up for too many courses. For me as a teacher, the effort to care involves focusing on one after another overlapping contexts in which both the student and I are situated: paying attention to the emotional impact of a given subject on the students, to how the economic squeeze is affecting students' lives, to how the neglect of caring within the institution leads to situations in which the students' needs overwhelm them. Taking these contexts into account, I decide what I should do in this situation (talk with the student, the class, the building manager's office, the head of undergraduate advisement) and what I might do in the long run (agitate for greater student subsidies, meet with the committee on undergraduate requirements, etc.).

Although refocusing attention may lead me toward actions I might otherwise not take, the work of both different voice and lesbian feminist ethicists reminds me that I need not "do something" for caring attention to have value. Under some conditions, attention itself is a form of caring. For students for whom visibility has been difficult to achieve, for those from groups whose realities have been systematically ignored or denied, for women whose "private" concerns are deemed irrelevant to public discourse, the attention of teachers or other students constitutes a powerful form of caring, a kind of ethical and political witness.[25] I do not have to "do" something about my student who was raped. By reading her journal and indicating that I have paid serious attention to her story, pain, and attempts at healing, I am doing a great deal. By paying attention to the fact that students are falling asleep or shivering in class, I already have changed the conditions under which the class operates. Indeed, by raising the questions of comfort, I may find that one of the students gets up to open or close a window simply because the room temperature now has become an overt concern for the class.

As this last example suggests, attention often leads to other caring activities, but it does not determine who shall do them. Much of the time, the structures in which we operate, together with the ideas we have about who is responsible for caring, results in certain people being designated as carers. To feminists, this logic has clear dangers. It erases the shared responsibility to respond to human needs, and it tends to support a rigid and self-sacrificing model of care. The more people are trapped in caring roles, especially when they are ill rewarded and unsupported in their work, the more likely they are to abuse those to whom they give care. The more they know that there are others to share the caring, like the "othermothers" in an African American community, the less oppressive that work may seem.

Thus, the second concept I suggest, *flexibility in the division of caring labor*, speaks to this state of affairs.[26] Teachers of all kinds find themselves trapped in a division of caring labor not of their making and struggling with ideals of caring they do not want to or cannot achieve. The notion that a teacher must accomplish caring tasks by herself is especially damaging. Often other carers can and should be called into play: students, sympathetic administrators, and staff. Rather than taking for granted how caring labor is distributed, teachers can initiate discussions about how the needs of students, staff, faculty, and others can be met.

Ideally, such discussions could result in a flexible and self-conscious division of caring labor. For example, if a student talks in class about being sexually harassed, many people may become involved in caring activities. Both the students who listen attentively to a classmate's story and the student herself have needs met through this discussion. At best, many people take responsibility for improving the conditions of care. Thus, the student who has been harassed may join with her classmates in a delegation to the student affairs office to discuss how sexual harassment policies can be improved. This approach can be highly creative in the sense that it allows for new definitions and ways of caring to emerge, rather than making caring and being cared for into an oppressive routine. While one student finds sexual harassment painful and humiliating, another may find it ridiculous and infuriating. While the first may need gentle attention to her experience before any further actions might be taken, the second might be looking for some peers to join her in some spontaneous guerrilla theater.

The possibility of participants in feminist discourse making an immediate, spontaneous response to an expressed need points to a third overarching concept: *improvisational caring*. Feminist discourse itself has a highly improvisational character. In ways, it parallels Elsa Barkley Brown's account of her approach to teaching African American women's history.[27] These classes, says Brown, resemble an African American quilt-making process in which materials are chosen for their liveliness and contrast rather than for their contribution to a traditional pattern. As a result, a vibrant and pleasing design emerges through the interplay of unpredictable and distinct elements. By giving a great deal of the responsibility for both learning and teaching to the students, Brown helps them create a "polyrhythmic, 'nonsymmetrical,' nonlinear structure" out of apparent chaos. Vitality and creativity give birth to their own order as the students make their ways through the subject of the course.

My own notion of the role that spontaneity can play in feminist teaching is influenced by my studies in dramatic and movement improvisation. The movement technique called *contact improvisation* provides an especially important model.[28] As in the quilt making described by Brown, there is no predetermined pattern. Throughout the improvisation, a group of movers remains in close contact with each other. They may lean on, sit on, push against, pull on, or wrap themselves around each other. All of them share a basic need, which is to deal with the effects of gravity. Each mover must find some way in which her weight can be supported. In the course of trying to take care of themselves in this way, each person follows her own body impulses and thus speaks to and validates her own needs. Yet each mover also must continuously be aware of and respond to the movement of those with whom they are in contact. One person's movement affects that of others and vice versa. On the most immediate physical level, these movements express interdependence. If one person does not pay attention to the movements of others, that person undermines her own balance. Viewed from the outside, the movers look like a single moving organism.

Viewed from the inside, they constitute a creative synthesis of self-care and caring for others.

That is precisely what happens in the story I tell about the class in which I suggest that the students begin by meeting their own needs. After nearly a semester of talking about the meanings of and responses to women's oppression, many students have a clearer image of what might constitute their own needs and those of others. Through a combination of following their own impulses and maintaining contact, each person meets her needs as best she can in this situation. These include but are not limited to needs related to the course materials. The class has a deeply gratifying quality. Our discourse thrives. I am doing the work I love. I believe that whatever needs arise, a combination of self-care and caring for others will speak to them.

This, of course, is not a typical class but a story about a treasured teaching moment in which individual and collective needs, as well as theory and practice, come into an especially fruitful relationship. As I have noted already, a great deal can stand in the way of that outcome. One of the major impediments to feminist discourse concerns the feelings of danger that students and teachers often experience. When I suggest to the class that we follow Trinh's lead and see the extent to which it is possible to combine caring with political discourse, I take a modest risk. In the worst scenario I can imagine, the students all leave the class or turn it into a joke on me. These risks do not seem great. I have a lot of teaching experience, and I believe I know these students. I do not spend time thinking about the risks because I feel relatively safe in this class and because I sense the students do as well. Yet, as with the concept of care, there is nothing self-evident about the meaning of safety. What does it mean to make "safety" a feature of feminist classrooms? Is it good for students and teachers to feel safe? These perplexing questions are the topic of my next chapter.

— 5 —

DANGEROUS CURVES

Safety and Self-Disclosure

After a go-around in which students talk about experiences with violence, Vera, a white and apparently middle-class woman, comments on how white, middle-class assumptions pervade several of the stories. Sarabeth, who is also white, becomes so agitated she can hardly stay in her seat. "I thought this was a safe place," she says, "that we were not supposed to judge each other." Vera leaps to her own defense: "I thought it was safe to say what we think!" I become anxious about my responsibility toward each of these students and toward the class as a whole. "What is 'safety' really about?" I wonder out loud. As we go around the class, Felice says safety has to do with knowing that I as the teacher will not let things get "out of control." Lourdes comments that she always feels safer when people are speaking Spanish, as she does with her family and friends. Bruce remarks that as the only man in the room he would feel safer if there were "more of us." It is clear that "safety" does not mean the same thing to everyone.

Why is safety so important to many feminist teachers and their students, and why is it so hard to find an adequate response to this concern? Is safety an intrinsic problem for classes in which teachers and students talk about their own experiences and feelings? Is safety a false goal used to suppress dissent?

For me, safety is neither a false nor a simple issue. When I first tried to integrate my own experiences and feelings into my feminist teaching, I found myself tongue-tied. I was astonished to discover that words that flowed so easily in conversations with friends and feminist comrades clung to my lips, reluctant to enter the classroom. Talking about myself seemed indecent as well as unprofessional. I was afraid of being hurt or at least seriously embarrassed. Throughout my years of teaching women's studies, the problem of safety for the students as well as myself has persisted. As

I follow the interchange between Sarabeth and Vera, a part of me sighs inside with weariness. "Why doesn't this issue of safety just disappear?"

Some feminists try to make the problem disappear by arguing that it is created by teachers. In *Professing Feminism*, Daphne Patai and Noretta Koertge imply that if teachers like me just stuck to the real purpose of higher education, to teach critical thinking and transmit scholarship, students would not be forced to disclose private matters. If feminist teachers respected the boundaries between private and public, we would not have to deal with safety.[1]

One appeal of this argument is the safety it provides the teacher. I could keep a "safe" distance from students to avoid having to deal with any messy or volatile experiences and feelings. But the attempt to seal off students and teachers from potentially threatening responses by banning self-disclosure has limited usefulness. Education cannot take place without some degree of self-disclosure.[2] To function effectively as a teacher, I must ask students to reveal what they have understood of the course content. They continuously ask me to reveal my intentions and judgments about the class and their success in it. These mundane and necessary self-disclosures often become problematic. A student may do everything she can (from mild dissembling to outright plagiarism) to avoid revealing how hard she has found the course material because she is afraid she will get a bad grade or be judged "stupid" by me or her peers. I, in turn, may dissemble when students ask me to clarify my intentions or judgments (Why *did* I put that reading on the syllabus? What *is* the difference between a B + and an A − ?), and I am afraid that my uncertainties will lead them to think I am a bad teacher.

Thus, like all teachers, I am faced with the necessity of developing and constantly reevaluating the *disclosure rules* that the students assume or that I convey to them.[3] How much of her lack of knowledge should I pressure the fearful student to expose? To whom and under what conditions? When will such revelations lead to greater learning and when to intellectual and psychological harm? Similarly, how many of my own uncertainties should I reveal to students or, for that matter, my impatience or boredom? When will such revelations facilitate learning and when impede it?

For someone seeking to teach through feminist discourse, such questions become even more complicated. As a course addresses area after area that the dominant culture considers "personal," teachers and students face endless choices about what experiences, feelings, thoughts, and actions to disclose. Even a formal lecture on the division of domestic labor, for instance, may induce anxiety in both women and men students about what this topic means for them personally. If, in addition, the teacher asks students to disclose or even merely reflect on the meaning of the division of domestic labor for their lives, many students may feel unsafe. The teacher herself, who may be in the middle of a knock-down-drag-out fight with her partner about who will do the dishes, may find her heart pounding as she speaks. She may learn, after the lecture, that a student who has had so much trouble writing her paper is puzzled or frightened by the meaning of this research for her own impending marriage. Reiterating the value of the public/private distinction cannot create safety within a feminist teaching project that invites radical rethinking of that distinction.

Some feminists have an additional concern: that the effort to ensure safety in feminist discourse results in denying difference and suppressing dissent. Bernice Reagon and bell hooks each argue vigorously that white feminist activists and academics often evoke the need for safety as a way of avoiding the issue of racism.[4] In my experience, too, this a serious issue. Let us say, in my opening story, that Sarabeth is white and Vera black and that I defend Sarabeth on the grounds that Vera's remark about white middle-class assumptions makes the classroom unsafe for sharing experiences. In my eagerness to make the classroom safe for Sarabeth and for myself as a white, middle-class woman, I am making it less safe for Vera to bring her ideas about class and race into that setting.

Susan Jarratt makes a parallel point when she suggests that feminist attempts to make classrooms safe for expression often eliminate or suppress pedagogically valuable conflicts.[5] To the degree that my efforts to bring Vera and Sarabeth into the same universe of discourse keep them from fully arguing out their respective values, I may contribute to suppressing conflict and dissent. As the story proceeds, however, I judge that they cannot learn from this conflict because it is not yet clear what it is about. I ask them and other class members to share their definitions of safety because I think that, until we understand what is at stake for not just Vera and Sarabeth but other class members, our discourse cannot continue fruitfully.

The argument that concern with safety suppresses conflict seems to me both convincing and insufficient. The norm of safety can be used oppressively. Yet this does not mean it should be discarded, and hooks grants as much when she notes as part of her argument about safety that faculty themselves may require a kind of safety from attacks by students and from professional humiliation to talk about volatile topics such as racism. She acknowledges that students, too, need a certain degree of safety but insists that it come from "a feeling of community" rather than suppressing difference.

As hooks suggests, building classroom community is a far better alternative to dealing with fears about safety than suppressing dissent. Efforts toward community building also tap into the *political* meaning of safety as it has evolved in the context of activism. Safety is always a concern for people who gather together to discuss oppression, because such talk threatens those in power. During the civil rights movement of the 1960s, gathering together to engage in political talk about resistance could lead to getting killed. Black churches and certain communities or houses provided "safe spaces," places in which people could discuss injustice and plan oppositional actions with some *physical safety*.[6]

New left, civil rights, community organizing, feminist, and other activists of the 1960s and 1970s emphasized the closely related notion of "free space." In this view, free spaces were created when these social movements drew people together to talk about what was wrong and what could be done. As Sara Evans and Harry Boyte put it, free spaces enable people to learn and practice a kind of citizenship denied to them by an unjust system.[7] In the course of addressing their social injustice issues, participants can call on community traditions of cooperation or learn to cooperate in new ways. Through such political discourse, they can create what could be described as *social safety*. The sense of social safety grows out of participants recognizing certain shared values and being able to count on each other. This is, I believe, the feeling of community bell hooks alludes to in her analysis of what makes a classroom "safe."

Many grassroots feminists of the period also valued safety. In particular, they sought a form of talking that would protect women from the verbal abuse they suffered (being shouted down, ridiculed, or ignored by male activists) when they tried to raise questions of gender justice. To counter this kind of suppression, feminist activists quickly concluded that women needed their own spaces in which to discuss the political meaning of their experiences. These free spaces enabled women to tell their stories without feeling intimidated or judged. The consciousness-raising caution against women responding to each other in a "judgmental" way provided the kind of *psychological safety* needed to address the questions so central to women's oppression.

Finally, the political experience of second-wave feminism suggests a fourth meaning of safety that I think of as *discourse safety*. In her analysis of consciousness-raising, Pamela Allen touches on this factor when she stresses the importance of honesty.[8] Honesty, she suggests, helps create the trust needed to develop truly free space. Trust is required to take oneself seriously, take the other women's thinking seriously, and make a commitment to the group. Although Allen does not address why women, in particular, might be dishonest with each other, feminist analyses of the period were filled with references to this problem. Dependence on male power, competition over the sexual attentions of men, and fears of male violence all led women to lie to each other as well as to men. In this respect, many women used dishonesty as a strategy for individual survival.

But this point also meant that women had to pay close attention to the problems posed by dishonesty for political discourse and seek to develop honest expression of their experiences, feelings, thoughts, and notions of action. To the extent that political discourse provides the basis for judgments about action, it is downright dangerous to rely on participants who share anything other than their best understanding of the situation the group is addressing. Dishonesty corrupts that understanding. Honesty, however, is hard to define, which is, perhaps, why Allen does not try to define it. It is easier for us to indicate what honesty is not.[9]

Honesty does not require that every discourse participant say what is on her mind all the time. At any point in the discussion she may ask herself whether what she might say would make a useful contribution to the discussion. I do not mean to suggest that a participant weighs every word through some kind of rational calculus or that everything she might want to say is consistent or even rational. Rather, by honesty I mean a giving rather than withholding attitude toward the discourse that, when generally shared, instills in everyone confidence that it can increase understanding and promote wiser judgments.

Honesty also does not require that discourse participants reveal a coherent, let alone a "true," self. *Self-disclosure is a process* through which different aspects of the self—not just identities but experiences, feelings, ideas, and actions—are exposed and responded to. In the context of second-wave feminism, consciousness-raising gave women an opportunity to discover and pay attention to selves that had been denied or barely acknowledged because the consequences of doing so were threatening or outright dangerous. The value of self-disclosure lay in its contribution to developing collective interpretations of and opposition to women's oppression. Honest participation in feminist discourse meant bringing as much of yourself as you could to such discussions, drawing on experiences, feelings, and ideas that might promote liberating actions.

Although in the earlier story Vera and Sarabeth each express anxiety about their safety in the class, they are both safe in many ways. Neither stops talking because she feels physically endangered. This is not always the case. For instance, in another class, Mia says she is going to drop the course because her husband has been physically threatening her for deciding to go to graduate school and taking women's studies classes. Vera and Sarabeth also feel a fair degree of social safety. In their own ways each of them views this classroom as "free" enough to explore ideas that challenge the dominant order. In contrast, Nellie says that the more her classmates in her professional program tease her about becoming a "radical feminist," the less free she feels in our discussions. Despite Sarabeth's and Vera's claims that they are being prevented from saying what is on their minds, both of them feel enough psychological safety to argue about whether the classroom is "safe." Yet, Sybil remains silent the whole semester; when I question her and offer help, she tells me she is far too afraid of being judged by other students to speak out.

Finally, in the context of my story, Vera and Sarabeth are in the process of developing greater discourse safety because they honestly state what they need to remain participants. Unlike Uta, a student in another course who says to me at the end of the semester that she was never willing to say what was really on her mind, Sarabeth declares that for her safety involves careful attention and response to what she is saying. Vera explains that for her safety means being able to take her ideas as far as she can without fear of reprisal. As members of the class explore the meanings of safety, we begin to consider how each definition might be taken into account in our discourse.

After this discussion, I ask the students to divide into pairs and return to the topic of violence that they had been discussing. I recommend that both partners remain aware of what it would take for each of them to feel relatively safe throughout their discussion. I note that safety can include strong disagreements as long as we maintain this kind of awareness. I ask Vera and Sarabeth to work together and make myself available to them if they find their talk breaking down. The room buzzes with intense conversations. After class, Vera and Sarabeth tell me how much better their discussion had gone. Sarabeth had a chance to describe her childhood experience with domestic violence, with which Vera could empathize. Vera spelled out her argument that middle-class notions of violence ignored the daily economic violence done to poor people. Sarabeth says she has difficulty understanding this definition of violence, but she is making a real effort to listen. I suggest that in the next class we explore with the others the possible relationships between these different forms of violence and what might be done in response to them.

In this classroom story, discourse becomes increasingly safe in part because Vera, Sarabeth, and others are gradually able to listen to each other more carefully and fully. Such *"political listening,"* to draw on Susan Bickford's analysis, does not assume or aim at complete agreement.[10] Rather, it involves the effort to focus attention on each speaker as a full participant in political discussion and on aspects of her speech that we may be inclined to misread or dismiss because of how relations of domination distort our expectations and interpretations. Thus, while such listening increases discourse safety, it also may challenge the ideas, interpretations, and beliefs that we bring to our classroom interactions. Political listening, as Bickford points out, is risky. In this story, I feel deeply gratified at the way in which Sarabeth and Vera have begun to listen to each other, and I am eager to see how this experience affects their subsequent discussion.

As this vignette suggests, safety becomes an issue precisely where community has failed to protect its members or where community has not yet come into existence. Classroom interactions often give rise to the feeling of being endangered. But problems of safety and self-disclosure also arise from the interactions between the class and the various contexts in which it is situated. In the remainder of the chapter, I first will look more closely at safety in classroom relationships. Then I will turn to the ways in which our concerns about safety are shaped by broader institutional and social conditions.

SAFETY WITH EACH OTHER

In a discussion of a feminist text on the meaning of family, Shayna describes taking her woman lover home for a family holiday and how her mother (who said "it would kill" Shayna's grandmother) refused to acknowledge the lesbian relationship. When Shayna finishes speaking, there is a long silence. Finally, I suggest a go-around, to encourage people to continue the discussion. Several students pass. Finally, Rita gently says that she understands Shayna's mother. In her family and culture, she says, old people are respected and you do not put such distressing facts "in their face." Shayna says she is shocked by Rita's homophobia (the implied acceptance of Shayna's mother's distaste for the relationship). I, who am struggling with coming out to my own aging mother, say nothing. After class, Shayna tells me that the class feels less safe. She expected more from Rita and from me, of all people.

Feminist teaching often generates intense expectations about what the teacher will do or the class be like. One student assumes that other students will automatically understand her experiences. Another expects the teacher to support everything she, the student, says. Some students also have negative expectations which provide them with a certain degree of safety. They have had hurtful experiences in similar situations (in groups of women, groups of feminists, or groups that were white dominated or mostly heterosexual), and their mistrust warns them not to take too many risks in class. Idealized expectations, on the other hand, virtually guarantee a certain degree of failure and, as in this story, raise the question of safety. Shayna's disappointment with me and her withdrawal of trust is based in part on the expectation that as a lesbian as well as a feminist I will support the values implied by her self-disclosure.

Students often come to feminist classrooms with mixed expectations about self-disclosure and its consequences. Those who have been exposed to some versions of feminist pedagogy may assume that expressing strong feelings is the norm for feminist classrooms. Beginning students, on the other hand, may be shocked with the level and kind of self-disclosure, or they may be starved for a chance to tell their stories and convinced by advance publicity that feminist classrooms are the place in which they can do so. They may be equally shocked when I set conditions for their self-disclosures—for example, if I ask them to connect their experiences to ideas, texts, or the experiences of others.

Since I realize that the students' various expectations may differ greatly from what I know or suspect may unfold in the class, I need to think about preparing them to engage in classroom activities. At the beginning of the semester, I talk about the strong feelings that may be evoked by material that has such personal relevance. I try to prepare students for the anger or shame they may feel in reading or talking about injustice. I let them know what I expect from them and the difficulties they may have in finding a productive relation to those expectations. I tell them that there is almost always room to explore, discuss, and negotiate when their expectations of me or other students do not match what they find in the classroom.

Over a semester, students in my women's studies classes usually develop a greater commonality of expectations. They catch on to the culture I am promoting in the classroom (whether they like it is another question), and I get to know them better, to understand their stories and their passions. But many factors limit the degree to which expectations can be shared. There may be too many of us to develop a shared culture easily. We are not together very long. Our stories and motivations are too complicated to know in depth. The very format of a class that gives prominence to experience and feelings weakens the ability to predict what will happen next. At any moment, a new story may reveal an unexpected facet of a person, or a strong feeling may break through the normal classroom regime to force us to question what we are doing. These sometimes dramatic twists and turns generate in both the students and me a certain amount of performance anxiety—not because we are afraid that we will forget our lines but because we do not know ahead of time what those lines will have to be.

Given this aura of uncertainty, the participants confront choices about how to respond when the classroom suddenly seems unsafe to them. Consciousness-raising assumed totally voluntary participation, but teaching in degree-granting institutions always involves an element of coercion. Increasing the range of choices about how to engage with the material gives students a chance to enter classroom discourse in a spirit of desire, just as women were drawn to consciousness-raising out of desire for knowledge and change and the desire to have some control over their lives. But offering students such choices as to "pass" in a go-around, or to observe rather than join a dramatic exercise, or to choose how much personal material they will include in a journal does not eliminate the coercive element. As teachers, we can make these constraints the focus of classroom discourse. How do differently situated students view their "choice" to participate in a given exercise? What does this mean about how the material might be taught?[11]

Expectations and choices interweave in complex ways. When expectations about the roles of teachers or students are disrupted, choices become increasingly problematic. For instance, if a student cries, as happens sometimes in my women's studies classes, what should teachers or students do? Should the teacher comfort her? Should some of the students? If the teacher fails to do so, what does this signal to students about what they should expect in feminist classrooms? If the teacher does comfort the student, does this imply that only the teacher may do so? Given the conflicting values related to caring that I explored in the last chapter, a feminist stance alone does not produce an unambiguous answer to these questions. A teacher may fail in caring both by taking an active role in comforting the student (thus undermining the student's self-care and the capacity of the students to care for each other) and by not showing concern about the student (thus, perhaps, signaling to others in the class that caring is not part of feminist pedagogy). How the teacher and the students respond in such a situation helps define how safe it is in this class to reveal painful feelings.

When students cry in class, I often have an impulse to comfort them physically as I would a friend who was in pain. I restrain myself not only because touching women students has implications for my own safety (as a lesbian teacher, my touching women is open to potentially damaging interpretations) but because I want to normalize the expression of such emotions in class, maximize student choice, and leave room for a more egalitarian model of caring. I do not see crying as an inappropriate response to some of the topics and dynamics that develop in class. Moreover, other students often make comforting gestures that the student who cries can more easily accept or reject. I confine myself to acknowledging the feeling with a supportive look and to checking with the student after class. Through these actions, we are together defining the parameters of safety.

Choices may become narrowed despite our intentions. I fail to intervene in the discussion between Shayna and Rita because I fear my own complex feelings about coming out to my mother will spill out in an uncontrolled way. After the course is over, I consider whether talking about these feelings would have promoted fuller and deeper discussion. What if I could have described to the class both the proud and angry lesbian in myself and the good daughter, who wanted to keep my old connection to my mother? Perhaps, if I had been able to own my kinship with both Shayna's and Rita's experiences, I could have promoted genuine feminist discourse about such contradictions.

But the choice to share my feelings or experiences fully does not necessarily promote shared expectations or increase feelings of safety. In another graduate class, students find themselves deeply divided over whether the autobiographical statements I have asked them to write for distribution should remain anonymous, which was my past procedure, or whether they should put their names on their papers. The more I listen to their arguments, the more convincing both sides seem. Because of the nature of this question, majority rule does not help us. If only a few choose anonymity, their identities will soon become apparent. After several agonizing discussions, I finally perform a dialogue I have written about my internal debate. I admit I cannot decide what alternative is best. The class stumbles on using my old method, but none of us is truly happy.

Anguished as this process might be, many of the students and I, too, feel that we have learned something about the complexity of our values and lives. We have discovered for ourselves that, as feminist and many other theorists argued, choice making is not simply a matter of rational calculation or the application of universal rules. We have learned how important it is to listen to each other's conflicting and overlapping voices.

I also learn that I cannot make a more informed choice about safety without examining more fully the assumptions underlying my values in feminist teaching. My preference for anonymity, I realize, has been based on the belief (reinforced by interactions with former students) that most students feel safer if they do not put their names on these particular papers. From the standpoint of learning from experience, it has seemed to me less important that we as a class know who said what than that we are able to reflect together on what these statements mean. But as the discussion proceeds, the students teach me that anonymity also may be a privilege linked with being "the same as others." The only visibly disabled woman in such a class, the only African American man, or the only out lesbian cannot write fully about themselves and remain anonymous. I learn that for some other students, anonymity also makes them feel less safe because they view it as erasing their unique voices.

In hindsight, I believe I should have argued against anonymity and sought another solution with the students. We might have talked about why, so far along in the course, many of the students felt frightened to reveal themselves in writing on this topic. We also might have discussed different versions of this autobiographical assignment, say, in a combination of writing and discussion or in discussion in pairs or very small groups rather than with the whole class. I might have been convinced to drop the assignment entirely. If I had remained focused on what I valued most in that situation—on finding a structure that included everyone's story as they chose to tell it—we together might have imagined these options.

Two aspects of this experience seem to me to have broad implications for feminist teachers grappling with problems of safety and self-disclosure. One concerns *setting limits* and the other concerns the *openness of teaching structures*. There is no easy formula for how a teacher can set limits and at the same time promote the value of choice making by her students. Setting limits makes some students and teachers feel more and others less safe.[12] As many feminists have argued, women may need to draw certain lines to create a space for developing our selves, rather than automatically putting others' requirements ahead of our own. When women always put others first and cannot limit the demands of others, we lose the opportunity to think about and act on our own desires and welfare.

If a feminist teacher is unwilling to set limits to how students express themselves, the classroom may become progressively *less* safe for describing and discussing feelings, experiences, and ideas. A student whose pain or anger is so great and whose resources for dealing with these feelings are so meager that she constantly demands that everyone respond to her feelings or listen to her stories can seriously undermine feminist discourse. A teacher who has difficulties placing limits on the expression of such feelings faces a situation not so different from that of a wife, mother, aunt, grandmother, or sister who is constantly expected to respond to her family's needs. If the teacher is unable to set limits, it is unlikely that her students will risk trying to do so. When I have had trouble establishing clear limits, students usually come to me after class, pleading for me to set limits that they feel unable to set themselves.

Yet an emphasis on setting limits has clear disadvantages. As bell hooks and others note, limit setting in the interests of making the classroom safe can reinforce the power of white or otherwise privileged students and teachers. Setting limits often suppresses the emotional expression so crucial to feminist discourse. If safety is approached only through establishing explicit or implicit rules, students and teachers may soon become reluctant to share new or radical ideas.

For these reasons, setting limits needs to go hand in hand with challenging or transgressing limits.[13] Feminist teachers, by definition, transgress limits when they confront sexism and misogyny and the racism, homophobia, and other forms of oppression interwoven with them. Students challenge limits when they question the basic categories around which discussion is being conducted (as hooks herself did when she challenged racism in white-dominated women's studies classes). Resistance to limitations does not take one unambiguous form, however. For instance, in one class, I might receive a nod of recognition from students of color when I stop a white student from trying to make an African American student into a "race expert"—that is, stop the white student from assuming that a black student can and should speak with authority about all African Americans. In another class, an African American student who welcomes the chance to tell the truth of her life might see my intervention as white maternalism. Such contradictions keep me from thinking in terms of a simple limits versus no limits opposition and assuming that one set of limitations will serve in every situation.

Feminist discourse also requires open and grounded teaching structures. The meaning of "openness" is far from self-evident. The lecture format may suppress student participation or encourage it, depending on how the lecturer handles her subject and relates to students. Discussion in a circle may invite student participation or create an atmosphere of surveillance, so that students feel that their every word or gesture is being judged. Feminist teachers concerned with safety need to ask themselves and their students not whether a particular teaching structure is inherently safe but how open it has become or can remain—open to both teacher and students making additional choices about what promotes the best kinds of participation in the class process.[14]

The structure of a given exercise can be modified by students themselves who refuse to participate. If no one volunteers, I immediately begin thinking about the structure I have proposed. Students can initiate change by raising certain objections ("We can't do that because") or by identifying certain features as problematic ("I could only do this part of it but not that"). Students also may spontaneously open a given structure as they use it, making it conform to their own choices about safety and self-disclosure. I encounter this pattern of spontaneously opening a teaching structure in a workshop I attend on multicultural issues. The small group of which I am a member grapples with the assignment to "tell the stories of our families" when one person in our group announces angrily that she did not have a "family." So our group begins by talking about what it means to feel that we have or lack a "family." We have transformed the workshop structure to keep talking.

Structures need to be grounded as well as open. In the classroom story in which neither the students nor I can find a way of dealing with anonymity, the structure is quite open to modification. I constantly ask for help to deal with the impasse and introduce my dramatic dialogue to try to deepen discussion. But in pursuing the problem, the discussion begins to resemble a kind of zero-sum conflict between positions.[15] The debate becomes increasingly abstracted from our actual lives, from the meaning of this choice for the students or me, from what we hoped or feared about this class and why. To ground our discussion, we need a structure that enables us to go back to these lives and the concrete meanings of our classroom discourse for them.

Keeping structures open and grounded supports the potential for making feminist classrooms safe for each individual to participate. Ideally, the more fully that process of feminist discourse is pursued, the safer the classroom becomes for expressing ideas, experiences, feelings, and images of action in response to gender injustice. But no class is an island entire of itself. Even at its best, feminist discourse takes place in institutional contexts that may render self-disclosure dangerous. Classroom disclosures can have substantive impact on students' and teachers' lives outside the classroom. Looking at classrooms in isolation prevents us from understanding the many meanings of safety.

SAFETY IN SCHOOL AND WORLDS BEYOND

Near the end of the semester, two students suggest that we perform a ritual as part of the class closure. Since everyone seems amenable, these women take off with their project. They plan and finally guide us through a process of remembering and honoring our experiences in the class. On the floor of the classroom they put down a cloth on which many of us place objects symbolizing our time together: notebooks, photos of family members, a book that has been particularly meaningful. I am generally comfortable with feminist ritual, and I am moved by what we say as we gather around the cloth. When I reflect on the ritual later on, however, I get scared. I imagine a colleague bursting into the room with a look of horror on his face as he cries out, "Really, Professor Fisher!"

Amelia's jaw tightens when I come out as a lesbian teacher, and she spends the first weeks of class looking at me with an expression of raw disgust. By the end of the semester, she astonishes me. She describes to the class how she went home for the spring break and defended me to her parents, who thought I had no business bringing my (immoral) sexuality into the classroom. She told them it was good for her education, and she was learning a lot!

My fantasy and fear of getting caught in the act of a spiritual, intensely emotional, and distinctly "unscholarly" feminist ritual taps into a reality that strongly shapes considerations of safety and self-disclosure.[16] No matter how committed to feminist discourse class participants may be, our institutional and social locations, as well as the world in which we live, preclude absolute safety.

Several factors seem especially key to me. Prospects for safety in self-disclosure are affected by *asymmetries of privilege* and the *differential vulnerabilities* that flow from them. Because of my position of relative power in the institution, which, in turn, is related to class and race advantages, I can risk "getting caught" in somewhat suspect classroom activities. An untenured faculty member who is a person of color and/or from a working-class background might choose to take the same risk. But her vulnerability would be greater. Yet, as a woman, a feminist, and a lesbian teacher, I also lack the privileges and relative security that go with masculinity, mainstream politics, and heterosexuality. Talking about my beliefs or life becomes an act of disclosure, as opposed to a taken-for-granted fact, and such disclosure can, in turn, be used to undermine my power and authority in the institution. Thus, safety operates on several levels simultaneously. My safe job might support me in disclosing more of myself, but it does not protect me from the threat of isolation or ridicule and the career costs that might accompany them.

Students' privilege and vulnerability also affect their willingness to disclose. Some students have the relative luxury of knowing they have a second chance. If they "mess up" in this school or this class, they can always shift schools or make up the course by taking another one. Other students have few if any second chances. If they do not make a certain grade or complete their program in a certain period, the enormous time and effort and resources they or their families are investing in their schooling go for naught.

What happens to a student in one course often affects what happens to her elsewhere in school, work, or life. A student taking a women's studies course or a feminist course that uses "touchy-feely" methods may be stigmatized by her adviser, other faculty, students, or even staff. In one undergraduate course, a white student talks about her white coworkers' hostile responses to a black feminist book she has brought to her part-time job. In another class, a heterosexual graduate student describes how difficult it is for her to carry the book we are reading currently, which has the word *lesbian* in the title, into a class whose other students, who are all women in her profession, look at the book cover with great discomfort.

The institutional climate also determines how comfortable students and teachers feel disclosing ideas or feelings. Some schools, departments, or programs encourage self-expression of many kinds. Others make disclosing anything personal difficult if not impossible. Students or faculty in a racial/ethnic or religious minority may be physically threatened or ostracized. Women of all backgrounds may be ridiculed or harassed. Students or teachers who disclose a queer sexual orientation may be sent to student counseling or fired.[17]

In my story about the class in which a feminist ritual is performed, the fears I experience afterward are vague and relatively shapeless. While I know that some colleagues might raise an eyebrow, others would smile and compliment me for encouraging student initiative and putting educational theory into practice. My fears, I sense, have much more to do with underlying questions about whether I, as a woman and a lesbian, truly can be a "professor." These fears, in turn, are generated and reinforced every time I enter a professional context in which women or lesbians are not visible or are not treated with respect. When I go to an academic conference, I consciously or unconsciously check to see who is there and in what position, just as I know many colleagues of color do as they enter an academic arena. Similarly, when I pick up a journal or anthology, I automatically scan the names to get a sense (to the extent that I can from names alone) of who is seen as worthy of inclusion. The degree of safety we feel in our professional contexts is bound to affect how teachers view safety in the classroom.

Similar concerns apply to an institutional context. If there are few women in authority, if there are few people of color, if there are virtually no out lesbians or gay men, self-disclosure for teachers who belong to such groups becomes highly problematic. Of course, the level of institutional safety can be raised through the efforts of students, teachers, and administrators. They can promote schoolwide campaigns to reduce bigotry. They can attempt to create "safe spaces" within an institution such as a women's studies program; a lesbian, gay, and bisexual student association; or a multicultural faculty seminar.[18] Increased safety may help some students or teachers talk about a wider range of ideas, experiences, or feelings in class. Or safety zones may serve as merely temporary refuges that make self-disclosure safe in very limited ways.

Regardless of the degree of safety that feminist discourse itself seems to support, the various worlds to which students and teachers belong outside school still greatly influence their sense of what they can and should disclose in class. For some, a feminist classroom provides a far safer space to talk about certain topics than do other parts of their lives. For others, such a classroom may seem a very dangerous place to talk about these same topics compared to family, community, friendship, or workplace settings. In effect, feminist classrooms become sites in which students and teachers can *form* connections or sites that threaten to *disrupt* connections in the outside world.[19] Forming connections through joining in discussions, sharing desires, taking responsibility, and/or paying attention to needs can create a relatively safe space for talking about feminist issues. But a yearning for stable relationships (unlike the mostly transient ones of the classroom), fear about economic well-being (which may be heightened by a feminist analysis of women's economic vulnerabilities), and the need for social approval (which association with feminism can call into question) all may threaten to disrupt connections outside class. "I can't keep reading these articles or participating in discussion," Flora says to me, "or my whole life will fall apart."

Conflicting assumptions about classroom safety in relation to the worlds outside have a strong impact on classroom interaction. In a graduate course in which we are discussing gender and economic exploitation, one group of students, who work as teaching assistants at the school, are eager to talk about their experience of exploitation. Another group, who work as administrative assistants, shy away from disclosing their experiences, feelings, and ideas. The teaching assistants welcome this discussion because they have been talking outside the classroom about the possibility of organizing. The administrative assistants avoid disclosure because their positions preclude them from organizing, and they do not even have the security of a semester-long contract. Moreover, these varying institutional locations may intersect differently with social worlds beyond the classroom. One administrative assistant from a working-class background may be frightened to even engage in such a discussion because of her family's anxiety about whether she will lose her job and thus her sole opportunity to complete her education. Another student whose working-class parents are staunch unionists may insist that the assistants speak out or even organize themselves.

Tensions over self-disclosure may signal to a teacher that it is time to back off, but they often suggest the need for more discussion about classroom process. I might ask the class, "What is the problem here?" or "Why do you find it so difficult to talk about this?" or "Why might some people find it difficult to talk about this?" Talk about "process" irritates some students, but I think that often this irritation flows from the difficulties students are having in addressing the underlying questions. In this discussion about gender and exploitation at work, loyalties outside the room threaten the bonds forming within the room. But there is no way these latter bonds can be sustained without addressing the fundamental issue of whether women can cooperate across occupational and class lines. This problem persists both outside and inside our classroom.

Willingness to take risks concerning safety in self-disclosure grows in part from whether teachers or students interpret vulnerability as a danger or an opportunity. Although vulnerability is commonly viewed as dangerous, Carter Heyward and Beverly Wildung Harrison argue that vulnerability enables people to form relationships based on "solidarity and compassion."[20] Such vulnerability, they point out, is not inconsistent with power. Revealing certain things about oneself may increase one's power, including one's power to make connections with others. This is, in fact, what happens with Amelia, who ends up defending me as a lesbian teacher. Because I disclose something about myself in class and she discloses something about her classroom experience to her family, our shared vulnerabilities enable us to connect to each other. Her willingness to be vulnerable to their criticism also enables Amelia to connect to her parents in a new way.

As many feminists have noted, however, the wisdom of making oneself vulnerable depends a great deal on context. Attitudes to risk taking may be shaped by not only our childhood experiences but how our overlapping social worlds reinforce or conflict with each other. Amelia's life is not confined to our classroom and her home. In conversations with her both inside and outside class, I learn that her life includes a church group (where the issue of sexual orientation has come up at a singles retreat), a group of friends (one of whom now seems to be moving toward same-sex relationships), and attendance at other university classes in which sexual orientation is occasionally mentioned. Given these overlapping affiliations, the line between what is inside and outside the classroom dissolves into a far more complex interplay of forces among which Amelia can test out what she thinks and who she wants to be.

Nevertheless, many students fear that self-disclosure means betraying connections to their worlds outside the classroom. Such betrayals were normative for early consciousness-raising, in which women sought to question as deeply as possible traditional connections that both women and men took for granted. In this spirit, Adrienne Rich could argue that women should be "disloyal to civilization" by joining together across race, class, and other lines to fight patriarchal domination.[21] A feminist pedagogy that takes consciousness-raising as its inspiration carries with it the impulse to "betray" ordinary relationships between women and men and among women themselves by subjecting these relationships to serious scrutiny rather than taking them for granted. Feminist discourse by definition disrupts the connections that perpetuate gender injustice. That is why taking a feminist course still remains a courageous or at least somewhat risky act for many students and why teaching such a course remains a risky act for many teachers.

As Rich acknowledges in her later writing, however, and as many white, middle-class, and/or heterosexual feminists have discovered in their efforts to build connections with women different from themselves, the threat of betraying inherited ties involves complex issues. The colleague I imagine storming into my seemingly safe classroom during a feminist ritual represents not only the disapproving gaze of administrators ("This is *not* what professors are supposed to do!") and colleagues ("This is *not* what scholars are supposed to do!") but the disapproving gaze of my Jewish parents, catching me in an act of "gentile" worship in which I am betraying two thousand years of Jewish survival under persecution, succumbing to the temptations of conversion, worshipping multiple gods ("No, Mom, I'm not praying to anyone!") and graven images ("No, Dad, those are just photos of people we love!").

Underestimating the force and meaning of family and community ties and their implications for safety and self-disclosure has led a lot of feminists into trouble. Students who sympathize with many feminist aims often come to view feminists as contemptuous of relationships that lie at the core of many people's lives. This kind of trouble may be necessary and good in the sense that it requires deeper inquiry into the meaning of women's oppression, but it leaves many problems in its wake. When young, heterosexual women from many backgrounds draw back from talking too much about their relations with young men, they indicate not only a fear that such discussions will undermine their chance of finding a husband but even deeper fears that failure to make an appropriate marriage will rob them of a place in their respective worlds. When Asian American, African American, or Hispanic students draw back from talking about family relationships, they may not only be protecting their kin from potential criticism but responding to fears that the cultural fabric that sustains these relations will be rent by such disclosures. Fear of disloyalty to one's family and community or ethnic group provides a powerful incentive for nondisclosure.

Yet, as Gloria Anzaldúa remarks, the impetus for betrayal may itself be built into the whole project of higher education. For many women of color from working-class backgrounds, she argues, becoming a "thinking subject" often means going against parental expectations "by exceeding them."[22] The desire to become a thinking subject requires such women to challenge both family expectations and dominant institutional and social values. Thus, in trying to carve out a transformative path between these different worlds, Anzaldúa's analysis implies, there can be no truly "safe" resting place.

When early proponents of consciousness-raising talked about safe or free space, they imagined a world in which the need for such space was a step on the way to creating a new political reality. In less revolutionary times, the prospect of such a transformation may seem utopian. Speaking too freely might well result in cutting oneself off from ongoing connections and ending up without any safe space at all. Yet viewing the future in terms of either total transformation or the necessity of hanging onto established connections underestimates the complexity of social change. Most social worlds are not homogeneous or perfectly coherent. They contain potential or actual fissures that can become the focus for collective efforts to promote social justice. Rather than simply exacerbating tension between social change movements and the home communities from which students or their teachers come, feminist discourse can help class participants explore the complexities and intersections of these worlds. For instance, a student raised in a Catholic community may feel it is unsafe to discuss reproductive rights in class. But the discussion might also lead to her discovering Catholic feminists who question church policies on gender. She might end up exploring formal and informal groups in which people like her are both rejecting certain religious tenets and struggling to affirm their connections to their tradition.

In my life as a feminist and a feminist teacher, self-disclosure has played a vital role in connecting to other people. This does not mean that I "tell all" in my classes. I choose not to disclose many things because I think they will hurt me, students, colleagues, or people in my worlds outside school. However, I have noticed over the years that I am less reluctant to disclose an experience, feeling, thought, or desire to act because I fear it will rupture ties. I have learned that the social worlds to which I belong are less fragile than I feared and my relation to them less tenuous. My feeling that I am betraying valued connections is more likely to occur when I cannot imagine how to change relationships or when I think I have to change them alone. I am willing to risk disclosing my feelings and experiences in the story I tell about the feminist classroom ritual in part because I have discovered that feminism and Judaism need not be incompatible, that there is a movement of Jewish feminists trying to bridge this gap. The contradictions of safety for my self-disclosure, I realize, are always changing.

SAFETY IN SOCIETY

Until our women's studies faculty group organizes the event on sexual harassment in the wake of the Clarence Thomas confirmation hearings, I find it difficult to get students to talk about the subject. After days of workshops, speeches, and discussions, the secrets start to surface. With everything I know, I am still shocked. Students beckon me into corners to tell ugly stories. More emerge daily.

My head is filled with the grotesque imagery of war as I carry my poster down the elevator: "At this very minute," it says, "U.S. troops are killing children, women, men, old people." A teacher I know winces as she reads

*the sign and avoids my eyes. After I stand for an hour with a small group
of colleagues protesting the Gulf War, I go to class. I do not know whose
lover or sister or husband has been called up. In an atmosphere of tremendous tension, I introduce the subject of women in the military.*

Just as the institutional climate and the worlds to which students and teachers belong affect classroom interactions around self-disclosure, so does society at large. The Clarence Thomas confirmation hearings bring out stories of sexual harassment in which race is also a key element. An Asian
American student talks about being harassed by her white professor. A
white student wonders about how her race both targets her for such harassment and protects her from it. The hearings have ambiguous consequences
for African Americans. Does this highly publicized event reinforce stereotypes of black male sexuality? Does it increase tensions between black
women and men?[23] Clearly it fosters awareness and debate about sexual
harassment in offices, in homes, and on street corners. Suddenly, feminist
classrooms do not seem special, presumably safe spaces in which to discuss this difficult subject but just another arena in which to work out its
political meaning.

When the United States goes to war in the Persian Gulf in 1991, the
groundswell of nationalism and militarism has a nearly opposite effect on
public discussion. In many places, to question the war means to take your
life in your hands. Even in sites noted for their tolerance, public discourse
shrinks dramatically. When I gather together with a group of like-minded
teachers to talk about the political, personal, and pedagogical meaning of
this military action, I find myself wondering whether we will end up in
jail. I wonder whether the space we have created will soon be invaded by
government agents charging us with treason in the manner of the political
witch-hunts of the post–World War II era.

When I raise the topic of the war in my women's studies classes, I do
so with great care, from concern for both my own safety and that of the
students. I want them to know that my speaking out against the war will
not lead to my punishing students who do not agree with me. I want to
defend the connections that have developed in the class and the possibility
of our continuing to talk with each other in a serious and full manner. To
protect these bonds and to initiate discussion in a way that does not reproduce the dominant rhetoric of patriots versus traitors that surround us, I try
to approach the war through the topic of gender discrimination. We discuss
and argue over when military service benefits women and how it hurts or
helps their families. We talk about how the war might affect women and
their families who live in the Persian Gulf area. We consider what is involved for women to take orders, to feel committed to a cause. I describe
what it means for me as a woman to dissent from public opinion. We bring

our own lives into the discussion with care. Tensions arise, but we keep the discussion going. I realize we know how close we have come to not being able to talk at all.

Many political, economic, social, and cultural conditions influence safety and self-disclosure in the classroom. *Competition* for economic rewards and status increases the risks associated with self-disclosure.[24] The person who discloses "too much" or "the wrong thing" decreases her likelihood of winning whatever scarce resources are at stake. This is as true for feminist teachers competing for a limited number of jobs and promotions as it is for students competing for financial aid or admission to programs or for rewards and honors. The more such competition remains underground, the more damage it is likely to do to feminist classroom discourse. In one class, I am unaware that the students from a certain program are competing for limited fellowships and sponsorship. As a result, I cannot understand why they are being so cautious about the way they frame some of the main issues in their field. In another class, I rather sharply attack a feminist project that some of the students find appealing before I realize how envious I am: this project has obtained the funding that I hoped to win for a project of my own. If as both students and teachers we could direct some of our feminist discourse to this underlying competition, we might at least be able to take its effects into account. At the most, we might propose alternative academic structures that would reduce the destructive effects of competition.

The tension between self-disclosure and competition is magnified by internal movement competition. This kind of competition emerges not only over access to positions (Who will lead a feminist organization? Who will get the women's studies job?) but over whose contributions are of greatest value to the movement: whose actions most radical, whose theories most sophisticated, whose resources most useful. This sort of competition makes it especially difficult to create what Alison Jaggar describes as "a safe space for in-house discussions among feminists."[25] Along the same lines, internal movement competition can affect feminist classroom discourse by making both students and teachers fearful that if they do not line up with the winning strategy, theory, or faction, they will be left out of the movement altogether. These concerns not only undermine the possibility of feminist discourse (if we already knew the "winning" strategy, theory, or faction, we would have no need for feminist political talk) but testify to the importance of continuing such talk. What issues, I ask the class, are being ignored by the "winning" viewpoint? What important points might be lost by dismissing the "losing" one?

Social and cultural *co-optation* also make classrooms seem dangerous for self-disclosure. The media, in particular, have played a powerful role by sensationalizing and trivializing personal experience and a feminist movement that values it. The remarks of a group of women talking on television about their experiences, feelings, ideas, or political actions are often reframed by the program "host" as confessions or foolishness. Soap operas, talk shows, and even "serious" news programs can be used by directors and producers, if not also boards of directors and owners, to make points with which those in power agree or at least that they believe will lead to high ratings and sales. Numerous feminist academics have gone on television only to find their words twisted, their statements cut off, or their concerns about social justice ridiculed. Whether they have participated in or merely watched such programs, feminist teachers increasingly see how private experience is manipulated in public arenas.[26]

Yet, by becoming aware of these patterns, feminist teachers also have the opportunity to confront them as they are reflected in feminist discourse. A group of students express their reluctance to speak out about their concerns on a student-run radio station, and I am able to share with them the advice of a political comrade who taught me how to prepare an effective statement in case I were interviewed during a demonstration. A student expresses her disdain for a popular talk show's presentation of sexuality issues, and I can raise the question of whether and where it is important to talk frankly about sexuality.

Wariness about self-disclosure also stems from the ways it has been used to motivate or justify state, corporate, or professional *intervention and control*. When poor women tell social workers about the real conditions of their lives, they may be cut off from needed welfare assistance. When women of color who have been assaulted reveal to the police what has happened to them, such incidents may be used to justify more white police violence in communities of color. When women workers complain to their bosses that they are being sexually harassed, they may find themselves without a job. When students or teachers disclose things about themselves in class, such information may be used against them in bureaucratic decisions about their competence.

As someone who teaches through feminist discourse, I cannot guarantee to students that what is said in class will not be picked up by someone inside or outside the class and used to harm either them or me. But, if I encourage grounded self-disclosure that acknowledges both the limits and value of risk taking, the potential for harm may be reduced. If anything, the students and I are often prone to overestimate the harm that will result from self-disclosures and to underestimate the contributions they can make to building resistance to injustice.

Another feature of feminist activism that impacts on patterns of safety and self-disclosure in feminist classrooms is *movement visibility*. When U.S. television news of the 1970s was filled with marching women demanding reproductive rights and salary equity, neither students nor teachers had to look far for support. Something that might have remained a private matter suddenly became a part of public discussion. Feminist classrooms often overflowed with stories of exploitation, domination, and violence against women. Without dramatic visibility, feminist teachers and students in their classes may believe that the movement is over and that in taking the risk of self-disclosure they are on their own.

The question of how to define the parameters of a social movement is complex and open to much debate, but feminist sociologists Myra Marx Ferree and Patricia Yancey Martin make a persuasive case for seeing second-wave U.S. feminism as a movement that has in large part transformed itself into a series of organizations that are "doing the work of the movement."[27] Feminist teachers need to take this pattern into account in our thinking about safety and self-disclosure. If a broad, visible movement does not provide a certain measure of safety for self-disclosure in the process of feminist discourse, we and our students may still be able to rely on feminist organizational resources. A women's studies program can validate the importance of making experiences and feelings a part of political discussion. A women's center or feminist counseling service can encourage students to speak up on gender and other forms of injustice. Feminist community organizers can help sustain critical attention to women's poverty. Women's caucuses and sections of academic associations can promote feminist critiques of academic disciplines and institutions. As students become aware of institutional supports for feminist discourse, through readings, lectures, projects, and so forth, classrooms become safer for discussing women's oppression.

Finally, one more important aspect of feminist activism affects the dynamics of safety and self-disclosure: *relations among social movements.* As I have noted repeatedly, feminist movements interact with other social movements in various ways. These patterns have direct effects on safety and self-disclosure in feminist classrooms. In the context of a developing movement of Asian Americans, a student of Chinese American heritage may speak up in class about the absence of attention to women like herself. She may discover bonds as well as tensions with Japanese American students or with students from Southeast Asian countries. In the context of a disability rights movement, a student with a disability may question her access not only to the classroom but to the discussion itself, whether its assumptions prevent or facilitate her sharing her experiences.

Forms of expression fostered by various social movements may support different facets of feminist discourse. A movement against child abuse may validate talking about certain kinds of pain in feminist classrooms. A movement for Native American rights that emphasizes storytelling as an aspect of political empowerment may support the sharing of experiences. A movement for black liberation that includes righteous anger at centuries of domination may motivate many African Americans to bring that passion to class. A movement to defend white male privilege may validate white men's rage at losing it, so that students who believe that white men have been unjustly treated feel safer to express their rage at feminists.

These encounters between social movements and feminist classrooms do not (as my example of white male rage especially suggests) always generate smooth interactions. A student involved in a strongly nationalist movement may see feminist internationalism as a threat. A student who has been committed to a labor movement that has paid little attention to gender issues might hesitate to join in a feminist discussion. A movement that makes it safer for some students to speak up may make it feel unsafe for others. The confluence of movements may lead to considerable conflict about what to disclose.

I have experienced such conflict myself as I have tried to put together my involvement with feminism, on the one hand, with my identification with the lesbian/gay/bisexual/transgender movement, on the other. These movements both reinforce and conflict with each other. They both speak to gender rights, but they often frame issues of gender justice differently. They argue for sexual freedom but interpret it in dissimilar ways.[28] Each movement may inspire me to disclose certain thoughts, feelings, and experiences, but the tensions between these movements also set up an internal struggle about disclosing my longings for both gender justice and freedom of sexual expression. I am willing to disclose, but I cannot figure out what to say that makes honest sense of my life. Only as I keep seeking points of contact between the movements do I discover what stories I want to tell and feel safe enough to tell them.

I will end this chapter with one such story. In the late 1990s, I am going to speak at a conference on queer pedagogy that will look at how academics teach lesbian and gay studies. I want to participate because I believe that feminist thinking about education should be represented in this discussion. I also want to try to find a place where these movements come together in me as a lesbian teacher of women's studies. In preparing for the event, however, I begin to think less about how feminist pedagogy applies to queer educational contexts and more about how these parallel movements have affected my sense of myself as a teacher.

In my early teaching years as a heterosexual woman fleeing from the domestic fate of the white middle-class women of my generation, I was drawn to an image of Socratic discussion. I encountered only a few women academics and none with the kind of self-confidence my male teachers projected. Many of my college teachers were excellent discussion leaders. I wanted to follow their path. Like the gay male intellectuals of Athens, I wanted to engage in passionate talk about serious matters. I did not want to be mistaken for a harried housewife. For years, I taught my own classes in this Socratic spirit, reveling in dialogue with my students.

The reemergence of the U.S. women's movement forced me to rethink some of my barely conscious assumptions. I was no longer comfortable distancing myself from other women and perpetuating the misogyny with which I was raised. I began to question the idealization of Socrates, who in my new, feminist eyes had begun to seem less of a culture hero and more of an intellectual batterer. Feminism led me to broaden my notion of inquiry to include the value of caring as well as the insistence that women were thinkers. Yet, when I came out as a lesbian, the lesbian and gay movement also helped me to revalue the same-sex love that informed Socratic teaching. This love, I finally realized, could be directed by women toward women. The gay male teacher in me gradually became a gay woman teacher who tried to incorporate caring into her educational work and who well might be called a "maternal butch." As I prepare to speak at the conference, I have come to a safe harbor in the arms of these two not always loving movements.

In the face of the socially structured dangers associated with self-disclosure, it is not surprising that many students as well as teachers fear that revealing too much about ourselves may be harmful. Yet, despite the potential costs, many feminist teachers and students continue sharing personal experiences and feelings, incorporating them in their attempts to think about and respond to gender injustice. This process continues both because its value is constantly rediscovered and because it can still receive support from a social movement dedicated to women's liberation. Although competition, co-optation, and controlling intervention narrow the range in which many teachers and students feel comfortable disclosing things about themselves, feminist activity and women's movements in general keep alive the value of self-disclosure to women's political engagement. As Aída Hurtado writes, "women have acquired strength through collective nakedness."[29]

Her language reminds me that many years ago, I spent a number of days with a friend in a resort area for nudists. I never will forget how this experience transformed the relationship between my body and the environment, what it felt like for every part of my body's surface to be in contact with the world. I marveled at how within a short period of time I became accustomed to the great diversity of human bodies and to accept that my own body represented only one of an almost infinite number of such variations. I was well aware of the limits to our safety. We had to avoid particular locations and remain a bit vigilant. But I was also reassured by the fact that the others who had come to this area shared our desire for such physical and social freedom and would defend it. We were surrounded, in effect, by a kind of community.

Community building not only supports safety but the likelihood that participants in feminist discourse will be able to disclose, think through, and act on their desires for gender justice. There is nothing simple about creating or sustaining community, however. If community is to play a role in feminist teaching, its ambiguities must be explored. That task I undertake in the next chapter.

— 6 —

"WOMEN DO NOT SAY 'WE'"

Difference and the Ideal of Community

Most of the white women in this class are health care professionals who express a lot of anger about male doctors ordering them around. When I bring up the topic of racial difference, these women turn their ire against the black women who work as hospital aides. Adele, the most outspoken student, says with venom that the aides are "stupid and lazy." No African American students are in this class. The two Asian American health professionals look away. An icy silence creeps over the room.

During our discussion of an African American feminist text, several white women keep suggesting that race is no longer a serious issue. Others try to focus talk on their own oppression as Jews or Italian Americans or white lesbians. Flo, who is white, becomes upset because she does not know "what I can do about all this." Charlene, a somewhat older black woman, voices irritation. She is tired, she says, of white classmates not "getting it." She thought the course was about women's issues, but she can see that this does not include women like her.

Why should feminist pedagogy direct attention to differences among women? How can feminist teachers help students "get" these differences? The answer to the first question lies in the history of feminism. For more than a century and a half, U.S. feminism has been shaped through its interaction with other movements for social justice. The nineteenth-century movement for the abolition of slavery gave birth to the women's rights struggle, and at times black and white women became political allies in these causes. Near the end of that century, middle-class women reformers and women labor activists formed cross-class coalitions to gain justice for women workers. Such encounters revealed substantial areas of shared commitment to social change. Yet, too frequently, as Paula Giddings points out in her history of black women in the United States, women with greater class and race privileges ended up putting their own interests ahead of the women they claimed as sisters. By the time Simone de Beauvoir wrote *The Second Sex* at the end of World War II, it was difficult to envision a feminist movement to which women could bring both their commonalities and differences.[1]

Although she later energetically joined in support of second-wave feminism, Beauvoir's postwar classic implied that collective action was likely to be futile. Women, she wrote, never developed the kind of "we" characteristic of class, racial, or ethnic groups. Women did not perceive themselves as having problems in common. They only said "we" at feminist congresses. In everyday life, women were "dispersed among the males" of their cultures and classes and felt a greater bond with the men of their group than with women outside it. Moreover, Beauvoir's analysis held out little hope for the "we" that women who belonged to the same groups might develop. After all, mothers perpetuated oppression by training their daughters to be members of "the second sex." For the postwar Beauvoir, the lesson was clear: each woman had to struggle individually to transcend her subjugated situation.

Two decades after the publication of her feminist treatise, many proponents of consciousness-raising both claimed Beauvoir's pioneering analysis and rejected her solution.[2] Through comparing their experiences of oppression, feminist activists sought to generate a new "we": a "we" that would attract increasing numbers of women; a "we" committed to collective as well as individual resistance; a "we" that could discuss the character of gender injustice and how to remedy it. This we-in-the-making created numerous tensions among women and men of the groups in which women were "dispersed." The mere act of women "taking time away from" their established relationships to talk about gender often created new conflicts with families and friends. This tension increased as women voiced the pain and anger they experienced in their gendered lives.

These experiences and feelings did not always take the same form, however. Women whose lives closely resembled each other in important respects might quickly encounter the differences that divided them. For instance, Norah, a middle-class white woman, joins a consciousness-raising group with women from similar backgrounds. For many weeks they share stories about their difficult relationships with men. Eventually, the women start to share their feelings of shame about their bodies. The discussion focuses on their legs—how the dominant ideals of beauty make them feel that their legs are "too fat" or "too hairy." Norah says she has some of these feelings too, but they do not play a very large role in her life. After all, as the group members are well aware, her legs have been affected by polio. Because of this, she walks with crutches. She is treated differently and excluded from many places. The other women pause awkwardly and then go back to talking about the politics of shaving their legs. They do not want to talk about pain they do not share or anger that might be directed toward them. They do not want to acknowledge that Norah is "different" or that their physical abilities give them privileges in a society organized around certain abilities. Norah has created a *discourse crisis* that calls into question the direction of the discussion, and the members of the group try to ignore it.[3]

The two classroom stories I tell at the beginning of the chapter involve similar discourse crises. In Adele's class, the white women health care workers eagerly criticize the male doctors' power and authority to tell them, as female subordinates, what to do. In Charlene and Flo's class, students begin their discussion with the sense that women have some common interests in changing patriarchal structures. Yet, when racial differentiation is introduced, most students in both classes refuse in one way or another to look at what difference this socially constructed difference makes.[4]

Ruth Frankenberg's analysis of how white women manifest racism is helpful in thinking about how members of privileged groups often balk at discussing the meaning of difference.[5] Adele, who characterizes black hospital aides as "stupid and lazy," manifests what Frankenberg describes as *"essentialist racism."* That is, Adele simply asserts the basic inferiority of these other women and insists that we as the audience for her remarks recognize this inferiority. She is not interested in discussing the matter further. She shows no awareness of racism as a social and historical phenomenon or how her own implied claim to superiority perpetuates racism. In contrast, the story about Charlene and her classmates illustrates what Frankenberg calls *"power evasive racism."* In this class, the white students generally affirm the importance of racial justice, but they obscure their own relationship to injustice by a series of evasions. They declare that social progress has rendered racism obsolete. They try to divert attention to their own experiences with social injustice. They voice despair. In general, power evasive responses deny that the person speaking in any way profits from racism or has the power to affect it. In Charlene's class, Flo, who says she does not know what to do, comes closest to acknowledging that she bears some responsibility for racism, but her lack of a sense of agency keeps her from pursuing the issue.

These stories bring out different aspects of the struggle to engage students in feminist discourse on difference. As Adele's teacher, I recognize that at this moment she cannot possibly consider the question Flo has raised in the other class about what she can do to remedy racism. Adele and a good number of her white classmates do not care about racism in the sense that they are not willing to pay serious attention to this social phenomenon. My attempts to lecture them, to make them look more closely at the readings, to engage them in exercises that will break through their bubble of white privilege only strengthen their resistance to my efforts. Meeting after meeting, Adele is so hostile and the classroom air is so thick with resentment that I could cut it with the proverbial knife. I can barely restrain myself from using my pedagogical power to stick a verbal knife into her. I sense that in attacking Adele individually, however, I would not only give up being her teacher but lose most of the other white students as well. I worry, too, about the meaning of this discussion for the two Asian American students, who have remained silent throughout this period.

Finally, by listening more closely to what Adele and her colleagues are saying, I find a way to approach this class. Whatever bastion of privilege they have constructed for themselves, they indicate that it does not fully protect them. The predominantly male medical staff treats them as incompetent to make many decisions and therefore keeps them from doing what they consider their professional work. Although they may subvert the doctors' orders, their position does not permit them to attack the doctors themselves. The white health care workers can more easily direct their anger toward the aides, blaming them for the difficulties encountered at work.

Thinking through the situation these students describe, I realize that in my zeal to address racial prejudices I have neglected the importance of gender, class, and ethnic diversity in their workplaces. I have failed to pay attention to their caring ideals. I need to take another tack. Most of the women in this class have a strong desire to act and be recognized as human service professionals. So I encourage them to talk about caring and what they are trying to accomplish in their work. I find an extra reading on the division of caring labor in health care institutions and how it is often stratified along gender, race, and class lines. I talk about the development of the women-predominant professions and about how the civil rights movement spurred the unionization of hospital workers. The students begin to look at their workplaces a little differently, noticing gender, race, and class segregation as well as patterns that cross-cut it. A Chinese American student speaks up, describing her problematic relationship with a Chinese American male doctor who is both an ally and a superior. One of the white women talks about her good working relationship with a black woman doctor who is especially interested in what the other health professionals as well as the patients have to say. Another mentions one African American aide who was helpful in a crisis.

As we begin discussing how institutional stratification inhibits or supports cooperation in caring, I finally can ask class members to think about the point of view of the aides, how they are treated and the kind of work they do. Two students begin to talk about how cleaning-up work is done in their hospital, who does what kind, and how they may feel about it. These students start to imagine a project in which they interview a number of people in their workplace, including several aides, about the problems involved in keeping the work setting clean and orderly. I do not know where Adele is in this conversation, because she has become unusually quiet. I hope that she is starting to think more dynamically about her workplace. It is almost the end of the semester, and things are finally moving.

The class with Charlene and Flo is far easier for me to teach because many students begin by acknowledging the value of racial justice. To those students who insist that injustice is no longer a problem, I can recommend readings and suggest projects that expose them directly to the fact that racial injustice persists. When white students try to redirect the discussion of gender and race by focusing on other experiences of injustice, I can ask them directly, "Why do you think we are having so much trouble sticking with the subject of race and gender?" To Flo, who feels overwhelmed by the enormity of racial injustice, I can list readings on the lives of white women who have been antiracist activists. All of us can discuss what can be done to combat racism and the role that women and men of different colors and backgrounds have taken in these efforts. This class is not a breeze to teach, but its problems are more familiar to me.

What I personally bring to each of these classes strongly shapes my responses to their respective discourse crises. At moments, I am barely able to teach Adele's class. When her racial rage first surfaces, I freeze. I see her racism as closely intertwined with the hatred that fuels anti-Semitism and homophobia. For a paranoid instant, I imagine Adele riding in with the Ku Klux Klan to kill me and the Asian American students along with the black hospital aides. To proceed in that class, I need to summon a kind of pedagogical courage that is composed of part power, part authority, and part hope. I do not want to abandon my belief that this group of students can engage in a feminist discourse on difference, but I recognize that I will have to deal with my own fears and judgments as well as theirs. If I want the students to consider the hospital aides as people who are also struggling with caring problems, I will have to approach the students as people, too.

I am more comfortable with the crisis that develops in Charlene and Flo's class not only because it is a common occurrence in my feminist courses but because it echoes my own upbringing. As with many children from white, middle-class homes, my education in social justice grew out of having to face the contradictions between my family's liberal values and our complicity in class oppression and institutionalized racism. From my own experience, I know that dealing with these contradictions can be painful, but I also believe it is possible. I share Charlene's frustration, but I trust that the white students can go through this process. I believe that Charlene will learn something valuable from it as well.

My basic approach as a teacher in these stories is to engage in a serious, complex and often very problematic search for common ground, one on which the desires and situations of discourse participants sufficiently connect with different others (whether or not they are present in the room) for discussion to continue. This pedagogical approach does not dissolve differences in power and privilege. It simply helps participants see a reason to keep on talking about injustice and what might be done to respond to it. The progress of such discourse, however, depends on the answer to a number of questions, three of which I will look at more closely in the remainder of this chapter. What is involved in knowing different others? What does difference mean in our relationships with others? Can differently situated people cooperate in talking and acting to bring about social justice? Although these are vast questions, it seems possible to get a small but firm hold on them by turning again to practice.

THE PROBLEM OF KNOWING OTHERS

I think I know a lot about Magda, who has taken several courses with me and talked with me about her research. During a meeting in my office, she tells me that for years she has had a chronic illness that impacts on her daily life. At last I realize that many of her decisions to take or postpone a course, ask for an incomplete grade, or work alone rather than with a group—decisions that I viewed as "merely academic"—have been shaped by her efforts as a woman with a physical disability to complete her doctorate. I suddenly see that neither I nor the students in the feminist class she is currently taking know Magda as well as we thought.

In the middle of a discussion of a lawsuit brought by an African American woman over the right to wear braids at her workplace, Soo, whose parents immigrated from Korea, raises an objection. She has serious reservations about bringing such suits. She herself would prefer to talk quietly with the employer until he understood her point of view. Ruby, who is African American, demurs. She believes that strong measures like legal actions are often needed to deal with prejudiced bosses. An Asian American woman who usually sits next to Soo in this undergraduate course comes to Soo's defense. One of Ruby's African American friends supports Ruby's position. I start to get anxious that yet another racial polarization is emerging.

As someone seeking to teach through feminist discourse, I assumed for many years that students would get to know each other and me through our sharing experiences, feelings, ideas, and notions of how we might act. The story about Magda, however, raises a number of questions about what it means to know others in such a classroom context. My analysis of safety in the previous chapter identifies many factors that discourage or prevent discourse participants from speaking openly. Magda's revelation about her disability introduces another problematic element—that is, *to reveal is not the same as being known.* Even though Magda shares certain facts about herself with me, I still may not know her very well. This point becomes evident to me when I come out as a lesbian in an undergraduate class where we are talking about the meaning of "family." I hope my description of how my lover and I comprise a family will not only enable students to know me better but to think more broadly and critically about this concept. For some students my revelation is pedagogically effective, but for others it simply feeds into their stereotype that lesbians do not want to relate in any way to men. The result of my coming out, at least for the moment, is that some of the students adopt a new set of misconceptions about me.

As Magda talks with me at various times during the semester, I learn that her disability has developed and changed over the years and actually varies on a daily basis. Her "disabled self" has a fluid and complex character depending on how she feels during a given week or day.[6] Yet, this fluidity of self is not infinite. When she gets up in the morning, Magda tells me, her eye falls on a cane in the corner of her bedroom, ready for use if her legs do not feel steady. When she makes financial plans, she must figure out how she will be able to afford an electric wheelchair should that become necessary. Both the instability and the stability of her identity as a person with a disability play into the academic decisions she makes, including her decision to tell me, as her teacher, about her condition.

Magda explains to me that her decision to talk about her disability was not an easy one. For a long time, she automatically censored any expression at school that would hint of her condition. But, on the day of the class meeting that preceded our discussion in my office, she had found it particularly difficult to get to class. She felt weaker than usual and had to struggle to get on the crowded elevator taking students to our classroom. As that day's discussion on reproductive rights turned to the question of abortion and one of the students began to argue for the importance of women being able to "eliminate abnormal children," Magda could hardly bear her own silence. Her desire to be known became overwhelming, and she wanted my support for coming out in class.

This desire, however, was not a simple one because of the ways in which power and privilege affect the possibility of knowing others. Magda tells me that she has kept her illness hidden from her department because she fears that it might adversely affect their view of her as a promising graduate student. Even at this point, she is not sure what and how much she wants them to know or how their knowledge could impact on her future. Moreover, what she might say to others about "who" she is remains ambiguous. She is, as she describes her disability, many things: some seem essential to her and her life; others are contingent, some simple, and others complex. Given the academic power differentials, her concern that she will be turned into a stereotypically "disabled woman," misunderstood and stigmatized in terms of both her disability and her gender, are quite reasonable.

As Magda describes the conflicting impulses that play into her wish to speak out in class, I am reminded of how similar *identity tensions* pervade my concept of who I am and how I want to express myself. I have a lesbian self that sometimes feels essential to my being (when I tap into the deepest roots of my sexual desire) and sometimes feels contingent (when I think back over my heterosexual years). In many ways, I feel essentially Jewish, deeply connected to both the people who died in the concentration camps and to a family that bound itself together through Jewish ritual. Yet I can choose to feature or downplay my Jewishness in a manner not available to more orthodox coreligionists. Moreover, my lesbian and Jewish selves are fragmented by cross-cutting identities that generate additional tensions. The socialist lesbian in me bristles when I take her to a high-priced lesbian benefit. The observant Jew in me balks when I make her attend a left-Jewish event at which religious ritual is treated with a certain disdain. Like Magda, I worry that non-lesbians and non-Jews will use a stereotyped interpretation of my identity to perpetuate social hierarchies. Like Judith Butler, I am concerned that the assumption of a stable, solid, and homogenous self may narrow the scope of my freedom and diminish my capacity for political resistance.[7]

Yet, as feminists of color and lesbians of all colors often have pointed out, such tensions signal points at which identity can become a political resource for feminist talk and action.[8] Gloria Anzaldúa traces in passionate and precise terms her internal struggle to find a way through the tensions among the Chicana, Anglo, and lesbian aspects of her identity to a more integrated and activist relation to the world.[9] bell hooks argues that claiming identity can lead to recovering "the legacy of defiance, of will, of courage," as well as of healing the splits caused by oppression. Minnie Bruce Pratt explores how her upbringing as a white, southern woman came into collision with her desire for love and friendship with women of other cultures. Anneliese Truame describes how her multiple identities as a "mixed-blood, disabled, lesbian student" become sites of struggle against multiple forms of injustice and points of connection to others who may join her in opposing those injustices. Identity in these instances is not a set of labels but a multifaceted subjectivity that can be actively shaped and utilized in confronting oppressive structures of power.

Such identity tensions are resolved in different ways at different times, in an individual's life story. Although each resolution may have an element of contingency, in the sense that this particular solution does not define us fully, our responses to identity tensions are not simply arbitrary. At best, they include self-conscious judgments. Magda's decision to reveal more of herself as part of making her political argument involves weighing her desire to be better known against the possible costs to her professional self. Her choice is not a matter of simple, abstract, and rational calculation. Her passions, her sense of her relation to her changing body and her varying social and physical environments all play a role in how that judgment is formed.

I, too, make identity judgments when I bring one aspect of myself to the fore rather than another. The same week in which I make a point of dancing with my lover at a family wedding because I adore dancing with her and want our family to embrace us as a Jewish lesbian couple, I downplay the lesbian part of me in a classroom discussion of Jewish identity. At this particular moment in the course, I want to focus on how anti-Semitism impacts on feminism. I sense that if we move too quickly to discussing differences among Jews, students will abandon the attempt to understand Jewish difference and find comfort in another old stereotype: that Jews never agree with each other.

Thus, as Magda is forming judgments about conflicts among different aspects of her self and their relation to our feminist classroom discourse, I am struggling with how I, as her teacher with my own identity tensions, can better understand her. One of the main cultural options available to me, in particular, as a woman raised to be caring, is that of empathy. However, empathy is a very tricky concept to employ in political contexts. What passes for empathy, as Sarah Hoagland points out, often masks attempts to control others, to get them to meet the needs of the empathizer. Dagmar Schultz and Gail Pheterson describe how in their feminist workshops, white, Christian, and heterosexual women often try to get their own capacity for empathy and understanding validated by women who lack these privileges.[10] In my classes, white women drawn to education and human service occupations through a deeply felt concern for others may be shocked to discover that students of color will not necessarily validate such empathy. For the feelings evoked in the more privileged students do not necessarily match the realities experienced by those with less privilege. Empathy can be not only manipulative but based on misconceptions.

Given these dangers, what, if anything, can a *politically oriented empathy* contribute to a feminist discourse on difference? Several feminist theorists provide concepts that help us answer this question. Diana Meyers points out that to empathize well, we may need to restrain our immediate emotional response to the other and mobilize our "powers of attentive receptivity and analytic discernment."[11] For example, when Magda first tells me about her disability, my heart goes out to her, and I begin to join her in what feels to me like shared pain about the difficulties she faces. But, as Meyers notes, this kind of response assumes knowledge that I do not have. Developing genuine empathy with Magda requires "protracted observations and painstaking imaginative reconstruction of the minutiae of the other's viewpoint." I have to be willing to go in this direction, of course, and my affection for Magda orients me toward learning more about her realities. But the initial feeling is not enough.

For this reason, imagination is both a powerful and limited faculty for promoting politically oriented empathy. Imagination can provide a potent force to break through the denial that the students and I often bring to our encounters with difference. Because Magda does not "look disabled," it is tempting to deny that she has any disability at all. In class, I sometimes use techniques like visualization to help students imagine what it might be like, for example, to live a life as someone who cannot be sure of whether her legs will sustain her on a given day. But I am cautious about how I use such teaching strategies. As Elizabeth Spelman and others warn, we are always in danger of imagining the others' realities in ways that suit our own needs. Overcoming the barriers of difference requires us to "apprentice" ourselves to the other.[12] In teaching students through their imaginations, I try to make sure that they test out any quick leaps of apparent understanding against careful listening, further reading, and broadened experience.

My own experiences and feelings can provide a certain impetus to understand Magda's situation. As she tells me her story, I immediately think back to the problems I had with mobility after I had a broken hip. Imagining another's situation with the help of analogies is useful though dangerous. I may get some insight into Magda's situation, but I am also tempted to remain focused on my own. When I turn my attention to my past or current difficulties, I do little for her. As Spelman argues, politically effective empathy supports the agency of others in their attempts to deal with their own oppression.[13] To support Magda, I need to engage in a detailed discussion about what she and I might say or do in class and why.

María Lugones enriches the notion of politically oriented empathy with her concept of " 'world'-travelling" (*sic*) as a way in which women can learn from and love each other across the barriers of race and culture.[14] World-traveling suggests that those with power and privilege must be willing to change their own position so that they can perceive things that they do not normally see. This traveling is an appealing idea, and it is warmly embraced by many students in my feminist classes. Yet, at first, they may not necessarily grasp that world-traveling involves hard work. Some of this work is emotional, such as dealing with fears of difference. Some is a matter of cultural knowledge about how to act in a situation in which you do not know the rules. Some of it involves learning what it is like to be viewed with admiration, envy, or hatred or how it feels to be totally ignored by people who see a given traveler as belonging to a more or less powerful or privileged world. Some traveling work involves dealing with the disruption of relationships that results from leaving one world to sojourn to another.

In one class, in which students greet Lugones's article with enthusiasm, I ask them to divide into small groups to discuss it. After enough time has elapsed for the groups to be deeply engaged in discussion, I spontaneously interrupt them and instruct at least one person from each group to "travel" to another group. Almost no one is willing to do this. It will disrupt their talk, they say. They do not know what is going on in the other groups. They have not been warned that they might be asked to change groups. In the discussion afterwards I ask them to reflect on their responses. What keeps people involved in certain ongoing social relations? Why might they not want to disrupt them? Why does it seem difficult to know what is going on in other groups? Which choices do people have about whether or not to "travel"? I suggest we consider different scenarios. What about the woman who has to leave her children in the Caribbean to come to the United States to earn enough money to support them? Or the girl child from a poor family in Southeast Asia who is forced into sexual slavery to meet the demands of the tourist market? Or the tourist whose race, class, or other privileges make it possible for her to visit the worlds of those with fewer material resources? I note that the desire to travel also can grow out of a political commitment and a longing for greater emotional closeness and connection. As a feminist, Lugones bids women to travel despite the difficulties and risks, to try to get to know others by joining them in their worlds.

The story I tell about Soo and Ruby at the beginning of this section involves two students who are struggling to enhance their agency in the context of different worlds. Both express a certain empathy with the protagonist of the article I had assigned about a woman who brought a lawsuit against her employer for the right to wear an African hairstyle to her job. Ruby tells the class she had a similar experience when she tried to wear an African-style dress to work. Soo says that she feels tremendous pressure at work to look as much as she can like the young, white women at her job.

Yet both accounts also suggest certain differences in how they are treated at their workplaces. Ruby is told that wearing a "costume" will distract her and others and undermine her efficiency. Soo is reminded that she is headed for great success in the company and should do everything she can to show that she is a "team player." Stereotypes of African Americans as inefficient workers and Asian Americans as the model minority resonate in these stories. The tensions between African American customers and Korean American shopkeepers in our city are mirrored in the growing tension in our classroom.

How can I as their teacher support Soo's and Ruby's agency and encourage other students to do so without exacerbating racial/ethnic hostility and stereotyping? How can each of these women and their classmates better understand Ruby's and Soo's situations and their responses to injustice? Since I sense that the members of this class are sufficiently comfortable with each other, I decide to try a role play. Some students indicate shyness, but both Ruby and Soo and a number of others are eager to participate.

I begin by asking the two women to each pick a student to represent her and to coach that person in the "Soo" or "Ruby" role. I also ask Ruby and Soo to coach volunteers who will play their bosses and parents. I stress the fact that players do not have to "be like" the person they are playing. Although Ruby and Soo each pick their supportive classmates to play themselves, there is a lively mix of people with roles, including a black male student playing Soo's mother and a white female student playing Ruby's white male boss. Soo and Ruby direct the role players in how to act as "Soo" and "Ruby" when they talk with their "bosses" and "parents."

While the role play unfolds with clumsy intensity, several points emerge. By directing the characters representing them, Soo and Ruby illuminate the quality of their own agency and the character of their situations. They have to clarify to those playing them what they say and do and why. They also spell out some of the contradictions of self that such agency may involve, say, between their work selves and their family selves. Although Ruby may consider Soo as far too accommodating in her response to her boss, Soo's mother may see her as far too aggressive, and Soo may be torn between several ways of feeling and acting. Although Soo may see Ruby as too aggressive, some of Ruby's family members may expect her to be more militant in dealing with the racism she so often encounters.

In the discussion following the role play, students express considerable understanding of the difference in Ruby's and Soo's situations and begin to think together about action strategies that will support agency for each of them. Soo's Korean American friend, Brenda, says that playing Soo's role helped her realize how her relationship with her own parents had improved by asking them to talk to her about their own histories. These conversations, she says, enabled her to speak out more strongly in work and school situations in which she was being seen as a stereotype rather than a person. She now can imagine joining a lawsuit against a discriminatory boss. Ruby's ally, Dinitra, describes her mixed feelings in playing Ruby's role because she often does not want to deal with prejudice against her as a black woman in a head-on manner and has been looking for other alternatives. Yet she wonders whether Soo's approach would be effective where a boss treats black workers with contempt. Walter, the black male student who played Soo's mother, talks about how drawn he was to the role and thinks it might reflect his own concern that in trying to "fit into" the larger society, he might give up too much of his cultural tradition. I invite Soo to comment on how her mother views her own history.

As the class proceeds, I congratulate them on how beautifully they have handled the role play. I am pleased because I know that role-playing strategies can backfire in many ways.[15] When I first started to experiment with dramaturgical techniques in my feminist teaching, I was distressed by how some students drew on racial or sexual stereotypes to play someone "different." I discovered that both I and the students needed to talk about how a role was played, how it felt to the player as well as to the other participants. In this class, Soo and Ruby help keep the role play on track by picking empathetic alters to play their roles and by carefully coaching each participant. Soo's and Ruby's agency is enhanced in this process, but not to the extent that they control all of its outcomes. Brenda, Dinitra, and Walter start thinking along lines that none of us might have predicted and that bring additional perspectives to bear on our political judgments.

In leading the discussion, I encourage students to identify and compare the features of Ruby's and Soo's situations. In what ways do patterns of denigrating African American workers and idealizing Asian American workers produce the same or different results? How do the employment options available to women of different racial/ethnic groups affect their willingness and capacity to engage in different forms of resistance to discrimination and exploitation? How might the family and political histories of these groups shape the potential for such resistance? How would all these factors encourage or discourage workers from different gender and racial/ethnic groups to collaborate in confronting injustice? I raise this question toward the end of class because I hope to orient the students to thinking about our next topic—unionization. I also want them to think further about how power affects our relationships and privileges.

DIFFERENCE AS RELATIONSHIP

Despite the fact that I have assigned several provocative readings by lesbian theorists, I cannot get this group to talk about lesbians. Some of the students point out the disadvantages of being heterosexual women. Others insist that the heterosexual/homosexual distinction is not useful. As far as I know, I am the only lesbian in the room, and I am beginning to feel increasingly invisible.

As the tension increases in our discussion of race and gender, Malka suddenly turns to me accusingly and wants to know why I have not included a reading on women in the Holocaust. Jewel, who wants to remain focused on our reading about African American women, breaks in with a challenge to Malka to come to visit the social agency at which she, Jewel, works, to see how poor women of color are "suffering right now." Hannah, an experienced activist, tries to calm the waters. "Let's not start an 'oppression derby' here. Nobody wins when you start a competition over who's the most oppressed."

As I struggle to lead the class discussion in which students studiously avoid talking about lesbians, I feel not only invisible but disconnected. I have assigned readings by different lesbian theorists because I hope that the class will come to grips with the issues of difference that the lesbian feminist and queer movements have raised for feminism. But, the students, none of whom have identified as lesbian, gay, bisexual, or transsexual, use the readings to focus discussion on heterosexuality. They cite Adrienne Rich's classic essay on "the lesbian continuum" to support their claim that there is little real difference between heterosexual and lesbian women.[16] They call on Judith Butler's critique of gender categories to insist that terms like *lesbian* and *straight* be discarded. I am familiar with this move: heterosexuals often want to deny that there is a difference in our situations. But, in doing so, they also deny relationship—the relationship of heterosexual privilege in relation to homosexuals and the relationships of equality and cooperation that might develop between us when our different situations are acknowledged.

In frustration, I start talking about my experiences. I tell them about a recent assault on a lesbian couple in a nearby neighborhood. I describe my hesitation in reaching for my lover's hand in public places, how my fear of homophobic violence and denigration informs many of my choices. I say how angry I have been with the backlash against gay civil rights legislation and ask the students to think about the reasons for this opposition. The class is quiet, and then one woman says, "It upsets me that you have to be afraid that way." My speech has opened up a space for thinking about the relationships that difference entails.

My move to assert my identity as a lesbian has a lot in common with Magda's coming out as a woman with a disability. Like her, I want to be known. In addition, I am purposefully making political use of my sexual identity in a manner that often has been associated with "identity politics." Although this term has acquired different meanings, it usually refers to a politics in which groups of oppressed people mobilize resistance around a shared identity. As academic critiques of the notion of a stable, unified identity increased in the 1980s, more and more feminists joined others in questioning not only the notion of identity but its value as the basis of political thought and action.

Criticisms of identity politics, as feminist political theorist Susan Bickford notes, have been made on several grounds.[17] One approach contends that an emphasis on the suffering of oppressed people breeds a mentality of victimization and resentment. Another line of thinking suggests that claims to justice on the part of identity groups such as blacks or women lead to laws and regulations that merely strengthen the control of the state or other institutions over people's lives. Still others portray identity politics as pitting groups against each other, ignoring our common interests as citizens in striving for social justice. Also important, I would add, are the observations by many feminists of color and working-class and lesbian feminists that white, middle-class, and heterosexual women tend to equate the identity "woman" with their own particular situations.

Some of my students express similar criticisms of identity politics. They, too, are distressed when they encounter anything they associate with victimization. "Feminists are so negative," they say. "Why do black women have to be so angry?" asks a white member of one class. Students also draw away from readings and discussions that seem exclusionary or divisive. "I feel so left out," says one heterosexual woman, "when we read about lesbians." Says a white, heterosexual man, "Doesn't all this negative stuff just deepen the splits between men and women or between whites and blacks?" Some also fear that attention to difference leads to authoritarianism. "All these rules and regulations about affirmative action," says a white student, "just give the government more control over our lives." "I don't want to be trapped in any of these categories," says a student who describes herself as bisexual. Students value cooperation and equality in our discourse and often believe that the emphasis on difference gets in the way of productive discussions.

I am willing to grant that these criticisms have some merit, although I do not think they should lead to a wholesale rejection of identity politics. As a feminist teacher, I do not aim at convincing students that identity categories make good or bad politics. This seems to me a question best answered in the context of concrete attempts to promote social justice. Rather, I hope that a feminist discourse on difference will help students incorporate into their judgments about gender injustice an understanding of what these judgments mean for differently situated people. Difference, as June Jordan and Naomi Scheman each have pointed out, has a great deal to do with our effect on others.[18]

One main criticism of identity politics has been that when a group of people makes social justice claims on the basis of a single identity, it suppresses the fact that those included in the given category (e.g., women or blacks) also have other identities that may put them in a position of privilege rather than oppression. A white lesbian like myself benefits from white skin privilege. A heterosexual Chicana benefits from heterosexual privilege. Moreover, at least some of these identities may change over time. The white lesbian may change her orientation and marry a man; the Chicana may come out as a lesbian. Thus, not only our identities but our relationships with different others are complex, fluid, and unstable.

This picture of shifting identities and relationships is helpful to me as a teacher in the class that will not talk about lesbians. I can talk about how my midlife shift in sexual orientation illuminated aspects of heterosexual privilege that I suppressed or was unable to grasp as a heterosexual woman. I also can encourage students to think about how new relationships can be formed to challenge oppression. For instance, when a lesbian and a gay male student in another class propose an action project to demand domestic partnership benefits for same sex couples in their workplace, I ask them to think about the complexities and fluidity of the sexual identities of their colleagues—how they as organizers might gain the support of people who are unsure of their sexual orientation. I also suggest to the students that they think about the pros and cons of joining with some heterosexual colleagues to press for benefits for all unmarried couples.

Although my awareness of fluidity and complexity aids me in making such pedagogical judgments, it does not dissolve many of the conflicts over difference that arise in my classes. The story about Jewel and Malka, who clash over whether we should focus discussion on injustices done to poor U.S. women of color or to European Jews, suggests the depth of some of these conflicts. In effect, each of these women puts forth a social justice claim. By doing this, they bring into focus the fact that movements often forward different and potentially competing definitions of justice. The progressive political movements that emerged after World War II all tended to support equality under law. But their notions of justice were far from identical. Feminists often emphasized "personal" matters that had been relegated to the private realm. Black liberationists frequently insisted that community play a leading role in social change. Disability rights advocates sought to redefine opportunity to include physical access. Although taken together these and similar movements remind teachers that injustice takes many forms, we are still faced with the question of how to respond to the kind of classroom conflict over priorities that Jewel and Malka represent.

In their detailed study of feminist college and university classrooms, Frances Maher and Mary Kay Thompson Tetreault employ the concept of "positionality" or intersectionality (adopted by Laurie Finke and others) to describe how feminist teachers can approach racial, gender, class, and similar inequities.[19] By stressing positionality, Maher and Tetreault suggest, teachers can help students understand that each person is located at the intersection of a number of systems of oppression: any individual may be both privileged and oppressed according to how they are positioned. This understanding, in turn, can enable students to reflect on how their particular locations shape both their definitions of knowledge and their relationships with others. A teacher who guides such explorations sees questions of difference through what one professor cited by Maher and Tetreault describes as "the third eye"—a perspective that offers her a wider view of these complex and often shifting relationships.[20]

The image of a more comprehensive viewpoint from which to interpret an ongoing discourse on difference is an appealing one, especially given the seemingly irresolvable clashes about who is to blame for injustice that often emerge through such discourse. But the belief that teachers and students can transcend competing definitions of social justice presents problems. The goals and arguments articulated through the social justice movements of the past decades have not coalesced into a single, common program on which activists agree. In its absence, academics continue to argue about which eye might be the third eye through which to view oppression.[21] Concepts like intersectionality or positionality do not resolve these differences. Rather, they provide a political and ethical orientation toward difference that bids us ask how we are profiting as well as suffering from systems of oppression and what responsibilities we may have to oppose them.

My story about Jewel and Malka speaks to this issue. When Malka tries to change the subject from current racial and gender oppression to the mass murder of European Jews, I interpret her move as power evasive. Because I have so often seen white students try to change the subject when that subject is race, I join Jewel's effort to get Malka to look at how racism and poverty intersect with gender injustice in the lives of the women who are clients of Jewel's social agency. But I still feel uncomfortable with my pedagogical move. I worry about whether I have automatically rather than thoughtfully deferred the issue of Jewish oppression. I wonder whether my own internalized anti-Semitism, including a stereotypical belief that Jews in the United States are now so privileged that they have no right to make social justice claims, is playing a role in how I am responding in class. I also ask myself whether I am afraid of making myself and other Jews too visible, instead of keeping the kind of low profile that I was taught to keep as a child. I sense that I am anxious to prevent this class from turning into a contest of social justice claims, the kind of "oppression derby" that Hannah wants to avoid. Like Hannah, I am well aware that conflict over such claims can be very destructive: we live in a city in which people who have suffered different forms of injustice have ended up killing each other.

As a teacher, where do I go from here? When I reflect on the class, I still feel that my initial decision to focus this section of the course on African American women is a sound one. Our course takes place in a national context of intensified racist rhetoric and backlash against the gains made by people of color. Like many women's studies teachers, I see the intersections among gender, race, and class as crucial areas for feminist scholarship and teaching. My students are predominantly white and middle-class women. Many of them do professional work in education and the human services that impacts on the lives of poor people of color. Feminist discourse on our professional responsibilities cannot avoid coming to grips with racism. I say all of this to Malka in a talk we have at the end of class. She agrees that context should play an important role in deciding which injustices to emphasize in our discussion. But she also describes how the concentration camp experiences of her grandparents continue to resonate within her family and again questions my excluding Jewish oppression from the discussion.

As I walk home, the image of Malka as a child, frightened and confused by her family's history, keeps coming into my mind. I suddenly realize that Jewel, too, has emphasized how the oppression of poor African American women has an especially strong impact on children. At last, I begin to imagine a common ground on which these two students can talk and from which we could continue our discussion.

At the next meeting, I begin by posing the problem of how children are affected by racial, economic, and other forms of violence. I ask Jewel to describe her agency's clients in these terms and for us all to think about situations in which unequal privilege and power have caused harm to children. Malka recounts her family experience, as does Harmony, who was raised in a very poor, white, rural family. Then, taking Jewel's description as a beginning point, I ask the class to consider several questions. How well do our readings on race and gender account for the situation Jewel describes? Jewel herself is dissatisfied with the readings because she does not think that these authors show sufficient awareness of the class differences among African Americans. She wants us to pay attention to the poverty of the women with whom she works and its impact on their ability to care for their children. Harmony, who also wants to see more emphasis on class, notes that as a child she found some solace in her deprivation through friendships with black children whose families were equally poor.

Malka says that although she sees the value of an economic argument for the situations described by Jewel and Harmony, she is less sure of its meaning for her own history. The fact that her great-grandfather owned a factory did not prevent the Nazis from annihilating him and most of his family. She has been reading theories about child abuse in her psychology classes, and she thinks that the culture of abuse described in some of these readings better accounts for the kind of oppression that led to the Holocaust. Jewel acknowledges that certain abuses in the exercise of power by officials in her agency contribute to clients' difficulties in taking care of their children, but she still sees economics as a key factor: she wonders whether Malka's great-grandfather's success might have made him a target of racist violence.

As the students explore the relationships among different forms of oppression, they are also testing out their own potentials for collaboration across differences. On one level, collaboration is basic to the discussion itself. If each person cannot both speak and listen, the discussion cannot go forward. When Malka feels silenced, she cannot listen. While Jewel feels disregarded, she is not interested in what Malka has to say. Each participant in the discussion needs to see that her concerns about difference can be made part of the discussion. This does not mean that they always must be at the center. Once Malka understands that her experience with oppression will not be ignored or denigrated, she becomes far less anxious. Once Jewel understands that the focus will not shift away from race, she feels far more open to comparisons.

The discussion of relationships among different forms of oppression also opens up the potential for further collaboration. Toward the end of the semester, Malka says that our discussions have helped her decide to do doctoral research on the ways in which child abuse may be related to anti-Semitism and racism. Jewel offers to help find clients in her agency who might be willing to be interviewed, but she feels that Malka is making a mistake if she leaves economics out of her study. By the time their conversation is over, I have begun to imagine them as comrades, joining together to do research, formulate policies, and fight for some of the fundamental changes our society needs. My imagination flies far from the classroom and a good deal beyond its current reality. I am excited by their discussion because my eagerness to promote a discourse on difference is informed by my longing to build community.

CHAPTER 6

COMMUNITY AS REALITY AND IDEAL

At the end of the final class meeting, a group of women hangs around the room. They have formed a noticeable bond over the semester and represent many parts of the world. Rashmi's parents immigrated from India. Larissa comes from the disintegrating Soviet Union. Augusta has moved to New York from a small town in the southern United States. Edna was born in Puerto Rico. Yoko comes from Japan. These students do not want the course to end, and neither do I. Something special has happened here, a moment of coming together across vast differences.

I have asked the class to divide themselves into small groups to discuss a text on the intersection of racism and sexism. A group of white students approach me with a request. They want me to make sure that at least one of the four students of color in the class joins their group so that they can learn more about the topic. My immediate, inner response is anger. What do you think we have here, I want to say, a street corner on which to pick up day laborers you need for a quick, cheap job?

Drawing on the deeply religious sources that helped fuel the civil rights movement of the 1950s and 1960s, activists sometimes referred to themselves as a "beloved community." This image had special power for people faced with continuous threats of beating, maiming, and murder. If activists could not count on community among comrades, they could not count on anything.[22]

Where threats are less visible and violent, the need for close ties among those working for social justice may be less obvious although still vital. In the new left and feminist movements, activists tended to emphasize a form of community that Wini Breines describes as "prefigurative politics"—that is, the commitment to practice with each other the egalitarian and cooperative values activists hoped to realize in the broader society.[23] Many second-wave feminists were deeply affected by this vision. Small political groups as well as established feminist organizations often viewed their efforts through the lens of prefigurative community. Consciousness-raising, too, reflected this ideal. As feminists talked together about their oppression and how to end it, they sought to practice the honesty, equality, and comradeship that they were demanding from the larger world. In this respect, my telling the story about Rashmi and her classmates also reflects a second-wave feminist dream: that despite Simone de Beauvoir's observation that women were profoundly "dispersed," they could join in community.

The ideal of community proved difficult to sustain, however. As many proponents of social change experienced disappointments with each other and conservatives charged activists with social subversion, two main criticisms emerged. The first portrayed community as dangerous because it suppressed freedom and individuality. The second conceded that although the ideal might be laudable, it could not be realized in practice. These concerns echoed the experience and thinking of feminist theorists who started to criticize the second-wave ideal of community as promoting conformity and utopianism.[24] The goal of creating community, they feared, suppressed important differences among women. Utopianism bred authoritarianism and incited feminists to force other women into a uniform mold. In contrast to this communal vision, Iris Young suggested, feminists might take inspiration from the ideal of the city, with its acceptance of heterogeneity and tolerance for individual expression.[25]

As a virtue, tolerance plays an especially important role in feminist discourse because to talk about differences, participants require a great deal of patience and forbearance.[26] We need to be willing to put up with each other's errors and misperceptions long enough to find a constructive way to talk about them. We have to accept a certain amount of our own pain and confusion to have a chance to reflect on them.

Cities, and the kind of tolerance that the ideal of the city symbolizes, also support greater freedom. After a number of years as a single woman living in the university community of a small city, I fled to a large urban center where I could live as I wished without everyone knowing my business or how I deviated from the traditional norm. Small, tight community structures can perpetuate and mask many forms of oppression and abuse. But the urban style of tolerance, too, has its price. It can hold others at a distance, draw potentially harmful boundaries between public and private, and permit us to ignore the individual or collective needs of others. Tolerance for the homeless people that sleep in the streets of my city is perfectly compatible with my stepping over their bodies on the way to teach my women's studies classes.

The line between community and individual freedom does not have to be so tightly drawn, however. Young acknowledges this in her idea of building political solidarity through "affinity groups" that could form or dissolve around particular issues and leave room for fluidity and complexity in the identities of their members. Patricia Hill Collins provides another helpful image of community, based in African American experience, in which individuality is respected and appreciated because of the ways that individuals can contribute to the community's survival.[27] Inspired by such ideals of collaboration, teachers promoting feminist discourse might strive for an idea of *community that supports individuality* rather than standing in opposition to it.

This kind of classroom community lies somewhere between a beloved, prefigurative community, in which participants can be assumed to share common values, and an association of disconnected individuals, who happen to join around their particular interests. For a community that supports individuality to evolve, members would have to discover or develop a shared interest in gender injustice, even though they may have deeply differing ideas about both gender and injustice. They would have to recognize on some level that they needed each other's participation to pursue that interest, to enlarge their own ideas and to make wise individual and collective decisions in this area.

Classroom community may coalesce quickly or slowly, completely or only partially. Sometimes individual students persist in preserving a separation between themselves and other class members for the entire length of the semester. Crystal, who is not a "minority" member of the class in any obvious sense, tells me that she is "not a group person" and joins in small-group discussions only because I require this activity as part of the course. She says she simply wants to do "her work." She does not seem to grasp at all the collaborative dimension of the course. I do not push the point, but I keep an eye out for another individual student with whom Crystal might engage in conversation.

In certain classes, some students come in with or form tight subgroups that enable them to resist or relate to my attempt to build classroom community. Adele and her white classmates—the health professionals who criticized the black hospital aides—were already part of a group before they came to class. These bonds made my effort to foster a wider, feminist discourse more difficult. In another class, an alliance of doctoral students forms who see themselves as having different interests from the other graduate students. I agree with them up to a point, and we talk about how they can use the course to their best advantage as well as contribute to the larger group. I am also wary of the ways in which this tight minicommunity may operate. In fact, the subgroup makes a carefully prepared and stimulating presentation to the rest of the class at the end of the semester, although later I discover that one member did virtually none of the work because the others agreed that preparing for her candidacy exams should be her priority.

As this last example suggests, then, the extent to which students want to and can participate in classroom community building depends to a great extent on the context. Some contexts are far more hospitable to community building than others. Bureaucratic structures, educational and job competition, and racial and other conflicts bring out or create barriers to such efforts. Trudy, for instance, is enrolled in a program that requires her to take an unusually heavy load of courses. This is why, she explains to me, she can spend so little time preparing and hardly joins in the class discussions. Brett, who is trying to get into a highly competitive graduate program, is working so hard for an A that she does not want to let me or other students know that she is confused about the answers to some vital questions raised in the class. Paulette leaves a message for me, after the brutal beating of a black citizen by white police officers, saying she cannot talk with white people about race or anything else for a while. Lucinda, a white woman whose white son was just hurt in a fight with a black schoolmate, tells me that she cannot attend another class in which we are discussing a major black feminist text.

These ruptures suggest the extent to which political discourse depends on certain minimally shared values about what is worth discussing when and with whom. No political discourse can take place without this willingness. But willingness is not enough. Building and sustaining sufficient community to engage in feminist discourse requires a good deal of collaborative work on the part of participants.[28] Such discourse work, as I have suggested throughout this volume, includes holding (to sustain belief in and engagement with the purpose of the discourse), narration (relating of experiences), emotional work (expressing feelings), theorizing (sharing ideas and development of arguments and analyses), action (insistence on an orientation toward what is to be done), caring (attention and response to the caring needs that arise in the discourse process), and listening.[29]

The importance of one or another form of discourse work may increase or decrease as talk proceeds. Thus, as I also have argued earlier, flexibility is an important quality in the division of discourse labor. But flexibility without reflection and a sense of direction can do considerable harm to feminist discourse on difference. This becomes evident in the story I tell at the beginning of this section about the white students who want to have a student of color in their small-group discussion of race. These white students, in effect, propose a division of labor based on their belief that students of color will do a certain kind of work within the group. This belief, in turn, requires me to reconsider my rather casual assumption that students could organize their discourse work unproblematically. Although my first, angry impulse is to squelch these white students' initiative, by pointing to the racist assumption that the function of students of color is to serve the educational interests of white students, I need to reflect further on what division of labor might best promote everyone's learning and engagement in discussion.

Anne Phillips's distinction between a "politics of ideas" and a "politics of presence" is useful here.[30] A politics of ideas derives from the liberal tradition of political discourse and argues that all relevant ideas should be expressed in the process of arriving at political judgments. This concept assumes that any rational individual could and should speak for any point of view that might enlarge the understanding of the participants. According to this argument, individuals engaged in political talk can readily replace each other. They are, in Seyla Benhabib's term, "fungible."[31]

A feminist teacher whose leadership is informed by a politics of ideas would encourage all of the students to articulate as many relevant arguments as possible. She would not pay attention to who presented what idea; indeed, she would carefully avoid assuming that a student would or should bring in a given point of view because they have a certain sexual orientation or come from a particular economic class or racial/ethnic group. She might, in fact, press students to make arguments that they or others might not expect them to promote, exercise their ability to understand, and bring a wide range of positions into the discussion.

This interchangeability of persons has definite advantages for developing a division of labor in political discourse. Anyone who judges that an important point of view is missing may volunteer or encourage other members who may be more familiar with that position to provide it. Viewing the story about the white students who want a student of color to join their group through this lens, my teaching job would involve making sure that someone presents the relevant ideas about racism and sexism. I could do this through a lecture. The students could learn about these ideas through reading. Students of color or white students could decide to voice such ideas. I could assign any or all of the students to make reports. In any case, I would never make these assignments on the basis of race or assume that a group of white students needed the presence of students of color to engage in productive discussion.

From the viewpoint of a politics of presence, however, the idea-centered approach has serious problems. The first has to do with how discourse participants determine what arguments are relevant. As both activists and academics of many sorts have pointed out, our beliefs in what ideas are relevant are highly dependent on the shared values of those who are talking together. Whether they are a longtime group of friends or members of a scientific discipline, participants often resist the introduction of ideas that run counter to the shared understandings. In the case of scientific communities, group members frequently resist new ways of talking as well. Some of the discourse activities that I associate with feminist political talk still seem alien to the communication style of many academic disciplines. Thus, people who try to introduce unfamiliar ideas or a new approach to discourse may be excluded or kept at the margins of discussion because their ideas or ways of expressing them are not deemed "relevant."

Breaking through an established discourse culture is often difficult and perhaps at times impossible. It may take some overwhelming counterevidence, a disaster, or the power of a highly visible social justice movement to create the space for a new kind of discussion. Thus, the physical presence of certain individuals does not guarantee that the differences they bring to the discussion will make an impact. They have to see themselves and be seen as valuable contributors to this discourse work.

A feminist teacher whose work is informed by a politics of presence would be especially attuned to the differences that her students and she might make a part of the discourse, in particular, the differences that they as people with distinct histories, ideas, and sets of experiences might share with the group. She would also remain aware that presence implies absence and take note of who was not present in the classroom as well as who was there. Like many women's studies teachers, she would attempt to incorporate as many voices as she could, through readings, films, guest speakers, and other means. She would try to show the relevance of these absent voices to the ongoing discussion.

Yet she would also run into difficulties that are not so different from those encountered by teachers whose work is informed by a politics of ideas. The effort to include more voices does not change the basic exclusionary system within which higher education usually takes place. Nor does it tell us which voices need to be present. As critics of identity politics point out, simply attempting to include "all" voices in a given discussion may result in superficiality or chaos, with no issue receiving real attention.

Moreover, a politics of presence raises serious questions concerning *representation*. Readings, films, and so forth, can never fully speak for themselves. Teachers must in some sense engage in re-presenting these voices. As Liza Fiol-Matta points out with respect to white teachers attempting to represent women of color, however, such representation often involves distortion.[32] If experiences, feelings, ideas, and judgments about action are interwoven as complexly as I have suggested, speakers may not be so easily interchangeable in their presentation of particular positions. In this respect, the white students who approached me about including a student of color in their group may have been right: none of them could have represented or interpreted their reading about race and gender as well as a student of color or someone highly and personally familiar with this intersection of oppressions.

A politics of presence has other problems. One, two, or three "minority" students cannot represent all the different values or practices of their given cultures or groups. Categories such as "Asian American" or "Hispanic" often do not reflect the cultural realities of the people grouped within them. The expectation or demand that they identify with a given social category may be painful or otherwise distressing to those biracial, transgender, or other students whose identities are frequently subject to misreadings or hostile challenges. As feminist and social justice teachers often argue, we may do considerable damage to students by assuming that they want to represent a given group. In discussions of social justice teaching, it has become a maxim that teachers should not call on students to speak for or about a group to which they presumably belong.

Yet, for feminist teachers, this is a problematic maxim. From the early years of second-wave feminism, many black feminists worked hard to educate their white counterparts about the impact of racism on African American women's lives. Then, in disappointment and anger, they often gave up on this effort, telling white women to work on their own racism and the racism of their sisters and brothers. This move, in turn, has led to a good deal of valuable antiracist work by white feminists, particularly work aimed at understanding white privilege.[33] But, as bell hooks argues, it also led some white feminists to erase the black feminist thinking that lies at the heart of such antiracist discussions.[34] A feminist discourse on difference that proceeds without acknowledging the leadership of feminists of color cuts this critique off at its source. Without the continued participation of women of color, such a discourse becomes increasingly defined by white women.

This argument does not imply that women of color would or should put the work of educating whites ahead of other work, particularly the work of talking with each other about how to interpret and respond to racism. Chela Sandoval stresses the importance of "U.S. Third World feminists" developing their own "oppositional consciousness" in response to the dominance of white Western feminists.[35] Patricia Hill Collins points to the need for black feminists to talk through their own differences. hooks herself has promoted discussion among black women about shared issues. For feminist teachers, hooks's concern that women of color not be omitted from the work of education about racism implies a caution: feminist teachers should neither assume that students want to speak from their histories and experiences of racism (or other forms of oppression) nor assume that they do not. In fact, some students may welcome the prospect of using their presence and identities as resources in political discussion. If we are too quick to rule out the idea that they could speak as members of a social group, we may silence them in yet another way.

In the story in which the white students want to hear from students of color, I do not know how each of the few students of color feels about speaking from her experiences and ideas about race until she indicates this to me or the class. Similarly, in another course, I do not know how a lesbian student may think and feel about her participation in the classroom division of labor. Moreover, students' ideas about how they want to speak may shift in one or another direction over the semester. I can watch closely. I can talk with students outside class. I can support without requiring. I can leave the door open for a student to take up the invitation or refuse it. Above all, as I have argued with respect to caring, I need to preserve flexibility in the division of discourse labor so that students can either disconnect certain "selves" from the discussion or bring some aspects of themselves into the discussion when they want to.[36]

This line of argument suggests other forms of work that play a role in classroom community building. One is *bridging work*. The commitment to build bridges has been named and practiced in many contexts by feminists (including many lesbians) of color. By describing their activist role in terms of "this bridge called my back," Cherríe Moraga and Gloria Anzaldúa, editors of the well-known volume that bears that name, imply both that bridging involves work and that such work may be virtually backbreaking to those who do it.[37] Anzaldúa takes this insight farther by arguing that the bridge image may be too limited. Sometimes, she says, it is neither possible nor desirable to act as a regular bridge. A drawbridge would provide a better image because it makes a connection and then withdraws; or an island, where the person who makes bridges can retreat; or a sandbar that allows making bridges in a more fluid, flexible way. Building bridges best promotes classroom community when it takes into account the needs and desires of those doing the work.

Some work involves bridging the various selves that are brought to the discussion of difference. When the white students ask me to make sure that their group will "have its own" student of color, I get angry at them for perpetuating the racist assumption that people of color are at the disposal of white people. Yet in my heart of hearts I recognize that their request taps into the ways that I, too, have tried to make my own uses of people of color. I have sought the presence of people of color to express vitality I myself wanted to feel. I have hoped for the involvement of women of color in feminist activities because I have wanted "my" movement to be multiracial. My anger at the white students is partly fueled by anger at these aspects of myself. To teach such white students, I need to make a bridge to the part of me that I would like to disown: the part that is still shaped by a white privilege that tempts me to act against my social justice values.

Bridging also takes the more public form of discovering and building alliances at the intersections of systems of oppression. In a feminist classroom, everyone may not leap at the chance to create such alliances. Yet they may gradually emerge in the difficult process of probing these intersections. Max, who I learn through a discussion in my office was badly abused by his father, slowly discovers the similarities between his experience and stories he hears or reads in class. He asks Midge, who has spoken up on the subject, to do a project with him on feminist theories of violence. Rashmi (who is at the center of the international group of students that I describe at the beginning of this section) engages in both internal and external bridging as the daughter of immigrant parents and as a woman who wants to talk about gender injustice with people from different backgrounds.

Effective bridging work also involves making connections between classroom discussions of difference and worlds outside the classroom. In the class with the students from so many parts of the world, Augusta recounts how she has raised several gender issues in her black student group. Rashmi takes our feminist discourse on difference back into her family and her work life. Yoko will take it back home to Japan, when she returns there after her studies. This bridging work is neither simple nor inevitable: it may die quickly without support and sustenance. Building bridges to worlds outside class often helps build community within the classroom. For students who see themselves building bridges to other groups, discourse work has a clear purpose. The better that work can be done in class, the more useful it will be outside.

Finally, community building requires *continuity work*. Feminist classes at best constitute temporary communities, bounded by the limits of the semester and the relations beyond the classroom that participants are able and willing to maintain. Like other transient communities (e.g., a workplace with fairly rapid turnover or a group that comes together to work on a particular political project), the temporary classroom community has both advantages and disadvantages for promoting feminist discourse. The transiency of many classroom relationships inspires some students to take risks they might not take in other settings. Yet, if the bonds seem too ephemeral or slight, discussion becomes superficial.

Everyone in the classroom can work to maintain continuity, but teachers are normally best positioned to do this. I must show up for each class, with my mind as well as my body. I have to respond in some way to each crisis that develops, whether or not students perceive it as a crisis or offer responses of their own. But students also do a good deal of continuity work. Lenore, an African American student, and Allegra, an Italian American student, make friends during the semester. They form a unit within the class and carve out for themselves a definite sphere of work, challenging other students who evade or misrepresent ideas about the intersection of racial and gender injustice. Their presence and their voices, which are strong and deeply felt, speak of their commitment to the classroom process. They do not always agree with each other, but their ability to maintain their connection while they disagree inspires other students to see our work as an ongoing project.

Continuity work also requires me to view my teaching in a way that gives our transient classroom community greater meaning. Such a framework helps me see the class in relation to my own academic life and involvement in the feminist movement, to locate my feminist pedagogy within an ongoing history.

— 7 —

INNOCENTS AND INTELLECTUALS

Is There Hope for Feminist Teaching?

Rashmi, Larissa, and their friends drift out of the classroom, and I am left gathering up my books and papers. The image of these women from so many places and cultures sticks in my mind, strangely familiar. In a flash, I recognize an old dream, deeply rooted in my childhood experience of World War II. As I listen to the news of death and suffering, I keep telling myself that things will get better. I hear the grown-ups say that after the war there will be a United Nations, and I can see it in my mind's eye: a world where different peoples talk rather than fight, a world where everyone lives a decent life.

For over an hour, the members of our faculty group have been analyzing a complex clash of values that has emerged in one of our women's studies classes. We listen to each other closely. We bring in different perspectives. The teacher whose class we are discussing gets some good ideas. Just as we are breathing a collective sigh of relief, another teacher, Gwen, bursts out with an agonized cry, "It's so bad out there! What difference can some little classroom discussion make?"

Movements for social justice require hope, although as events unfold, this hope may appear shallow and overblown. My childhood optimism about peace and justice was painfully tempered by the outbreak of the Korean War and the rise of right-wing witch-hunts against advocates for social change. Yet I clung to the conviction that with serious effort, life could be made better for everyone.

The social justice movements that burgeoned in the 1950s, 1960s, and 1970s in the United States also confronted events and trends that called into question the viability of hope. By the 1980s, political and cultural backlash made many liberatory dreams of the previous two or three decades seem outdated, misguided, or simply wrong. Reactionary critics claimed that people of color and white women were now getting more than their share of society's resources, that social justice demands were based on false values, or that such movements actually harmed those they claimed to represent. Activism was often portrayed as utopian, romantic, and ignorant. People who in an earlier period might have identified with social justice efforts began to view them as fruitless. In my feminist classes, students saw themselves as increasingly powerless to change the dominant social order and anxious about how they as individuals could survive.

Many activists, too, lost hope, and increasing numbers of academics began to rethink their colleagues' or their own earlier optimism. The critique of "progress," to which feminists had contributed some important ideas, grew apace, and advocates of progressive social change began to qualify their aspirations. Ferenc Fehrér suggested that proponents of social justice replace their idealized "great hope" for change with a "rational hope" that brings our capacity for reasoning to bear on the possibilities for a problematic future.[1] Michel Foucault's argument for locally based rather than large-scale resistance bred a certain skepticism toward social justice movements that made broad demands. Many feminists started to look askance at what Frances Bartkowski calls the "promissory hope" implicit in some second-wave thinking: the belief that the movement would lead to a near-perfect social order. Instead, to keep their commitments alive, feminists often exchanged idealism for a "cautionary hope" that might have a chance of being fulfilled.

This move to reduce the breadth of hope has definite advantages in periods when activist efforts seem to produce little basic change. For feminist and other activist-oriented academics, the strategy of reducing hope fits well with the limitations of the classroom: the fact that only a small number of issues can be covered and most of our steps toward social justice are small ones. Yet, in both the classroom and the wider world, the distinction between great and limited hopes cannot be so easily sustained. A student who starts describing the job discrimination she encounters may find herself thinking about the changes that could be made in her workplace. As she reads various writings and talks with others about the issue, she may consider broader changes that could be made in other workplaces as well. Discussions about how to transform workplaces may lead to students invoking different economic ideas or imagining different organizations of work.

This connection between more limited and greater hopes can have contradictory results. For example, in one class we are talking about feminist ideas of caring. Many students are drawn to these theories and find ample support for them in their own lives as they care for children, parents, students, or clients. Such relationships give them small but significant hopes.

As our discussion begins to address the economic conditions required to support caring activities and make caring accessible to everyone, the students become somber and then depressed. They cannot imagine themselves trying to make fundamental economic changes. Their small hopes shrivel, no longer so secure.

Great hopes can also collapse when their dependence on smaller hopes is revealed. Two women in another class have been chosen to join in a large-scale experiment for curricular reform that will be tried in a number of secondary schools. They are thrilled to become a part of this project and filled with hope. They bring their new ideas into class, critique them in the light of the class readings, and refine them in discussion with their classmates. They charge ahead with great enthusiasm until they discover that a male colleague on the project does not want to treat them as his equals. In addition, one of the women starts fighting with her husband about the extra time that she is spending on the project, while the other student clashes with a white woman supervisor who seems uncomfortable with people of color. The future now looks more doubtful, because the interpersonal relationships on which the larger project depends prove problematic.

As a teacher, I can do a great deal to nurture or discourage both small and great hopes for social justice, through my choice of readings, how I direct discussions, through formal presentations and what I reveal about my own life and values. I cannot create hopes out of whole cloth, however. They depend not only on how I conduct the class but on what the students make of the course, not only on what the students imagine possible but on what they discover to be viable as they interact in the world.

Moreover, my capacity to present social justice issues in a hopeful light depends on my ability to sustain my own greater and more limited hopes for change. One evening, I guide students through an exciting discussion of feminist issues and the next morning open the newspaper to discover that an affirmative action law has been struck down, a vast number of women and children have been driven into refugee camps, and a "welfare reform" law has been enacted that turns poor women in my city into a new type of indentured servant. Like Gwen, I want to cry out, "What's the point of this teaching?" I imagine myself quitting on the spot and leaving the academy forever to become a full-time activist in the "real" world.

My internal dialogue about the value of teaching is not new, to either me or the feminist movement. Radical activists of the 1960s and 1970s often accused academics of complicity with dominant institutions, of being part of the problem instead of part of the solution. This charge stemmed in part from the well-founded criticism of the split between mental and manual work and Marx and Engels's important caution that philosophizing alone does not change the world.[2] Yet, where it is not clear what actions do change the world for the better, the distinction between philosophy and action becomes problematic. We need to talk together to be able to act. While I agonize about the distance between feminist discourse in the classroom and the serious state of the world outside it, the students often comment on how much of the real world is brought into the classroom, how difficult it is to face these problems. Sometimes they say that I am pushing them to deal with too many painful realities.

Teachers committed to social justice respond to tensions between the classroom and activism in the world outside in a variety of ways. One is to accept this split and focus on what can be done outside. From this perspective, teaching is simply one way to earn a living: the real action lies elsewhere. Like artists who clean houses or wait on tables to support their art, teaching becomes instrumental to other ends. It enables us to survive so that we can invest our energies where they will make a difference. It involves *deferred hope*, in contrast to the *present hope* that motivates political action.[3]

This distinction between deferred and present hope can be very persuasive under certain historical conditions. Where movement for social justice is slight and institutional conditions are highly constrained, feminist and kindred teachers may want to put limited political energy into their teaching. However, teaching conditions also vary greatly over time and place, and hopes that have been deferred may begin to find fertile soil in what once seemed a relatively barren situation. Dramatic transformations may happen over the course of a semester. In one class, many of the students may start out with a hostile, skeptical, or frightened attitude. I can say to myself, "This is hopeless; just try to get yourself through the semester and concentrate on other things." Yet, if I am able to live with the tension in myself between deferred hope for change outside the classroom and a present hope that the class will truly engage with feminist issues, a far more *grounded hope* may evolve. This sense of promise is neither great nor small but grounded in the continued interactions among class members, myself, and the world.

In the class that includes Rashmi and Larissa in which the students bond so closely by the end of the semester, I do not expect my teaching to form them into a miniature United Nations. I assume these students will go through many struggles about how they relate to each other and to me. At first the class moves haltingly, but about halfway through the semester, something begins to happen during our discussion of a reading about motherhood. Rashmi is quite disturbed because the reading assumes that mothering is a one-to-one activity in contrast to how child care is shared in her extended family. Augusta says this is true of many families she knows as well, but very poor women need more than shared child care to survive. Larissa describes her own mother's unhappy experiences with the child care provided by the state. I point out the complex conditions and clash of values involved in developing child care policies and how some of our other readings speak to these issues. As their discussion proceeds, the students are listening to each other closely. They care deeply about this issue and see the possibility of figuring out together what can be done. I never could have brought this process into being by evoking my ancient dream of a just and peaceful world and trying to make their discourse conform to it. Rather, it is they who have reawakened that hope in me by finding, with my help, a way to talk with one another.

Another way in which teachers working for social justice can respond to the tensions around higher education and activism in the nonacademic world is by employing the *logic of preparation*. The logic of preparation permeates dominant educational discourse, with its emphasis on preparing students for citizenship, economic self-sufficiency, and leadership. Hannah Arendt and other social theorists have employed this logic when they insist that a firm line be drawn between educational preparation for citizenship and the social justice activities in which adults might engage.[4] Early proponents of feminist consciousness-raising made similar assumptions when they envisioned consciousness-raising as a way to prepare women for activism. However, some women who participated in these groups already engaged in feminist politics and had begun to struggle with male domination in their homes, workplaces, and nonfeminist activism. In this respect, consciousness-raising did not so much prepare members for activism as accompany ongoing action: help women attend to, analyze, and cultivate their political agency.

Given the mixed messages that consciousness-raising implies about the meaning of "preparation," it is not surprising that feminist classroom discourse both prepares students to make judgments and take actions in the world and requires them to do so in the classroom itself.[5] Injustices suffered in class are as real as injustices suffered in any other venue. When a student interrupts our talk about the intersection of race and gender to call attention to how racism is affecting our interaction, we need to deal with this issue in the moment. When another student says that we are not being caring toward each other, we need to discuss and possibly act on the matter.

The world outside the classroom also prepares us to participate in feminist discourse. Continued incidents and organized opposition to racial injustice outside the classroom may prepare some students to pursue their concerns about racism within it. The struggle of single mothers to raise their children may prepare a student who is a single mother to engage in discourse on women's caring in relation to the structure of communities and of the state. By relying solely on the logic of preparation, we obscure the interaction between our talk and society and assume a linear progression from education to social justice.

In making this argument, I do not mean to diminish the role of academic disciplines or interdisciplinary scholarship in enriching and strengthening feminist discourse. As a feminist teacher in higher education, I require students to consider gender injustice in the light of particular academic traditions, and I seek to strengthen the academic skills students need to engage with those traditions. These are only some of the many traditions and skills relevant to participating in feminist discourse, however. It can be deepened through the creative arts, planning political actions, talks with partners or family or friends, diversity workshops, conferences, and women's service projects. Viewing feminist teaching in terms of a strong split between preparation and action not only obscures the connections among these arenas but limits the depth of discussion.

Moreover, feminist teachers cannot be certain which forms of action will be most effective in achieving gender and other kinds of social justice. Second-wave activists spent a lot of political energy making claims for the superiority of one over another kind of political work. Direct action, such as civil disobedience and demonstrations, was pitted against electoral politics and lobbying. Working in established educational, health, and human service organizations was considered antithetical to creating alternative organizations. Labor organizing was deemed more central than other political efforts. Arts-related activism was posed against mere service work. Yet the value attributed to one or another form of activism might change with social conditions. Organizing or participating in a demonstration might seem a significant action when many people attended it and look like a waste of time when few people turned out. Classroom activities might feel vital to achieving justice when a movement is swelling and like a puny effort when no one is talking about social change.

When I ask Gwen (who anguishes over the social ineffectiveness of our feminist teaching) to say more about the difference between her classroom activities and political work in the world outside, she comments that real activism involves a high level of risk. Teaching is fairly tame stuff, she says, compared to joining a picket line or climbing the fence at a military installation. I know what she means. In my heart, or at least part of it, I share her assessment. I always feel more "political" holding a picket sign or "putting my body on the line" along with my comrades. When I feel more political, I feel more hopeful. This comparison, though, takes a number of things for granted: that only high-risk political activities are truly significant, that risks involved in social justice work can be measured on a single scale, and that our personal histories are not relevant to what constitutes a risk. These are questionable assumptions.

The notion that only high levels of risk count politically undermines the possibility of collaborative political work in which each person takes the risks she is willing and able to take. The story I tell in the second chapter about participating in an affinity group for a women's peace action makes this point. As our discussion process reveals, some of the women who have gathered to plan for the action are far more fearful than others of the physical injury we might suffer during the civil disobedience. Dominant norms of heroism, which draw heavily on military imagery, lead many of us to feel that if we are not willing to take such physical risks, we cannot make a significant contribution. Nevertheless, as we continue our talk about the action, we are able to find important roles for each woman who wants to participate. If we had ruled out this division of labor and emphasized only certain kinds of risk taking, we would have diminished the political agency of some of our members and of the group as a whole.[6]

The belief that risk taking can be measured on a uniform scale involves additional problems. Political activism may entail not only physical but economic, psychological, spiritual, social, and/or intellectual risks. The quality of these risks differs greatly. The physical risk of participating in a demonstration to a woman who has fragile bones cannot be easily compared to the economic risk of signing a union card to a woman who is the sole support of several children. The risk of standing up to a sexually harassing supervisor for a woman who was sexually abused as a child cannot easily be compared to the risk of presenting a feminist term paper to a misogynist professor for a woman whose higher education hangs on maintaining a financial scholarship.

As these examples suggest, the meaning of political risk taking is connected to individual life stories as they intersect with historical and social circumstances. For one feminist teacher, coming out as a feminist or an antiracist teacher or a lesbian may be a relatively low-risk activity because she has a lot of support in taking such stances or because she expects the costs to her sense of self or her career to be minimal. For another feminist teacher, any one of these steps may be momentous because it risks psychological or social or economic damage from which she may slowly if ever recover. If we view political risk taking as situated along many dimensions rather than as a series of acts to be measured against a single ideal, we become more aware of the relation between the risks a feminist teacher or her students take in the classroom and those they take in daily life. Classroom risk taking is not inherently more or less politically valuable than risk taking in the "real" world. What political risks mean to variously situated individuals is a problem to be addressed by feminist discourse rather than an assumption on which it can be founded.

For many teachers, one of the greatest risks involved in practicing the kind of feminist teaching I have been describing is the risk to legitimacy as an academic. Academics are supposed to be experts in a particular area of knowledge, and that expertise lends legitimacy to actions inside and outside the classroom. The pressure to achieve legitimacy is particularly great on teachers who deviate in any way from the prevailing models of academic appropriateness: on those who enter academia as outsiders or who challenge the dominant social structures and values. A feminist academic, particularly if she is also a woman of color and/or from a working-class background and/or a lesbian, is under special pressure to demonstrate her expertise. If her teaching does not confirm her claims to expertise—worse still, if it arouses the suspicion that she is an amateur or mere dabbler in fields in which she is not an expert—she risks unemployment or at least ostracism.

Whether this risk is worth taking depends on the teacher's particular situation and on how she views her work in a larger social and historical context. The risks I take as a tenured professor teaching through feminist discourse relate to diminished status rather than unemployment. I am not sure whether I would feel so free to teach in this way if I felt that my job were at stake. But the fear of being devalued has its own price. When an academic, in particular a feminist academic, attacks feminist pedagogy as "therapy" or "psychobabble," I wince and ready myself to fight or flee, taking my feminist essays on teaching with me. To keep thinking and acting politically, I have to remind myself of what I am doing and why. This is where my sense of the larger meaning of my work becomes relevant. Seeing it as part of a movement for social change reminds me that my commitment, by definition, involves risks to legitimacy. This perspective helps me think again about my ideals for social change and who else, to different degrees, shares them. It helps balance my fears with the reminder that I am not alone.

As this argument suggests, risks to legitimacy are closely associated with risks to political agency. By this I mean the risk entailed in expressing beliefs and taking actions that at some later time may prove an actor so incompetent in her judgments that her assumption of agency is discredited. Something approaching this situation occurred for me toward the end of the 1980s, when the impact of political reaction against 1970s feminism reached my own corner of the academic world. As many academic feminists launched stronger and stronger attacks on preceding styles of feminist thought and action, I could not help wondering whether I had made a terrible mistake. I am not alluding here to the many mistakes that I had to painfully acknowledge in the course of my own feminist education—the lessons I had to learn about women differently situated from myself and ways to think and act more effectively as a feminist. Rather, I mean the kind of massive error that would have rendered my years of feminist work foolish, useless, or downright destructive.

Although this prospect was fairly terrifying, it had certain useful outcomes. It made me look much more closely at how I conceived of my own political agency, both within and outside academia. I had to think again about what had drawn me to feminism, what I considered its strengths and weaknesses as a social movement, and how I positioned myself in relation to it. I had to ask myself which kinds of support were important to me and which less, about what forms of evidence count in deciding whether certain social justice actions are worth the risk or simply should be scrapped.

My thinking about what constitutes evidence is key here. In the context of the classroom, I have almost always felt that my efforts were worthwhile, that they enhanced feminism as a social movement. Even when students expressed conservative clichés that were rampant in the society, the process of promoting classroom discourse based in experiences, feelings, and ideas strengthened my belief that the risk of feminist teaching was justified. This belief had to encompass the students as well. That is, I needed to hear from them that the risks I was asking them to take in class and that they also might be taking outside the classroom contributed in some way to social justice. In short, I could not make sense of my pedagogical risk taking without relying on some larger images of social change, without some notion of progress.

FEMINIST DISCOURSE AND THE PROBLEM OF PROGRESS

For weeks I have been looking forward to this event at which three prominent feminist theorists are scheduled to speak. The auditorium buzzes with excitement as each woman rises to make her complex argument. When the speakers finally respond to each other, the atmosphere changes. Each one points to faults in the other two positions. One speaker after another claims that her own position has been grossly misunderstood. When members of the audience are invited to join in, they attack one or another speaker. I leave the auditorium with a sinking feeling.

Olga comes up to me after class with a serious grievance. She has a substantial background in women's studies and tells me that this graduate course is not sufficiently advanced for her. Although I stressed at the beginning of the semester that this class included students who vary widely in their familiarity with feminism, she thinks "their naiveté is boring." She is not interested in "reinventing the wheel," she says. I am eager to respond to her but also disturbed. I tell her I would like to think about it and talk with her in a few days.

As many social commentators have noted, the loss of hope that followed the 1960s and 1970s wave of social activism entailed a growing skepticism about progress. Feminist academics contributed to this skepticism by pointing out the androcentric assumptions entailed in claims about "progress."[7] Economic reforms often made men richer and women poorer. Political gains could mean an increase in male dominance. Many new health care technologies resulted in women having less control over their bodies. As a widespread and visible U.S. feminist movement waned and as increasing numbers of feminists recognized its failings, criticism of progress turned more sharply toward the movement itself. In the area of education, the assumption that second-wave ideals and practices would lead to progress was challenged by feminist academics like Jennifer Gore, who argued that feminist and other social critics ought to heed Michel Foucault's warning that "all things are dangerous." Similarly, postcolonial academics like Indira Karamcheti argued that "minority teachers" could teach more effectively through "subversion, interrogation, critique" than by evoking positive models of change.[8]

Such warnings remind teachers committed to social justice that we cannot casually assume that our work will lead to progress. We need to direct critical analysis toward both our pedagogical practices and any notion of progress that informs them. Yet a strong emphasis on criticism alone, just like practice alone, ruptures the interdependence between intellectual and political work. Criticism and political activism are put in competition. Feminists become concerned that an explicitly political pedagogy, in Wendy Brown's words, ends up "privileging the political over the intellectual." Or they fear, in Rosi Braidotti's view, that intellect will seek to "legislate" feminist political practice.[9]

From the standpoint of feminist discourse, the tendency to split intellectual and political activity undermines both feminism as a social movement and the thinking that can critically illuminate that movement. Although second-wave feminism included some strains of anti-intellectualism—such as activists who attacked thinking of any kind as patriarchal or saw academic work as standing in the way of feminist progress—the movement also laid the groundwork for a great deal of subsequent academic work. Indeed, a number of second-wave activists were or became academics whose research and teaching was thoroughly informed by their political commitments. The sense of rupture between intellectual and political work, I would argue, stems less from limits inherent in either activity than from a clash of values between the activist impulse and higher education institutions.

Academic culture remains suspicious of movements for social change, except to the extent that we as researchers and scholars seek to guide or warn against such changes. Academics, however, do not agree among ourselves about what constitutes intellectual progress. Our standards of intellectual progress are shaped by differing disciplinary backgrounds and commitments to different schools of thought as well as by our various political values. This sort of disagreement surfaces in the story I tell at the beginning of this section about the panel of feminist theorists who clash over whose theory is superior.[10] As I listen to their debate, I find myself wondering what kind of intellectual or political progress, if any, is being made through this discussion. Will it advance our understanding of feminist issues? Will it in some way contribute to feminism as a social movement?

My own motives for attending this event are somewhat less lofty than these questions suggest. I am curious about the speakers. I am eager to get a sense of them as people as well as authors. I am frankly titillated by the prospect of a contest between leading feminist theorists who espouse conflicting positions. I am also curious about where those positions might come together and what their conjunction might mean for feminist thought and action.

Some of my expectations are readily fulfilled. The presentations are brilliant. An air of competition pervades the auditorium, as the speakers point out each others' unarticulated assumptions and contradictions. These exchanges, however, seem to push the speakers farther apart. Competition gives way to greater distance. Speakers complain that their thinking is not being sufficiently respected. The prospect of their working cooperatively to find ways in which these positions complement each other, or to identify the conditions under which one theory or another might be more salient to particular feminist issues, becomes increasingly remote.

In the context of this story, what I miss is the sense that the discussants have a common political goal. I do not mean that they must agree on every political principle or strategy. Politics itself invites the articulation of many differences, and the political goal may be a very general one. But without some common beliefs and a shared commitment to social change, it is not clear why these speakers are talking to each other at all. I want to rush up to the stage and, playing the teacher, ask each one to tell us what feminism means to her. I am certain that if they described their desires for gender justice and how they see their intellectual work helping achieve it, some points of contact would emerge. I sometimes see this happen in discussions among feminist academics, when participants are able to own the connections among competing positions, to see how all their positions are contingently situated. I want such values to pervade this gathering.

I do not rule out competition or a process of setting limits to what will be included in the discourse. A speaker could argue passionately for her point of view and hope that others would come to share her position. She could point out limitations in the thinking of her rivals. The group as a whole could decide on clearly articulated grounds that they would exclude certain positions from the discussion, for instance, that it was not the time and place to take on the arguments of feminists opposed to abortion. Because such limits so often undermine social justice, however, it would be important to consider any decision as a temporary one. This cooperative debate would have many of the features that Bernice Reagon ascribes to coalition, including acknowledgment of the deep differences that divide feminists.[11] It would be conducted in the spirit of discovering how intellectual differences could contribute to needed political activism rather than focusing on which position should predominate.

As my story about Olga who wanted me to be teaching a more advanced course suggests, the problem of the relation between feminist intellectual and political progress pervades feminist teaching as well. I empathize with Olga. I feel her desire to engage with new ideas, go more deeply into old ones, and share this process with others who have the same eagerness. I see her passion as intimately connected with her feminism. She cares about these ideas because she cares about gender injustice and vice versa. In previous years, I have tried to create the kind of course she yearns for, but complicated institutional factors have stood in the way. Luckily, I have the opportunity to work with doctoral students, to both guide their work and engage with them in discussions that require a more extensive background than those that take place in our class. Olga has indicated an interest in going on for a doctorate, and we talk about how that route might provide her a more sophisticated intellectual community. However, I emphasize to her that I cannot transform this particular class into such a community or talk with her in class in a way that the other students cannot join.

Moreover, I have learned an important political and intellectual lesson from teaching these "mixed-level" classes that I see of value to Olga as well. Disciplinary communities and schools of academic thought tend to create common cultures with shared sets of assumptions that provide the framework for assessing what is considered an advance in the given area.[12] Because the students in these mixed classes come from widely different disciplines and social backgrounds, they do not share a specialized academic culture. From the standpoint of one or another kind of specialized study, many student comments and questions are "naive." Students often ask what some basic concept means or why something that seems obvious to them is not being acknowledged. Such "innocent" questions may, of course, be filled with prejudice and misinformation and can be responded to in ways that seek to identify and get students to reflect on their assumptions. Yet naive comments also may break through the pretense that we advanced students understand more than we actually do or that our assumptions can be defended at every turn. As Audre Lorde remarked, naiveté implies that we are not "programmed" to defend ourselves before we have time to explore what another speaker means.[13] In this respect, feminist discourse requires a substantial dollop of naiveté. Such discourse does not advance in a linear fashion. Rather, it frequently asks us to retrace our steps and ask where we are going. It might be described better as *widening*, because its focus fluctuates with the participants, the points of view they bring into the discussion, and the particular issues we face.

At the same time, it is still possible and necessary to think in terms of progress in feminist discourse. Discussion always requires a certain degree of focus. If I am trying to direct a discussion on the intersection of race and gender and some of the students try to change the subject, I am willing to rule their comments "out of order." I do not think we can make progress on this topic unless everyone is willing to attend to it, look at it from different perspectives, and feel and think through its meaning for them and others. Only in this way will we develop and deepen our judgments. Yet, as I have suggested earlier, my own pedagogical judgments about what is relevant to this topic and what will advance our discussion need to be viewed as contingent. My decisions about what to exclude or include in a given discussion are too easily driven by my hope and fears about its outcome. I often fail to hear a point that could enrich the discussion. In this respect, students who insist on the relevance of their point of view may, by forcing all of us to refocus and think more deeply, also contribute to our progress. The measure of that progress derives from process itself. Feminist discourse makes progress to the extent that it helps individuals and groups respond to injustice in an honest, truthful and effective way.

I am convinced by this argument, but I suspect that Olga may not be. I imagine her saying, "This is all very well, but most of the students in this class don't know what is *really* going on in the field because they are just learning to read this material." She is right, in some ways, and I feel the same frustration. During the semester that Olga takes my class, I have been attending a faculty seminar on feminist theory that captures the sense of serious intellectual play with peers that Olga is looking for. I often think about the seminar as a sort of racquetball court with many players. The ball speeds around the court, being smacked with precision by one player after another, bouncing off the wall at wild angles and keeping everyone on their toes. At the end of the seminar meetings, I am exhausted and exhilarated. I have articulated my own ideas more fully, acquired some new ideas, and seen limitations to my current thinking. In its own way, I love this game, and I do not want anyone interfering with my excitement or my hope that I will score lots of points. I think my ideas are valuable, and I want others to listen to them. I also do not want to be slowed down by clumsy beginners. No wonder Olga is impatient. Viewed in this light, I, too, can lose patience with the work of helping students acquire the background and skills they need to read complex feminist arguments.

The difference between the feminist seminar in which I am participating and the classroom in which Olga is a student echoes the distinction that María Lugones and Elizabeth Spelman make between "excelling" and "doing excellently."[14] *Excelling* means winning the game or at least being a runner-up. In the feminist seminar I describe, each player's expectation that she will win points assumes that it is also possible to lose them. If someone loses consistently, she starts to be seen as "a loser." In contrast, *doing excellently* does not create winners and losers. This way of relating assumes that if participants in a feminist project support the agency of anyone eager to join it, the project will benefit. If a newcomer lacks skills, the success of the project requires helping her get those skills. If she lacks understanding, it is each person's responsibility, as best she is able, to help cultivate that understanding.

My discussion of the role of caring in feminist discourse can be used to develop this argument. From one perspective, the problem posed by Olga is how can she be freed of caring responsibilities so that she can follow her own desires. She is like an older daughter in a houseful of children. I am the mother who asks her to help with the younger ones while she wants to be out playing with her friends. My caring work makes it possible for the other children to progress in the strength and skills needed to join in those games. I cannot easily join in games with my own peers as long as there is caring work to be done.

But, as a teacher who learns from her teaching and hopes that Olga, too, will learn from this class, I want to find an alternative way to talk about progress: an image that requires neither winners and losers nor a fixed hierarchy of carers and those needing care. The closest I can come at the moment is to follow the lead of Paula Gunn Allen as she discusses the American Indian concept of ceremonial time.[15] This notion of time, she points out, is radically different from a colonialist and imperialist idea of time, with its emphasis on productivity and individual control over the environment. Instead, American Indian ceremonial time involves a "timely movement, knitting person and surroundings into one."

In terms of feminist discourse, the concept of *timeliness* may provide a more valuable guideline than the concept of progress. Timeliness fits with the need to develop judgments about specific social justice issues that are rooted in our particular temporal and spatial realities. A person or group of people cannot respond well to those realities unless they are able to connect their thinking, experiences, feelings, and plans for action to that environment. Moreover, since the environment of social justice concerns continues to change and with it our individual life stories and group histories, the challenges to political judgment and action will change as well. As Allen's analysis implies, the Western notions of being "ahead" or "behind" in an intellectual contest may be far less relevant to feminist discourse than a developed sense of the appropriateness of a particular response to a particular situation.

My hope for Olga is that she can find a way to integrate her intellectual thirst with a kind of political collaboration that reaches beyond her academic specialty. I realize that other feminist academics are seeking to generate such collaboration and that in her own field of study, Olga may find a mentor among them. Knowing this, I feel a certain envy. I wonder what it would have been like to have had a feminist mentor. How would my teaching and writing have differed? How might it have helped me to bridge the gap with the older generation?

FEMINIST TEACHING ACROSS THE GENERATION GAP

It is 1965 and my first year of university teaching. I am one of two women who have just been hired in this virtually all-male department. A third woman who recently has retired from a job outside academia teaches part-time. She is what my father would have called an "odd duck." She is gray-haired, white-skinned, unstylish, and very outspoken. One day in a department meeting she catches me by surprise. As we are talking about the current effort to recruit a new dean, the chairman turns to my older colleague and says in a teasing tone that she probably would not be satisfied unless the new dean were a woman. "No," she replies smartly, "you're wrong. She would have to be a Negro woman." I am delighted and embarrassed by her candor.

My lover and I are leading a workshop for women on the topic of aging activists. One at a time, the women tell their stories. Suddenly in the middle of describing her years of work on reproductive rights, a woman named Maud cries out in despair. She cannot believe how her activism has been ignored by younger women. She is greatly angered by their contempt. They do not appreciate the fragility of the gains our generation has made. They refuse to join her. As the years go by, she watches her political sisters drop away because of burnout, economic pressures, illness, and death. If the younger women continue to distance themselves, she fears, she will soon be alone.

Although students keep veering away from economic inequalities, Verne has caught fire on this topic. She criticizes the text. She points to the devastating effects of economic difference. She brings in other assigned readings. She acknowledges the painful contradictions involved in her own class position. Her persistence finally enlivens the class. Some students cite their own quite different experiences as well as the text. They disagree with some of her interpretations. She listens and answers. At the end of the period, she comes up to me to tell me that she is thinking about doing further work in women's studies. Could she come and talk with me? As I nod, I say to myself, "That is what I wanted, not to be a mother but to have children of the spirit."

My delight and embarrassment as a twenty-nine-year-old teacher in the mid-1960s stem from a combination of my latent feminism and my strong desire to be accepted as a woman in academia. I have fought a number of battles to arrive at a full-time academic appointment. But I believe that the tide of history is with me. I can feel it. I am part of a small, Depression-born generation that added relatively small numbers to the labor force and produced few doctorates. I am in demand. Large universities like the one at which I recently have obtained an appointment are just beginning to face the tidal wave of children born after World War II. In response to the civil rights movement, urban riots, and other pressures for progressive change, the government is pouring money into higher education. Intimations of feminist activism are increasing.

I do not feel at home in academia, however. Although I enjoy the status of an "exceptional woman," I sense my vulnerability. At any moment "they" could take it away from me. I am relatively isolated, despite the fact that within two years I become deeply involved in campus political activities. There are few women my age and almost none who are older. My older woman colleague embarrasses me because I do not want the others, the men, to think that I am like her: unattractive and unpolished. The academics around me are quick to assess people in terms of whether young academics are rising stars. Unless they are prestigious, the oldest faculty members are often referred to as "deadwood."

Although I cannot articulate it to myself at the time, I sense a kind of competition between generations that informs my relationship with this older woman. I want to shape the definition of "woman," to challenge the misogynist stereotype of intellectual women as ugly, sexless, and graceless. She hinders my attempt to control this definition by presenting herself as what seems to me a caricature of the woman academic. She also threatens my individual style of feminism with her political pronouncements. Part of what makes me "exceptional" is my insistence on feminist principles. But I convey these principles through brief and sober statements. I am not prepared to "wave flags" or be subjected to the kind of teasing the department chairman directs at this old woman. Identifying with her might make me, too, into a joke. I am all too eager for her to disappear so that I can make my unique mark.

The advent of the feminist movement made this competition between generations more complicated. Women like me often engaged in a struggle to both collectively assert our feminism and maintain ties to our mostly nonfeminist mothers and other important members of the older generation. As the movement began to create successive generations of feminists, this competition took an even more complex turn.

Julia Kristeva's essay on the relation of women to time helps clarify this pattern.[16] Mainstream feminism, she argues, is an effort to insert women into history. Although this effort has brought about crucial reforms, it has distinct liabilities. One of these is the attempt of one generation to control the activities of the next, to use the next generation to fulfill the earlier generation's political goals. This move violates a basic premise of feminism. If feminism grows out of women's deep desires to expand and change their options in the world, any attempts to control subsequent feminist generations profoundly undermine the movement.

Kristeva's point is an important one and speaks directly to Maud's reaction in the story about the workshop for aging activists. Maud wants to see a straight line between her activism and that of the next generation. There is something to be said for such linear progress. A feminist movement that did not pay attention to the impact of its ideas and actions on the next generation, that showed no interest in the future, would suffer from an exceedingly narrow vision. Political agency requires attention to the consequences of our actions, including the consequences for those who come after. Thus, each feminist generation faces the problem of how to exercise agency without undermining its relationship to succeeding generations.

What kind of relationship should this be, and what are its implications for feminist teaching? In expressing her distress, Maud makes a series of assumptions. She thinks younger women should share her anger at the fact that full reproductive rights are still not established for all women. She expects younger women to share her analysis of women's continued lack of control over their bodies. She insists that the next generation join the activist efforts that she and other feminist pioneers initiated. Her despair includes some elements of seeking to control others. It also implies that others should feel anger at gender injustice, that they should think about how such injustice is sustained and be willing to take the risks entailed in fighting it.

I, too, have gone through periods of despair and rage about the direction that many feminists of the next generation have taken. Like Maud, I have longed to see political daughters marching to my drumbeat into the future.

I have been hurt and confused when they either ignored the work that our generation had done, turned it into some simple formula, or ridiculed it as outdated. At times, my distress has been so deep that I have not known how to put it into words. The workshop on aging activists makes this matter clear to me. Neither I nor many of my generational peers know how to talk about this issue. We have powerful feelings, but we as feminists have not developed a discourse about generational relationships.

To talk about these differences, we need to begin by paying more attention to our definitions of "the generation gap." Maud assumes that a generational difference means women young enough to be her daughters, and this familial meaning resonates in her anguished argument. As she talks, I think about how my mother's oldest sister, Sophie, who virtually raised my mother, insisted (when my mother had turned eighty and Sophie was over ninety) that my mother take care of her. Historically, relations of reciprocal caring often have tied generations of women together, and the reproaches that surface in our workshop on aging activists reflect this pattern: "We took care of you by winning many feminist battles; now you should take care of us, by supporting us and our cause."

There are many problems here. One stems from identifying generation with age. Although age frequently plays a role in defining feminist generations, it is often complemented or even overridden by other factors. Following Karl Mannheim's analysis of generations, they can be conceived of as groups of people who share common sets of historical experiences.[17] Since individuals born at the same time may have radically different social locations, they divide into what Mannheim calls "generational units." Certain historical experiences may persist over a number of generations so that members of one generational unit may have much more in common with the corresponding unit in the previous or next generation than with differently located people of their age. This point is often made by African American feminists when they note that the continued necessity of dealing with racism creates strong ties among generations in black communities.[18]

Moreover, speaking outside the framework of age, generations may be very long or very short, depending on historical circumstances. In Nancy Whittier's analysis of one feminist community, for example, feminist activists fall into generational groups of only a few years in length.[19] Some women see themselves as part of the pioneer generation, protesting and pushing for radical political changes. A few years later, a new feminist generation begins to build feminist institutions. Several years after, the next generation joins them, and so forth. Although perhaps close in chronological age, activists often define generations in terms of the movement. Their view of relations among feminist generations depends to a great extent on the historical direction they believe the movement should take: its political goals and how different strategies might serve these goals.

Like many members of the pioneer generation interviewed by Whittier, Maud feels deeply betrayed because the feminist institutions in her community do not mirror her particular feminist values and type of activism. Her community, like Whittier's, is fairly small, so that if Maud is not willing to join the main feminist organization, she remains relatively isolated. As the workshop discussion continues, however, it becomes clear that by looking beyond their local communities, other participants have been able to discover members of a new activist generation who share their values. True, the numbers may be small, but the mutual validation involved in these successor generational units keep some of these aging activists' hopes alive.

Without due caution, however, a relationship of mutual validation between generational units can become destructive. Verne's announcement (in the third story) that she wants to do further work in women's studies might delight me, but my pleasure can be misleading. Perhaps taking a degree in women's studies will not be the best choice for her. If I am not careful, perhaps the warmth I feel toward her may prevent me from paying close enough attention to the critical arguments raised by other students in the class. Perhaps I have projected too many of my own hopes onto Verne. Our cross-generational bond may help both of us survive, but its value may reside less in our similarities than in the way in which it encourages us to engage in our different kinds of feminist work.

The feminist discourse on difference that I discuss in the previous chapter usually centers on social space: how our experiences, ideas, and actions are related to our overlapping or conflicting locations. The long talk I finally have with Verne in my office suggests how our understanding of difference needs to include the dimension of time: where individuals and groups have come from, where they are heading, and how their different histories or stories contribute to political discussion.

As Verne and I exchange stories, it becomes clearer how the eras in which we were born, the state of social justice movements, and the development of women's studies as a field have brought us by different paths into the same classroom to voice our concerns about class inequities as part of feminist discourse. I came of age in the 1950s, when my responses to economic injustice were silenced by national prosperity and McCarthyite repression. Verne came of age in the 1980s, when the collapse of Eastern bloc countries and untrammeled capitalist expansion made it extremely difficult to articulate an alternative economic vision. I connected to movements for social justice in the 1960s and to feminism in the 1970s when I finally encountered a version of it that included attention to

CHAPTER 7

economic exploitation. Verne found her way to the class issue in feminism in the late 1980s, through working with a Central American women's cooperative and meeting U.S. feminists doing international work.

When I started teaching women's studies, I tell Verne, feminists of many kinds were talking about the impact of class on women's liberation (reproductive issues, racism, working conditions), and I took it for granted that class should be a part of feminist discourse. When I thought about feminist academic organizing, I drew on Adrienne Rich's vision of women in higher education uniting across class and professional lines.[20] When Verne started to take women's studies, she tells me, many of her teachers paid little attention to the socialist tradition, and she found herself becoming a sort of inside agitator to include economic issues in women's studies discussions. When she thought about feminist academic organizing, she called on a vision of global feminism developed in great part through her internet relationships with activists in other countries.

Our family stories, we acknowledge to each other, had considerable impact on our choices. My eagerness to emancipate myself from being dependent on middle-class men led me to ignore the class privileges on which my independence was built. As my lengthening career created more middle-class assets, I found myself asking what this change implied for relationships to, say, feminist friends from working-class backgrounds or women who were raising children by themselves or trying to live on welfare checks. Verne tells me that although she spent her early childhood in a white, middle-class suburb, her family lost its money because of her father's death and the discovery of his huge debts. Rather than my question about what middle-class feminists can do with their resources, her leading question is how to free poor people from their increasing burden of debt. Her global conversations focus on the relationship of women in Third World countries to the policies of the International Monetary Fund. At the end of several hours of talk, we consider whether she might pursue a doctoral degree specializing in international women's studies and what she might do with it.

When Verne leaves my office, I sit there musing. It is evening now, and the office suite has become quiet. I think about how the generation gap between us has both disappeared in the course of our discussion, when we shared similar experiences or ideas, and has opened up, when we discover that we do not share others. I can see that my initial response to Verne, as a member of a successor generation who carries forward the spirit of my teaching, is only partly true. Although white and middle-class in origin and even possibly a lesbian, she is not my younger self. We are moving in different directions, and our relationship is transient. Yet I suspect that her voice and her story will remain part of my internal dialogue and that my voice and story may remain a part of hers. I even could imagine us work-

— 210 —

ing together. In my fantasy, Verne returns to teach at my school, bringing into my life as a teacher a fresh perspective, a different angle on teaching and feminism.

As Verne and I are talking, time takes on different dimensions as well. It passes so quickly that I cannot believe that our talk has lasted this long. It slows down to accommodate our intense discussion. I realize how infrequently I have the time to talk with students as long as I would like. I think about how institutional time crowds feminist discourse into semesters and hours. I remind myself that the schedules kept by adjuncts or community college teachers create even greater pressures on them. I remember how students often race through their courses to cope with school costs and pay off the massive educational debts they are accruing. It becomes harder and harder to carve out enough feminist discourse time to share and reflect on experiences, express and discuss a wide range of feelings, explore analyses, and consider options for action. It takes a lot of time to cultivate judgments about gender justice.

Yet I do not see such discussions as a leisurely, timeless conversation about ideas. Feminist political discourse has developed around the felt need for action: around women's demands for a fair and equal place in the world, greater control over the conditions of our lives, broad social changes that benefit society as a whole, and the chance to speak and be spoken to as full citizens. The desire and need to act implies that feminist discourse is intrinsically linked to action: it contributes what it can at a given moment to individual and collective judgments. These judgments and actions cannot be deferred until feminist discourse has reached some ultimate conclusion. And action itself always requires further discourse—to interpret and assess the new experiences that arise through one or another actions, to pay attention to the feelings evoked, to think through the implications for current analyses and how they might need to be changed.

A few days after I talk with Verne about her life and her plans, our class meets again. It is difficult for me not to pay special attention to her because I feel I have come to know her so much better than the other students. As we launch again into the topic of class and gender, however, I notice new things about the other students as well. Talking with Verne has made me think more about the specific historic conditions under which each of us has encountered questions of economic inequality and their relation to gender.

I slow the speed of the discussion because I sense that some of the resistance to participating in last week's meeting stemmed from continued confusion and disagreement about the meaning of "class." I ask the students to think about a woman they know well: how they would describe her economic class and why. We talk about these various women and identify a number of problems involved in conceptualizing their class situations. We go through the text more carefully, and one of the students who remained silent last week finally grasps how she can respond to Verne. The discussion takes off again, this time with a greater number of voices taking part and being heard. I will leave this room with its discussion resonating in my mind. So, I believe, will many of the students. This prospect gives me hope and the spirit I need to keep going.

— Postscript —

WHERE CAN I GO FROM HERE?

At the last class meeting, I ask the students to join in a ritual of closure and separation. We go around the circle so that everyone who wishes to can say something about what they will be taking away with them and something about what they did not get from the course. The students and I express delight and a sense of loss as well as disappointment and anger. During this ritual we are reminded that this particular constellation of people will not come together in this way again. If these students find in feminist discourse a source of hope, they will now have to find it elsewhere. So will I.

I often feel sad at the end of a semester, even depressed. I know I will miss the students and the kind of discussions that have been developing in my classes. The sadness makes me especially conscious of how isolated the practice of teaching can be: of how much I yearn to talk to others about the puzzling, disturbing, and exciting interactions that so often take place in my feminist classrooms.

As this book demonstrates, I have spent a lot of time talking with myself about teaching. I replay classes in my head. I chew over whether I made the right or wrong move. Many times I discuss these issues with my students and engage them in helping me teach more successfully. But my relationship with a given class is transient, and my teaching practice calls out for deeper and more continuous discussion of what I am doing. For teachers committed to teaching social justice topics, this kind of discussion is not simply a good idea; it is crucial. To the extent that we see ourselves as doing political work, we need to talk with others. Politics is not an activity that can be pursued in isolation. It requires both discourse and action.

In this brief postscript, I want to describe a seminar on social justice teaching I developed to create an arena for such discourse. The idea grew out of my own pedagogical loneliness as a feminist teacher. Although I had organized and participated in numerous workshops and sessions on feminist pedagogy at conferences and meetings, I recognized in myself a need to talk with other teachers about the problems that arise on a day-to-day level and the underlying political questions they raise.

I came to this realization through a series of discussions that developed rather spontaneously with a graduate student who acted as my assistant in a large undergraduate women's studies class. Despite my long years of teaching, I never had had a teaching assistant and had no preconceptions about the role. Quite naturally, we fell into long regular talks about the course. Some of our interchanges could have been described as mentoring in the sense that I offered her advice about teaching based on my own experience. But what interested me most about our discussions was the chance to explore together what had gone on in a specific class: what teaching choices one or the other of us had made and why, what thinking, feelings, and values had played into these decisions and what implications flowed from them.

The next semester I expanded these discussions to include two adjuncts who were now teaching this course, and I soon began to imagine an ongoing seminar in which women's studies teachers from across the institution would meet to discuss our work. Just as this idea was taking shape, several other teachers of multicultural and lesbian and gay subjects approached me and asked whether they could join our discussions. For a brief time I hesitated, because this meant giving up my image of creating a haven for feminist teachers. Then I realized the extent to which this evolving seminar mirrored my own feminist teaching values. It always had been less important to me whether students considered themselves "feminist" than whether they were willing to engage in serious discussion about the issues raised by feminism and other social justice movements. So, I started the Seminar on Teaching Social Justice to promote such discussion among interested teachers.[1]

The seminar meets every other week for about two hours. Between seven and fifteen people participate each semester, including full-time faculty and doctoral students who are adjunct instructors. As the seminar grew, we developed two simple rules: *confidentiality* and *continuity*. Our concern with confidentiality grew out of our understanding that we could not treat information and judgments about our interactions with individual students in a casual manner. There were issues of institutional safety here, for both the students and ourselves. Our concern with continuity grew out of the realization that continuous attendance over at least one semester conveyed commitment to the seminar and increased the trust we felt for each other. Neither these nor other rules we discussed turned out to be simple guidelines. For example, what if someone who is clearly very committed to the seminar is assigned additional academic duties and has to miss a number of sessions? As our discussions continued, we had to talk about our relationships to each other.

Over the life of the seminar, we have engaged in a number of activities together. We exchange syllabi and articles on teaching social justice subjects, report on and attend conferences, guide the group through experiential exercises we use with students, and give advice about classroom crises that require immediate response. These activities help us to get to know each other better and to appreciate one another's strengths as teachers. By carefully attending to and discussing our stories, we are encouraged to take risks that we might not otherwise take in both the seminar and our classes. This process of validating our teaching skills and our capacity to grow even stronger as teachers plays an important role in the seminar because we usually focus on the problems we encounter in social justice teaching. It is all too tempting to view such problems as a sign of our failure as teachers rather than as intrinsic to our project of addressing political issues. We need to remind ourselves that we are only able to engage in this thinking together because the usual theories and practices of "good teaching" are not adequate to the social justice issues we face in our classrooms.

Most often, we concentrate our discussions on a particular problem that has arisen in one of our courses. We treat it as a beginning point for an in-depth discussion rather than as an issue for the individual teacher. As we talk, we gradually begin to identify a common concern we may face in our social justice teaching. We describe various teaching experiences that relate to this common problem and explore the different circumstances and values that enter into our pedagogical decision making.

Several features stand out in these discussions. One is the importance of *describing teaching problems in detail*. Details about exactly what was being done or discussed in the class, who the students are and what they said and did, what we as teachers thought and felt, or institutional factors such as the time of the semester or the other courses the students were taking all contribute to our understanding of how to approach a given teaching situation. On a deeper level, a discussion of details often requires us to reconsider how we are defining "the problem." It is tempting to assume, for example, that the pedagogical difficulty in a given class is one of student "resistance" when the problem might also be defined as one of the teacher's anger toward a student for not accepting her point of view. Such anger might well be justified (from a social justice viewpoint, it makes sense to be angry when people do not seem to care about the suffering of others), but its political and pedagogical meaning still requires reflection and discussion. Thus, it is important *what constitutes the problem*, to allow for the possibility that what we consider a social justice teaching issue may be framed and reframed a number of times throughout the discussion.

This approach entails an assumption that I see as crucial to a feminist discourse on social justice teaching: *political questions* need to take priority over *managerial questions*. By managerial questions, I mean those that focus on how to make classes run smoothly and produce the kinds of outcomes at which teachers, educational institutions, and powerful sectors of the society are aiming.[2] When we are pedagogical managers, we take our educational ends for granted and put our energy into perfecting appropriate means to reach those ends. Of course, management is a basic feature of all teaching in the sense that teachers need a clear vision of what they want to accomplish and the skills to work toward that end. Teaching social justice is no different in this respect. But social justice teaching also requires that teachers continuously reflect on the values that underlie our work, on the practices of the institutions for which we teach and the social forces that impact on those institutions and the people in them. When as teachers we assume that we already know the nature of a given pedagogical problem, we risk shortcutting the political and ethical questions that our social justice approach should be rendering problematic.

For example, the discourse on teaching social justice that has evolved in our seminar has focused not on how to get students to respect our authority as teachers of social justice subjects but on how we understand our own authority. To what ends do we exercise or fail to exercise it in classrooms? How do we feel about that authority? How do the students respond to it? How do differences in race, gender, class, and political values between ourselves and our students affect interpretations of our authority? How is our authority affected by the kind of institutions in which we teach and our locations within them? Such discussions require us to articulate our basic assumptions about social justice and about teaching, as well as to make connections between our individual stories and the social structures that help to shape them.

Like the feminist classroom discourse I have described in this volume, our seminar talk invites a good deal of "personal" disclosure. Without such disclosure it is impossible to describe in detail and discuss the issues that arise in classroom practice. If it turns out that a teacher is very angry that a student voices certain opinions or refuses to comply with certain assignments, the problem cannot be grasped until we talk about anger toward students, not only the anger of the particular teacher toward a particular student but the anger we may each feel from time to time in response to situations that arise in social justice teaching. Where does this anger come from? What does it mean? What does it indicate about ourselves and how we are dealing with our classes?

Talking about experiences in which we as teachers are angry, frightened, or ashamed renders us very vulnerable. This may be why we do it so rarely. Such vulnerability grows out of both our individual histories and the institutional contexts in which we are talking with each other. Thus, the same questions concerning safety and self-disclosure that pervade feminist classroom discourse also shape our seminar discussions of teaching practice. In the seminar, too, individuals make choices about what to reveal to our colleagues based on expectations about what might happen to us in this particular institutional setting, our relationships outside that setting (whom might we betray?), and the level of trust we have developed with each other.

The logic of sharing experiences and feelings also applies to our discussions of social justice teaching. For participants to be willing to speak from experience and feelings, we must assume that others will do the same and that such expressions will be treated with respect for the speaker. We analyze our experiences not from a position of superiority but from one of *mutual vulnerability*. We all hold assumptions that we can reflect on critically. Some of these assumptions may reveal substantial differences and disagreements among us, despite our common commitment to social justice teaching. One member of the seminar may value caring over equality or vice versa. Another may value harmonious social relations over the development of individuality. We may all honor knowledge and the search for truth, but we may weigh truths differently as we seek to develop politically and pedagogically sound judgments. We may all have been touched by social justice movements that have emerged over the past thirty or forty years, but our different relations to various of these movements might lead us to emphasize one or another set of political priorities.

This process of talking with colleagues about social justice teaching does not always run smoothly. The narration of experience may operate to squelch analysis. Analysis may be used to discredit the description of experience. Relations of authority may serve to undermine as well as support equality and trust. Differences of race, class, gender, sexual orientation, and age among teachers may all create tensions that shape the direction of our discussions. Caring needs generated by our discourse may remain unacknowledged and unmet and influence the discussion on a subterranean level. The relation between our relatively smooth-flowing discussion and the "outside world" may be seen as problematic because in other settings our frank and open discussion of teaching practices seems dangerous or utopian. Compared to the social justice issues that keep emerging outside that classroom, our talk about teaching may seem trivial. Yet the outside world is never far away.

Our discussions inevitably lead to talking about the institutional and other structures of power that affect our lives as teachers. If we are discussing a crisis of authority for a teacher of color in relation to a predominantly white class or a white teacher in relation to a class that includes many students of color, we must talk about the impact of institutionalized racism on the project of teaching social justice subjects. If we focus on a teacher's safety in such classrooms, we need to ask, Who studies and teaches there? Is the teacher new to the institution or an old hand? Is she part-time or full-time, on a tenure line or tenured? In what field does she teach? How do such factors shape what she or others consider norms for her teaching? In our seminar, we have had not only teachers in a variety of positions in the same institution but teachers who have taught in a wide variety of higher and other institutional settings. This factor enables us to attend to a range of institutional constraints, as well as to the meaning of wider political and economic trends, such as the increased use of part-time teachers or cutbacks in public higher education, on our teaching.

We also have addressed the relation between our seminar and the outside world by developing "open workshops" to which teachers who do not belong to the seminar have been invited to attend. Although so far our group has offered only two of these workshops, they promise to expand our discussions.

When we offer an open workshop, we begin by briefly describing our seminar process. Then we demonstrate it by talking with each other about a particular classroom problem. In meetings before the open workshop, we have identified a classroom situation with which we want to begin. But we do not rehearse the discussion. We let the discourse evolve as it does in our regular meetings, with all the jagged edges, the pauses, the miscommunications, and the diversions that accompany our talk. After we talk this way for a while, we invite any audience members who wish to do so to join us. We try to leave time at the end of the workshop to talk about its process.

Discussing our social justice teaching in front of a group of other teachers raises some very important questions. To begin with, the open workshops increase vulnerability and raise the question of "safety" to a new level. Although as individuals we may not reveal the same or as much about ourselves as we do in our less public discussions with each other, we must be willing to engage in some degree of self-revelation to demonstrate our discussion process. On the surface, this would seem an easy thing to do, because so far we have offered our workshops to people whom we view as sympathetic to our broader social values. But the moment we expose our process to others who have not been a part of it, we face greater challenges.

For instance, sometimes members of our audience respond to our personal revelations, our descriptions of teaching experiences and the feelings and meanings that accompany them, by personalizing our problems and giving us advice. From the standpoint of the seminar, the difficulty here is not that the advice is bad or good but that it rests on the assumption that the given teaching problem stems from the individual teacher's failings rather than representing pedagogical issues that our seminar needs to address. Just as early proponents of consciousness-raising insisted that their process was not "therapy" (i.e., devoted to solving individual problems), we try to convey to our audience the value we attach to exploring the larger social justice questions implicit in our individual teaching problems.

While we attempt to teach our audience, they also teach us. A group of any kind tends to perpetuate certain assumptions that support its continuity and coherence. Whatever tensions and disagreements may emerge among us, the members of our seminar tend to develop our own culture. Insiders may easily minimize disagreement. Outsiders, who though sympathetic to our purposes are not a part of this culture, more readily question our assumptions. Some of these may be political. For instance, someone in the audience who espouses a nationalistic politics questions what appears to be our dismissal of nationalism. Someone else may question the belief expressed by many seminar members about the centrality of "experience" in social justice teaching. Still another person in the audience may question an institutional condition we take for granted by pointing out that in her small college, the teachers could not possibly engage in such self-revelatory discussion because it would render individuals too vulnerable in their already intimate environment.

Such questioning forces us to clarify our thinking and values and begins to bridge the gap between our seminar and the "outside world." It may bridge this gap temporarily through outsiders joining our discussion during the period of the open workshop. Or the bridge may be made on another level if a former audience member ends up becoming a seminar member or the seminar members continue discussing the challenge to our assumptions after the open workshop is over.

The process of "outsiders" raising questions to seminar members assumes a fundamentally respectful and friendly relationship between outsiders and seminar members. Yet this assumption has limits as well. To expose any political discussion to a larger and larger audience increases the possibility of genuine attack, not merely the questioning of assumptions but the attempt to undermine speakers. In academia, undermining often takes the form of delegitimation, in particular the charge that an individual is an incompetent academic. But it can be interwoven with other political or economic factors bearing, for example, on the prospects of being reappointed or getting promoted that might make it especially difficult for part-time teachers or junior faculty to speak honestly about their teaching. Thus, members of the seminar have real reason to fear the increased vulnerability that "going public" with our process entails.

When our seminar members talked about the issue of vulnerability before the first of our open workshops, I was struck by the similarity between our concerns and the concerns about performance that had been voiced by members of the feminist theater ensemble to which I belong. In both cases, performance renders individual members and the group as a whole increasingly vulnerable to criticism from others who might judge us either in terms of values we already hold or in terms of values quite different from our own. That judgment might be useful in improving our work, but it also might be personally and, in the case of the academic context in particular, professionally damaging. In both groups, members have to figure out as best we can how to protect each other and the integrity of the group without suppressing the vitality of spirit that each of us brings to the performance. We have to figure out how to let outsiders into our performance, to allow their responses to what we are doing inform our efforts, without losing the focus on our particular performative task. We do not always succeed in doing this well, of course, especially since in both cases we are relative beginners. Yet, when the seminar or the ensemble manages to achieve a balance between protecting the expression of individual members and preserving the integrity of the group, between keeping a focus on the group task and allowing the responses of "outsiders" to permeate and redefine our boundaries, we are on our way to developing a new mode of discourse on politics and pedagogy.

At the beginning of a new century, there is nothing self-evident about how to pursue social justice. The problems of knowledge, power and authority, caring, safety, difference, and whether we can maintain hope for change permeate the global environment as thoroughly as they permeate a feminist classroom or a seminar devoted to social justice teaching. Neither feminist discourse nor a discourse on teaching social justice can provide final answers. They can only, at best, provide some wisdom to guide us in whatever choices we have the opportunity to make. Some of the most important of these choices concern how we treat each other, as members of a class, a seminar, or a common world.

A common world needs to be created and re-created rather than taken for granted. It is a fragile project that can quickly disintegrate under the pressures of fear, greed, hatred, and ignorance. We teachers committed to teaching social justice have a lot of work ahead of us without any guarantees of success. Although I see this as a realistic assessment, it is not a counsel of despair. Work of any kind offers us a chance to make our individual and collective marks on the world. If we work collaboratively, we can learn from, support, and enjoy each other. If we are successful, we can celebrate our accomplishments. If we do not quite achieve everything we had hoped to, we can remind ourselves that we are simply humans, not angels, and that out of our multifaceted and contradictory humanity our best teaching grows.

Notes

INTRODUCTION

1. The long list of resources on teaching in higher education includes Barbara Gross Davis, *Tools for Teaching* (San Francisco: Jossey-Bass, 1993); Wilbert J. McKeachie, *McKeachie's Teaching Tips: Strategies, Research, and Theory for College and University Teachers*, 10th ed. (Boston: Houghton Mifflin, 1999); C. Roland Christensen, David A. Garvin, and Ann Sweet, eds., *Education for Judgment: The Artistry of Discussion Leadership* (Boston: Harvard Business School Press, 1991); and publications such as *The Teaching Professor*.

2. Current discussions of participatory democracy and citizenship often take as their reference point Benjamin Barber's *Strong Democracy: Participatory Politics for a New Age* (Berkeley: University of California Press, 1984), which clearly seems inspired by U.S. grassroots organizing in the civil rights, new left, and feminist movements of the 1960s. See also John S. Dryzek, *Discursive Democracy: Politics, Policy, and Political Science* (Cambridge: Cambridge University Press, 1990); Gayatri Chakravorty Spivak and David Plotke, "A Dialogue on Democracy," *Socialist Review* 24, no. 3 (1994): 1–22; James Bohman, *Public Deliberation: Pluralism, Complexity and Democracy* (Cambridge, Mass.: MIT Press, 1996); Amy Gutmann and Dennis Thompson, *Democracy and Disagreement* (Cambridge, Mass.: Belknap Press, 1996); Seyla Benhabib, ed., *Democracy and Difference: Contesting Boundaries of the Political* (Princeton, N.J.: Princeton University Press, 1996); and Nancy Fraser, *Justice Interruptus: Critical Reflections on the "Postsocialist" Condition* (New York: Routledge, 1997). Many feminist discussions of participatory democracy take as a reference point the work of Hannah Arendt. See, for example, Patricia Moynagh, "A Politics of Enlarged Mentality: Hannah Arendt, Citizenship, Responsibility, and Feminism," *Hypatia* 12, no. 4 (Fall 1997): 27–53 (special issue: "Citizenship in Feminism: Identity, Action, and Locale," ed. Kathleen B. Jones), as well as the other excellent essays in that volume.

3. Laurel N. Tanner's reflections on the "Lab School" (*Dewey's Laboratory School: Lessons for Today*, foreword by Philip W. Jackson [New York: Teachers College Press, 1997]) contain interesting accounts of the school's theory and practice. Dewey's vision for this school is conveyed through his essays *The Child and*

the Curriculum and *The School and Society* (Chicago: University of Chicago Press, 1956), first published in 1902 and 1900, respectively.

4. The dominant values concerning gender in that period were dramatically criticized by Betty Friedan in her groundbreaking book *The Feminine Mystique* (New York: Norton, 1963) and described in their social context by Wini Breines in *Young, White, and Miserable: Growing up Female in the Fifties* (Boston: Beacon, 1992). As Breines points out, however, this dominant imagery entailed white middle-class assumptions. Alternative paths were being carved out by black women, including black lesbians (see Audre Lorde, *Zami: A New Spelling of My Name* [Watertown, Mass.: Persephone, 1982]), cultural rebels (see Hettie Jones, *How I Became Hettie Jones* [New York: Dutton, 1990]) and working-class women with socialist ideas (see Vivian Gornick, *The Romance of American Communism* [New York: Basic, 1977]). Even within the world of mainstream middle-class white women, there were important stirrings of dissatisfaction and the beginnings of activism, as evidenced in Jane S. Gould's autobiography, *Juggling: A Memoir of Work, Family and Feminism* (New York: Feminist Press, 1997).

5. The "Hutchins B.A." at the University of Chicago had been abandoned just before I entered the college in 1954, but the "great books" courses and philosophy of an integrated curriculum were still in place, as was the unconventional student population. Robert M. Hutchins's argument for educational reform is spelled out in *The Higher Learning in America* (New Haven, Conn.: Yale University Press, 1936), and the history of the Hutchins College is described in William H. McNeill, *Hutchins' University: A Memoir of the University of Chicago, 1929–1950* (Chicago: University of Chicago Press, 1991).

6. In a series of essays, Anselm and I discussed the main ideas of the Chicago school of sociology with which he was identified and that in many ways shaped my thinking. See, for example, Berenice M. Fisher and Anselm L. Strauss, "Interactionism," in *A History of Sociological Analysis,* ed. Tom Bottomore and Robert Nisbet (New York: Basic, 1978), 457–98. I was drawn to George Herbert Mead's symbolic interactionism and John Dewey's philosophical pragmatism because of their down-to-earth quality and emphasis on understanding the viewpoints of others. I also was attracted to the value placed on building community, the attempt to see beyond binary oppositions, and the orientation toward process and change. As I note later, I had and continue to have strong reservations about the tendency in these theories to bypass questions of unequal power, including but not confined to the area of gender. In both philosophy and sociology, feminists have been exploring the potentials of the interactional tradition for feminist thought and research. See, for example, Mary Jo Deegan and Michael R. Hill, eds., *Women and Symbolic Interaction* (Boston: Allen & Unwin, 1987), and Charlotte Haddock Seigfried, *Pragmatism and Feminism: Reweaving the Social Fabric* (Chicago: University of Chicago Press, 1996).

7. Such work included Kate Millett's landmark book, *Sexual Politics* (New York: Avon, 1970); Charlotte Bunch's essays in the Washington-based journal *Quest* (some of which were reprinted in her volume, *Passionate Politics: Feminist Theory in Action* [New York: St. Martin's, 1987]; and Robin Morgan's edited collection, *Sisterhood Is Powerful: An Anthology of Writings from the Women's Liberation Movement* (New York: Random House, 1970).

NOTES

8. Heidi Hartmann's essay "The Unhappy Marriage of Marxism and Feminism: Towards a More Progressive Union," in *Women and Revolution: A Discussion of the Unhappy Marriage of Marxism and Feminism,* ed. Lydia Sargent (Boston: South End, 1981), 1–41, suggests the strains involved in trying to develop an analysis that embraced the thinking of both social movements. For a sense of this important (but, in the United States, too often neglected) political project, see Karen V. Hansen and Ilene J. Philipson, eds., *Women, Class, and the Feminist Imagination: A Socialist-Feminist Reader* (Philadelphia: Temple University Press, 1990). Areas of convergence between different feminist positions are also often neglected. As Carol Anne Douglas notes in *Love and Politics: Radical Feminist and Lesbian Theories* (San Francisco: ISM Press, 1990), radical and socialist feminist politics sometimes overlap on both a theoretical and practical level. Though considering myself a socialist feminist, I kept turning to radical feminists for their clear and powerful indictment of male domination (see Anne Koedt, Ellen Levine, and Anita Rapone, eds., *Radical Feminism* [New York: Quadrangle, 1973]), to the emerging group of black feminists for their analysis of race and gender (see, e.g., Audre Lorde's earlier pieces in *Sister Outsider: Essays and Speeches* [Trumansburg, N.Y.: Crossing, 1984]), and to the pages of *Quest* for a radical lesbian feminist discussion of the intersection of sexual orientation, class, and gender. Jewish feminist consciousness-raising sessions at the National Women's Studies Association pushed me to think more deeply about the relations among religion, ethnicity, and gender.

9. See Florence Howe, "Women and the Power to Change," in *Women and the Power to Change,* ed. Florence Howe (New York: McGraw-Hill, 1975), 127–71; Howe's account of the impact of the civil rights movement on her teaching in "Mississippi's Freedom Schools: The Politics of Education" (1964) in her *Myths of Coeducation: Selected Essays, 1964–1983* (Bloomington: Indiana University Press, 1984), 1–17; and the special anniversary issue of *Women's Studies Quarterly* 25, nos. 1 & 2 (Spring/Summer 1997), "Looking Back, Moving Forward: 25 Years of Women's Studies History," ed. Elaine Hedges.

10. As the anniversary issue of *Women's Studies Quarterly,* "Looking Back, Moving Forward," indicates, women's studies first developed in the United States in a wide variety of liberal arts settings. Relatively little has been written about the history of women's studies in professional schools, where feminist faculty have had to evolve distinct strategies for incorporating questions of gender justice. I have long suspected that faculty devoted to preparing students for women-predominant professions encounter special problems in bringing feminist thinking and research into the curriculum—problems linked to concerns about the legitimacy of women-predominant fields within higher education, to the pressures and restrictions stemming from state credentialing requirements, and to the particular ways in which homophobia are manifest in women-predominant environments.

11. In addition to Robert M. Hutchins, *The Higher Learning in America,* see Hutchins, *The Conflict in Education in a Democratic Society* (New York: Harper, 1953); Mortimer J. Adler, *Reforming Education: The Opening of the American Mind,* ed. Geraldine Van Doren (New York: Macmillan, 1977); and Adler, *The Conditions of Philosophy: Its Checkered Past, Its Present Disorder, and Its Future*

Promise (New York: Atheneum, 1965). In *Hutchins' University*, William McNeill presents a rather highly critical picture of the reforms promoted by these men.

12. See Richard McKeon, "Dialogue and Controversy in Philosophy," in *Freedom and History, and Other Essays: An Introduction to the Thought of Richard McKeon*, ed. Zahava K. McKeon, with an introduction by Howard Ruttenberg (Chicago: University of Chicago Press, 1990), 103–25.

13. In addition to our joint writings on the Chicago school cited in note 5, see accounts of Strauss's classroom teaching and collaborative research style in Anselm L. Strauss, *Qualitative Analysis for Social Scientists* (Cambridge: Cambridge University Press, 1987). As an individual student working primarily with historical material, I had a somewhat different experience of his teaching, although he brought the same pedagogical spirit to his guidance of my work.

14. Criticisms of higher education in the 1960s proceeded in two directions simultaneously: toward revealing the limits and hidden educational agendas being promoted by capitalism (e.g., Samuel Bowles and Herbert Gintis, *Schooling in Capitalist America: Educational Reform and the Contradictions of Economic Life* [New York: Basic, 1977]) and toward creating new educational forms that were intended to cultivate participatory democracy (e.g., Michael Rossman's *On Learning and Social Change* [New York: Random House, 1972]). Paulo Freire's *Pedagogy of the Oppressed* (New York: Herder & Herder, 1971) offered a theory for the literacy education of adults that was then applied by critical academics like Ira Shor to higher education. See his *Critical Teaching and Everyday Life* (Boston: South End, 1980).

15. Ella Baker's career, political philosophy and impact on younger activists are described in essays by Ellen Cantarow, with Susan Gushee O'Malley and Sharon Hartman Strom, *Moving the Mountain: Women Working for Social Change* (Old Westbury, N.Y.: Feminist Press, 1980); Charles Payne, "Ella Baker and Models of Social Change," *Signs* 14, no. 4 (1989): 885–99; Barbara Omolade, *The Rising Song of African American Women* (New York: Routledge, 1994); and Joanne Grant, *Ella Baker: Freedom Bound* (New York: Wiley, 1998).

16. Berenice Fisher, "What Is Feminist Pedagogy?" *Radical Teacher* 18 (1981): 20–24. In the process of writing this essay, I visited the Highlander Folk School and spoke with founder Myles Horton about education for social change. On Highlander's work with labor, community, and civil rights organizers, see John Matthew Glen, *Highlander: No Ordinary School, 1932–1962* (Lexington: University Press of Kentucky, 1988).

17. Barbara Scott Winkler, "Raising C-R: Another Look at Consciousness-Raising in the Women's Studies Classroom," *Transformations, a Resource for Curriculum Transformation and Scholarship: The New Jersey Project Journal* 8, no. 2 (Fall 1997): 66–85.

18. *Women's Ways of Knowing: The Development of Self, Voice, and Mind*, by Mary Field Belenky, Blythe McVicker Clinchy, Nancy Rule Goldberger, and Jill Mattuck Tarule (New York: Basic, 1986), takes off from the argument that Carol Gilligan made in *In a Different Voice: Psychological Theory and Women's Development* (Cambridge, Mass.: Harvard University Press, 1982), but it shifts the focus from the contribution that women (given our generally different responsibilities

and experiences from men) could make to questions of social justice to how women's experiences suggest a deeper understanding of creative learning. One early collection, *Learning Our Way: Essays in Feminist Education,* ed. Charlotte Bunch and Sandra Pollack (Trumansburg, N.Y.: Crossing, 1983), suggests how closely some second-wave educational theory was linked to activism. Another early anthology, *Gendered Subjects: The Dynamics of Feminist Teaching,* ed. Margo Culley and Catherine Portuges (Boston: Routledge & Kegan Paul, 1985), includes a range of theories and practices. Only a few feminists have paid attention to the ways in which diverse feminist viewpoints might lead to different interpretations of education: see Sandra Acker, "Feminist Theory and the Study of Gender and Education," *International Review of Education* 33, no. 4 (1987): 419–35; and Gaby Weiner, *Feminisms in Education: An Introduction* (Buckingham, England: Open University Press, 1994). In general, feminist writing about education either assumes a single feminist viewpoint on education or pluralizes "feminist pedagogy" without exploring very fully how "feminist pedagogies" differ.

19. Daphne Patai and Noretta Koertge, *Professing Feminism: Cautionary Tales from the Strange World of Women's Studies* (New York: Basic, 1994). See also Christina Hoff Sommers's even more pugilistic attack on what she takes to be feminist pedagogy in *Who Stole Feminism? How Women Have Betrayed Women* (New York: Simon & Schuster, 1994). The contradictions involved in these critiques are skillfully revealed by Elizabeth Kamarck Minnich in "Feminist Attacks on Feminisms: Patriarchy's Prodigal Daughters," *Feminist Studies* 24, no. 1 (Spring, 1998): 159–75.

20. For an overview of postmodern and poststructuralist themes in feminist thinking, see Jane Flax "Postmodernism and Gender Relations in Feminist Theory," in *Feminism/Postmodernism,* ed. Linda J. Nicholson (New York: Routledge, 1990), 39–62. Although the varieties of postmodern and poststructuralist thinking seem endless, they tend to be associated with the theoretical work of French intellectuals like Michel Foucault, Jacques Derrida, and Jean François Lyotard and the critique of the eighteenth-century enlightenment and liberalism. Feminist and other activists concerned with the conservative implications of some postmodern criticism sometimes distinguish between "right" and "left" postmodern thought. Cynthia Kaufman provides a useful left and feminist interpretation in "Postmodernism and Praxis: Weaving Radical Theory From Threads of Desire and Discourse," *Socialist Review* 24, no. 3 (1994): 57–80. Feminist postmodern or poststructuralist educational theory certainly belongs to the left category, because it preserves an orientation toward achieving gender justice. See, for instance, Jennifer M. Gore, *The Struggle for Pedagogies: Critical and Feminist Discourses as Regimes of Truth* (New York: Routledge, 1993), and essays in Carmen Luke and Jennifer Gore, eds., *Feminisms and Critical Pedagogy* (New York: Routledge, 1992). By the late 1990s, increasing numbers of feminist academics were trying to find a way between second-wave and postmodern or poststructural analyses. See, for example, Susan Leigh Foster, "Choreographies of Gender," *Signs* 24, no. 1 (Autumn 1998): 1–33; and Elizabeth Wingrove, "Interpellating Sex," *Signs* 24, no. 4 (Summer 1999): 869–93.

21. For an example of feminist academics struggling with the question of

criticism, see Natalie Zemon Davis et al., "Feminist Book Reviewing (a Symposium)," *Feminist Studies* 14, no. 3 (Fall 1988): 601–22.

22. I met Barbara Deming in the early 1980s at a meeting to discuss the impact of the women's peace protests at Greenham Common, England, on U.S. activism, and I had the privilege of marching with her in women's peace protests in the United States. Her long activist history is sketched out in *We Are All Part of One Another: A Barbara Deming Reader,* ed. Jane Meyerding, with a foreword by Barbara Smith (Philadelphia: New Society, 1984). I was moved by her deep commitment to nonviolent social action and to telling one's truth simply and clearly, even to those who might be seen as enemies.

23. I first encountered Gestalt psychotherapy through working with New York City psychotherapist Jane Vern in the mid-1970s. Rather than focusing on Fritz Perls's technique of developing a dialogue between an internal "top dog" and "underdog," Vern helped me explore the multiple internal voices that comprised my inner and often barely conscious conversations. For the theoretical basis on which Gestalt therapy was constructed, see Frederick S. Perls, Ralph F. Hefferline, and Paul Goodman, *Gestalt Therapy: Excitement and Growth in the Human Personality* (New York: Julian, 1951). Although a number of feminists have remarked on the importance of internal or internalized voices to our thinking about political issues, the relationships among such voices is subject to debate. As Naomi Scheman points out in "Though This Be Method, Yet There Is Madness in It: Paranoia and Liberal Epistemology" in *Engenderings: Constructions of Knowledge, Authority, and Privilege* (New York: Routledge, 1993): 75–105, acknowledging internal multivocality does not tell us how such voices should relate to each other. How feminists answer this question depends partly on the degree of integration among voices we consider possible or desirable. Norma Alarcón cautions that the struggle with internalized discourses with which women of color must constantly engage contradicts the dominant white feminist assumption that these voices must add up to a single unified self; see her "The Theoretical Subject(s) of *This Bridge Called My Back* and Anglo-American Feminism," in *Making Face, Making Soul/Haciendo Caras: Creative and Critical Perspectives by Feminists of Color,* ed. Gloria Anzaldúa (San Francisco: Aunt Lute, 1990), 356–69. Feminists also differ in their appraisal of how oppressive or liberatory our internalized voices calling for activism may be. Susan Griffin's piece "The Way of All Ideology" in *Feminist Theory: A Critique of Ideology,* ed. Nannerl O. Keohane, Michelle Z. Rosaldo, and Barbara C. Gelpi (Chicago: University of Chicago Press, 1982), 273–92, suggests that the voice of political correctness about what we should be thinking, feeling, and doing as feminists can itself begin to oppress important aspects of our "denied" selves. M. Jacqui Alexander and Chandra Talpade Mohanty argue that the voice of our political consciousness can help internally colonized women develop "non-hegemonic selves" that work to achieve both internal and external decolonization. See the introduction to their edited volume *Feminist Genealogies, Colonial Legacies, Democratic Futures* (New York: Routledge, 1997). Finally, it seems valuable to look at the extent to which the cultural context of activism supports or denigrates internalized multivocality. Karen McCarthy Brown provides a provocative account of multiple voices in Haitian spiritual practice in *Mama Lola: A Vodou Priestess in Brooklyn* (Berkeley: University of California Press, 1991).

24. My introduction to movement improvisation came through teachers at the Laban/Bartenieff Institute of Movement Studies and Movement Research in New York City—in particular, Paulette Sears, Robert Dunn, and Simone Forti. My transition into dramatic improvisation was prompted by Gestalt psychotherapeutic work with Jane Vern, workshops in psychodrama, study with Ruth Zaporah, and the Groupe Boal in Paris (see next note). The feminist theater ensemble, Shock of Gray, is directed by Stephanie Glickman, who draws heavily on the improvisational techniques of Joseph Chaiken's Open Theater. I am grateful to Karen K. Humphrey for calling my attention to the early connection between Gestalt psychotherapy and theater in "Theater as Field: Implications for Gestalt Therapy," *Studies in Gestalt Therapy* 8 (1999): 172–81.

25. See Augusto Boal, *Theater of the Oppressed*, trans. Charles A. and Maria-Odilia Leal McBride (New York: Urizen, 1979). For a description of my encounter with Boal's work, see "Feminist Acts: Women, Pedagogy, and Theatre of the Oppressed," in *Playing Boal: Theatre, Therapy, Activism,* ed. Mady Schutzman and Jan Cohen-Cruz (London: Routledge, 1994). My experience of adapting some of his techniques to my feminist teaching is described in "The Heart Has Its Reasons: Feeling, Thinking, and Community-Building in Feminist Education," *Women's Studies Quarterly* 21, nos. 3 & 4 (Fall/Winter 1993): 75–87.

26. In the words of its biannual newsletter, The Crystal Quilt, Inc., is a "nonprofit, feminist community-based organization that brings women together for cultural and educational programs." The name was inspired by Adrienne Rich's poem "Toward the Solstice," in *The Dream of a Common Language: Poems 1974–1977* (New York: Norton, 1978). Linda Nathan Marks founded the Crystal Quilt in 1981, shortly before we became life partners. The multimedia workshops I created for the Crystal Quilt are described in "Enhancing Feminist Pedagogy: Multimedia Workshops on Women's Experience with the Newspaper and Home," in *The Feminist Teacher Anthology: Pedagogies and Classroom Strategies,* ed. Gail E. Cohee et al. (New York: Teachers College Press, 1998), 98–113.

27. Donald Schön, *The Reflective Practitioner: How Professionals Think in Action* (New York: Basic, 1983). Also see Deborah P. Britzman, *Practice Makes Practice: A Critical Study of Learning to Teach* (Albany: State University of New York Press, 1991), on the theory–practice split among and within university disciplines.

28. Elizabeth Ellsworth's piece, "Why Doesn't This Feel Empowering? Working through the Repressive Myths of Critical Pedagogy," was originally published in the *Harvard Educational Review* 59, no. 3 (August 1989): 297–324, and reprinted in a number of anthologies on education and social (including feminist) change. It is frequently mentioned in support of criticisms of 1960s and 1970s critical and feminist pedagogies as being inadequately or undertheorized, in particular with respect to the actual position of the teacher (institutional, racial, class, etc.) in relation to her students.

29. Feminist academics have worked on curriculum reform on many fronts, including the justification and development of interdisciplinary women's studies and discipline-based feminist curricula. Elizabeth Kamarck Minnich's *Transforming knowledge* (Philadelphia: Temple University Press, 1990) proposes a philosophical

foundation for both kinds of curricular reforms. Anthologies such as Christie Farnham, ed., *The Impact of Feminist Research in the Academy* (Bloomington: Indiana University Press, 1987), and Cheris Kramarae and Dale Spender, eds., *The Knowledge Explosion: Generations of Feminist Scholarship* (New York: Teachers College Press, 1992), suggest how feminists have sought to change the curriculum in specific fields. Liza Fiol-Matta and Mariam K. Chamberlain, eds., *Women of Color and the Multicultural Curriculum: Transforming the College Classroom* (New York: Feminist Press at the City University of New York, 1994), demonstrate the impact of movements for antiracist and multicultural teaching on the conceptualization of women's studies curricula. The question of a feminist approach to textual interpretation has been pursued most ardently by feminist academics in literary fields. Judith Fetterley's *The Resisting Reader: A Feminist Approach to American Fiction* (Bloomington: Indiana University Press, 1978) is a classic in this area, as are Barbara Christian, *Black Women Novelists: The Development of a Tradition, 1892–1976* (Westport, Conn.: Greenwood, 1980), and Elaine Showalter, ed., *The New Feminist Criticism: Essays on Women, Literature, and Theory* (New York: Pantheon, 1985).

30. Kathleen Weiler's early study, *Women Teaching for Change: Gender, Class and Power* (South Hadley, Mass.: Bergin & Garvey, 1988), examines the experiences of feminist teachers in high schools. On feminists teaching in higher education, see Frances A. Maher and Mary Kay Thompson Tetreault, *The Feminist Classroom* (New York: Basic, 1994); Becky Ropers-Huilman, *Feminist Teaching in Theory and Practice: Situating Power and Knowledge in Poststructural Classrooms* (New York: Teachers College Press, 1998); Frances L. Hoffmann and Jayne E. Stake, "Feminist Pedagogy in Theory and Practice: An Empirical Investigation," *NWSA Journal* 10, no. 1 (Spring 1998): 79–97. Cheryl L. Sattler, *Talking about a Revolution: The Politics and Practice of Feminist Teaching* (Cresskill, N.J.: Hampton, 1997), compares the ideas and practices of secondary school and academic teachers. Although she does not frame her discussion in terms of feminist teaching, Michelle Fine in "Sexuality, Schooling, and Adolescent Females: The Missing Discourse of Desire," *Harvard Educational Review* 58, no. 1 (February 1988): 29–53, suggests an approach to sex education that stresses the importance of supporting discourse on sexuality that empowers developing women.

31. Feminist academics continue to develop theories and practices of feminist teaching for a wide range of disciplines. See, for example, April Laskey Aerni and KimMarie McGoldrick, eds., *Valuing Us All: Feminist Pedagogy and Economics* (Ann Arbor: University of Michigan Press, 1999); and Maralee Mayberry, "Reproductive and Resistant Pedagogies: The Comparative Roles of Collaborative Learning and Feminist Pedagogy in Science Education," in *Meeting the Challenge: Innovative Feminist Pedagogies in Action*, ed. Maralee Mayberry and Ellen Cronan Rose (New York: Routledge, 1999), 1–22.

32. I see these vignettes functioning in a manner somewhere between case studies, fiction, and thought experiments. Like a case selected for study (say, in legal or business education), they are an account based in experience. Like many novelists, I also have created characters and situations out of my experiences. I have transformed my experiences to respect my relationships to individual students

(which was not one of researcher-subject) and to emphasize what to me was the key question or contradiction in a particular type of classroom interaction. I have felt free, as in philosophical thought experiments, to imagine perplexing situations to explore their consequences for my argument. But I have tried to keep my stories truthful by always asking myself whether such-and-such an incident or response really could have happened in one of my classes. In some instances, I have drawn on my memory of actual events, but in these stories I do not name and describe individual actors as I do in the strictly fictional vignettes. On a technical level, I have referred to class lists for my women's studies courses from 1982 to the time I have submitted this manuscript for publication in order not to employ the names of actual students. Because these lists do not cover my earlier women's studies classes and my efforts to cross-check names with the manuscript may be subject to error, the attempt to avoid actual student names may not be completely effective. In the vignettes concerning other teachers, specific characters also are entirely invented, although some feminist teachers may share the names I have assigned these characters.

33. Cohee et al., eds., *The Feminist Teacher Anthology,* and the *Women's Studies Quarterly* 21, nos. 3 & 4 (Fall/Winter 1993), include many examples of teaching strategies. So do general essays on teaching social justice, like bell hooks, *Teaching to Transgress: Education as the Practice of Freedom* (New York: Routledge, 1994), and books devoted to specific aspects of teaching social justice subjects, like Katherine J. Mayberry, ed., *Teaching What You're Not: Identity Politics in Higher Education* (New York: New York University Press, 1996).

34. The role of male teachers in women's studies proves both problematic and interesting. See, for example, essays in Katherine J. Mayberry, ed., *Teaching What You're Not,* including J. Scott Johnson, Jennifer Kellen, Greg Seibert, and Celia Shaughnessy, "No Middle Ground? Men Teaching Feminism," 85–103; Craig W. Heller, "A Paradox of Silence: Reflections of a Man Who Teaches Women's Studies," 228–37; and Gary L. Lemons, "'Young Man, Tell Our Stories of How We Made It Over': Beyond the Politics of Identity," 259–84. Also see Stephen R. Marks's thoughtful reflections on teaching a sociology of gender course in "The Art of Professing and Holding Back in a Course on Gender," in *Family Relations* 44, no. 2 (April 1995): 142–48. The male students who sign up for my women's studies/feminist classes tend (as best I can tell from their speech, writings, and actions) to be motivated by the desire to sort out personal issues (especially relationships with women), to understand better their own sexuality (usually gay or bisexual men or men who are uncertain of their orientation), to understand better gender issues being raised in their professional field (e.g., educational administration or counseling), to understand gender images and problems presented by the media and/or in general conversation, and, occasionally, either to fulfill a credit requirement or to have the opportunity to attack feminists and/or women. Feminist teachers facing classes filled with apathetic, resentful, and/or aggressive male students may require a feminist pedagogy quite different from the one I propose here.

35. Iris Marion Young's analysis of the structural features of oppression is contained in her *Justice and the Politics of Difference* (Princeton, N.J.: Princeton University Press, 1990), 39–65. In "Culture, Political Economy, and Difference: On

Iris Young's *Justice and the Politics of Difference*," Nancy Fraser points out how promising Young's distinctions are for analyzing the differences among gender, racial, class, and other forms of oppression in *Justice Interruptus,* 189–205. I would add that we also need to look at the different meanings of these "faces" of oppression. For example, "violence" may mean the violence involved in rape, the violence suffered by working in unhealthy or unsafe work environments, the violence experienced by not having enough to eat, as well as the violence of being treated as though one were less than human. Because the political resonance of these terms changes over time, such explorations can be particularly complex. This point applies to not only the language of gender but that of racial and other oppressions. In my use of terms such as *Asian American, African American, black, white,* or *people of color,* I want to acknowledge that ongoing political discussions accompany the use of such expressions and that none remains unproblematic.

36. Juliet Mitchell, *The Longest Revolution: Essays on Feminism, Literature, and Psychoanalysis* (London: Virago, 1984).

CHAPTER 1

1. Betty Friedan's discussion of women's education in *The Feminine Mystique* (New York: Norton, 1963) combines an indictment of female and male college and university educators for not taking women students of the 1950s seriously. Friedan's criticism also aims at middle-class, white suburban women for yielding to the temptations of what Friedan sees as an intellectually shallow and dependent life. She is equally hard on some versions of progressive education, in particular the contemporary life adjustment movement that sought to give students skills to cope with everyday life. She expresses contempt for techniques like role playing and the inclusion of personal and emotional material in class. From her standpoint, women's adjustment to their lives is a problem, not a solution. Friedan's famous predecessor, Mary Wollstonecraft, made her case for women's educational equality in *A Vindication of the Rights of Women,* ed. Miriam Brody Kramnick (Middlesex, England: Penguin, 1975), first published in 1792.

2. Carol Gilligan's groundbreaking research, *In a Different Voice: Psychological Theory and Women's Development* (Cambridge, Mass.: Harvard University Press, 1982), has its counterpart in the work of feminist educational philosopher Nel Noddings's *Caring: A Feminine Approach to Ethics and Moral Education* (Berkeley: University of California Press, 1984). The values associated with what feminist theorists sometimes call "the ethic of care" weave in and out of many feminist educational arguments. In her *The Dialectic of Freedom* (New York: Teachers College Press, 1988), Maxine Greene both incorporates and suggests the limits of these values in her vision of women's liberation as part of a communally oriented "'existential project.'"

3. See bell hooks, *Teaching to Transgress: Education as the Practice of Freedom* (New York: Routledge, 1994); Patricia Hill Collins, *Black Feminist Thought: Knowledge, Consciousness, and the Politics of Empowerment* (Boston: Unwin Hyman, 1990); Michèle Foster, "Constancy, Connectedness, and Constraints in the Lives of African-American Teachers," *NWSA* Journal 3, no. 2 (Spring 1991): 233–

61; and her *Black Teachers on Teaching* (New York: New Press, 1997). Gloria T. Hull and Barbara Smith indicate that renewed black feminist interest in black women as learners and teachers developed the confluence of the black liberation and women's liberation movements. See their introduction to Gloria T. Hull, Patricia Bell Scott, and Barbara Smith, eds., *All the Women Are White, All the Blacks Are Men, But Some of Us Are Brave: Black Women's Studies* (Old Westbury, N.Y.: Feminist Press, 1982).

4. The character and meaning of social movements have long been the topic of debate among social science researchers and theorists. Sociologists have looked at the relative importance of consciousness, self-interest, human and material resources, identity formation, and ethical values in the mobilization and development of such movements. For a sense of the feminist contribution to these debates, see Myra Marx Ferree's "The Political Context of Rationality: Rational Choice Theory and Resource Mobilization," as well as related articles in *Frontiers in Social Movement Theory*, ed. Aldon D. Morris and Carol McClurg Mueller (New Haven, Conn.: Yale University Press, 1992), 29–52. Many theorists argue that movements for social justice can play a critical role in bringing about genuine democracy and social justice, but relations among such movements (e.g., should a movement for economic justice take precedence over others?) and how they should proceed (e.g., should they collaborate with capitalist or governmental structures?) remains the subject of continued disagreement. For discussion of the political meaning of feminism and other "new social movements" (an expression often used to describe the social justice movements of the 1960s and beyond), compare Chantal Mouffe, "Feminism, Citizenship and Radical Democratic Politics," in *Feminists Theorize the Political,* ed. Judith Butler and Joan W. Scott (New York: Routledge, 1992), 369–84, with Nancy Fraser, "Multiculturalism, Antiessentialism, and Radical Democracy: A Genealogy of the Current Impasse in Feminist Theory," in Fraser, *Justice Interruptus: Critical Reflections on the "Postsocialist" Condition* (New York: Routledge, 1997), 173–88.

5. The range of articles in Myra Marx Ferree and Patricia Yancey Martin, eds., *Feminist Organizations: Harvest of the New Women's Movement* (Philadelphia: Temple University Press, 1995), suggests some of these complexities, including how feminists have divided not only along the lines of social identity (race, class, sexual orientation being the most often cited) but in terms of their involvements in one or another kind of political work, including grassroots organizing, building complex organizations, and confronting or attempting to work with the state and with nonfeminist women's groups. Ferree and Yancey also argue that to a great extent, second-wave feminism transformed into a movement that operated through a series of organizations. This formulation makes social movement sense of projects like feminist teaching. On feminist movements in various national contexts, see Amrita Basu, ed., *The Challenge of Local Feminisms: Women's Movements in Global Perspective* (Boulder, Colo.: Westview, 1995). As the title of this latter volume suggests, the relation between "feminist movements" and "women's movements" remains ambiguous. When the early second-wave expression "women's liberation movement" was shortened to "women's movement," this change not only dulled the expression's radical edge but led to greater confusion between

NOTES

feminist movements that by definition seek some form(s) of gender justice and women's movements that may seek other types of social justice or may not be seeking justice at all (such as fascist women's movements). Yet, as Mary Pardo points out in "Doing It for the Kids: Mexican American Community Activists, Border Feminists?" in *Feminist Organizations*, ed. Ferree and Martin, 356–71, the feminist/women's movement distinction often dissolves on closer inspection. Celene Krauss's research on women activists in the movement against dumping toxic waste in residential neighborhoods suggests the wide variety of ways in which gender identities and categories can function to support or impede the activism of women from different racial/ethnic groups and, therefore, where gender justice may not or may be seen as part of the social problem. See her "Women of Color on the Front Line," in *Race, Class, and Gender: An Anthology*, 3rd ed., ed. Margaret L. Andersen and Patricia Hill Collins (Belmont, Calif.: Wadsworth, 1998), 540–51. One additional issue relevant to the definition of feminism as a social movement concerns when a given movement begins and when it is over. With regard to the social justice movements that gained public attention in the 1960s, some activists argued that the movements only lasted as long as their most visible or radical (by one or another definition) periods, while others have stressed the continuity of social movements, including those periods in which activists continue their work without very much or any public visibility. My theory of feminist teaching draws on the latter interpretation, although I recognize that claims about what counts as "the movement" and what figures or actions are included in the effort to trace its continuity are open to considerable debate. For a sense of the complexities bearing on this question, see Verta Taylor and Leila J. Rupp, "Lesbian Existence and the Women's Movement: Researching the 'Lavender Herring,' " in *Feminism and Social Change: Bridging Theory and Practice*, ed. Heidi Gottfried (Urbana: University of Illinois Press, 1996), 143–59, as well as *Feminist Organizations*, ed. Ferree and Martin.

6. See Gloria Anzaldúa, ed., *Making Face, Making Soul/Haciendo Caras: Creative and Critical Perspectives by Feminists of Color* (San Francisco: Aunt Lute Books, 1990). In her introduction, Anzaldúa, who has herself played a leading role in giving the voices of feminists and lesbians of color a wider hearing, emphasizes how differences in power and privilege (in particular, as shaped by racism) impact on who gets to speak where and who is heard by whom. She also argues for thinking in terms of a multiplicity of movements, rather than a single movement. Although I have chosen to use the formulation "feminist movement" to emphasize the necessity and possibility of women who identify as feminists talking with each other, there are many contexts in which it may be more useful to think in terms of a series of overlapping (and often conflicting) movements. The line between these two ways of conceiving feminism can be as blurry as the line between feminist and women's movements.

7. Garth Boomer et al., eds., *Negotiating the Curriculum: Educating for the 21st Century* (London: Falmer, 1992). I am indebted to Becca Chase for calling this book to my attention. Together with Becca and other members of the Seminar on Teaching Social Justice described in the postscript to this book, I have wrestled with the question of what is and is not negotiable in the curriculum. In the end, I

— 234 —

believe the answer for teachers of social justice subjects relies as much on belief as on knowledge. That is, unless I am able to sustain my belief that it is worthwhile engaging in teaching that focuses on gender and other forms of injustice, I have no "bottom line" from which to negotiate. Although students may contribute to that belief, they also can undermine it. This is yet another reason that the kind of feminist teaching I describe requires the support of a social movement and does not simply emerge as the result of individual, pedagogical choice making.

8. See John Dewey, *Democracy and Education: An Introduction to the Philosophy of Education* (New York: Free Press, 1966), and *The Public and Its Problems* (Chicago: Swallow, 1927). Gramsci's educational writings can be found in *Selections from the Prison Notebooks of Antonio Gramsci*, ed. and trans. Quintin Hoare and Geoffrey Nowell Smith (New York: International Publishing, 1971). Paulo Freire's *Pedagogy of the Oppressed,* trans. Myra Bergman Ramos (New York: Herder & Herder, 1971), should be read along with his later writings, such as *The Politics of Education: Culture, Power, and Liberation*, trans. Donaldo Macedo with an introduction by Henry A. Giroux (South Hadley, Mass.: Bergin & Garvey, 1985). Ira Shor's *Empowering Education: Critical Teaching and Social Change* (Chicago: University of Chicago Press, 1992) and Henry A. Giroux's *Schooling and the Struggle for Public Life: Critical Pedagogy in the Modern Age* (Minneapolis: University of Minnesota Press, 1988) continue Freire's project by developing critical social justice pedagogies. For an educational reading of Dewey, Gramsci, and Freire that favors Gramsci's thought in developing a feminist adult education, see Diana Coben, *Radical Heroes: Gramsci, Freire, and the Politics of Adult Education* (New York: Garland, 1998). Also see Jeanne Brady, *Schooling Young Children: A Feminist Pedagogy for Liberatory Learning* (Albany: State University of New York Press, 1995), for a feminist application of Freirean thinking to elementary education. Kathleen Weiler locates the effort to develop a feminist pedagogy in its context of social justice movements and points to the limits of Freire's original theory as a basis for feminist teaching in her "Freire and a Feminist Pedagogy of Difference," *Harvard Educational Review* 61, no. 4 (November 1991): 449–74. However, feminist teachers also have integrated the work of one or another of these thinkers into their own. See, for example, bell hooks's discussion of the influence of Freire's writing on her own feminist pedagogy in *Teaching to Transgress*, 6ff.

9. Although the expression *second wave* or *second-wave feminism* had become fairly widespread among feminists and activists by the 1980s, its meaning remains ambiguous. Sometimes the term is used by feminists to situate U.S. and other feminist movements in relation to the nineteenth-century movements for women's rights whose leaders are seen as "foremothers." Sometimes the term is used to imply that the feminist wave of the 1960s and 1970s has been superseded by "post-feminist" realities. Sometimes second-wave feminism is differentiated from the activities of "third-wave" feminists who became involved in the 1980s and 1990s and who variously built on and criticized their second-wave predecessors. Nancy F. Cott, *The Grounding of Modern Feminism* (New Haven, Conn.: Yale University Press, 1987), which treats the U.S. feminist "wave" of the 1920s, suggests how dividing feminism into such waves necessarily involves historical assumptions. Despite these complexities, I have decided to use the expression *second wave*

NOTES

because I have not encountered one that better represents the activism of the 1960s through at least the early 1980s.

10. For portraits of the 1950s atmosphere of repression and attempts to confront it, see I. F. Stone, *The Haunted Fifties* (New York: Random House, 1963), and Ellen Schrecker, *Many Are the Crimes: McCarthyism in America* (Boston: Little, Brown, 1998). Although academics continue to debate the causes and locus of blame for the political purges of the fifties, there seems little question that they made any discourse on social justice highly problematic.

11. Ella Baker's impact on the student civil rights movement and its subsequent meaning for black feminists is described in Barbara Omolade, "Ella's Daughters," in Omolade's *The Rising Song of African American Women* (New York: Routledge, 1994), 161–77. For a series of interpretations of the social justice movements of the 1960s, including a sense of how political talk operated or failed to operate, see Sohnya Sayres, Anders Stephanson, Stanley Aronowitz, and Frederic Jameson, eds., *The 60s without Apology* (Minneapolis: University of Minnesota Press, 1984). Alice Echols argues for the need to reinterpret the feminist and other sixties movements in "'We Gotta Get Out of This Place': Notes toward a Remapping of the Sixties," *Socialist Review* 92, no. 2 (April–June 1992): 9–33. Some of these movements eventually produced guidelines and handbooks to help activists to talk with each other. In addition to the writing on consciousness-raising cited later, see for example, Gracie Lyons, *Constructive Criticism: A Handbook* (Oakland, Calif.: Issues in Radical Therapy, 1976); Virginia Coover, Ellen Deacon, Charles Esser, and Christopher Moore, *Resource Manual for a Living Revolution*, 2d ed. (Philadelphia: New Society Press, 1978); Karen Brandow, Jim McDonnell, and Vocations for Social Change, *No Bosses Here! A Manual on Working Collectively and Cooperatively*, 2d ed. (Boston: Alyson and Vocations for Social Change, 1981); Joanna Rogers Macy, *Despair and Personal Power in the Nuclear Age* (Philadelphia: New Society, 1983); and Charlene Eldridge Wheeler and Peggy L. Chinn, *Peace and Power: A Handbook of Feminist Process* (New York: National League for Nursing, 1989). As these citations suggest, U.S. activists (including feminist activists) clearly drew on a variety of contemporary sources in developing their notions of political talk. In addition to the models social justice movements offered each other (e.g., the civil rights emphasis on community-based discussions and the peace movement's emphasis on consensus), other influences often mentioned are the national liberation movements that developed after World War II (in particular, Mao Tse-tung's Chinese communist movement) and Kurt Lewin's theory and practice of group dynamics. Kathie Sarachild, Juliet Mitchell, and other early radical feminists note the influence on consciousness-raising of Mao's approach of urging oppressed peasants to "speak bitterness." Ann Popkin also mentions the influence of both the Chinese revolutionary model and the impact of the black liberation movement in "The Personal Is Political: The Women's Liberation Movement," in *They Should Have Served That Cup of Coffee: 7 Radicals Remember the 60s*, ed. Dick Cluster (Boston: South End, 1979), 183–222. Lewin's group dynamics fed directly into organizing methods through institutions like the Highlander Folk School, which Rosa Parks had attended prior to her historic refusal to move to the back of the bus in Montgomery, Alabama. Lewin's social philosophy and

— 236 —

practice is described in Alfred J. Marrow, *The Practical Theorist: The Life and Works of Kurt Lewin* (New York: Teachers College Press, 1977).

12. Given the enormous impact of consciousness-raising on the lives of women who were or became active in second-wave feminism, there is surprisingly little description of how consciousness-raising actually functioned in various groups. My own discussions with women who participated in such groups suggest considerable variation. Memoirs and feminist fiction also offer various accounts. See, for example, Maureen Brady's novel, *Give Me Your Good Ear* (New York: Spinsters, 1979), and its valuable afterword by Bonnie Zimmerman. Barbara Epstein, "Ambivalence about Feminism," 124–48; Priscilla Long, "We Called Ourselves Sisters," 324–37; and Shirley Geok-lin Lim "'Ain't I a Feminist?' Re-forming the Circle," 450–66, point to the failures of consciousness-raising in *The Feminist Memoir Project: Voices from Women's Liberation,* ed. Rachel Blau DuPlessis and Ann Snitow (New York: Three Rivers, 1998). Nancy Azara and Roxanne M. Green, "Working with the Light: Women of Vision," 33–42, and other contributors to *Feminist Foremothers in Women's Studies, Psychology, and Mental Health,* ed. Phyllis Chesler, Esther D. Rothblum, and Ellen Cole (New York: Harringon Park, 1995) indicate the important role played by consciousness-raising in their subsequent activities as feminists. Among academics, the greatest interest in consciousness-raising seemed to have developed among feminist psychologists who saw a therapeutic potential in this process. Such research also suggests that as consciousness-raising became more widespread in the 1970s, its original political impulse often became obscured by an emphasis on the personal rather than on the personal-political connection. See Diane Kravitz, "Consciousness-Raising Groups in the 1970's," *Psychology of Women Quarterly* 3, no. 2 (Winter 1978): 168–86, for an analysis of this shift.

13. African American activist Cellestine Ware, who belonged to one of the early radical feminist groups, expressed both approval of consciousness-raising, for its power to politicize women, and criticism of the process, for its failure to promote a sufficiently intellectual, activist, and antiracist politics. See Cellestine Ware, *Women Power: The Movement of Women's Liberation* (New York: Tower, 1970).

14. The *NOW Guidelines for Feminist Consciousness-Raising* (Washington, D.C.: National Organization for Women, 1983) were first published in 1975 and expanded over the years to include material on men's consciousness-raising (NOW always has been a mixed organization), race, and other topics. Although this booklet includes a good deal of material that derives from and overlaps earlier consciousness-raising statements, the process it describes draws heavily on socialization theory and is oriented toward getting women to recognize the degree to which they have been gender socialized. It is also oriented toward recruiting women to become active in NOW. The distinction between NOW's approach to consciousness-raising and the early radical feminist approach has blurred over the years. A flyer for a 1998 consciousness-raising workshop cosponsored by the Gainesville Women's Liberation and the Florida State branch of NOW quotes Kathie Sarachild's goals for consciousness-raising.

15. Kathie Sarachild's piece, "A Program for Feminist Consciousness-Raising," was reprinted in *Feminist Revolution,* ed. Redstockings (New York: Ran-

dom House, 1978), 202–03, together with other essays related to consciousness-raising by Sarachild, Barbara Leon, Anne Forer, Carol Hanisch, and Ellen Willis. Like a number of second-wave feminists, Sarachild substituted a matronymic or woman-identified name for her patronymic, Amatniek. At times in her writing, she put the term *class* in quotation marks, indicating both the contribution of Marxist thought to radical feminist analysis and the rejection of that thought as an adequate framework for feminist activists. This move, like a good deal of description of consciousness-raising, hints at the large, underlying questions for which consciousness-raising did not supply ready-made answers. See also Ellen Willis's essay "Radical Feminism and Feminist Radicalism," in *The 60s without Apology*, ed. Sayres, Stephanson, Aronowitz, and Jameson, 91–118, in which she points to the differing "political and philosophical assumptions" that feminist activists brought to their political discussions. Most interesting from the standpoint of my notion of feminist discourse, Willis (a one-time member of the radical feminist group Redstockings) remarks that "there was an unarticulated assumption that we could work out our differences solely within a feminist framework and ignore or agree to disagree on other political issues" (95). I am struck by Willis's points, first, that there were political differences for consciousness-raising to resolve and, second, that to make more progress feminist discourse had to go beyond the confines of its own movement and assumptions. This, as Willis notes, included the need to confront the heterosexist prejudices that became increasingly evident in the speech and writings of some radical feminists. In reaction to this heterosexism, some lesbians formed their own consciousness-raising groups.

16. Pamela Allen, *Free Space: A Perspective on the Small Group in Women's Liberation* (New York: Times Change, 1970). Alice Echols, in her account of consciousness-raising in relation to radical feminist political struggles, notes that Allen's interpretation focused more on the need for personal empowerment and Sarachild's more on the need to develop an analysis to support feminist activism (see Echols, *Daring to Be Bad: Radical Feminism in America, 1967–1975* [Minneapolis: University of Minnesota Press, 1989], 74–92). Although Echols's work is very helpful in setting consciousness-raising in its political and historical context, any simple typology of consciousness-raising styles seems insufficient. For instance, in some ways the difference between Sarachild's and Allen's approaches reflects the former's commitment to what some radical feminists called the "pro-women" line. In that analysis, women's responses to oppression were viewed as conscious and often realistic decisions (e.g., about whether to leave an abusive husband) in contrast to an analysis that stressed "brainwashing" or internalized oppression—a feature of oppression emphasized by Allen. Yet, while Allen stressed the need for women to empower themselves intellectually and emotionally, she also paid serious attention to the value of political analysis as a collective process.

17. Sarachild's notion that consciousness-raising could provide scientific grounding for feminist activism echoes those strains within the Marxist tradition that emphasize the need to first develop a scientific analysis on which to base political organizing and action. But the radical feminism that Sarachild and others were creating also drew on contemporary new left critiques of party elites who based their programs on theory alone rather than on the voices and actions of the op-

pressed. See English Marxist E. P. Thompson's *The Poverty of Theory and Other Essays* (New York: Monthly Review Press, 1978). For the background of this critique of scientism in radical movements, see Lorraine Cohen's study of Rosa Luxemburg, "Reinterpreting Rosa Luxemburg's Theory of Social Change: Consciousness, Action and Leadership" (Ph.D. dissertation, City University of New York, 1987). Grassroots activists of the 1960s continuously sought ways to make scientific analysis inclusive, interactive, and contingent. As women from different backgrounds became involved in feminist activism, the notion that consciousness-raising could produce scientific results in any simple sense of that term became increasingly debatable. This discussion continued in another form when feminist academics sought to give a political account of their research methods. See Gottfried, ed., *Feminism and Social Change,* in particular pieces by Sherry Gorelick "Contradictions of Feminist Methodology," 23–45; Judith Stacey, "Can There Be a Feminist Ethnography?" 88–101; and Nancy Naples with Emily Clark, "Feminist Participatory Research and Empowerment: Going Public as Survivors of Childhood Sexual Abuse," 160–83.

18. A process of critiquing consciousness-raising and exploring the possibilities of resolving its contradictions was implicit in the writings of second-wave feminists such as Charlotte Bunch. See her *Passionate Politics,* 27–45 and 81–92.

19. The meaning of "consciousness" as attention, awareness, perception, and/or knowing varies greatly with different political and intellectual contexts, any of which is potentially relevant to developing an interpretation of "consciousness-raising." Bernard J. Baars, *In the Theater of Consciousness: The Workspace of the Mind* (New York: Oxford University Press, 1997), describes consciousness as "the publicity organ of the brain . . . a facility for *accessing, disseminating, and exchanging information* and for *exercising global coordination and control*" (7). This interpretation also leaves room for "fringe consciousness," as a sort of penumbra that involves "feelings of knowing" but not "detailed, structured experiences." More than the psychoanalytic distinction between conscious and unconscious, this gray area between attention and inattention, awareness and nonawareness, seems to me a crucial locus for consciousness-raising. Sandra Lee Bartky's *Femininity and Domination: Studies in the Phenomenology of Oppression* (New York: Routledge, 1990) points to the origins of much political discussion of consciousness in Marx's analysis of the contradiction between existing social relations and emerging material conditions. Paying attention to the contradiction between social relations and the realities of daily life enables oppressed groups to understand and resist domination. For Bartky, however, women's consciousness of their oppression leads less readily to a clear analysis of unjust social relations than to what she calls "anguished consciousness," in which women face an intense confusion about who they are and what they should be doing, and in which the answers to their questions cannot be known in advance. If consciousness is identified with attention, this confusion can be seen as stemming from our paying attention to contradictory social relations for which there is no clear or uniform resolution, because they point to conflicting desires among and within various women (e.g., the question of how child care can and should be arranged).

20. See Jane O'Reilly, *The Girl I Left Behind* (New York: Macmillan, 1980). Although Reilly's image of consciousness-raising as a "click" gained popular currency, virtually no attention was paid to her accompanying observation: "Every time I get my consciousness raised, I find another, stubborner, layer beneath" (169) or to her description of the "clunk"—that is, the backsliding, depression, and so forth, at discovering that there are no magic solutions. "Clicks are enraging and stimulating and tend to strengthen us for the task of making straight the path of reform. The trouble is, we tend to forget that the path is not very well marked" (170).

21. Friedan, *The Feminine Mystique*. Although I have found some of her work problematic, Mary Daly courageously pioneered the effort to reconceptualize gender justice and injustice through renaming women's experiences of oppression and liberation. See her book with Jane Caputi, *Webster's First New Intergalactic Wickedary of the English Language* (San Francisco: HarperCollins, 1994).

22. Patrocinio P. Schweickart makes an important case for the value to feminist discourse of active listening in "Speech Is Silver, Silence Is Gold: The Asymmetrical Intersubjectivity of Communicative Action," in *Knowledge, Difference, and Power: Essays Inspired by* Women's Ways of Knowing, ed. Nancy Rule Goldberger, Jill Mattuck Tarule, Blythe McVicker Clinchy, and Mary Field Belenky (New York: Basic, 1996), 305–28. Also see Susan J. Bickford, *The Dissonance of Democracy: Listening, Conflict, and Citizenship* (Ithaca, N.Y.: Cornell University Press, 1996).

23. My emphasis on the role of judgment in consciousness-raising fits with an ongoing feminist discussion about the potential and limits of Jürgen Habermas's theory of communicative action (also called "discourse ethics" or "communicative ethics") for feminist political thought and action. See Jürgen Habermas, *Moral Consciousness and Communicative Action* (Cambridge, Mass.: MIT Press, 1990) and *Justification and Application: Remarks on Discourse Ethics*, trans. Claran Cronin (Cambridge, Mass.: MIT Press, 1993). In contrast to philosophers such as Alasdair MacIntyre (*After Virtue: A Study in Moral Theory* [Notre Dame, Ind.: University of Notre Dame Press, 1984]), who stress the importance of shared values as the basis for political discussion and collective action, Habermas has argued for the potential of cooperatively conducted rational discourse to provide a process through which quite differently situated people can reach agreement. For a very useful description and interpretation of Habermas, in relation to communitarian thinkers such as McIntyre, see William Rehg, *Insight and Solidarity: A Study in the Discourse Ethics of Jürgen Habermas* (Berkeley: University of California Press, 1994). For some of the current debates on this issue, see Ellen Frankel Paul, Fred D. Miller Jr., and Jeffrey Paul, eds., *The Communitarian Challenge to Liberalism* (Cambridge: Cambridge University Press, 1996). Feminist philosophers Seyla Benhabib and Nancy Fraser have pointed out how Habermas's argument for the universality of discourse results in erasing what Benhabib calls "concrete, embodied selves" and what Fraser points to as the differences among publics that must interpret their own needs. See Seyla Benhabib, *Situating the Self: Gender, Community and Postmodernism in Contemporary Ethics* (New York: Routledge, 1992), and Nancy Fraser, *Unruly Practices: Power, Discourse, and Gender in*

Contemporary Social Theory (Minneapolis: University of Minnesota Press, 1989). Also see Iris Young's critique of Habermas in *Throwing Like a Girl and Other Essays in Feminist Philosophy and Social Theory* (Bloomington: Indiana University Press, 1990), 102*ff.* I am particularly struck by Ruth Lister's comment that for feminists who have drawn on Habermas's theory, "the point of such dialogue is not to arrive at agreement on 'the' general interest but instead to promote the development of view and the exercise of judgment, having taken into account different viewpoints" (14) in "Dialectics of Citizenship," in *Hypatia* 12, no. 4 (Fall 1997): 6–26 (special issue: "Citizenship in Feminism: Identity, Action, and Locale," ed. Kathleen B. Jones).

24. Hannah Arendt's theory of action also features reciprocity between speakers, who disclose their identities through political talk, and their fellow citizens, who listen to and interpret this talk. Both feminist and other academics who have been drawn to Arendt's political theory point to the tension within it between a heroic model of politics (in which actors disclose and display their unique qualities) and a participatory one (in which actors create community). My rereading of consciousness-raising more resembles the participatory dimension of Arendt's argument although it includes elements of both models. See Arendt, *The Human Condition* (Chicago: University of Chicago Press, 1958); and for a range of feminist interpretations of her work, Bonnie Honig, ed., *Feminist Interpretations of Hannah Arendt* (University Park: Pennsylvania State University Press, 1995), in particular, Mary G. Dietz, "Feminist Receptions of Hannah Arendt," 17–50, and Hanna Fenichel Pitkin, "Conformism, Housekeeping, and the Attack of the Blob: The Origins of Hannah Arendt's Concept of the Social," 51–81.

25. See Sarachild, "A Program for Feminist Consciousness-Raising," in *Feminist Revolution*, ed. Redstockings, 202–03. Alice Echols suggests that the radical feminist emphasis on consciousness-raising stood in an uncomfortable relation to direct action; see Echols, *Daring to be Bad*, 85–86. In this same period, I encountered both activists who were caught up in the need to act regardless of meaning or consequences of their actions and activists who were unwilling to act until they had worked out a complete analysis of the situation. Whatever ambiguities persist concerning the definition of *action,* I see consciousness-raising as an attempt to find a way between the two extremes of action-for-its-own-sake and action-fully-governed-by-analysis.

26. Anita Shreve makes the idea of a click central to her interpretation of consciousness-raising in *Women Together, Women Alone: The Legacy of the Consciousness-Raising Movement* (New York: Viking, 1989). The image of consciousness-raising as an instant "click" resembled the comparison sometimes made between consciousness-raising and religious conversion and to the later feminist criticism (which emerged in the 1980s under the influence of Michel Foucault's theory of disciplinary power) that consciousness-raising required a kind of "confession." Although it seems likely that confession (both in the form of coerced speech and of catharsis) played some role in the consciousness-raising experiences of some women, the attempt to reduce this process to cathartic confessions erases important features and ignores its ongoing quality. Charlotte Bunch, among others, noted that consciousness-raising is "an unending process" (see *Passionate Politics*, 32).

27. Carol Hanisch's "The Personal Is Political" was originally published in 1969 and reprinted in *Feminist Revolution*, ed. Redstockings, 204–05. In this piece, she defends consciousness-raising groups from the charge of "therapy" that was being leveled by feminist and nonfeminist activists. One of the major points at issue was whether consciousness-raising spoke to merely "personal problems" that could be solved on an individual level. "One of the first things we discover in these groups," writes Hanisch, "is that personal problems are political problems. There are no personal solutions at this time. There is only collective action for a collective solution" (204). Consciousness-raising, she argues, was an important form of action, because women (like blacks and workers) tended to blame themselves for their situation. As "political therapy," through which women would develop an understanding of their oppression, consciousness-raising enabled women to "stop blaming ourselves." Until this was accomplished, Hanisch argues that the attempt to create "alternative life-styles" (she put this expression in quotes) could not succeed. Nor would it be possible to understand why so many women, despite their oppressed situation "don't want to do action. Maybe there is something wrong with the action or why the action is necessary is not clear enough in our minds" (205). In subsequent feminist discussions, the terms *personal* and *private,* like the terms *political* and *public,* often have been conflated. In exploring these distinctions, Patricia J. Williams (*The Alchemy of Race and Rights* [Cambridge, Mass.: Harvard University Press, 1991]) eloquently describes how "the personal" involves the self and the personality for which privacy may be both a protection and a prison. "I share the lawyerly resistance," she writes, "to the windy, risky plain of exposure that the 'personal' represents. I am just as fearful of my own personality having been put into public debates as my critics are of theirs" (91). The term *public* often embraces far more than what is normally considered "political," but as Nancy Fraser and others have argued, feminism as a social movement contributes to the continuous redefinition of both these terms (see Fraser, "Women, Welfare, and the Politics of Need Interpretation," in *Unruly Practices,* 144–60).

28. Sheila Rowbotham talks about the importance of paying attention to the "minutia" of daily life for developing a consciousness in her socialist feminist analysis, *Woman's Consciousness, Man's World* (Middlesex, England: Penguin, 1973), and *The Past Is Before Us: Feminism in Action Since the 1960s* (Boston: Beacon, 1989). In contrast to the United States, socialist movements and parties in other English-speaking countries and western Europe have provided a central location within and against which feminist activists have worked out their thinking and practices. On the ambiguous consequences for feminism of the late twentieth-century crisis in socialist thought and practice, see Nanette Funk and Magda Mueller, eds., *Gender Politics and Post-Communism: Reflections from Eastern Europe and the Former Soviet Union* (New York: Routledge, 1993).

29. See Fraser, "Women, Welfare, and the Politics of Need Interpretation," in *Unruly Discourses,* 144–60. In this piece Fraser points out that "the public sphere of discourse" as conceived by Jürgen Habermas is not adequate to the discussion of the needs of different segments of the population. This requires, among other things, social movements (e.g., feminism) that can offer and contest need interpretations. Although such movements may succeed in putting certain needs on the

political agenda, they are still open to debate—as well as co-optation by experts, reformers, state agencies and the like.

30. See Aída Hurtado, "Relating to Privilege and Political Mobilization: Toward a Multicultural Feminism," in Aída Hurtado, *The Color of Privilege: Three Blasphemies on Race and Feminism* (Ann Arbor: University of Michigan Press, 1996), 1–44. The emphasis in this argument on surviving racial and class oppression also invites discussion about how strategies for survival differ among poor and working-class women and men. See Katie Geneva Cannon, *Katie's Canon: Womanism and the Soul of the Black Community* (New York: Continuum, 1995), on religious and ethical dimensions of black women's survival. In discussions among lesbians of different colors and classes, I have been struck by how often interracial and intergenerational partnerships virtually force lesbians into a posture of political resistance to assure the survival of the relationship. Also see Adriana Hernández's argument that the public/private distinction needs to be explored rather than assumed in feminist pedagogy in *Pedagogy, Democracy, and Feminism: Rethinking the Public Sphere* (Albany: State University of New York Press, 1997), a study of the Madres of Argentina as an oppositional group. Magda Gere Lewis, *Without a Word: Teaching beyond Women's Silence* (New York: Routledge, 1993), observes that women often lack privacy *within* their homes and that for her going to graduate school gave her some private space. Ideas about what constitutes "privacy" and how much women expect or demand clearly differ cross-culturally. See, for instance, Isabel Fonseca, *Bury Me Standing: The Gypsies and Their Journey* (New York: Random House, 1995), 24ff., and Leela Fernandes, "Beyond Public Spaces and Private Spheres: Gender, Family and Working-Class Politics in India," *Feminist Studies* 23, no. 3 (Fall 1997): 525–47.

31. I recognize that this interpretation emphasizes certain features of "kitchen table talk" and runs the risk of both generalizing and idealizing it. Not by chance, however, a pioneering group of second-wave feminists of color named their publishing venture Kitchen Table: Women of Color Press. Many accounts also suggest that historically women have used such informal gatherings as a way of processing their experiences of injustice, with men and with other women. In "Magnolias Grow in Dirt: The Bawdy Lore of Southern Women," *Southern Exposure* 4, no. 4 (Winter 1977): 29–33, Rayna Green describes how the southern women she knew would gather around the table to entertain, teach, critique, and defy patriarchal conventions through tale-telling. Buchi Emercheti's novel set in Nigeria, *Double Yoke* (New York: Braziller, 1983), suggests some of the ambiguities concerning what constitutes "kitchen table talk" for women struggling to make their ways between traditional cultures and the pressures toward Western-style development.

32. Alice Echols cites an interview with Irene Peslikis to the effect that women like Kathie Sarachild, who went to Harvard, could easily afford to downplay a knowledge of past theories because they already took this knowledge for granted, while women from working-class backgrounds could not (see Echols, *Daring to Be Bad*, 85). Although such class-based criticisms of access to consciousness-raising were not uncommon, it is also dangerous to generalize about the limits of working-class women's knowledge and intellectual skills. For stories that not only expose the class bias in higher education but suggest the wide variety of abilities

and knowledges that working-class women bring to it, see Michelle M. Tokarczyk and Elizabeth A. Fay, eds., *Working-Class Women in the Academy: Laborers in the Knowledge Factory* (Amherst: University of Massachusetts Press, 1993).

33. Elisabeth J. Johnson, "Working-Class Women as Students and Teachers," in *Working-Class Women in the Academy*, ed. Tokarczyk and Fay, 197–207.

34. Barbara Omolade, "A Black Feminist Pedagogy," in Omolade, *The Rising Song of African American Women* (New York: Routledge, 1994), 129–36. Feminists with a radical perspective have long struggled with the issue of access. See, for example, Dale Spender, *Invisible Women: The Schooling Scandal* (London: Readers & Writers Publishing Cooperative Society, 1982).

35. See Gilligan, *In a Different Voice*; Noddings, *Caring;* and Noddings, *The Challenge to Care in Schools: An Alternative Approach to Education* (New York: Teachers College Press, 1992). For a number of feminist essays both critiquing and extending Noddings's argument, see Ann Diller, Barbara Houston, Kathryn Pauly Morgan, and Maryann Ayim, eds., *The Gender Question in Education: Theory, Pedagogy, and Politics* (Boulder, Colo.: Westview, 1996). Because of the emphasis in Gilligan's work on gender differences and the competing social values of individualization and relation, it is sometimes difficult to recognize how much she herself values *creating a political discourse* in which women's "different voices" are integral.

36. See Terry L. Haywoode and Laura Polla Scanlon, "World of Our Mothers: College for Neighborhood Women," in *Women's Studies Quarterly* 21, nos. 3 & 4 (Fall/Winter 1993): 133–41. Although the theme of community appears frequently in discussions of feminist pedagogy, it often refers neither to the kind of local community described by Haywoode and Scanlon nor to a specifically feminist political community but rather to communal values as a prerequisite for democratic society. See, in this same volume, Carolyn M. Shrewsbury, "What Is Feminist Pedagogy?" 8–16, and Nancy Schniedewind, "Teaching Feminist Process in the 1990s," 17–30.

37. For a striking example of how lecturing can incorporate many features of consciousness-raising, see Wendy Ball, "Feminist Teaching in a Law Faculty in New Zealand," in *Meeting the Challenge: Innovative Feminist Pedagogies in Action*, ed. Maralee Mayberry and Ellen Cronan Rose (New York: Routledge, 1999), 299–316. Estelle B. Freedman suggests how small consciousness-raising groups can be combined with large lectures in "Small-Group Pedagogy: Consciousness Raising in Conservative Times," in *Tilting the Tower,* ed. Linda Garber (New York: Routledge, 1994), 35–50.

38. In their argument for a "connected teaching" that fosters connected knowing and constructed knowledge, Mary Field Belenky, Blythe McVicker Clinchy, Nancy Rule Goldberger, and Jill Mattuck Tarule stress that a teacher should reveal the "process of gestation" that has led to "his" thinking. In this approach, the teacher models appropriate thinking and emphasizes that everyone is engaged in learning and constructing knowledge. See *Women's Ways of Knowing: The Development of Self, Voice, and Mind* (New York: Basic, 1986), 214–29.

39. See Jane Gallop, "Im-personation: A Reading in the Guise of An Introduction," in *Pedagogy: The Question of Impersonation,* ed. Jane Gallop (Blooming-

ton: Indiana University Press, 1995), 1–18, as well as Indira Karamcheti, "Caliban in the Classroom," 138–46. As Gallop's introduction notes, Karamcheti's essay conveys some of the ambivalence that many teachers seem to feel about whether an authentic self lies behind their pedagogical performance. I am indebted to Catherine Green and her ongoing development of a lesbian–feminist pedagogical theory of image-text for insight into Gallop's argument. In her memoir, *Life in School: What the Teacher Learned* (Reading, Mass.: Perseus, 1996), 62*ff.*, Jane Tompkins gives an interesting account of how she was attracted to a performance model of university teaching.

40. For a cross section of the current arguments about the character of critical thinking, see Richard A. Talaska, ed., *Critical Reasoning in Contemporary Culture* (Albany: State University of New York Press, 1992). The use of *critical* in the second sense has been given wide educational currency by Henry Giroux, who has followed the Marxist lead of the Frankfort School. See Henry A. Giroux, *Theory and Resistance in Education: A Pedagogy for the Opposition,* foreword by Paulo Freire (Amherst, Mass.: Bergin & Garvey, 1983). Later, Giroux added feminist and postmodern arguments to his interpretation of critical pedagogy in Henry A. Giroux, ed., *Postmodernism, Feminism, and Cultural Politics: Redrawing Educational Boundaries* (Albany: State University of New York Press, 1991). See also Jennifer M. Gore, *The Struggle for Pedagogies: Critical and Feminist Discourses as Regimes of Truth* (New York: Routledge, 1993), for a feminist postmodern critique of both Giroux and proponents of feminist pedagogy as being insufficiently critical. Kerry S. Walters notes in her edited volume *Re-Thinking Reason: New Perspectives in Critical Thinking* (Albany: State University of New York Press, 1994), 1–24, how failing test scores in the United States in the 1970s led to a focus on "critical thinking" by many educational reformers. The essays in this volume also highlight the debate about whether critical thinking is discipline specific or cross-cuts disciplinary boundaries.

CHAPTER 2

1. My argument follows the path laid out by William James in his famous 1896 essay "The Will to Believe" in James, *The Will to Believe and Other Essays in Popular Philosophy* (New York: Longmans, Green, 1908), 1–31, in which he argues that scientific work is grounded in beliefs and that these, in turn, require a sort of leap of faith. Thomas Kuhn, *The Structure of Scientific Revolutions* (Chicago: University of Chicago Press, 1970), popularized a sociological version of this argument by placing the emphasis on the collective beliefs of scientific communities. For my purposes here, I prefer James's argument because it heightens the sense of individual moral responsibility entailed in making decisions in the classroom. James C. S. Wernham's *James's Will-to-Believe Doctrine: A Heretical View* (Kingston, Canada: McGill-Queen's University Press, 1987) reviews the many interpretations of James's essay, including conflicting interpretations of the term *belief.* The aspect of James's argument that seems to me most relevant to consciousness-raising and feminist classroom discourse is that which links knowledge with passion and action. On the epistemological strengths and weaknesses of

coherence theories of truth that emphasize a "web of belief," see Linda Alcoff, "Justifying Feminist Social Science," 85–103, and Lisa Heldke, "John Dewey and Evelyn Fox Keller: A Shared Epistemological Tradition," 104–15 in *Feminism and Science,* ed. Nancy Tuana (Bloomington: Indiana University Press, 1989).

2. Following the lead of feminist psychotherapists, I have appropriated the notion of "holding" from the object relations tradition of psychotherapy, in particular, feminist readings of D. W. Winnicott. See his "The Theory of the Parent–Infant Relationship," *International Journal of Psycho-Analysis* XLI (November–December, 1960): part 6, 585–95. In her critical interpretation of Winnicott, Jane Flax emphasizes the "transitional space" created by the mother's capacity to psychologically hold her child and thus allow for creative interplay between them. Applying this model to psychoanalysis, she characterizes it as "relational work in which theory and practice constantly inform, correct, and depend on each other," see Flax, *Thinking Fragments: Psychoanalysis, Feminism, and Postmodernism in the Contemporary West* (Berkeley: University of California Press, 1990), 107*ff.* This seems relevant to teaching through feminist discourse because the teacher's commitment to "hold" a class (dependent on her own belief in its purpose and process) does not imply that she can or should be able to predict the direction of the discourse as it unfolds.

3. This conclusion bears on the ongoing debate referred to in note 23, of chapter 1, over whether, to pursue political or ethical discourse, it is more important for discussants to share certain substantive values (in particular, their definition of what is "good") or to follow particular procedures (e.g., making sure that everyone has a chance to speak). In the classroom context, as illustrated here, I do not assume that the students and I share a common definition of what is good in the realm of social justice, only that the class generally agrees that there is some degree of injustice in gender relations and that this is worthy of talk and action. Moreover, any rigid adherence to a feminist notion of the good (as exemplified by Titania) would undermine the purpose of teaching through feminist discourse. On the other hand, as I will argue in a few pages, the entire project depends on the feminist social movement assumption (so fundamental to my belief in what I am doing) that gender relations are deeply affected and harmed by systemic injustices—an assumption that I share with other feminists. This assumption, however, does not so much precede feminist discourse or take logical priority to it as fully permeate it.

4. See Lynn Hankinson Nelson, "Epistemological Communities," in *Feminist Epistemologies,* ed. Linda Alcoff and Elizabeth Potter (New York: Routledge, 1993), 121–59. Nelson defines an epistemological community as one that "constructs and shares knowledge and standards of evidence" (124). She argues that it is the community itself, rather than individuals, that must be seen as the knower and that feminist academics should be especially concerned about how various disciplinary communities (knowers) define evidence. Although she acknowledges disagreement within feminist epistemological communities and that a pattern of splitting over differences can create "subcommunities," the question of how members of the same feminist epistemological community can and should conduct their discourse remains (as in many similar investigations) unanswered. Marilyn Frye

notes the impediments to women forming an epistemological community and struggles with how this can be done given the differences of experience, in "The Possibility of Feminist Theory," *Willful Virgin: Essays in Feminism 1976–1992* (Freedom, Calif.: Crossing, 1992), 59–75.

5. Many second-wave activists went on to pursue academic careers or were already engaged in them and, for a number of years, tried to preserve the ties between the manifestos and essays that activists had produced in the 1960s and 1970s and the academic writing that grew out of them. See, for instance, Vivian Gornick and Barbara K. Moran, eds., *Woman in Sexist Society: Studies in Power and Powerlessness* (New York: Basic, 1971), in which the tie between academic analyses and activism is still owned and discussed (although some issues important for both activism and academia—in particular, differences among women—are barely discussed).

6. See Catharine A. MacKinnon, "Feminism, Marxism, Method, and the State: An Agenda for Theory," *Signs* 7, no. 3 (Spring, 1982): 515–44. The notion of a standpoint epistemology has been thoroughly criticized by feminist academics working from a variety of positions who see the notion of unqualified political standpoint as epistemologically distorted and politically authoritarian. See, for instance, Bat-Ami Bar On's "Marginality and Epistemic Privilege" in *Feminist Epistemologies*, ed. Alcoff and Potter, 83–100; and Judith Butler, *Gender Trouble: Feminism and the Subversion of Identity* (New York: Routledge, 1990). My effort to carve a pedagogical path between these opposed camps resembles Davida Alperin's call for a model of dealing with difference that builds on the thinking of Audre Lorde, Bernice Reagon, and Charlotte Bunch. This approach emphasizes *interaction* among social justice movement standpoints, in contrast to the claim that a single standpoint conveys the truth. See Davida J. Alperin, "Social Diversity and the Necessity of Alliances: A Developing Feminist Perspective," in *Bridges of Power: Women's Multicultural Alliances,* ed. Lisa Albrecht and Rose M. Brewer (Philadelphia: New Society, 1990), 23–33. Also see Sandra Harding's critical assessment and recuperation of standpoint theory in *Whose Science? Whose Knowledge? Thinking from Women's Lives* (Ithaca, N.Y.: Cornell University Press, 1991), 164*ff.*

7. In addition to Harding, *Whose Science? Whose Knowledge?* and Butler, *Gender Trouble,* see Elizabeth Kamarck Minnich, *Transforming Knowledge* (Philadelphia: Temple University Press, 1990); Patricia Hill Collins, *Black Feminist Thought: Knowledge, Consciousness, and the Politics of Empowerment* (Boston: Unwin Hyman, 1990); Chandra Talpade Mohanty, "Under Western Eyes: Feminist Scholarship and Colonial Discourses," in *Third World Women and the Politics of Feminism,* ed. Chandra Talpade Mohanty, Ann Russo, and Lourdes Torres (Bloomington: Indiana University Press, 1991), 51–80; Elizabeth V. Spelman, *Inessential Woman: Problems of Exclusion in Feminist Thought* (Boston: Beacon, 1988); Maria Lugones, "Playfulness, 'World'-Travelling, and Loving Perception," in *Lesbian Philosophies and Cultures,* ed. Jeffner Allen (Albany: State University of New York Press, 1990), 159–80; and Denise Riley, *"Am I That Name?" Feminism and the Category of "Women" in History* (Minneapolis: University of Minnesota Press, 1988).

8. My approach to the concept of experience draws heavily on John Dewey's discussion of this concept in *Art as Experience* (New York: Minton, Balch, 1934) and to a lesser extent, his *Experience and Nature* (New York: Dover, 1958). In *John Dewey and the Paradox of Liberal Reform* (Albany: State University of New York Press, 1990), William Andrew Paringer argues that Dewey's account of experience lacks attention to the "felt contradictions of experience" (124); but in *Pragmatism and Feminism: Reweaving the Social Fabric* (Chicago: University of Chicago Press, 1996), Charlene Haddock Seigfried reads Dewey as saying, "Experience is not just naively undergone; it is overlaid and saturated not only with previous philosophical interpretations but also with past beliefs, values, and classifications" (156). Early in the academic feminist debates on subjectivity, Teresa de Lauretis made a connection between the tradition of philosophical pragmatism (by way of philosopher Charles Sanders Peirce rather than Dewey) and the feminist attempts to understand women's experience in *Alice Doesn't: Feminism, Semiotics, Cinema* (Bloomington: Indiana University Press, 1984). Here she defines *experience* as "a *process* by which, for all social beings, subjectivity is constructed" (159) and then, in discussing the crucial role of language or signs in this process, offers an interpretation of consciousness-raising as enabling a shift in the "'ground' of a given sign (the conditions of pertinence of the representation in relation to the object)," allowing participants to "effectively intervene upon the codes, codes of perception, as well as ideological codes" (178).

9. See Dorothy E. Smith, *The Conceptual Practices of Power: A Feminist Sociology of Knowledge* (Boston: Northeastern University Press, 1990), 25*ff*. Seyla Benhabib points out that everyday practices involve their own forms of theorizing and standards of legitimation, some of which serve feminist criticism and action better than others. See "Feminism and Postmodernism: An Uneasy Alliance," in *Feminist Contentions: A Philosophical Exchange,* ed. Seyla Benhabib, Judith Butler, Drucilla Cornell, and Nancy Fraser (New York: Routledge, 1995), 17–34.

10. See Susanne Bohmer, "Resistance to Generalizations in the Classroom," in *The Feminist Teacher Anthology,* ed. Gail Cohee et al. (New York: Teachers College Press, 1998), 61–69. Susan Bordo points out that without generalization, we are limited to discussing individual cases in "Feminism, Postmodernism, and Gender Skepticism," in *Feminism/Postmodernism,* ed. Linda J. Nicholson (New York: Routledge, 1990), 133–56.

11. Elizabeth Minnich, *Transforming Knowledge,* 52–81. Kathryn Pyne Addelson, however, suggests that early feminist statements about "all women" were not so-called claims to "'objective knowledge of true propositions about women'" but "rallying cries for political unity and defining the direction strategy and reform should take." See her *Impure Thoughts: Essays on Philosophy, Feminism, and Ethics* (Philadelphia: Temple University Press, 1991), 235; and Pamela Allen, *Free Space,* 42. In "Introducing a New Course: Muslim Women in Twentieth Century Literature," *NWSA Journal* 9, no. 1 (Spring 1997): 76–88, Fawzia Afzal-Khan notes that non-Muslim students may both exoticize and distance the lives of Muslim women, to keep from really engaging with their experiences or admitting that Western women are oppressed in any way similar to Muslim women.

12. See Harilyn Rousso, "Daughters with Disabilities: Defective Women or Mi-

nority Women?" in *Women with Disabilities,* ed. Michelle Fine and Adrienne Asch, 139–71; and Roberta Galler, "The Myth of the Perfect Body," in *Pleasure and Danger: Exploring Female Sexuality,* ed. Carole S. Vance (London: Harper-Collins, 1992), 165–72.

13. In the groundbreaking book edited by Gloria T. Hull, Patricia Bell Scott, and Barbara Smith, *All the Women Are White, All the Blacks Are Men, But Some of Us Are Brave: Black Women's Studies* (Old Westbury, N.Y.: Feminist Press, 1982), Tia Cross, Freada Klein, Barbara Smith, and Beverly Smith describe their work of women's consciousness-raising on racism and suggest a group of questions that can be addressed by such groups. See "Face-to-Face, Day-to-Day—Racism CR," 52–56. In *Teaching to Transgress: Education as the Practice of Freedom* (New York: Routledge, 1994), bell hooks describes using an exercise similar to the one I use in this story (84).

14. See Joan W. Scott, " 'Experience,' " in *Feminists Theorize the Political,* ed. Judith Butler and Joan W. Scott (New York: Routledge, 1992), 22–40; and Diane Fuss, *Essentially Speaking: Feminism, Nature & Difference* (New York: Routledge, 1989), 113–19. Elaborating on Scott's critique, Judith Grant develops an extensive criticism of women's experience as a focus of feminist theory and action in *Fundamental Feminism: Contesting the Core Concepts of Feminist Theory* (New York: Routledge, 1993). Grant draws a firm line between women's experiences and a process of reflecting on them—that is, between "women" as a socially constructed category requiring deconstruction and feminists, who have adequately theorized "women" and are therefore prepared to act in a liberatory manner.

15. See Sherry Gorelick, "Contradictions of Feminist Methodology," in *Feminism and Social Change: Bridging Theory and Practice,* ed. Heidi Gottfried (Urbana: University of Illinois Press), 23–45, in which Gorelick wrestles with the tension between the need for critical theories like Marxism and the importance of making women's different experiences of oppression central in feminist research.

16. Susan E. Babbitt discusses the epistemological function of experience as critique in "Feminism and Objective Interests: The Role of Transformation Experiences in Rational Deliberation," in *Feminist Epistemologies,* ed. Alcoff and Potter, 245–64.

17. The study of personal narratives suggests how people shape their stories according to individual desires, social contexts, and what storytellers hope to achieve within them. See Mark B. Tappan and Lyn Mikel Brown, "Stories Told and Lessons Learned: Toward a Narrative Approach to Moral Development and Moral Education," in *Stories Lives Tell: Narrative and Dialogue in Education,* ed. Carol Witherell and Nel Noddings (New York: Teachers College Press, 1991), 171–92; and the Personal Narratives Group, ed., *Interpreting Women's Lives: Feminist Theory and Personal Narratives* (Bloomington: Indiana University Press, 1989). Margaret Urban Walker makes a strong case for the role of narrative in moral discourse in "Picking Up Pieces: Lives, Stories, and Integrity," in *Feminists Rethink the Self,* ed. Diana Tietjens Meyers (Boulder, Colo.: Westview, 1997), 62–84.

18. See Fuss, *Essentially Speaking,* chap. 7.

19. See Helen E. Longino, "Subjects, Power, and Knowledge: Description and Prescription in Feminist Philosophies of Science," in *Feminist Epistemologies,* ed.

Alcoff and Potter, 101–20; and Elizabeth Potter, "Modeling the Gender Politics in Science," in *Feminism and Science,* ed. Tuana, 132–46, for discussions of how experience and consciousness impact on theory choice and development in the natural sciences.

20. Trinh T. Minh-ha, *Woman, Native, Other: Writing Postcoloniality and Feminism* (Bloomington: University of Indiana Press, 1989), 47–76. Similarly, Sandra Harding argues that the subject and object of knowledge need to be approached on the same causal, critical planc in "Rethinking Standpoint Epistemology: What Is 'Strong Objectivity'?" in *Feminist Epistemologies,* ed. Alcoff and Potter, 49–82. Articles in both Heidi Gottfried, ed., *Feminism and Social Change,* and the Personal Narratives Group, ed., *Interpreting Women's Lives,* suggest the wide range of discussion among feminist social scientists about the possibility or impossibility of doing research on/for women without turning subjects into "natives." And bell hooks warns against the assumption that while some academics and/or students do the theorizing, others should provide the experiences in "Feminist Theory: A Radical Agenda" and other essays in *Talking Back: Thinking Feminist, Thinking Black* (Boston: South End, 1989), 35–41.

21. The theorist was Jean Bethke Elshtain (see Scott Heller, "Finding a Common Purpose: U. of Chicago Scholar Has Become a Key Advocate of Communitarianism," *Chronicle of Higher Education,* March 31, 1995, A10, A16), and I believe this ambivalence toward disclosing or not disclosing what she considers private matters runs throughout her work. See her "The Social Relations of the Classroom: A Moral and Political Perspective," *Telos* 27 (Spring 1976): 97–110; her now classic study *Public Man, Private Woman: Women in Social and Political Thought* (Princeton, N.J.: Princeton University Press, 1981); and *Power Trips and Other Journeys: Feminism as Civic Discourse* (Madison: University of Wisconsin Press, 1990). I have discussed some problems in incorporating physical movement work in feminist pedagogy in "Enhancing Feminist Pedagogy: Multimedia Workshops on Women's Experience with the Newspaper and Home," in *The Feminist Teacher Anthology,* ed. Cohee et al., 98–113.

22. See John Dewey, *Art as Experience,* 42, where he describes emotion as "the moving and cementing force" of experience. Charlene Haddock Seigfried interprets Dewey's approach to feeling as follows: "Emotions are not in the first place private, subjective events, but are revelatory of situations in which we find ourselves" (see her *Pragmatism and Feminism,* 159).

23. See Kathie Sarachild, "A Program for Consciousness-Raising," in Redstockings, ed., *Feminist Revolution* (New York: Random House, 1978). In her feminist adaptation of Michel Foucault, Jana Sawicki suggests, "At its best, feminism has been very effective at realizing methods for sharing strong feelings in order to foster shared political commitment. We need to return to this model of consciousness-raising to learn from our differences and use them to enrich our politics." See Sawicki, *Disciplining Foucault: Feminism, Power, and the Body* (New York: Routledge, 1991), 46.

24. See Arlie Russell Hochschild, "The Sociology of Feeling and Emotion: Selected Possibilities," in *Another Voice: Feminist Perspectives on Social Life and Social Science,* ed. Marcia Millman and Rosabeth Moss Kanter (New York: An-

chor, 1975), 280–307; and Alison M. Jaggar, "Love and Knowledge: Emotion in Feminist Epistemology," in *Gender/Body/Knowledge: Feminist Reconstructions of Being and Knowing,* ed. Alison M. Jaggar and Susan R. Bordo (New Brunswick, N.J.: Rutgers University Press, 1989), 145–71.

25. See Morwenna Griffiths, "Feminism, Feelings and Philosophy," in *Feminist Perspectives in Philosophy,* ed. Morwenna Griffiths and Margaret Whitford (Bloomington: Indiana University Press, 1988), 131–51; and Martha Nussbaum, "Emotions and Women's Capabilities," in *Women, Culture and Development,* ed. Nussbaum and Glover, 360–95. I had used a similar argument in "Guilt and Shame in the Women's Movement: The Radical Ideal of Action and Its Meaning for Feminist Intellectuals," *Feminist Studies* 10, no. 2 (Summer, 1984): 185–212. Sara Ruddick points to the crucial role of feeling and feeling interpretation in the practice of mothering in *Maternal Thinking: Toward a Politics of Peace* (Boston: Beacon, 1989), 67*ff.*

26. I am indebted to Gill Wright Miller's ongoing research on the choreographing and performing of pregnancy dances (created and danced by pregnant dancers) for expanding my own understanding of what might be "realistic" choices in the dance world.

27. See Sue Campbell, *Interpreting the Personal: Expression and the Formation of Feelings* (Ithaca, N.Y.: Cornell University Press, 1997).

28. See Audre Lorde, *Sister Outsider: Essays and Speeches* (Trumansburg, N.Y.: Crossing, 1984), in particular, "Eye to Eye: Black Women, Hatred, and Anger," 145–75. Diana Meyers argues for the importance of both "vanilla" and "vindaloo" emotions that enable us to be both receptive listeners and angry participants in ethical discourse in "Emotion and Heterodox Moral Perception: An Essay in Moral Social Psychology," in *Feminists Rethink the Self,* ed. Meyers, 197–218. Lorde's argument may call into question the distinction between these two emotional states.

29. The figure most closely associated with initiating feminist discussions of the object–subject relation in research is Evelyn Fox Keller, *Reflections on Gender and Science* (New Haven, Conn.: Yale University Press, 1985), whose analysis draws on the object relations tradition in psychotherapy and who suggests that "the questions asked about objects with which one feels kinship are likely to differ from questions asked about objects that are seen as unalterably alien" (167). See also Donna Haraway's "Situated Knowledges: The Science Question in Feminism and the Privilege of Partial Perspective," *Feminist Studies* 14, no. 3 (Fall, 1988): 575–99, in which she argues for "an embodied objectivity that accommodates paradoxical and critical feminist science projects. Feminist objectivity means quite simply situated knowledges" (581); and Sandra Harding, *Whose Science? Whose Knowledge?*

30. See Lorraine Code's comparison of seeing, touching, and hearing as modes of getting to know objects in *What Can She Know? Feminist Theory and the Construction of Knowledge* (Ithaca, N.Y.: Cornell University Press, 1991), 149*ff.* Sara Ruddick makes the interesting suggestion that students' own separation processes may influence how close or far they want to be from a certain subject matter. For example, students who want to achieve some distance from their parents or com-

munity may prefer modes of learning that allow them to take a certain distance from familiar subject matter, in contrast to others who more resemble the "connected knowers" described by Mary Field Belenky, Blythe McVicker Clinchy, Nancy Rule Goldberger, and Jill Mattuck Tarule in *Women's Ways of Knowing: The Development of Self, Voice, and Mind* (New York: Basic, 1986). See Ruddick, "Reason's 'Femininity': A Case for Connected Knowing," in *Knowledge, Difference, and Power: Essays Inspired by* Women's Ways of Knowing, ed. Nancy Rule Goldberger, Jill Mattuck Tarule, Blythe McVicker Clinchy, and Mary Field Belenky (New York: Basic, 1996), 248–73.

31. This dialogic image of thinking, employed by a wide variety of theorists, is captured in Elisabeth Young-Bruehl's "The Education of Women as Philosophers," *Signs* 12, no. 2 (Winter 1987): 207–21. On philosophical thought as conversation, also see Jane Roland Martin, *Reclaiming a Conversation: The Ideal of the Educated Woman* (New Haven, Conn.: Yale University Press, 1985).

32. See Ellen Willis, "Radical Feminism and Feminist Radicalism," and Pamela Allen, *Free Space.* Sheila Rowbotham also warns that it was impossible to develop a sound analysis on the basis of a few groups of feminists, although it is clear that she hopes that developing a wider base will eventually produce or contribute to a more comprehensive libertarian socialism. See Rowbotham, "The Women's Movement and Organizing for Socialism," in *Beyond the Fragments: Feminism and the Making of Socialism,* ed. Sheila Rowbotham, Lynne Segal and Hilary Wainright (Boston: Alyson, 1981), 21–155.

33. Terry L. Haywoode and Laura Polla Scanlon include a brief but interesting discussion of classroom theory building in their essay "World of Our Mothers: College for Neighborhood Women," in *Women's Studies Quarterly* 21, nos. 3 & 4 (Fall/Winter 1993): 133–41. Their pedagogy involves students paying special attention to the different backgrounds and cultures in which they are situated, but the authors do not discuss here the possibility of students seriously disagreeing with each other about the interpretations of their research. This may stem in part from the research being focused on what have already been identified as common neighborhood concerns (e.g., the quality of the schools). Similarly, Mary Field Belenky, Lynne A. Bond, and Jacqueline S. Weinstock have little to say about disagreements among community women who come together to discuss common problems in *A Tradition That Has No Name: Nurturing the Development of People, Families, and Communities* (New York: Basic, 1997).

34. See Marilyn Frye, "The Possibility of Feminist Theory" in her *Willful Virgin: Essays in Feminism, 1976–1992* (Freedom, Calif.: Crossing, 1992), 59–75. M. Jacqui Alexander and Chandra Talpade Mohanty argue that "the *interpretation* of that experience within a collective context" is a crucial aspect of liberatory transformation in the introduction to their edited volume *Feminist Genealogies, Colonial Legacies, Democratic Futures,* xl.

35. See Barbara Christian, "The Race for Theory," in *Making Face, Making Soul/Haciendo Caras, Creative and Critical Perspectives by Feminists of Color,* ed. Anzaldúa (San Francisco: Aunt Lute, 1990), 335–45. With respect to the point about focus, I am indebted to an informal interview with Ellen Shumsky, who was part of the Radicalesbians group that wrote an influential 1970 essay "The Woman

Identified Woman," collected in *Radical Feminism*, ed. Anne Koedt, Ellen Levine, and Anita Rapone (New York: Quadrangle, 1973), 240–45. This conversation helped me to think about how the theorizing/theory building distinction was expressed in my classes.

36. Nancy Whittier, *Feminist Generations: The Persistence of the Radical Women's Movement* (Philadelphia: Temple University Press, 1995).

37. Susan Wendell offers an interesting analysis of agency in terms of the roles of victim, responsible actor, and observer of political engagement in "Oppression and Victimization; Choice and Responsibility" in *Hypatia* 5, no. 3 (Fall 1990): 15–46. Also see Judith Kegan Gardiner's introduction to her edited volume, *Provoking Agents: Gender and Agency in Theory and Practice,* ed. Judith Kegan Gardiner (Urbana: University of Illinois Press, 1995), on the effort to find a way to conceptualize agency that includes both the limits and potentials of a given situation.

38. As a pioneer of consciousness-raising, Charlotte Bunch made an early and strong argument for the value of both building and comparing feminist theories in their relation to action. See Charlotte Bunch, "Not By Degrees: Feminist Theory in Education," originally published in 1979 and republished in her *Passionate Politics: Feminist Theory in Action* (New York: St. Martin's, 1987), 240–53. At the end of this essay she writes, "The crux of teaching feminist theory is getting women to analyze and think about others' ideas as well as to develop their own" (253). In making her case for postmodern shifts and disunity, longtime activist and academic Joan Nestle argues for the importance of keeping all "the intellectual roads open," which enables us to gather the theoretical tools we need to confront oppression. See her "The Politics of Thinking" in *A Fragile Union: New and Selected Writings* (San Francisco: Cleis, 1998), 89–96. Elizabeth Durbin, Sonia Ospina, and Ellen Schall provide a valuable example of how students can be encouraged to interweave theory with action in "Living and Learning: Women and Management in Public Service," *Journal of Public Affairs Education* 5, no. 1 (Winter 1999): 25–41. Also see Jane A. Rinehart's thoughtful assessment of women's studies internships in "Feminist Wolves in Sheep's Disguise," in *Meeting the Challenge: Innovative Feminist Pedagogies in Action,* ed. Maralee Mayberry and Ellen Cronan Rose (New York: Routledge, 1999), 63–97.

39. Mitsuye Yamada, "Asian Pacific American Women and Feminism," in *This Bridge Called My Back: Writings by Radical Women of Color,* ed. Cherríe Moraga and Gloria Anzaldúa (Watertown, Mass.: Persephone, 1981) 71–75. Also see her "Invisibility Is an Unnatural Disaster: Reflections of an Asian American Woman," in the same volume, 35–45.

40. Patrocinio P. Schweickart, "What Are We Doing? What Do We Want? Who Are We? Comprehending the Subject of Feminism," in *Provoking Agents,* ed. Gardiner, 229–48.

CHAPTER 3

1. In *Making History: The American Left and the American Mind* (New York: Columbia University Press, 1988), Richard Flacks, a new left activist and aca-

demic, defines power as *"the capacity to make history—to influence the conditions and terms of everyday life in a collectivity"* (5) and distinguishes between power exercised by the few and the power of the people to block or challenge the rule of elites through various oppositional efforts. To both Flacks and many activists of the period, the "capacity to collectively innovate culturally" was "a primary resource of popular power" (7). Feminist activists and academics often followed a similar logic by distinguishing between patriarchal or capitalist patriarchal "power over" others and the "power to" liberate or the liberatory exercise of "power with" others. For example, see Nancy Hartsock, "Political Change: Two Perspectives on Power," in *Building Feminist Theory: Essays from* Quest: a feminist quarterly, ed. Charlotte Bunch et al.(New York: Longman, 1981), 3–19. Such arguments often placed strong emphasis on the power generated through consciousness, communication, and community building. But feminists also have adopted and developed a wide range of definitions of power, from collective to individual, from material to spiritual, from conscious to unconscious. In her critical assessment of psychological theories of power in relation to gender, Joan L. Griscom argues that the dichotomy between bad and good forms of power does not do justice to the multiplicity of power and its relational and dynamic character, in "Women and Power: Definition, Dualism, and Difference," *Psychology of Women Quarterly* 16, no. 4 (December 1992): 389–414. In *Power Trips and Other Journeys: Feminism as Civic Discourse* (Madison: University of Wisconsin Press, 1990), Jean Bethke Elshtain notes that feminists still lack a definition of power that takes into account the paradox of power and powerlessness experienced by many women. Building on the cultural theories of Antonio Gramsci and later Michel Foucault, Joan Cocks attacks what she takes to be the radical feminist notion of power-over by arguing that it simply reproduces the dominant masculine/feminine dichotomy (see Cocks, *The Oppositional Imagination: Feminism, Critique and Political Theory* [London: Routledge, 1989]), while Sandra Lee Bartky points to the limits of Foucault's diffuse notion of power in "Agency: What's the Problem?" in *Provoking Agents: Gender and Agency in Theory and Practice,* ed. Judith Kegan Gardiner (Urbana: University of Illinois, 1995), 178–93. Nancy Hartsock summarizes current feminist debates on power in "Community/Sexuality/Gender: Rethinking Power," in *Revisioning the Political: Feminist Reconstructions of Traditional Concepts in Western Political Theory,* ed. Nancy J. Hirschmann and Christine Di Stefano (Boulder, Colo.: Westview, 1996), 27–49.

2. Jo Freeman's well-known essay, "The Tyranny of Structurelessness," was published under her pseudonym "Joreen" in *Radical Feminism,* ed. Anne Koedt, Ellen Levine, and Anita Rapone (New York: Quadrangle, 1973), 285–99. A working-class and lesbian critique of middle-class discussion styles can be found in Caryatis Cardea, "Lesbian Revolution and the 50 Minute Hour: A Working-Class Look at Therapy and the Movement," in *Lesbian Philosophies and Cultures,* ed. Jeffner Allen (Albany: State University of New York Press, 1990), 193–217. In the same volume, Bette S. Tallen makes a similar point about Jewish versus gentile conversation styles in "How Inclusive Is Feminist Political Theory? Questions for Lesbians," 241–57. My comment on the impact of work connections on the dynamic in consciousness-raising groups is based on a number of informal interviews.

3. Simone de Beauvoir's *The Second Sex* (New York: Knopf, 1968) can be seen as an extended investigation of the problem of complicity. Madeleine R. Grumet's *Bitter Milk: Women and Teaching* (Amherst: University of Massachusetts Press, 1988) points to the betrayal of mothers and homemakers by daughters who become teachers and bow to the authority of patriarchal administrators. Jo Anne Pagano's critique of the rule against plagiarism makes a similar argument about women pressing other women into conformity to a patriarchal order in "Teaching Women," in *Exiles and Communities: Teaching in the Patriarchal Wilderness* (Albany: State University of New York, 1990), chap 6. Linda Carty points to the racial complicity of white women academics in "Black Women in Academia: A Statement from the Periphery," in *Unsettling Relations: The University as a Site of Feminist Struggles,* ed. Himani Bannerji, Linda Carty, Kari Dehli, Susan Heald, and Kate McKenna (Toronto: Women's Press, 1991), 13–44. Jennifer Gore's interpretation of second-wave feminist pedagogy in effect also charges its advocates with complicity in the dominant order in *The Struggle for Pedagogies: Critical and Feminist Discourses as Regimes of Truth* (New York: Routledge, 1993). Christine Overall's *A Feminist I: Reflections from Academia* (Peterborough, Canada: Broadview, 1998) conveys a keen awareness of how making a life in academic institutions entails endless complicity.

4. See Hannah Arendt, *On Violence* (New York: Harcourt, Brace & World, 1970). Arendt also claims that the concept of authority has lost its political meaning in modern society in "What Is Authority?" in *Between Past and Future: Six Exercises in Political Thought* (Cleveland: World, 1961), 91–141. On the other end of the spectrum, philosopher Vicki Hearne argues that we know but have been unable to claim the meaning of authority as the kind of command to which both dogs and humans consent when they recognize it as something "worth doing right." See "How to Say 'Fetch!'" in *Adam's Task: Calling Animals by Name* (New York: Knopf, 1986), 42–76. Also see Kathleen B. Jones (whose feminist rethinking of the concept of authority I will discuss more fully in the next chapter), "On Authority: Or, Why Women Are Not Entitled to Speak," in *Authority Revisited: Nomos XXIX,* ed. J. Roland Pennock and John W. Chapman (New York: New York University Press, 1987), 152–68. Jones herself revisits the topic in the light of current feminist theory in "What Is Authority's Gender?" in *Revisioning the Political,* ed. Hirschmann and Di Stephano, 75–93.

5. Abby J. Hansen offers a thoughtful description of the contract system in "Establishing a Teaching/Learning Contract," in *Education for Judgment: The Artistry of Discussion Leadership,* ed. C. Roland Christensen, David A. Garvin, and Ann Sweet (Boston: Harvard Business School Press, 1991), 123–35. Hansen points out that implied contracts often permeate classrooms and that making an agreement explicit does not eliminate the issue of trust. She argues that as conditions change and students grow, contracts can and should be renegotiated, "or revolution may be the result" (131). I find myself wondering what sort of revolution this might be and whether it might not sometimes be a good thing.

6. In her exploration of the complexities of trust in *Moral Prejudices: Essays on Ethics* (Cambridge, Mass.: Harvard University Press, 1994), Annette C. Baier argues that trust involves neither pure feeling nor pure reason but having "a belief-

informed and action-influencing attitude" (10). She also points out how trust is shaped by context and by our understanding of the part people play in a system of relationships. This understanding includes the extent to which we trust the roles that people play in various institutional contexts and the possibility of trying to redesign those roles. "We take risks," she notes, "when we redesign roles; we place our trust . . . in procedures as well as people" (201).

7. See Anne Seller, "Realism versus Relativism: Towards a Politically Adequate Epistemology," in *Feminist Perspectives in Philosophy,* ed. Morwenna Griffiths and Margaret Whitford (Bloomington: Indiana University Press, 1988), 169–86.

8. See Naomi Scheman, "Who Wants to Know? The Epistemological Value of Values," in *Engenderings: Constructions of Knowledge, Authority and Privilege* (New York: Routledge, 1993), 205–25. Patricia Hill Collins also stresses the relation between authority and accountability to the black community in *Black Feminist Thought,* where her description connects trust to both of these qualities. Sarah Lucia Hoagland, on the other hand, views accountability critically because of the connections she sees between it and an ethic of blame and excuse making. See her *Lesbian Ethics: Toward New Value* (Palo Alto, Calif.: Institute of Lesbian Studies, 1988). My notion of accountability is in many ways similar to Hoagland's concept of "intelligibility." Also see Kathryn Pyne Addelson, "Knower/Doers and Their Moral Problems," in *Feminist Epistemologies*, ed. Linda Alcoff and Elizabeth Potter (New York: Routledge, 1993), 265–94, on the accountability of academics to activists.

9. See Patrocinio P. Schweickart, "Speech Is Silver, Silence Is Gold: The Asymmetrical Intersubjectivity of Communicative Action," in *Knowledge, Difference, and Power: Essays Inspired by* Women's Ways of Knowing, ed. Nancy Rule Goldberger, Jill Mattuck Tarule, Blythe McVicker Clinchy, and Mary Field Belenky (New York: Basic, 1996), 305–31.

10. Also see Margaret Urban Walker's discussion of integrity as "reliable accountability" in "Picking Up Pieces: Lives, Stories, and Integrity" in *Feminists Rethink the Self*, ed. Diana Tietjens Meyers (Boulder, Colo.: Westview, 1997), 71*ff.*

11. Max Weber draws a firm line between politics and university teaching in "Science as a Vocation," in *From Max Weber: Essays in Sociology,* trans. and ed. H. H. Gerth and C. Wright Mills (New York: Oxford University Press, 1946), chap. 5. Hannah Arendt's argument appears in "The Crisis in Education," in *Between Past and Future*, chap. 5. Related to, but not the same as my point about persuasion, is the argument made by teachers who cite Socrates in support of seduction as a means of drawing students toward the pursuit of truth. Jane Gallop turns this argument on its head in *Feminist Accused of Sexual Harassment* (Durham, N.C.: Duke University Press, 1997), when she argues that students can compensate for inequality with their teachers through seducing them. In both feminist and lesbian terms, arguments for seduction seem to me highly problematic.

12. This point resonates with Max Weber's notion of charismatic authority. Although as I began to think about authority in feminist teaching I noticed a parallel to Weber's tripart distinction between traditional, charismatic, and bureaucratic au-

thority, my analysis eventually developed in a kind of counterpoint to his. See Max Weber, *The Theory of Social and Economic Organization*, Section III, "The Types of Authority and Imperative Co-ordination," ed. Talcott Parsons (New York: Free Press, 1947), 324–423. For feminist critiques of Weber, see Roslyn Wallach Bologh, *Love or Greatness: Max Weber and Masculine Thinking—A Feminist Inquiry* (London: Unwin Hyman, 1990), and Kathy E. Ferguson, *The Feminist Case against Bureaucracy* (Philadelphia: Temple University Press, 1984). Teresa L. Ebert presents a Marxist feminist critique of the decontextualization of desire in postmodern feminist analyses, in *Ludic Feminism and After: Postmodernism, Desire, and Labor in Late Capitalism* (Ann Arbor: University of Michigan Press, 1996). Pioneer feminist Carol Hanisch puts forward a radical feminist critique of "stars" and "leaders" that emerged in the 1970s in "The Liberal Takeover of Women's Liberation" in *Feminist Revolution*, ed. Redstockings (New York: Random House, 1978), 163–67.

13. I have pursued my thinking about role models in a series of essays: "Who Needs Women Heros?" *Heresies* 3, no. 1, issue 9, "Women Organized/Women Divided: Power, Propaganda & Backlash" (Fall 1980): 10–13; "The Models among Us: Social Authority and Political Activism," *Feminist Studies* 7, no. 1 (Spring 1981): 100–12; and "Wandering in the Wilderness: The Search for Women Role Models," *Signs* 13, no. 2 (Winter 1988): 211–33.

14. See also Joy James's discussion of activist role models "as conduits for reviewing our own political commitments rather than models to be emulated" in "Gender, Race, and Radicalism: Teaching the Autobiographies of Native and African American Women Activists," in *The Feminist Teacher Anthology*, ed. Gail E. Cohee et al. (New York: Teachers College Press, 1998), 234–58, 238. Stephen Marks points out that the impact on students of teachers expressing passionate convictions may vary with the teachers' own social location (e.g., a male teacher with mostly female students), in "The Art of Professing and Holding Back in a Course on Gender," in *Family Relations* 44, no. 2 (April 1995): 142–48.

15. My interest in initiation as an aspect of authority stems in important part from what I have learned about the role of initiation in movement improvisation from teachers at the Laban Institute (named for movement analyst Rudolph Laban and later called the Laban-Bartenieff Institute of Movement Studies) in New York City. I discuss idealization in both "Who Needs Woman Heros?" and "Wandering in the Wilderness."

16. bell hooks talks about excitement in the last chapter of *Teaching to Transgress: Education as the Practice of Freedom* (New York: Routledge, 1994). Also see Ebert's reservations in *Ludic Feminism and After*.

17. I have discussed the political dynamic of shame in more detail in "Guilt and Shame in the Women's Movement: The Radical Ideal of Action and Its Meaning for Feminist Intellectuals," *Feminist Studies* 10, no. 2 (Summer 1984): 185–212. In recent years, increasing interest has been shown both within and outside the psychoanalytic tradition in the topic of women and shame.

18. See Cynthia Harrison, *On Account of Sex: The Politics of Women's Issues 1945–1968* (Berkeley: University of California Press, 1988).

19. See Ferguson, *The Feminist Case against Bureaucracy*; and Hannah Arendt,

Eichmann in Jerusalem: A Report on the Banality of Evil, rev. ed. (New York: Viking, 1965). Although the Weberian model of bureaucratic rationality has been modified in many ways over the years to include a far wider range of motivations and meanings, many of its basic assumptions persist. See Esther Ngan-Ling Chow's critical assessment of bureaucratic roles in terms of their impact on both gender and ethnicity in "Asian American Women at Work," in *Women of Color in U.S. Society,* ed. Maxine Baca Zinn and Bonnie Thornton Dill (Philadelphia: Temple University Press, 1994), 203–27. Inasmuch as women's paid work and personal lives remain in constant structural tension with each other, bureaucratic workplace reforms can only go so far.

20. See Jo Freeman, *The Politics of Women's Liberation* (New York: McKay, 1975); and Ellen Messer-Davidow, "Acting Otherwise," in *Provoking Agents,* ed. Gardiner, 23–51. In the 1970s, many small feminist organizations and businesses found ways for women to work together collaboratively and effectively. See Eleanor Olds Batchelder and Linda Nathan Marks, "Creating Alternatives: A Survey of Women's Projects," and other articles in *Heresies* 2, no. 3, issue 7, "Women Working Together" (Spring 1979): 97–127. Such small groups provide an important setting in which to explore the potentials and problems of democratic management—a value too readily ignored when activists begin to focus on making a large-scale impact.

21. See Jane A. Rinehart, "Feminist Wolves in Sheep's Disguise" in *Meeting the Challenge: Innovative Feminist Pedagogies in Action,* ed. Maralee Mayberry and Ellen Cronan Rose (New York: Routledge, 1999), 66; and Hester Eisenstein's exploration of the contradictory role of "femocrats" trying to work within the Australian government in *Inside Agitators: Australian Femocrats and the State* (Philadelphia: Temple University Press, 1996).

22. See Ferguson, *The Feminist Case against Bureaucracy,* 87ff.

23. See Annette Kolodny, *Failing the Future: A Dean Looks at Higher Education in the Twenty-First Century* (Durham, N.C.: Duke University Press, 1998).

24. See Bologh, *Love or Greatness.*

25. The notion that feminist teachers should deal with grading in a way that fosters collaboration with and among students is widespread, but the issue of why we are grading at all (and in whose interests) is far more difficult to answer in a way that does not lead to serious political quandaries. See Jodi Wetzel's discussion of her college's development of a collaborative assessment plan in response to conservative pressures for academic "accountability" in "Assessment and Feminist Pedagogy," in *Meeting the Challenge,* ed. Mayberry and Rose, 99–119.

CHAPTER 4

1. Assumptions and arguments about what constitutes "need" weave in and out of a great deal of feminist theory and research. Martha C. Nussbaum and Jonathan Glover, eds., *Women, Culture, and Development: A Study of Human Capabilities* (Oxford: Clarendon, 1995), have argued for the importance of developing a general understanding of women's needs to create international aid programs that reduce gender inequities, while other critics are concerned that the process of gen-

eralizing about "women's needs" may suppress and ignore differences among women. Along these lines, Nancy Fraser introduces the concept of "need interpretation" in "Women, Welfare, and the Politics of Need Interpretation," in *Unruly Practices: Power, Discourse, and Gender in Contemporary Social Theory* (Minneapolis: University of Minnesota Press, 1989), 144–60, and womanist theologian Katie Geneva Cannon stresses the need to survive as the fundamental condition for black women in a racist society in *Katie's Canon: Womanism and the Soul of the Black Community* (New York: Continuum, 1995). Psychologists and philosophers who base their arguments on one-to-one caring relationships tend to assume universal physical and psychological needs; see, for example, Sara Ruddick, *Maternal Thinking: Toward a Politics of Peace* (Boston: Beacon, 1989). Feminist criticisms of "different voice" theory, on the grounds that it reproduces gender domination, come from many quarters. These criticisms range from the argument that women should not have a special relation to caring to the contention that categories such as "women" and "caring" should be treated with suspicion. For example, Jennifer M. Gore criticizes some of the early literature on feminist pedagogy for assuming that "nurturance" excludes "discipline" in her *The Struggle for Pedagogies: Critical and Feminist Discourses as Regimes of Truth* (New York: Routledge, 1993), 67*ff.*

2. On the image of woman as the angel in the house, see Sandra M. Gilbert and Susan Gubar, *The Madwoman in the Attic: The Woman Writer and the Nineteenth-Century Literary Imagination* (New Haven, Conn.: Yale University Press, 1979), 20*ff.*

3. Questions about the meaning of the public/private distinction become heightened when feminist and other teachers ask students to keep individual journals that may reveal painful or what the student considers shameful or even illegal experiences. As my approach in this story suggests, I think that it is important for feminist teachers to keep as their major focus the potential contribution of such journal keeping to feminist discourse. Figuring out how "private" thoughts can be incorporated into public discussion itself requires continuous, shared reflection. For an approach to journal keeping as a feminist pedagogical strategy, see Ellen Berry and Elizabeth Black, "The Integrative Learning Journal (or, Getting Beyond 'True Confessions' and 'Cold Knowledge')," *Women's Studies Quarterly* 21, nos. 3 & 4 (Fall/Winter 1993): 88–93. The role of autobiographical writing in exploring feminist and related issues is explored in Rebecca M. Chase, "Writing an Examined Life: A Lesbian Feminist Educator's Inquiry into Writing Autobiography" (Ph.D. dissertation, New York University, 1999); and Wendy S. Hesford, *Framing Identities: Autobiography and the Politics of Pedagogy* (Minneapolis: University of Minnesota Press, 1999).

4. See Rayna Green, "American Indian Women: Diverse Leadership for Social Change," in *Bridges of Power: Women's Multicultural Alliances,* ed. Lisa Albrecht and Rose M. Brewer (Philadelphia: New Society, 1990), 61–73.

5. See Kathleen B. Jones, *Compassionate Authority: Democracy and the Representation of Women* (New York: Routledge, 1993), and her essay, "What Is Authority's Gender?" in *Revisioning the Political: Feminist Reconstructions of Traditional Concepts in Western Political Theory,* ed. Nancy J. Hirschmann and

Christine Di Stephano (Boulder, Colo.: Westview, 1996). Also see Patricia Hill Collins's discussion of respect and dialogue within African American communities in her *Black Feminist Thought: Knowledge, Consciousness, and the Politics of Empowerment* (New York: Routledge, 2000) and Seyla Benhabib's "The Generalized and the Concrete Other: The Kohlberg–Gilligan Controversy and Moral Theory," in *Women and Moral Theory,* ed. Eva Feder Kittay and Diana T. Meyers (Totowa, N.J.: Rowman & Littlefield, 1987).

6. When students already know each other or have some connection through being in the same program or sharing other courses, the course–partner system works most dependably. But I give the students regular help in finding course partners and encourage them to tell me whether the system is breaking down. At the beginning of the semester, I ask students to fill out a "fact sheet" in which they describe their academic background and activities related to the course and can say something about their interest in or questions concerning the course. This gives me an opportunity not only to draw for myself a quick profile of the class but to help match up students who do not have course partners. The students also adjust the system by developing larger "partner" groups, using e-mail, for example.

7. Catharine E. Beecher and Harriet Beecher Stowe's classic treatise, *The American Woman's Home* (New York: Ford, 1870), assumes that "the American Woman" has immigrant or U.S. rural women servants to ensure the success of her domestic management. In *All-American Girl: The Ideal of Real Womanhood in Mid-Nineteenth-Century America* (Athens: University of Georgia Press, 1989), Frances B. Cogan points out that contemporary advice books gave nineteenth-century middle-class women practical advice about their own rather demanding work and did not project an image of such women as ethereal creatures.

8. See Carol Gilligan, *In a Different Voice: Psychological Theory and Women's Development* (Cambridge, Mass.: Harvard University Press, 1982); Nel Noddings, *Caring: A Feminine Approach to Ethics and Moral Education* (Berkeley: University of California Press, 1984); and Ruddick, *Maternal Thinking.*

9. See Joan C. Tronto, *Moral Boundaries: A Political Argument for an Ethic of Care* (New York: Routledge, 1993). As Tronto's subtitle suggests, feminist arguments for revaluing caring do not start from the same premises or lead in the same direction. Tronto points out that the association between women and caring is not an absolute one but evolved out of a series of historic circumstances that made women the bearers of morality at the same time women were excluded from emerging political discussions. Thus, developing an ethic of care need not rely on women's special virtues but can be developed through a discourse on care that challenges a gender-based division of caring labor.

10. See Noddings, *Caring,* 47ff.

11. See Berenice Fisher and Joan Tronto, "Toward a Feminist Theory of Caring," in *Circles of Care: Work and Identity in Women's Lives,* ed. Emily K. Abel and Margaret K. Nelson (Albany: State University of New York Press, 1990), 35–62.

12. See Ann Diller, "The Ethics of Care and Education: A New Paradigm, Its Critics, and Its Educational Significance," and "An Ethics of Care Takes on Pluralism," in *The Gender Question in Education,* ed. Ann Diller, Barbara Houston,

Kathryn Pauly Morgan, and Maryann Ayim (Boulder, Colo.: Westview, 1996), 89–104 and 161–69.

13. See Ruddick, *Maternal Thinking*, 65*ff*. In chap. 2, I have drawn on the feminist reading of the object relations school of psychoanalysis in arguing for the role of belief in "holding" the class. In the context of this chapter, I interpret "holding" in a way that more closely resembles the psychoanalytic interpretation of physical and emotional holding, introduced into the feminist debate on motherhood by Nancy Chodorow in *The Reproduction of Mothering: Psychoanalysis and the Sociology of Gender* (Berkeley: University of California Press, 1978), 58*ff*.

14. As part of their response to the widespread assumption that caring stems solely from emotional and/or intuitive responses to the needs of others, Sara Ruddick and others argue that caring has its own logic and rules. This argument that genuine caring often requires clear and overt rules has been pursued by educators such as Lisa D. Delpit, who has argued that presumably kind, caring, and supportive white, middle-class teachers often fail to read their black students and thus perpetuate white, middle-class domination. See her "The Silenced Dialogue: Power and Pedagogy in Educating Other People's Children," *Harvard Educational Review* 58, no. 3 (August 1988): 280–98.

15. See Sarah Lucia Hoagland, *Lesbian Ethics: Toward New Value* (Palo Alto, Calif.: Institute of Lesbian Studies, 1988); "Some Thoughts about Caring," in *Feminist Ethics*, ed. Claudia Card (Lawrence: University of Kansas Press, 1991), 246–63; Janice G. Raymond, *A Passion for Friends: Toward a Philosophy of Female Affection* (Boston: Beacon, 1986); and Jeffner Allen, "Motherhood: The Annihilation of Women," in *Mothering: Essays in Feminist Theory*, ed. Joyce Trebilcot (Totowa, N.J.: Rowman & Allanheld, 1983), 315–30. Although her argument develops from a quite different stance, Maxine Greene's concern that women's agency is undermined by the obligation to care for others parallels the lesbian feminist arguments made by Hoagland and others. See Maxine Greene, *The Dialectic of Freedom* (New York: Teachers College Press, 1988), chap. 3.

16. See Indira Karamcheti, "Caliban in the Classroom," in *Pedagogy: The Question of Impersonation,* ed. Jane Gallop (Bloomington: Indiana University Press, 1995), 138–46.

17. In contrast to the usual generalizations about "lesbian separatism," some lesbian feminists have argued for a complex notion of separatism and its benefits for the development of lesbian agency. See Claudia Card, "Pluralist Lesbian Separatism," in *Lesbian Philosophies and Cultures,* ed. Jeffner Allen (Albany: State University of New York Press, 1990), 125–41; and Dana R. Shugar, *Separatism and Women's Community* (Lincoln: University of Nebraska Press, 1995). Also see Carol Anne Douglas, *Love and Politics: Radical Feminist and Lesbian Theories* (San Francisco: ISM Press, 1990), 250*ff*., on the meaning of separatism and the criticisms of women of color.

18. Despite the fact that feminist theories overlap each other and do not always stay within neat and clear boundaries, I use descriptors such as *black feminist, socialist feminist, different voice,* and *poststructuralist* to indicate a general point of view on leading feminist issues. These terms are not meant to obscure the often substantial differences among academics and activists who might describe them-

NOTES

selves by a given label or to limit theoretical positions to members of a particular social group.

19. See Collins, *Black Feminist Thought*; Bonnie Thornton Dill, "Fictive Kin, Paper Sons, and *Compadrazgo*: Women of Color and the Struggle for Family Survival," in *Women of Color in U.S. Society*, ed. Maxine Baca Zinn and Bonnie Thornton Dill (Philadelphia: Temple University Press, 1994), 149–69; and Carol B. Stack, *All Our Kin: Strategies for Survival in a Black Community* (New York: Harper, 1974). The role of poor black women and poor women from other groups as domestic carers has been the subject of a number of feminist studies, including Judith Rollins, *Between Women: Domestics and Their Employers* (Philadelphia: Temple University Press, 1985).

20. See Michèle Foster, "Othermothers: Exploring the Educational Philosophy of Black American Women Teachers," in *Feminism and Social Justice in Education: International Perspectives*, ed. Madeleine Arnot and Kathleen Weiler (London: Falmer, 1993), 101–23. In her study of how black mothers teach their daughters about work and other aspects of daily life, Suzanne C. Carothers describes patterns relevant to the construction of care in African American communities. See her "Catching Sense: Learning from Our Mothers to Be Black and Female," in *Uncertain Terms: Negotiating Gender in American Culture*, ed. Faye Ginsburg and Anna Lowenhaupt Tsing (Boston: Beacon, 1990), 232–47.

21. In thinking about Jewish identity in relation to my feminist teaching, I am deeply indebted to pioneer work in Jewish feminist and Jewish lesbian feminist studies such as Evelyn Torton Beck, ed., *Nice Jewish Girls: A Lesbian Anthology* (Trumansburg, N.Y.: Crossing, 1982); Melanie Kaye/Kantrowitz, *The Issue Is Power: Essays on Women, Jews, Violence and Resistance* (San Francisco: Aunt Lute, 1992); and Irena Klepfisz, *Dreams of an Insomniac: Jewish Feminist Essays, Speeches and Diatribes* (Portland, Oreg.: Eighth Mountain, 1990). For a poststructural reading of Jewish identity, see Naomi Scheman, "Queering the Center by Centering the Queer: Reflections on Transsexuals and Secular Jews," in *Feminists Rethink the Self*, ed. Diana Tietjens Meyers (Boulder, Colo.: Westview, 1997), 124–62. Discussions with Sherry Gorelick about her ongoing research on Jewish women's political identities keeps me thinking about this issue. See her "Peace Movements," in *Jewish Women in America: An Historical Encyclopedia*, ed. Paula E. Hyman and Deborah Dash More (New York: Routledge, 1997), 1033–40.

22. See Fisher and Tronto, "Toward a Feminist Theory of Caring," in *Circles of Care*, ed. Abel and Nelson.

23. In addition to Nancy Fraser, "Women, Welfare, and the Politics of Need Interpretation," see her essay with Linda Gordon, "A Genealogy of 'Dependency': Tracing a Keyword of the U.S. Welfare State," in Fraser, *Justice Interruptus: Critical Reflections on the "Postsocialist" Condition* (New York: Routledge, 1997), 121–49.

24. Trinh T. Minh-ha, *Woman, Native, Other: Writing Postcoloniality and Feminism* (Bloomington: Indiana University Press, 1989), 1–2.

25. For an indication of the pedagogical problems associated with witnessing, see Shoshana Felman, "Education and Crisis, or the Vicissitudes of Teaching," in

Testimony, ed. Shoshana Felman and Dori Laub (New York: Routledge, 1992), 1–56; and Hesford, *Framing Identities,* 71*ff.*

26. See Fisher and Tronto, "Toward a Feminist Theory of Caring," on the notion that sisterhood, including our actual experiences of relationships among sisters, can contribute to a more flexible concept of the division of caring labor.

27. See Elsa Barkley Brown, "African-American Women's Quilting: A Framework for Conceptualizing and Teaching African-American Women's History," *Signs* 14, no. 4 (Summer, 1989): 921–29. Brown also draws on Creole conversation as a model of nonlinear communications in which people talk simultaneously, in the same fashion that different musical voices interweave in jazz improvisation.

28. See the pages of *Contact Quarterly* for discussions of contact improvisation as well as other improvisational approaches. I am indebted to Deborah Sherman for reintroducing me to contact improvisation in the context of our feminist theater workshop and ensemble, Shock of Gray. Cynthia J. Novack offers a historical, ethnographic account of this form in *Sharing the Dance: Contact Improvisation and American Culture* (Madison: University of Wisconsin Press, 1990).

CHAPTER 5

1. The criticism of feminist pedagogy as invasion into students' private lives has been developed by a series of feminist academics, including not only Daphne Patai and Noretta Koertge (*Professing Feminism: Cautionary Tales from the Strange World of Women's Studies* [New York: Basic, 1994]) but also Jean Bethke Elshtain (who already had begun to express such concerns in her groundbreaking volume, *Public Man, Private Woman: Women in Social and Political Thought* [Princeton, N.J.: Princeton University Press, 1981]); and Christina Hoff Sommers in her widely touted assault on "gender feminism" (*Who Stole Feminism? How Women Have Betrayed Women* [New York: Simon & Schuster, 1994]). Diane Fuss's attack on the "authority of experience" in feminist classrooms in *Essentially Speaking: Feminism, Nature & Difference* (New York: Routledge, 1989), 113–19, puts a postmodern spin on the question of privacy by stressing how norms of self-disclosure regulate the "personal"—although she also argues that the "personal" has no fixed content.

2. Heterosexual teachers are rarely aware of the many, sometimes subtle ways in which they reveal things about their presumably private lives, from wearing a wedding ring to mentioning "our" vacation, to assuming what kinds of relationships can be publicized in what contexts. AnnLouise Keating offers a provocative response to this situation and its pedagogical implications in "Heterosexual Teacher, Lesbian/Gay/Bisexual Text: Teaching the Sexual Other(s)," in *Tilting the Tower,* ed. Linda Garber (New York: Routledge, 1994), 96–107. My approach to the meaning of self-disclosure in social interaction draws on the symbolic interactionist tradition in sociology, in particular to George Herbert Mead (see, e.g., Mead, *George Herbert Mead on Social Psychology,* ed. Anselm Strauss, rev. ed. [Chicago: University of Chicago Press, 1964]); Georg Simmel (see Simmel, *The Sociology of Georg Simmel,* ed. Kurt H. Wolff [Glencoe, Ill.: Free Press, 1950]); and Erving Goffman, *Stigma: Notes on the Management of Spoiled Identity* (En-

glewood Cliffs, N.J.: Prentice Hall, 1963). These social theorists all lay the ground-work for a concept of self-disclosure that emphasizes both the complexity of self and the ways in which its definition depends on the interactional context.

3. My argument here parallels the attempt by Lorraine Code and others to identify "epistemic virtues"—that is, the moral qualities that participants must bring to their shared effort to increase knowledge. See Code, *Epistemic Responsibility* (Hanover, N.H.: University Press of New England, 1987).

4. Bernice Johnson Reagon's influential talk, "Coalition Politics: Turning the Century" (originally delivered in 1981), is included in Barbara Smith, ed., *Home Girls: A Black Feminist Anthology* (New York: Kitchen Table: Women of Color Press, 1983), 356–68. bell hooks's concerns about the value of safety are laid out in *Teaching to Transgress: Education as They Practice Freedom* (New York: Routledge, 1994), chap. 2 and throughout.

5. See Susan C. Jarratt, "Feminism and Composition: The Case for Conflict," in *Contending with Words: Composition and Rhetoric in a Postmodern Age,* ed. Patricia Harkin and John Schilb (New York: Modern Language Association of America, 1991), 105–23.

6. Although many participants and observers of the civil rights movement have described the tremendous dangers involved (see James Forman, *The Making of Black Revolutionaries* [New York: Macmillan, 1972]), I am especially indebted to my friend Roberta Galler for her insights into the importance of safety in the movement and the role of many women activists like herself in securing it.

7. The idea of free space for activism was developed in numerous forms during the 1960s and early 1970s in the context of community-based organizing as well as the nascent women's movement. See Sara M. Evans and Harry C. Boyte, *Free Spaces: The Sources of Democratic Change in America* (Chicago: University of Chicago Press, 1992); Harry C. Boyte, "The Pragmatic Ends of Popular Politics," in *Habermas and the Public Sphere,* ed. Craig Calhoun (Cambridge, Mass.: MIT Press, 1992), 340–55; and Nancy Fraser, "Rethinking the Public Sphere: A Contribution to the Critique of Actually Existing Democracy," in the same volume, 109–42. In *The Dialectic of Freedom* (New York: Teachers College Press, 1988), Maxine Greene describes public spaces as places "where individuals are impelled to come together in speech and action" (19).

8. See Pamela Allen, *Free Space: A Perspective on the Small Group in Women's Liberation* (New York: Times Change Press, 1970). Aída Hurtado uses the language of "disrobing" and "nakedness" to describe the process by which women reveal to each other those selves that are normally hidden in *The Color of Privilege: Three Blasphemies on Race and Feminism* (Ann Arbor: University of Michigan Press, 1996), 128*ff.* Such images of honesty have been developed in response to the fact that as long as members of a disempowered group perceive *individual* survival as their primary value, they mask their feelings, hide their experiences, censor their ideas, and thus generally inhibit the emergence of political discourse about their situation.

9. For example, in her *Lying: Moral Choice in Public and Private Life* (New York: Pantheon, 1978), Sissela Bok emphasizes intention as a main feature of truthfulness and the importance of thinking through the meaning of honesty versus

deception, for people's capacity to make moral choices in the context of our relationships. Allen, too, seemed to emphasize the meaning of honesty for the promotion of human bonds and the development of individual moral and intellectual integrity. Several viewpoints bearing on the classic (though endlessly debated) virtue of honesty appear to render it irrelevant: the psychoanalytic argument that unconscious forces often lead us to deceive ourselves and others about our supposedly truthful intentions (see Jane Flax, *Thinking Fragments: Psychoanalysis, Feminism, and Postmodernism in the Contemporary West* [Berkeley: University of California Press, 1990], 60*ff.*) and the poststructuralist argument that our attempts to communicate truthfully are determined by a sort of linguistic unconscious. In discussing the Lacanian emphasis on the power of language to shape human experience, Nancy Fraser criticizes the tendency to endow the symbolic dimension with "an exclusive causal power to fix people's subjectivities once and for all" in "Structuralism or Pragmatics? On Discourse Theory and Feminist Politics," in Fraser, *Justice Interruptus*, 151–70. These criticisms present teachers with a series of dilemmas concerning how we should act. Granted the role of the unconscious in our attempts to talk with each other and the ways in which unexamined categories may be shaping our political discourse, does awareness of these patterns help us to improve the quality of that discourse? Do we as participants in such discourse need the intervention of experts (e.g., psychoanalysts or academic specialists in deconstruction) to improve that discourse? If so, how should we, as groups of discussants, relate to these experts? Should feminist teachers themselves be such experts, and how should they then relate to their students? My sense of caution in attempting to answer these questions stems in part from memories of a period in which women's voices were readily discounted because they were seen as determined by our presumably unconscious drives. In "Teaching Women's Studies: The Repersonalization of Our Politics," *Women's Studies International Forum* 13, no. 5 (1990): 469–75, Chris Ruggiero comments, "Most students . . . are not demanding group therapy; they are demanding *honesty*" (473).

10. See Susan J. Bickford, *The Dissonance of Democracy: Listening, Conflict, and Citizenship* (Ithaca, N.Y.: Cornell University Press, 1996)—in particular, her argument that listening, like seeing, requires that *"for the moment* I make myself the background, the horizon, and the speaker the figure I concentrate on" (23) and that "I think and speak for myself while listening to others" (90).

11. The concept of choice, which is so permeated by the assumptions of the liberal tradition, gets redefined and contested by feminists trying to reconcile women-as-choice-makers with feminist notions of the self that emphasize connection. Contrast, for example, the argument made by Nel Noddings for the ethical justification of abortion in *Caring: A Feminine Approach to Ethics and Moral Education* (Berkeley: University of California Press, 1984), with Patricia S. Mann, "Cyborgean Motherhood and Abortion," 133–51, in *Provoking Agents: Gender and Agency in Theory and Practice,* ed. Judith Kegan Gardiner (Urbana: University of Illinois Press, 1995). Feminist theory bearing on expectation is not as plentiful, although this topic surfaces in a wide variety of contexts. One interesting example concerns the impact of the electronic media on expectations about self-disclosure. See, for example, Kathleen A. Boardman, Jonathan Alexander, Marga-

ret M. Barber, and Peter Pinney, "Teacher Involvement and Transformative Power on a Gender Issues Discussion List," in *Meeting the Challenge: Innovative Feminist Pedagogies in Action,* ed. Maralee Mayberry and Ellen Cronan Rose (New York: Routledge, 1999), 169–90.

12. Feminist discussions about establishing limits often emerge from attempts to adapt and refashion certain psychotherapeutic traditions to the needs of feminist inquiry. Jean Baker Miller's pioneering argument about autonomy, *Toward a New Psychology of Women* (Boston: Beacon, 1976), and the work of other feminist psychologists address the issue of women's self-sacrificing relationships and the problem of how to gain fuller autonomy.

13. The posture of challenging or transgressing limits is strongly associated with postmodern arguments such as Judith Butler, *Gender Trouble: Feminism and the Subversion of Identity* (New York: Routledge, 1990), and Jane Gallop, ed., *Pedagogy: The Question of Impersonation* (Bloomington: Indiana University Press, 1995), but the impulse to challenge limits pervades many radical pedagogies—although the particular limits to be challenged vary from one political position to another.

14. Jennifer M. Gore, *The Struggle for Pedagogies: Critical and Feminist Discourses as Regimes of Truth* (New York: Routledge, 1993), makes the point that presumably democratic teaching structures can be used oppressively. I have discussed my own concerns about the dangers of pedagogical techniques like role playing in "Feminist Acts: Women, Pedagogy, and Theatre of the Oppressed," in *Playing Boal: Theatre, Therapy, Activism,* ed. Mady Schutzman and Jan Cohen-Cruz (London: Routledge, 1994), 185–97.

15. The growing interest in conflict resolution techniques among teachers of social justice subjects is relevant here. One conflict resolution approach, pioneered and popularized by Roger Fisher and William Ury with Bruce Patton, ed., in their book *Getting to Yes: Negotiating Agreement without Giving In,* 2d ed. (New York: Penguin, 1991), encourages opposed parties to become clear about their interests and search for ways of accommodating them. This approach is clearly useful in containing and reshaping serious conflicts that harm all parties concerned, and it has been applied with considerable success to conflicts among students at all levels of schooling. See Linda Lantieri and Janet Patti, *Waging Peace in Our Schools* (Boston: Beacon, 1996). But, I think it is important that feminist discourse not be quickly conflated with conflict resolution. The latter process assumes that participants can articulate their interests, whereas in feminist discourse, the meaning of "interest" in gender justice is itself at issue. In feminist classrooms, the pressure to reach accommodation (so vital to conflict resolution) could end up narrowing the scope and shortcutting the discourse process.

16. Jennifer Scanlon describes the incorporation of ritual into her feminist teaching in "Educating the Living, Remembering the Dead: The Montreal Massacre as Metaphor," in *The Feminist Teacher Anthology,* ed. Gail E. Cohee et al. (New York: Teachers College Press, 1998), 224–33. Just as the place of religious studies remains ambiguous in secular colleges and universities, so the place of the women's or feminist spirituality movement remains ambiguous in women's studies and the feminist disciplines. I actually have done little with the topic of feminist

spirituality in my teaching (and have occasionally been criticized for this by students), but I have gained self-understanding and had the opportunity to bond with others through engaging in feminist rituals outside the classroom. See Barbara Witenko, "Feminist Ritual as a Process of Social Transformation" (Ph.D. dissertation, New York University, 1992), and the work of Starhawk, who pioneered the attempt to combine feminist spirituality with activism in *Dreaming the Dark: Magic, Sex, and Politics* (Boston: Beacon, 1982). Although I share feminist concerns about the role of religion in perpetuating women's oppression, I also see the work done by feminists within their own religious groups of definite value to the movement. See, for example, Sister Patricia Mary Berliner, "Revaluing the Feminine: The Process of Psychospiritual Change in Contemporary Roman Catholic Women" (Ph.D. dissertation, New York University, 1990), for an account of feminist work with "traditional" Catholic women; Judith Plaskow, *Standing Again at Sinai: Judaism from a Feminist Perspective* (San Francisco: HarperCollins, 1990), for a feminist revision of Jewish theology; and Maria Harris for the implications of spirituality for education in *Women and Teaching* (New York: Paulist, 1988).

17. Annette Kolodny, "Paying the Price of Antifeminist Intellectual Harassment," in *Antifeminism in the Academy,* ed. VèVè Clark, Shirley Nelson Garner, Margaret Higonnet, and Ketu H. Katrak (New York: Routledge, 1996), 3–33. The institutional vulnerability of women and feminist academics is detailed in Magda Gere Lewis, *Without a Word: Teaching beyond Women's Silence* (New York: Routledge, 1993), chap. 3. The debate over harassment directed toward racial, sexual, and other campus minorities is represented in John Arthur and Amy Shapiro, eds., *Campus Wars: Multiculturalism and the Politics of Difference* (Boulder, Colo.: Westview, 1995).

18. I am grateful to Marcia Cantarella, who advised the student-run Academic Achievement Program at New York University, for insights into how creating safe spaces for African American and Latino students within a predominantly white institution can foster academic achievement without generating a sense of betraying one's community. It seems significant that this particular academic home was utilized and kept going mostly by women students.

19. The concept of connection has gained considerable currency in discussions of feminist and women's education, in great part due to Mary Field Belenky, Blythe McVicker Clinchy, Nancy Rule Goldberger, and Jill Mattuck Tarule, *Women's Ways of Knowing: The Development of Self, Voice, and Mind* (New York: Basic, 1986). *Connection* is often used in different ways, some emphasizing psychological aspects of learning, some emphasizing epistemological assumptions. Here, I am stressing the sociological sense of affiliation and the emotional ties that accompany ongoing relations with others.

20. See Carter Heyward and Beverly Wildung Harrison, "Boundaries: Protecting the Vulnerable or Perpetuating a Bad Idea?" in *Boundary Wars: Intimacy and Distance in Healing Relationships,* ed. Katherine Hancock Ragsdale (Cleveland: Pilgrim, 1996), 111–28. Although I find Heyward and Harrison's argument about vulnerability a very powerful one, I sense it may assume the existence of a community (such as a progressive Christian community) whose general commitments operate to "hold" individuals so that they can risk the kind of vulnerability Heyward

and Harrison prize. Because it is not necessarily desirable for people in disadvantaged positions to make themselves vulnerable to those with greater power, I also share the concerns voiced by other contributors to this fine volume—who argue for the need for professional ethics as an instrument for protecting both practitioners and those they seek to serve. We also need to continue to ask why codes of professional ethics fail to speak to the many ways in which professionals can harm their clients, students, or patients.

21. Adrienne Rich's essay, "Disloyal to Civilization: Feminism, Racism, Gynephobia," was published in Rich, *On Lies, Secrets, and Silence: Selected Prose 1966–1978* (New York: Norton, 1979), 275–310. Her reformulation can be found in "Notes toward a Politics of Location," in *Blood, Bread, and Poetry: Selected Prose 1979–1985* (New York: Norton, 1986), 210–31.

22. See the introduction, "Haciendo Caras, una Entrada," in *Making Face, Making Soul/Haciendo Caras: Creative and Critical Perspectives by Feminists of Color,* ed. Gloria Anzaldúa (San Francisco: Aunt Lute, 1990), xv-xxviii; and Kitty Tsui's eloquent account of trying to bridge worlds in "Breaking Silence, Making Waves and Loving Ourselves: The Politics of Coming Out and Coming Home," in *Lesbian Philosophies and Cultures,* ed. Jeffner Allen (Albany: State University of New York Press, 1990), 49–61.

23. See the essays in Toni Morrison, ed., *Race-ing Justice, En-gendering Power: Essays on Anita Hill, Clarence Thomas, and the Construction of Social Reality* (New York: Pantheon, 1992), on the point that no simple feminist lesson could be drawn from the confirmation hearings.

24. Valerie Miner and Helen E. Longino grapple with the problem of competition among women in "A Feminist Taboo," in *Competition: A Feminist Taboo?* ed. Miner and Longino (New York: Feminist Press, 1987), 1–37. Although I greatly value the work of these authors, I think that such discussions tend to downplay economic structures that put women in competition with each other and the possible strategies by which these structures might be challenged. In this respect, it also seems important to ask how the economic insecurity of adjunct, graduate student, and other transient, low-status, and underpaid teachers affects the question of how safe it is for them to engage in self-disclosure.

25. See Alison Jaggar, "Introduction: Living with Contradictions," in *Living with Contradictions: Controversies in Feminist Social Ethics,* ed. Jaggar (Boulder, Colo.: Westview, 1994), 2.

26. On co-optation by the media, see Laurel Richardson's essay, "Sharing Feminist Research with Popular Audiences: The Book Tour," in *Beyond Methodology: Feminist Scholarship as Lived Research,* ed. Mary Margaret Fonow and Judith A. Cook (Bloomington: Indiana University Press, 1991), 284–95.

27. See Myra Marx Ferree and Patricia Yancey Martin, "Doing the Work of the Movement," in *Feminist Organizations: Harvest of the New Women's Movement,* ed. Ferree and Martin (Philadelphia: Temple University Press, 1995), chap. 1. I do not mean to suggest that feminist discourse should embrace uncritically every feminist organization or that such organizations do not often have to be pushed by internal dissent or grassroots mobilizations to change organizational policies and practices. Feminist debates and studies suggest the need for continued political dis-

cussion of the problems of organizational failure and co-optation. In particular, activists have been long concerned about the role of state and corporate funding in distorting the feminist impulse that lies behind the building of such organizations. See Claire Reinelt, "Moving onto the Terrain of the State: The Battered Women's Movement and the Politics of Engagement," as well as other essays in *Feminist Organizations*, ed. Ferree and Martin, 84–104; and Mollie Whalen, *Counseling to End Violence against Women: A Subversive Model* (Thousand Oaks, Calif.: Sage, 1996).

28. For an example of how some feminist academics have tried to deal with the tension between these movements, see Jacquelyn N. Zita, "Gay and Lesbian Studies: Yet Another Unhappy Marriage?" in *Tilting the Tower*, ed. Garber, 258–76.

29. See Hurtado, *The Color of Privilege*, 128.

CHAPTER 6

1. See Paula Giddings, *When and Where I Enter: The Impact of Black Women on Race and Sex in America* (New York: Bantam, 1984). Simone de Beauvoir makes her argument about how women are "dispersed" in her introduction to *The Second Sex* (New York: Knopf, 1968), xix.

2. Feminists of many political varieties have discovered and rediscovered Beauvoir as a movement foremother. As Kathie Sarachild points out, Shulamith Firestone dedicated her pioneering feminist treatise, *The Dialectic of Sex* (New York: Morrow, 1970) to Beauvoir (see Sarachild, "The Power of History," in *Feminist Revolution*, ed. Redstockings [New York: Random House, 1978], 13–43) as part of a continuing, radical feminist tradition. Deirdre Bair describes Beauvoir's encounters with and support for second-wave feminism in *Simone de Beauvoir: A Biography* (New York: Summit, 1990), 543*ff.*

3. This story is adapted from an interview I did for an article with Roberta Galler, "Friendship and Fairness: How Disability Affects Friendship between Women," in *Women with Disabilities: Essays in Psychology, Culture, and Politics,* ed. Michelle Fine and Adrienne Asch (Philadelphia: Temple University Press, 1988), 172–94. In the context of the disability rights movement, activists developed consciousness-raising approaches. See Women and Disability Awareness Project, *Building Community: A Manual for Exploring Issues of Women and Disability,* rev. ed. (New York: Educational Equity Concepts, 1989).

4. Although I tend to avoid the language of social construction, because I think it is used too loosely and often obscures important differences among groups of people with different histories, the argument that U.S. racial categories have been shaped by political domination and an ideology of white supremacy seems to me irrefutable. See Timothy Maliqalim Simone, *About Face: Race in Postmodern America* (New York: Autonomedia, 1989) on not only the social determinants of racial categories but the ways in which a category such as "black" can provide to its members "cultural nurturance." See also bell hooks, *Killing Rage: Ending Racism* (New York: Holt, 1995) in which gender is consistently woven into the analysis.

5. See Ruth Frankenberg, *White Women, Race Matters: The Social Construc-*

tion of Whiteness (Minneapolis: University of Minnesota Press, 1993). Toni Morrison makes a compelling case for the way in which the "dark, abiding, signing Africanist Presence" informs the national literary heritage of the United States and indicts white literary critics for ignoring and distorting this presence. See Morrison, *Playing in the Dark: Whiteness and the Literary Imagination* (New York: Vintage, 1993), 5ff.

6. See Sandra Butler and Barbara Rosenblum, *Cancer in Two Voices* (San Francisco: Spinsters Book Company, 1991) for an account of what Barbara Rosenblum describes as "living in an unstable body" and its impact on their relationship. The lines between being able-bodied and having a stable disability or a time-limited, terminal, or a chronic illness are themselves often fluid. Barbara Hillyer discusses at length the language used to characterize disability in Hillyer, *Feminism and Disability* (Norman: University of Oklahoma Press, 1993), 20–46.

7. Judith Butler's now classic critique of identity categories and her argument for a fluid notion of the self is contained in *Gender Trouble: Feminism and the Subversion of Identity* (New York: Routledge, 1990). In her subsequent work, Butler struggles with the limitations of viewing all human experience (including experiences of identity and self) as contingent, social constructions. See Butler, *Bodies That Matter: On the Discursive Limits of "Sex"* (New York: Routledge, 1993); and Irene Costera Meijer and Baukje Prins, "How Bodies Come to Matter: An Interview with Judith Butler," *Signs* 23, no. 2 (Winter 1998): 275–86. Ann Ferguson, while suggesting that Butler never fully comes to grips with the question of agency, offers a materialist and relational model of "self" that leaves room for thought, judgment, feelings, and change in "Can I Choose Who I Am? And How Would That Empower Me? Gender, Race, Identities and the Self," in *Women, Knowledge, and Reality: Explorations in Feminist Philosophy*, ed. Ann Garry and Marilyn Pearsall, 2d ed. (New York: Routledge, 1996), 108–26. On the costs and repair of self-lessness, see Kathryn A. Gentile, "Healing through Lyrical Improvisations within the Transitional Space of a Diary" (Ph.D. dissertation, New York University, 2000).

8. Diane Fuss (*Essentially Speaking: Feminism, Nature & Difference* [New York: Routledge, 1989]) and other feminists identified with poststructuralism often use the language of "strategy" and "deployment" in trying to develop an antiessentialist concept of how identity can be used as a political resource. This military rhetoric has the advantage of reminding us that identity can be used to fight for social justice. However, such language tends to underplay the emotional and social meanings of acquiring, disowning, or wanting to maintain at least some of our identities. If the feminist goal is to abolish identity, then erasing these elements may be desirable. But, for many groups, including Native Americans and other indigenous peoples, the struggle for social justice involves the effort to protect cultural identity from erasure. See Leslie Marmon Silko, *Yellow Woman and a Beauty of the Spirit: Essays on Native American Life Today* (New York: Simon & Schuster, 1997); Chandra Talpade Mohanty's description of her identity and community affiliations as an immigrant as falling "somewhere between the histories and experiences we inherit and the political choices we make through alliances, solidarities, and friendships" in "Defining Genealogies: Feminist Reflections on Being South

Asian in North America," in *Our Feet Walk the Sky: Women of the South Asian Diaspora,* ed. Women of South Asian Descent Collective (San Francisco: Aunt Lute, 1993), 351–58, 357; and Nancy Fraser's relevant comments about Iris Young's "Five Faces of Oppression" in "Culture, Political Economy, and Difference: On Iris Young's *Justice and the Politics of Difference,*" in *Justice Interruptus: Critical Reflections on the "Postsocialist" Condition* (New York: Routledge, 1997), 189–205.

9. See Gloria Anzaldúa, *Borderlands/La Frontera: The New Mestiza* (San Francisco: Aunt Lute, 1987)—in particular, "La Herencia de Coatlicue/The Coatlicue State," 41–51; bell hooks, *Talking Back: Thinking Feminist, Thinking Black* (Boston: South End, 1989), 9; Minnie Bruce Pratt, "Identity: Skin Blood Heart," in *Yours in Struggle: Three Feminist Perspectives on Anti-Semitism and Racism,* ed. Elly Bulkin, Minnie Bruce Pratt, and Barbara Smith (Brooklyn: Long Haul, 1984), 11–63; and Anneliese Truame, "Tau(gh)t Connections: Experiences of a 'Mixed-Blood, Disabled, Lesbian Student,'" in *Tilting the Tower,* ed. Linda Garber (New York: Routledge, 1994), 208–14. See also Susan Bickford's reading of the politics of resistance in antiracist authors in "Anti-Anti-Identity Politics: Feminism, Democracy, and the Complexities of Citizenship," in *Hypatia: A Journal of Feminist Philosophy* 12, no. 4 (Fall 1997): 111–31 (special issue: "Citizenship in Feminism: Identity, Action, and Locale," ed. Kathleen B. Jones).

10. See Sarah Hoagland, *Lesbian Ethics: Toward New Value* (Palo Alto, Calif.: Institute of Lesbian Studies, 1988); and Dagmar Schultz, "Anti-Racism: The Challenge to Women's Studies," trans. Tobe Levin, *WISE Women's News* 4 (1992) and 1 (1993): 36–44. On the context of the antiracist work of Dagmar Schultz, Ika Huegel, and other German feminist activists, see Sara Lennox, "Divided Feminism: Women, Racism, and German National Identity," in *Rethinking Self and Society: Subjectivity, Gender and Identity,* ed. Electa Arenal, Senter for Humanistisk kvinneforskning, Skriftserien nr. 9 (Bergen, Norway: University of Bergen, 1997), 123–54. Gail Pheterson describes her workshops with Dutch women in "Alliances between Women: Overcoming Internalized Oppression and Internalized Domination" in *Bridges of Power: Women's Multicultural Alliances,* ed. Lisa Albrecht and Rose M. Brewer (Philadelphia: New Society, 1990), 34–48.

11. Diana Tietjens Meyers, *Subjection and Subjectivity: Psychoanalytic Feminism and Moral Philosophy* (New York: Routledge, 1994), 33*ff.*

12. Elizabeth V. Spelman, *Inessential Woman: Problems of Exclusion in Feminist Thought* (Boston: Beacon, 1988), 178*ff.* Drawing on Spelman's work, Sandra Lee Bartky argues that imagination needs to be supplemented by both "apprenticing" to learn others' realities and a "solidarity" with them. See Bartky, "Sympathy and Solidarity: On a Tightrope with Scheler," in *Feminists Rethink the Self,* ed. Diana Tietjens Meyers (Boulder, Colo.: Westview, 1997), 177–96. Also see Seyla Benhabib, "The Generalized and the Concrete Other: The Kohlberg–Gilligan Controversy and Moral Theory," in *Women and Moral Theory,* ed. Eva Feder Kittay and Diana T. Meyers (Totowa, N.J.: Rowman & Littlefield, 1987), 154–77; and Jessica Benjamin, *The Bonds of Love: Psychoanalysis, Feminism, and the Problem of Domination* (New York: Pantheon, 1988), on "mutual recognition," 23*ff.*

NOTES

13. Elizabeth V. Spelman, *Fruits of Sorrow: Framing Our Attention to Suffering* (Boston: Beacon, 1997).

14. See María Lugones, "Playfulness, 'World'-Travelling, and Loving Perception," in *Lesbian Philosophies and Cultures,* ed. Jeffner Allen (Albany: State University of New York Press, 1990), 159–80.

15. See my discussion of the use of Augusto Boal's forum theater in classroom contexts in "The Heart Has Its Reasons: Feeling, Thinking, and Community-Building in Feminist Education," *Women's Studies Quarterly* 21, nos. 3 & 4 (Fall/ Winter 1993): 75–87. Paula Ressler's "Queer Issues in Multicultural Teacher Education: Toward an Antihomophobic Educational Practice" (Ph.D. dissertation, New York University, 1999) suggests how dramaturgical techniques such as role playing can be used to help students to explore the multiple dimensions and meanings of sexual identity.

16. See Adrienne Rich, "Compulsory Heterosexuality and Lesbian Existence" (first published in 1980) in *Blood, Bread, and Poetry: Selected Prose 1979–1985* (New York: Norton, 1986), 23–75; and Butler, *Gender Trouble.* Harriet Malinowitz offers a rich analysis of the use of lesbian and gay student writing to explore the complexities of identity in *Textual Orientations: Lesbian and Gay Students and the Making of Discourse Communities* (Portsmouth, N.H.: Heinemann, 1995).

17. See Bickford, "Anti-Anti-Identity Politics," 111–31. Bickford focuses her summary on the criticisms of identity politics from left and feminist critics, including Todd Gitlin, Jean Bethke Elstain, and Judith Butler. But she does not try to define "identity politics," because of the many, thickly layered meanings that the term has acquired. I agree with Iris Young when she argues that group identity is not inherently essentialist or oppressive but contingent on a series of conditions that shape its meaning and effects. See Iris Marion Young, *Justice and the Politics of Difference* (Princeton, N.J.: Princeton University Press, 1990), 46*ff.* For additional discussions of "identity politics," see the essays in John Rajchman, ed., *The Identity in Question* (New York: Routledge, 1995). I am grateful to Sherry Gorelick for emphasizing to me the importance of the Combahee River Collective's "A Black Feminist Statement" (in *All the Women Are White, All the Blacks Are Men, But Some of Us Are Brave: Black Women's Studies,* ed. Gloria T. Hull, Patricia Bell Scott, and Barbara Smith [Old Westbury, N.Y.: Feminist Press, 1982], 13–22) in pioneering a radical and multidimensional notion of political identity. Their position evolved through a series of discussions that began in 1974 with consciousness-raising. Although Gayatri Chakravorty Spivak also criticizes identity politics, I like her suggestion that "essentialism" may be a "code word for a feeling for the empirical" in Spivak, *Outside in the Teaching Machine* (New York: Routledge, 1993), 7.

18. See June Jordan, "Report from the Bahamas," in Jordan, *On Call: Political Essays* (Boston: South End, 1985), 39–49. See Naomi Scheman, *Engenderings: Constructions of Knowledge, Authority, and Privilege* (New York: Routledge, 1993), 209*ff.* The importance and impact of privilege on others were also strikingly illustrated in a diversity workshop directed by Papusa Molina that I attended during the sixteenth annual meeting of the National Women's Studies Association in 1995. In this workshop, Papusa asked us to stand and form a circle. Then, she

proceeded to march around the inside of that circle, perilously close to our vulnerable toes, while she talked about how people often have no concept of how their power and privilege affects others. Because of her momentary position of power, our eyes remained fixed on the damage that she might do to our toes, while she herself continued to walk in seeming ignorance of her impact. With all its uncompromising message about the consequences of privilege, this workshop was conducted in a spirit of compassion and love that is captured in her piece "Recognizing, Accepting and Celebrating Our Differences," in *Making Face, Making Soul/ Haciendo Caras: Creative and Critical Perspectives by Feminists of Color,* ed. Gloria Anzaldúa (San Francisco: Aunt Lute, 1990), 326–31.

19. See Frances A. Maher and Mary Kay Thompson Tetreault, *The Feminist Classroom* (New York: Basic, 1994). Maher and Tetreault adopt the term *positionality* from Laurie Finke's argument that, in Maher and Tetreault's words, "people are defined not in terms of fixed identities, but by their location within shifting networks of relationships, which can be analyzed and changed" (164). Along these lines, they also cite Linda Alcoff, "Cultural Feminism versus Post-Structuralism: The Identity Crisis in Feminist Theory," *Signs* 13, no. 3 (Spring 1988): 405–36, who makes a similar point about the importance of context in interpreting oppression. Paula S. Rothenberg has done pioneering work in seeking "an integrated study of racism and sexism, within the context of class." See her edited volume *Race, Class, and Gender in the United States: An Integrated Study,* 2d ed. (New York: St. Martin's, 1992) 1. Also see Maurianne Adams, Lee Anne Bell, and Pat Griffin, eds., *Teaching for Diversity and Social Justice: A Sourcebook* (New York: Routledge, 1997), chaps. 1–4. Lindsay Pentolfe Aegerter presents an interesting example of getting students to look at their own multiple identities and the power relations involved in them in "Michelle Cliff and the Paradox of Privilege," *College English* 59, no. 8 (December 1997): 898–915.

20. See Maher and Tetreault, *The Feminist Classroom,* 201–02.

21. This pattern of competing notions of social justice is reflected in the area of multicultural education as well, where neo-Marxist interpretations that stress the impact of colonialism clash with psychological accounts of how oppression affects the formation of racial identity and the justice claims of indigenous peoples collide with those of immigrant groups that began their histories in a given national context as exploited laborers. See Christine E. Sleeter, *Multicultural Education as Social Activism* (Albany: State University of New York Press, 1996), for an attempt to distinguish radical from liberal and conservative theories while acknowledging differences within the radical perspective itself. James Banks, whose pioneering work in multicultural education helped to create the foundations for this field, has centered his own work firmly in the history and theory of African American social justice movements. See James A. Banks, *Educating Citizens in a Multicultural Society* (New York: Teachers College Press, 1997). Maxine Baca Zinn and Bonnie Thornton Dill offer a synthesis of principles developed by feminists of color in "Theorizing Difference from Multiracial Feminism," *Feminist Studies* 22, no. 2 (Summer 1996): 321–31.

22. Sara Evans discusses the relation between the notion of "beloved community" as it developed in the black church and was incorporated into civil rights

activism and the emerging feminist movement in *Personal Politics: The Roots of Women's Liberation in the Civil Rights Movement and the New Left* (New York: Vintage, 1980).

23. Wini Breines defines "prefigurative politics" as "the effort to create and sustain within the live practice of the movement, relationships and political forms that 'prefigured' and embodied the desired society," in *Community and Organization in the New Left, 1962–1968: The Great Refusal* (South Hadley, Mass.: Praeger, 1982), 6.

24. The post-1960s criticisms of community are closely related to the criticisms of identity politics and cover as wide a political spectrum. This includes conservatives, who see radical political communities as harming those they claim to be their members or as threatening "traditional" community life, and postmodern critics, who doubt the possibility of community in any form. Some feminist concerns are reflected in Nancie Caraway's *Segregated Sisterhood: Racism and the Politics of American Feminism* (Knoxville: University of Tennessee Press, 1991), who indicts the white feminist notion of community (i.e., "sisterhood") because she sees it based in "visceral affect" in contrast to more rationally assessed decisions about whether various feminists can or should work together. Mary B. McRae's analysis of teaching group counseling in interracial classrooms suggests that creating alliances across race lines involves a process that is both affective and rational. See McRae, "Interracial Group Dynamics: A New Perspective," *Journal for Specialists in Group Work* 19, no. 3 (September 1994): 168–74. For a range of feminist thinking on the possibility and problems of community, see Penny A. Weiss and Marilyn Friedman, eds., *Feminism and Community* (Philadelphia: Temple University Press, 1995).

25. See Young, *Justice and the Politics of Difference*, chaps. 6 and 8.

26. Elizabeth V. Spelman makes the point that tolerance has two faces: one reflecting the posture of privilege and the other as opening up space for what has been precluded. See her *Inessential Woman*. The notion of the city as a realm of freedom was explored by Georg Simmel in his classic essays on "The Stranger" and "The Metropolis and Mental Life," in Simmel, *The Sociology of Georg Simmel,* trans. and ed. Kurt H. Wolff (Glencoe, Ill.: Free Press, 1950). Benedict Anderson's influential study, *Imagined Communities: Reflections on the Origin and Spread of Nationalism* (London: Verso, 1983), points out that some communities are of necessity "*imagined*" because the members of even the smallest nation will never know their fellow members" (6).

27. See Young, *Justice and the Politics of Difference*, 168*ff*. One striking feature of Patricia Hill Collins's *Black Feminist Thought: Knowledge, Consciousness, and the Politics of Empowerment* (New York: Routledge, 2000) is how she portrays individuality as emerging through interactions both within the black community and between that community and the larger, racist society. Thus, for instance, a person's history with other community members, as well as the ways in which they have coped with racism outside the community, will affect how their words are weighed by others and the extent to which they are considered having wisdom. The community recognizes individuality, and individuality is defined in the context of the community and its situation in the society. See especially chap. 10. In this

book, Collins tends to downplay conflict and differential power within as well as diversity among African American communities, but in her *Fighting Words: Black Women and the Search for Justice* (Minneapolis: University of Minnesota Press, 1998), she begins to wrestle with the differences that emerge in black feminist discourse.

28. In general, working-class and/or feminist women of color seem far more aware than white, middle-class feminists of how much *work* is needed to sustain community. See Suzanne C. Carothers, "Generation to Generation: The Transmission of Knowledge, Skills, and Role Models from Black Working Mothers to Their Daughters in a Southern Community" (Ph.D. dissertation, New York University, 1987).

29. See Patrocinio P. Schweickart, "Speech Is Silver, Silence Is Gold," in *Knowledge, Difference, and Power: Essays Inspired by* Women's Ways of Knowing, ed. Nancy Rule Goldberger, Jill Mattuck Tarule, Blythe McVicker Clinchy, and Mary Field Belenky (New York: Basic, 1996), 305–31. The talking/listening division of labor also can support domination, of course; see Pamela M. Fishman's now classic research on male–female conversation patterns, for example: "Interaction: The Work Women Do," *Social Problems* 25, no. 4 (April 1978): 397–406.

30. See Anne Phillips, "Dealing with Difference: A Politics of Ideas, or a Politics of Presence," in *Democracy and Difference: Contesting Boundaries of the Political,* ed. Seyla Benhabib (Princeton, N.J.: Princeton University Press, 1996), 140–52. Regarding a politics of presence, I am struck by Native American lesbian writer Beth Brant's remark that rather than "come out," she prefers an approach in which you "present yourself to the Creator, not the people." This way, she argues, is more consonant with the value her people place on being a part of nature. See "Recovery and Transformation: *The Blue Heron,*" in *Bridges of Power,* ed. Albrecht and Brewer, 118–21.

31. Seyla Benhabib contrasts the notion of fungible persons with the "concrete other," in "The Generalized Other and the Concrete Other," in *Women and Moral Theory,* ed. Kittay and Meyers, 154–77.

32. See Liza Fiol-Matta, "Litmus Tests for Curriculum Transformation," *Women's Studies Quarterly* 21, nos. 3 & 4 (Fall/Winter 1993): 161–63, and Liza Fiol-Matta and Mariam K. Chamberlain, eds., *Women of Color and the Multicultural Curriculum: Transforming the College Classroom* (New York: Feminist Press at the City University of New York, 1994).

33. Ruth Frankenberg's *White Women, Race Matters: The Social Construction of Whiteness* (Minneapolis: University of Minnesota Press, 1993) is written in the spirit of educating whites about white privilege. Peggy McIntosh has given the critique of white privilege an influential pedagogical form in her essay "White Privilege and Male Privilege: A Personal Account of Coming to See Correspondences through Work in Women's Studies," in *Race, Class, and Gender: An Anthology,* ed. Margaret L. Andersen and Patricia Hill Collins, 3d ed. (Belmont, Calif.: Wadsworth, 1998), 94–105. Sandra M. Lawrence describes how as the result of using McIntosh's exercises in a mixed class, African American students became increasingly angry and more convinced than ever of the depth of racism as white students acknowledged their lack of awareness of how white skin privilege affects people

of color. See "Bringing White Privilege into Consciousness," *Multicultural Education* 3, no. 3 (Spring, 1996): 46–48. Lorraine Cohen presents a provocative model of pedagogical work on white privilege in "Facilitating the Critique of Racism and Classism: An Experiential Model for Euro-American Middle-Class Students," *Teaching Sociology* 23, no. 2 (April 1995): 87–93.

34. See bell hooks, "Revolutionary Feminism: An Anti-Racist Agenda," in *Killing Rage*, 98–107; and *Teaching to Transgress: Education as the Practice of Freedom* (New York: Routledge, 1994), 93*ff*.

35. See Chela Sandoval's indictment of the "hegemonic feminism" of privileged women in "U.S. Third World Feminism: The Theory and Method of Oppositional Consciousness in a Postmodern World," *Genders* 10 (Spring, 1991): 1–24, as well as Collins, *Fighting Words*. In writing like *Sisters of the Yam: Black Women and Self-Recovery* (Boston: South End, 1993), bell hooks, too, promotes discourse *among* black women.

36. Educators working in the group relations tradition point out that in group contexts, black and white women often develop an emotional division of labor in which black women express the anger while white women express the vulnerability. See Medria L. Connolly and Debra A. Noumair, "The White Girl in Me, the Colored Girl in You, and the Lesbian in Us: Crossing Boundaries," in *Off-White: Readings on Race, Power, and Society*, ed. Michelle Fine, Lois Weis, Linda C. Powell, and L. Mun Wong (New York: Routledge, 1997), 322–32. My thanks to Ellen Short for bringing this piece to my attention.

37. See Cherríe Moraga and Gloria Anzaldúa, *This Bridge Called My Back: Writings by Radical Women of Color* (Watertown, Mass.: Persephone, 1981); and Gloria Anzaldúa, "Bridge, Drawbridge, Sandbar or Island: Lesbians-of-Color: Haciendo Alianzas," in *Bridges of Power*, ed. Albrecht and Brewer, 216–31.

CHAPTER 7

1. See Ferenc Fehrér, "The Status of Hope at the End of the Century," in *The Left in Search of a Center*, ed. Michael Crozier and Peter Murphy (Urbana: University of Illinois Press, 1996), 31–42; and Michel Foucault, *Power/Knowledge: Selected Interviews and Other Writings, 1972–1977*, ed. Colin Gordon (New York: Pantheon, 1980). In the United States, Foucault's writing seems to have encouraged both pessimism and optimism about the prospects for social change, which may account for its adoption not only by people with a wide variety of political values but by academic proponents of social justice who themselves feel deeply conflicted about the prospects for change. Sue Middleton describes how the political backlash against social justice reforms in New Zealand undermined the hopes and ideals of left and feminist educators in *Educating Feminists: Life Histories and Pedagogy* (New York: Teachers College Press, 1993). See also Francis Bartkowski, *Feminist Utopias* (Lincoln: University of Nebraska Press, 1989).

2. See Karl Marx and Frederick Engels, *The German Ideology*, ed. C. J. Arthur (New York: International Publishing, 1978). The attempt to overcome the split between mental and manual work is typical of but not confined to socialist criticism and practices, and the results of trying to abolish this split have been very mixed.

Feminists have struggled with this issue in relation to caring. See Sara Ruddick, *Maternal Thinking: Toward a Politics of Peace* (Boston: Beacon, 1989); and Margaret Urban Walker, ed., *Mother Time: Women, Aging, and Ethics* (Lanham, Md.: Rowman & Littlefield, 1999).

3. My use of the term *deferred hope* owes a debt to "Dream Variations," a song composed and sung by the African American women's group Sweet Honey in the Rock and based on a poem by Langston Hughes (music by Charles Mann, "Sweet Honey in the Rock," Flying Fish Music, BMI 1976). The refrain of this song, "nothing lights a fire like a dream deferred," resonates strongly with the sense during the civil rights movement that deferring hopes for so long had created a passion for justice in the hearts of African Americans that finally demanded expression and real change.

4. The distinction between education and politics made by major social theorists such as Max Weber and Hannah Arendt and to which I alluded in my discussion of authority assumes that we can draw a clear line between adult citizens and children who do not have the capacity to participate as full citizens. Arendt's criticism of the participation of children in adult political activities may have stemmed from its association with the Nazi political "education" of children. See her "The Crisis in Education" in Arendt, *Between Past and Future: Six Exercises in Political Thought* (Cleveland: World, 1961), 173–96. The participation of children in the civil rights movement, as well as the fact that many children directly face issues such as drugs and poverty, has inspired activists and academics to take a closer look at children's relation to political activism in a variety of situations. See Jonathan G. Silin, *Sex, Death, and the Education of Children: Our Passion for Ignorance in the Age of AIDS* (New York: Teachers College Press, 1995); and Judith Y. Singer, "Fighting for a Better World: Teaching in an Inner-City Day Care Center" (Ph.D. dissertation, New York University, 1998).

5. The notion that education involves mere preparation or rehearsal for action becomes especially problematic when practices such as internships or required exercises done outside class have real political and ethical consequences for others. I have been particularly disturbed when workshops or courses in which I have been a student have involved actions such as guerilla theater that, because *we* were students, were treated as though they did not count as real actions. In these cases, the logic of preparation exempted us from engaging in much needed political discussion about what we were doing.

6. My concern with the question of heroism and risk taking in political action grew out of my self-questioning about what it meant to be a feminist activist and is reflected in my essay "Who Needs Woman Heros?" *Heresies* 3, no. 1 (Fall 1980): 10–13. The wonderful illustrations by Barbara Nessim that accompany this essay show a woman whose insistence on looking up to an imaginary female ideal make it difficult for her to look her women comrades in the eye. In making this argument, I do not mean to diminish the value of political courage but suggest that we view it broadly and complexly. See Holloway Sparks, "Dissident Citizenship: Democratic Theory, Political Courage, and Activist Women," *Hypatia* 12, no. 4 (Fall 1997): 74–110.

7. The concept of progress (like "community" and "identity") has been criti-

NOTES

cized from a variety of political angles. Joan Kelly-Gadol's classic piece "Did Women Have a Renaissance?" in *Becoming Visible: Women in European History,* ed. Renate Bridenthal and Claudia Koonz (Boston: Houghton Mifflin, 1977), 137–64, helped to initiate questions about women's relation to male-centered notions of "progress." Third World feminist arguments, like that of Uma Narayan, in "The Project of Feminist Epistemology: Perspectives from a Nonwestern Feminist," in *Gender/Body/Knowledge: Feminist Reconstructions of Being and Knowing,* ed. Alison M. Jaggar and Susan R. Bordo (New Brunswick, N.J.: Rutgers University Press, 1989), 256–69, have challenged Western feminist academic critiques of progress. Also see Jeffrey C. Alexander and Piotr Sztompka, eds., *Rethinking Progress: Movements, Forces, and Ideas at the End of the 20th Century* (Boston: Unwin Hyman, 1990).

8. See Jennifer M. Gore, *The Struggle for Pedagogies: Critical and Feminist Discourses as Regimes of Truth* (New York: Routledge, 1993), and Indira Karamcheti, "Caliban in the Classroom," in *Pedagogy: The Question of Impersonation,* ed. Jane Gallop (Bloomington: Indiana University Press, 1995). These and similar pieces also suggest the difficulty of teaching social justice materials in a period and place that provide such teachers little support, the support neither of a visible and effective social movement nor, in many cases, of enough like-minded colleagues to demand and help to bring about increased social justice within the institution. Acting alone or from a position of weakness increases the sense that all activities are dangerous. Being the only one or one of very few teachers who are distinguished by their race, ethnicity, gender, or sexual orientation reduces the possibility of exploring positive teaching models in which minority teachers put themselves at the center.

9. See Wendy Brown, "The Impossibility of Women's Studies," *Differences: A Journal of Feminist Cultural Studies* 9, no. 3 (Fall 1997): 79–101; and Rosi Braidotti, *Nomadic Subjects: Embodiment and Sexual Difference in Contemporary Feminist Theory* (New York: Columbia University Press, 1994), 209*ff.* In "Professing Feminism: Feminist Academics and the Women's Movement," *Psychology of Women Quarterly* 7, no. 1 (Fall 1982): 55–69, I argue that conflicts among feminist academics about what kinds of knowledge advances our politics are often rooted in part in disciplinary rivalries. This also applies to our notions of what constitutes an adequate feminist pedagogy, an argument I made in "Philosophy and Education in Feminist Pedagogical Practice," presented at the National Women's Studies Association in June 1999.

10. As with many of my stories, this rendering of the debate among feminist theorists draws on many feminist panels I have attended and does not refer to specific individuals. However, the ambiance of such occasions is suggested by a series of papers coming out of a conference that I did *not* attend that was published in *Feminist Contentions: A Philosophical Exchange,* ed. Seyla Benhabib, Judith Butler, Drucilla Cornell, and Nancy Fraser (New York: Routledge, 1995). The issue of who should be included in or excluded from a given feminist discussion is complicated. In her strong argument for inclusivity as an epistemological requirement for feminist thinking, Helen E. Longino nevertheless ends up excluding what she considers "crackpot theories," leaving us with the problem of how we determine

which theories are beyond the pale of consideration and which are not. See her "Subjects, Power, and Knowledge: Description and Prescription in Feminist Philosophies of Science," in *Feminist Epistemologies,* ed. Linda Alcoff and Elizabeth Potter (New York: Routledge, 1993), 101–20.

11. I am referring to Bernice Reagon's 1981 classic essay on differences among feminists, "Coalition Politics: Turning the Century," in *Home Girls: A Black Feminist Anthology,* ed. Barbara Smith (New York: Kitchen Table: Women of Color Press, 1983), 356–68. At the beginning of this piece, Reagon emphasizes that doing coalition work, as she describes it, is not a matter of what is appealing but of survival. "The only reason you would consider trying to team up with somebody who could possibly kill you, is because that's the only way you can figure you can stay alive" (356–57). Although this may be stretching the analogy, I suspect that the only reason that feminists with strong investments in competing theories would be willing to engage fully with each other in feminist discourse is if they saw their survival at stake in some important respects. Without such an incentive, there is no compelling reason for us as feminist academics to leave the theoretical and/or disciplinary homes we make for ourselves and to which we more or less belong. On some of the problems with and limits to the actual building of political coalitions, see Gretchen Arnold, "Dilemmas of Feminist Coalitions," in *Feminist Organizations: Harvest of the New Women's Movement,* ed. Myra Marx Ferree and Patricia Yancey Martin (Philadelphia: Temple University Press, 1995), 276–90.

12. Ellen Cronan Rose describes an interesting and troubling collision between "advanced" and "beginning" students in "'This Class Meets in Cyberspace': Women's Studies via Distance Education," in *Meeting the Challenge: Innovative Feminist Pedagogies in Action,* ed. Maralee Mayberry and Ellen Cronan Rose (New York: Routledge, 1999), 141–67.

13. Audre Lorde makes this comment in "Eye to Eye: Black Women, Hatred, and Anger," in *Sister Outsider: Essays and Speeches* (Trumansburg, N.Y.: Crossing Press, 1984), 157.

14. See María C. Lugones and Elizabeth V. Spelman, "Competition, Compassion, and Community: Models for a Feminist Ethos," in *Competition: A Feminist Taboo?* ed. Valerie Miner and Helen E. Longino (New York: Feminist Press, 1987), 234–47. Lugones and Spelman make the related argument that in order for some to play the competition game, others must work to sustain the structure that supports that game (who sweeps up the floor afterward, sews the teams' costumes, etc.?). Women trying to emancipate themselves from the caring role and eager to join the game itself often fail to ask about whose labor makes that game possible. Christine Overall is a keen critic of competition in academia in *A Feminist I: Reflections from Academia* (Peterborough, Canada: Broadview, 1998), while Janice Moulton points to the limits of certain forms of competition for the field of philosophy in "A Paradigm of Philosophy: The Adversary Method," in *Women, Knowledge, and Reality: Explorations in Feminist Philosophy,* ed. Ann Garry and Marilyn Pearsall, 2d ed. (New York: Routledge, 1996), 11–25.

15. See Paula Gunn Allen, "The Ceremonial Motion of Indian Time: Long Ago, So Far," in Allen, *The Sacred Hoop: Recovering the Feminine in American Indian Traditions* (Boston: Beacon, 1986), 147–54.

16. See Julia Kristeva, "Women's Time," in *Feminist Theory: A Critique of Ideology*, ed. Nannerl O. Keohane, Michelle Z. Rosaldo, and Barbara C. Gelpi (Chicago: University of Chicago Press, 1982), 31–53. Kristeva goes on to explore a notion of time geared to the symbolic rather than historical order.

17. See Karl Mannheim, "The Problem of Generations," in Mannheim, *Essays on the Sociology of Knowledge*, ed. Paul Kecskemeti (London: Routledge & Kegan Paul, 1952), 276–320.

18. See Gloria I. Joseph's "Black Mothers and Daughters: Their Roles and Functions in American Society," in *Common Differences: Conflicts in Black and White Feminist Perspectives,* ed. Gloria I. Joseph and Jill Lewis (New York: Doubleday, 1981), 75–126. The range and complexity of these intergenerational relationships are suggested in Patricia Bell-Scott et al., eds., *Double Stitch: Black Women Write about Mothers and Daughters* (Boston: Beacon, 1991).

19. See Nancy Whittier, *Feminist Generations: The Persistence of the Radical Women's Movement* (Philadelphia: Temple University Press, 1995).

20. Adrienne Rich, "Toward a Woman-Centered University" (1973–1974), in Rich, *On Lies, Secrets, and Silence: Selected Prose 1966–1978* (New York: Norton, 1979), 125–55.

POSTSCRIPT

1. Although it began as an independent faculty initiative, I was able to publicize and expand the scope of the seminar with the support of Mona Kreaden, director of the EQUAL Commission at New York University. Among its many activities, the commission sponsors a series of faculty development workshops and seminars. As the seminar grew, it became incorporated into the commission's work and acquired a formal title.

2. Critical educational theorists frequently point to the dangers of a managerial ethos in teaching as well as society in general. For example, in *Theory and Resistance in Education: A Pedagogy for the Opposition* (South Hadley, Mass.: Bergin & Garvey, 1983), Henry A. Giroux argues that instead of addressing questions of basic political values, "educators have generally retreated . . . to questions of technique, organization, and administration" (193).

Bibliography

Abel, Emily K., and Margaret K. Nelson, eds. *Circles of Care: Work and Identity in Women's Lives.* Albany: State University of New York Press, 1990.

Acker, Sandra. "Feminist Theory and the Study of Gender and Education." *International Review of Education* 33, no. 4 (1987): 419–35.

Adams, Maurianne, Lee Anne Bell, and Pat Griffin, eds. *Teaching for Diversity and Social Justice: A Sourcebook.* New York: Routledge, 1997.

Addelson, Kathryn Pyne. *Impure Thoughts: Essays on Philosophy, Feminism, and Ethics.* Philadelphia: Temple University Press, 1991.

———. "Knower/Doers and Their Moral Problems," pp. 265–94 in Alcoff and Potter (1993).

Adler, Mortimer J. *The Conditions of Philosophy: Its Checkered Past, Its Present Disorder, and Its Future Promise.* New York: Atheneum, 1965.

———. *Reforming Education: The Opening of the American Mind.* Ed. Geraldine Van Doren. New York: Macmillan, 1977.

Aegerter, Lindsay Pentolfe. "Michelle Cliff and the Paradox of Privilege." *College English* 59, no. 8 (December 1997): 898–915.

Aerni, April Laskey, and KimMarie McGoldrick, eds. *Valuing Us All: Feminist Pedagogy and Economics.* Ann Arbor: University of Michigan Press, 1999.

Afzal-Khan, Fawzia. "Introducing a New Course: Muslim Women in Twentieth-Century Literature." *NWSA Journal* 9, no. 1 (Spring 1997): 76–88.

Alarcón, Norma. "The Theoretical Subject(s) of *This Bridge Called My Back* and Anglo-American Feminism," pp. 356–69 in Anzaldúa (1990).

Albrecht, Lisa, and Rose M. Brewer, eds. *Bridges of Power: Women's Multicultural Alliances.* Philadelphia: New Society, 1990.

Alcoff, Linda. "Cultural Feminism versus Post-Structuralism: The Identity Crisis in Feminist Theory." *Signs: Journal of Women in Culture and Society* 13, no. 3 (Spring 1988): 405–36.

———. "Justifying Feminist Social Science," pp. 85–103 in Tuana (1989).

Alcoff, Linda, and Elizabeth Potter, eds. *Feminist Epistemologies.* New York: Routledge, 1993.

Alexander, Jeffrey C., and Piotr Sztompka, eds. *Rethinking Progress: Movements, Forces, and Ideas at the End of the 20th Century.* Boston: Unwin Hyman, 1990.

Alexander, M. Jacqui, and Chandra Talpade Mohanty, eds. *Feminist Genealogies, Colonial Legacies, Democratic Futures.* New York: Routledge, 1997.

Allen, Jeffner, ed. *Lesbian Philosophies and Cultures.* Albany: State University of New York Press, 1990.

————. "Motherhood: The Annihilation of Women," pp. 315–30 in Trebilcot (1983).

Allen, Pamela. *Free Space: A Perspective on the Small Group in Women's Liberation.* New York: Times Change, 1970.

Allen, Paula Gunn. *The Sacred Hoop: Recovering the Feminine in American Indian Traditions.* Boston: Beacon, 1986.

Alperin, Davida J. "Social Diversity and the Necessity of Alliances: A Developing Feminist Perspective," pp. 23–33 in Albrecht and Brewer (1990).

Andersen, Margaret L., and Patricia Hill Collins, eds. *Race, Class, and Gender: An Anthology.* 3d ed. Belmont, Calif.: Wadsworth, 1998.

Anderson, Benedict. *Imagined Communities: Reflections on the Origin and Spread of Nationalism.* London: Verso, 1991.

Anzaldúa, Gloria. *Borderlands/La Frontera: The New Mestiza.* San Francisco: Aunt Lute Books, 1987.

————. "Bridge, Drawbridge, Sandbar or Island: Lesbians-of-Color *Haciendo Alianzas*," pp. 216–31 in Albrecht and Brewer (1990).

————. "Haciendo Caras, una Entrada," pp. xv–xxviii in Anzaldúa (1990).

————, ed. *Making Face, Making Soul/Haciendo Caras: Creative and Critical Perspectives by Feminists of Color.* San Francisco: Aunt Lute Books, 1990.

Aptheker, Bettina. *Tapestries of Life: Women's Work, Women's Consciousness, and the Meaning of Daily Experience.* Amherst: University of Massachusetts Press, 1989.

Arenal, Electa, ed. *Rethinking Self and Society: Subjectivity, Gender and Identity.* Senter for humanistisk kvinneforskning, Skriftserien nr. 9. Bergen, Norway: University of Bergen, 1997.

Arendt, Hannah. *Between Past and Future: Six Exercises in Political Thought.* Cleveland: World, 1961.

————. *Eichmann in Jerusalem: A Report on the Banality of Evil.* Rev. and enlarged ed. New York: Viking, 1965.

————. *The Human Condition.* Chicago: University of Chicago Press, 1958.

————. *On Violence.* New York: Harcourt, Brace & World, 1970.

Arnold, Gretchen. "Dilemmas of Feminist Coalitions: Collective Identity and Strategic Effectiveness in the Battered Women's Movement," pp. 276–90 in Ferree and Martin (1995).

Arnot, Madeleine, and Kathleen Weiler, eds. *Feminism and Social Justice in Education: International Perspectives.* London: Falmer, 1993.

Arthur, John, and Amy Shapiro, eds. *Campus Wars: Multiculturalism and the Politics of Difference.* Boulder, Colo.: Westview, 1995.

Azara, Nancy, and Roxanne M. Green. "Working with the Light: Women of Vision," pp. 33–42 in Chesler, Rothblum, and Cole (1995).

Baars, Bernard J. *In the Theater of Consciousness: The Workspace of the Mind.* New York: Oxford University Press, 1997.

Babbitt, Susan E. "Feminism and Objective Interests: The Role of Transformation Experiences in Rational Deliberation," pp. 245–64 in Alcoff and Potter (1993).

Baca Zinn, Maxine, and Bonnie Thornton Dill. "Theorizing Difference from Multiracial Feminism." *Feminist Studies* 22, no. 2 (Summer 1996): 321–31.

———, eds. *Women of Color in U.S. Society*. Philadelphia: Temple University Press, 1994.

Baier, Annette C. *Moral Prejudices: Essays on Ethics*. Cambridge, Mass.: Harvard University Press, 1994.

Bair, Deirdre. *Simone de Beauvoir: A Biography*. New York: Summit, 1990.

Ball, Wendy. "Feminist Teaching in a Law Faculty in New Zealand," pp. 299–316 in Mayberry and Rose (1999).

Banks, James A. *Educating Citizens in a Multicultural Society*. New York: Teachers College Press, 1997.

Bannerji, Himani, Linda Carty, Kari Dehli, Susan Heald, and Kate McKenna, eds. *Unsettling Relations: The University as a Site of Feminist Struggles*. Toronto: Women's Press, 1991.

Bar On, Bat-Ami. "Marginality and Epistemic Privilege," pp. 83–100 in Alcoff and Potter (1993).

Barber, Benjamin R. *Strong Democracy: Participatory Politics for a New Age*. Berkeley: University of California Press, 1984.

Bartkowski, Frances. *Feminist Utopias*. Lincoln: University of Nebraska Press, 1989.

Bartky, Sandra Lee. "Agency: What's the Problem?" pp. 178–93 in Gardiner (1995).

———. *Femininity and Domination: Studies in the Phenomenology of Oppression*. New York: Routledge, 1990.

———. "Sympathy and Solidarity: On a Tightrope with Scheler," pp. 177–96 in Meyers (1997).

Basu, Amrita, ed. *The Challenge of Local Feminisms: Women's Movements in Global Perspective*. Boulder, Colo.: Westview, 1995.

Batchelder, Eleanor Olds, and Linda Nathan Marks. "Creating Alternatives: A Survey of Women's Projects." *Heresies: A Feminist Publication on Art & Politics* 2, no. 3, issue 7, "Women Working Together" (Spring 1979): 97–127.

Beck, Evelyn Torton, ed. *Nice Jewish Girls: A Lesbian Anthology*. Trumansburg, N.Y.: Crossing, 1982.

Beecher, Catharine E., and Harriet Beecher Stowe. *The American Woman's Home: Or, Principles of Domestic Science*. New York: Ford, 1870.

Belenky, Mary Field, Blythe McVicker Clinchy, Nancy Rule Goldberger, and Jill Mattuck Tarule. *Women's Ways of Knowing: The Development of Self, Voice, and Mind*. New York: Basic Books, 1986.

Belenky, Mary Field, Lynne A. Bond, and Jacqueline S. Weinstock. *A Tradition That Has No Name: Nurturing the Development of People, Families, and Communities*. New York: Basic Books. 1997.

Bell-Scott, Patricia, et al., eds. *Double Stitch: Black Women Write about Mothers and Daughters*. Boston: Beacon, 1991.

Benhabib, Seyla, ed. *Democracy and Difference: Contesting Boundaries of the Political*. Princeton, N.J.: Princeton University Press, 1996.

———. "Feminism and Postmodernism: An Uneasy Alliance," pp. 17–34 in Benhabib, Butler, Cornell, and Fraser (1995).

———. "The Generalized and the Concrete Other: The Kohlberg–Gilligan Controversy and Moral Theory," pp. 154–77 in Kittay and Meyers (1987).

———. *Situating the Self: Gender, Community and Postmodernism in Contemporary Ethics*. New York: Routledge, 1992.

Benhabib, Seyla, and Drucilla Cornell, eds. *Feminism as Critique: On the Politics of Gender*. Minneapolis: University of Minnesota Press, 1987.

Benhabib, Seyla, Judith Butler, Drucilla Cornell, and Nancy Fraser, eds. *Feminist Contentions: A Philosophical Exchange*. New York: Routledge, 1995.

Benjamin, Jessica. *The Bonds of Love: Psychoanalysis, Feminism, and the Problem of Domination*. New York: Pantheon, 1988.

Berliner, Sister Patricia Mary. "Revaluing the Feminine: The Process of Psychospiritual Change in Contemporary Roman Catholic Women." Ph.D. dissertation, New York University, 1990.

Berry, Ellen, and Elizabeth Black. "The Integrative Learning Journal (or, Getting beyond 'True Confessions' and 'Cold Knowledge')." *Women's Studies Quarterly* 21, nos. 3 & 4 (Fall/Winter 1993): 88–93.

Bickford, Susan. "Anti-Anti-Identity Politics: Feminism, Democracy, and the Complexities of Citizenship." *Hypatia: A Journal of Feminist Philosophy* 12, no. 4, special issue on "Citizenship in Feminism: Identity, Action, and Locale," ed. Kathleen B. Jones (Fall 1997): 111–31.

———. *The Dissonance of Democracy: Listening, Conflict, and Citizenship*. Ithaca, N.Y.: Cornell University Press, 1996.

Boal, Augusto. *Theater of the Oppressed*. Trans. Charles A. and Maria-Odilia Leal McBride. New York: Urizen, 1979.

Boardman, Kathleen A., Jonathan Alexander, Margaret M. Barber, and Peter Pinney. "Teacher Involvement and Transformative Power on a Gender Issues Discussion List," pp. 169–90 in Mayberry and Rose (1999).

Bohman, James. *Public Deliberation: Pluralism, Complexity and Democracy*. Cambridge, Mass.: MIT Press, 1996.

Bohmer, Susanne. "Resistance to Generalizations in the Classroom," pp. 61–69 in Cohee et al. (1998).

Bok, Sissela. *Lying: Moral Choice in Public and Private Life*. New York: Pantheon, 1978.

Bologh, Roslyn Wallach. *Love or Greatness: Max Weber and Masculine Thinking—A Feminist Inquiry*. London: Unwin Hyman, 1990.

Boomer, Garth, et al., ed. *Negotiating the Curriculum: Educating for the 21st Century*. London: Falmer, 1992.

Bordo, Susan. "Feminism, Postmodernism, and Gender Scepticism," pp. 133–56 in Nicholson (1990).

Bottomore, Tom, and Robert Nisbet, eds. *A History of Sociological Analysis*. New York: Basic Books, 1978.

Bowles, Samuel, and Herbert Gintis. *Schooling in Capitalist America: Educational Reform and the Contradictions of Economic Life*. New York: Basic Books, 1977.

Boyte, Harry C. "The Pragmatic Ends of Popular Politics," pp. 340–55 in Calhoun (1992).

Brady, Jeanne. *Schooling Young Children: A Feminist Pedagogy for Liberatory Learning*. Albany: State University of New York Press, 1995.

Brady, Maureen. *Give Me Your Good Ear*. New York: Spinsters, 1979.

Braidotti, Rosi. *Nomadic Subjects: Embodiment and Sexual Difference in Contemporary Feminist Theory*. New York: Columbia University Press, 1994.

Brandow, Karen, Jim McDonnell, and Vocations for Social Change. *No Bosses Here! A Manual on Working Collectively and Cooperatively*. 2d ed. Boston: Alyson and Vocations for Social Change, 1981.

Brant, Beth. "Recovery and Transformation: *The Blue Heron*," pp. 118–21 in Albrecht and Brewer (1990).

Breines, Wini. *Community and Organization in the New Left, 1962–1968: The Great Refusal*. New York: Praeger, 1982.

———. *Young, White, and Miserable: Growing up Female in the Fifties*. Boston: Beacon, 1992.

Bridenthal, Renate, and Claudia Koonz, eds. *Becoming Visible: Women in European History*. Boston: Houghton Mifflin, 1977.

Britzman, Deborah P. *Practice Makes Practice: A Critical Study of Learning to Teach*. Albany: State University of New York Press, 1991.

Brown, Elsa Barkley. "African-American Women's Quilting: A Framework for Conceptualizing and Teaching African-American Women's History." *Signs: Journal of Women in Culture and Society* 14, no. 4 (Summer 1989): 921–29.

Brown, Karen McCarthy. *Mama Lola: A Vodou Priestess in Brooklyn*. Berkeley: University of California Press, 1991.

Brown, Wendy. "The Impossibility of Women's Studies." *Differences: A Journal of Feminist Cultural Studies* 9, no. 3 (Fall 1997): 79–101.

Bulkin, Elly, Minnie Bruce Pratt, and Barbara Smith, eds. *Yours in Struggle: Three Feminist Perspectives on Anti-Semitism and Racism*. Brooklyn, N.Y.: Long Haul, 1984.

Bunch, Charlotte. *Passionate Politics: Feminist Theory in Action*. New York: St. Martin's, 1987.

Bunch, Charlotte, and Sandra Pollack, eds. *Learning Our Way: Essays in Feminist Education*. Trumansburg, N.Y.: Crossing, 1983.

Bunch, Charlotte, et al., eds. *Building Feminist Theory: Essays from* Quest: a feminist quarterly. New York: Longman, 1981.

Butler, Judith. *Bodies That Matter: On the Discursive Limits of "Sex."* New York: Routledge, 1993.

———. *Gender Trouble: Feminism and the Subversion of Identity*. New York: Routledge, 1990.

Butler, Judith, and Joan W. Scott, eds. *Feminists Theorize the Political*. New York: Routledge, 1992.

Butler, Sandra, and Barbara Rosenblum. *Cancer in Two Voices*. San Francisco: Spinsters, 1991.

Calhoun, Craig, ed. *Habermas and the Public Sphere*. Cambridge, Mass.: MIT Press, 1992.

Campbell, Sue. *Interpreting the Personal: Expression and the Formation of Feelings.* Ithaca, N.Y.: Cornell University Press, 1997.

Cannon, Katie Geneva. *Katie's Canon: Womanism and the Soul of the Black Community.* New York: Continuum, 1995.

Cantarow, Ellen, with Susan Gushee O'Malley and Sharon Hartman Strom. *Moving the Mountain: Women Working for Social Change.* Old Westbury, N.Y.: Feminist Press, 1980.

Caraway, Nancie. *Segregated Sisterhood: Racism and the Politics of American Feminism.* Knoxville: University of Tennessee Press, 1991.

Card, Claudia, ed. *Feminist Ethics.* Lawrence: University of Kansas Press, 1991.

———. "Pluralist Lesbian Separatism," pp. 125–41 in Allen (1990).

Cardea, Caryatis. "Lesbian Revolution and the 50 Minute Hour: A Working-Class Look at Therapy and the Movement," pp. 193–217 in Allen (1990).

Carothers, Suzanne C. "Catching Sense: Learning from Our Mothers to Be Black and Female," pp. 232–47 in Ginsburg and Tsing (1990).

———. "Generation to Generation: The Transmission of Knowledge, Skills, and Role Models from Black Working Mothers to Their Daughters in a Southern Community." Ph.D. dissertation, New York University, 1987.

Carty, Linda. "Black Women in Academia: A Statement from the Periphery," pp. 13–44 in Bannerji, Carty, Dehli, Heald, and McKenna (1991).

Chase, Rebecca M. "Writing an Examined Life: A Lesbian Feminist Educator's Inquiry into Writing Autobiography." Ph.D. dissertation, New York University, 1999.

Chesler, Phyllis, Esther D. Rothblum, and Ellen Cole, eds. *Feminist Foremothers in Women's Studies, Psychology, and Mental Health.* New York: Harrington Park, 1995.

Chodorow, Nancy. *The Reproduction of Mothering: Psychoanalysis and the Sociology of Gender.* Berkeley: University of California Press, 1978.

Chow, Esther Ngan-Ling. "Asian American Women at Work," pp. 203–27 in Baca Zinn and Dill (1994).

Christensen, C. Roland, David A. Garvin, and Ann Sweet, eds. *Education for Judgment: The Artistry of Discussion Leadership.* Boston: Harvard Business School Press, 1991.

Christian, Barbara. *Black Women Novelists: The Development of a Tradition, 1892–1976.* Westport, Conn.: Greenwood, 1980.

———. "The Race for Theory," pp. 335–45 in Anzaldúa (1990).

Clark, VèVè, Shirley Nelson Garner, Margaret Higonnet, and Ketu H. Katrak, eds. *Antifeminism in the Academy.* New York: Routledge, 1996.

Cluster, Dick, ed. *They Should Have Served That Cup of Coffee: 7 Radicals Remember the 60s.* Boston: South End, 1979.

Coben, Diana. *Radical Heroes: Gramsci, Freire, and the Politics of Adult Education.* New York: Garland, 1998.

Cocks, Joan. *The Oppositional Imagination: Feminism, Critique and Political Theory.* London: Routledge, 1989.

Code, Lorraine. *Epistemic Responsibility.* Hanover, N.H.: Published for Brown University Press by University Press of New England, 1987.

————. *What Can She Know? Feminist Theory and the Construction of Knowledge.* Ithaca, N.Y.: Cornell University Press, 1991.

Cogan, Frances B. *All-American Girl: The Ideal of Real Womanhood in Mid-nineteenth-century America.* Athens: University of Georgia Press, 1989.

Cohee, Gail E., et al., eds. *The Feminist Teacher Anthology: Pedagogies and Classroom Strategies.* New York: Teachers College Press, 1998.

Cohen, Lorraine. "Facilitating the Critique of Racism and Classism: An Experiential Model for Euro-American Middle-Class Students." *Teaching Sociology* 23, no. 2 (April 1995): 87–93.

————. "Reinterpreting Rosa Luxemburg's Theory of Social Change: Consciousness, Action, and Leadership." Ph.D. dissertation, City University of New York, 1987.

Collins, Patricia Hill. *Black Feminist Thought: Knowledge, Consciousness, and the Politics of Empowerment.* Boston: Unwin Hyman, 1990.

————. *Fighting Words: Black Women and the Search for Justice.* Minneapolis: University of Minnesota Press, 1998.

Combahee River Collective. "A Black Feminist Statement," pp. 13–22 in Hull, Scott, and Smith (1982).

Connolly, Medria L., and Debra A. Noumair. "The White Girl in Me, the Colored Girl in You, and the Lesbian in Us: Crossing Boundaries," pp. 322–32 in Fine, Weis, Powell, and Wong (1997).

Coover, Virginia, Ellen Deacon, Charles Esser, and Christopher Moore. *Resource Manual for a Living Revolution.* 2d ed. Philadelphia: New Society, 1978.

Cott, Nancy F. *The Grounding of Modern Feminism.* New Haven, Conn.: Yale University Press, 1987.

Cross, Tia, Freada Klein, Barbara Smith, and Beverly Smith. "Face-to-Face, Day-to-Day Racism CR," pp. 52–56 in Hull, Scott, and Smith (1982).

Crozier, Michael, and Peter Murphy, eds. *The Left in Search of a Center.* Urbana: University of Illinois Press, 1996.

Culley, Margo, and Catherine Portuges, eds. *Gendered Subjects: The Dynamics of Feminist Teaching.* Boston: Routledge & Kegan Paul, 1985.

Daly, Mary, with Jane Caputi. *Webster's First New Intergalactic Wickedary of the English Language.* San Francisco: HarperCollins, 1994.

Davis, Barbara Gross. *Tools for Teaching.* San Francisco: Jossey-Bass, 1993.

Davis, Natalie Zemon, et al. "Feminist Book Reviewing (a Symposium)." *Feminist Studies* 14, no. 3 (Fall 1988): 601–622.

de Beauvoir, Simone. *The Second Sex.* New York: Knopf, 1968.

de Lauretis, Teresa. *Alice Doesn't: Feminism, Semiotics, Cinema.* Bloomington: Indiana University Press, 1984.

Deegan, Mary Jo, and Michael R. Hill, eds. *Women and Symbolic Interaction.* Boston: Allen & Unwin, 1987.

Delpit, Lisa, D. "The Silenced Dialogue: Power and Pedagogy in Educating Other People's Children." *Harvard Educational Review* 58, no. 3 (August 1988): 280–98.

Deming, Barbara. *We Are All Part of One Another: A Barbara Deming Reader.* Ed. Jane Meyerding. Philadelphia: New Society, 1984.

Dewey, John. *Art as Experience*. New York: Minton, Balch, 1934.
———. *The Child and the Curriculum and The School and Society*. Chicago: University of Chicago Press, 1956.
———. *Democracy and Education: An Introduction to the Philosophy of Education*. New York: Free Press, 1966.
———. *Experience and Nature*. New York: Dover, 1958.
———. *The Public and Its Problems*. Chicago: Swallow, 1927.
Dietz, Mary G. "Feminist Receptions of Hannah Arendt," pp. 17–50 in Honig (1995).
Dill, Bonnie Thornton. "Fictive Kin, Paper Sons, and *Compadrazgo*: Women of Color and the Struggle for Family Survival," pp. 149–69 in Baca Zinn and Dill (1994).
Diller, Ann. "An Ethics of Care Takes on Pluralism," pp. 161–69 in Diller, Houston, Morgan, and Ayim (1996).
———. "The Ethics of Care and Education: A New Paradigm, Its Critics, and Its Educational Significance," pp. 89–104 in Diller, Houston, Morgan, and Ayim (1996).
Diller, Ann, Barbara Houston, Kathryn Pauly Morgan, and Maryann Ayim, eds. *The Gender Question in Education: Theory, Pedagogy, and Politics*. Boulder, Colo.: Westview, 1996.
Douglas, Carol Anne. *Love and Politics: Radical Feminist and Lesbian Theories*. San Francisco: ISM, 1990.
Dryzek, John S. *Discursive Democracy: Politics, Policy, and Political Science*. Cambridge: Cambridge University Press, 1990.
DuPlessis, Rachel Blau, and Ann Snitow, eds. *The Feminist Memoir Project: Voices from Women's Liberation*. New York: Three Rivers, 1998.
Durbin, Elizabeth, Sonia Ospina, and Ellen Schall. "Living and Learning: Women and Management in Public Service." *Journal of Public Affairs Education* 5, no. 1 (Winter 1999): 25–41.
Ebert, Teresa L. *Ludic Feminism and After: Postmodernism, Desire, and Labor in Late Capitalism*. Ann Arbor: University of Michigan Press, 1996.
Echols, Alice. *Daring to Be Bad: Radical Feminism in America, 1967–1975*. Minneapolis: University of Minnesota Press, 1989.
———. "'We Gotta Get Out of This Place': Notes toward a Remapping of the Sixties." *Socialist Review* 92, no. 2 (April–June 1992): 9–33.
Eisenstein, Hester. *Inside Agitators: Australian Femocrats and the State*. Philadelphia: Temple University Press, 1996.
Ellsworth, Elizabeth. "Why Doesn't This Feel Empowering? Working through the Repressive Myths of Critical Pedagogy." *Harvard Educational Review* 59, no. 3 (August 1989): 297–324.
Elshtain, Jean Bethke. *Power Trips and Other Journeys: Essays in Feminism as Civic Discourse*. Madison: University of Wisconsin Press, 1990.
———. *Public Man, Private Woman: Women in Social and Political Thought*. Princeton, N.J.: Princeton University Press, 1981.
———. "The Social Relations of the Classroom: A Moral and Political Perspective." *Telos* 27 (Spring 1976): 97–110.

Emercheti, Buchi. *Double Yoke.* New York: Braziller, 1983.

Epstein, Barbara. "Ambivalence about Feminism," pp. 124–48 in DuPlessis and Snitow (1998).

Evans, Sara M. *Personal Politics: The Roots of Women's Liberation in the Civil Rights Movement and the New Left.* New York: Vintage, 1980.

Evans, Sara M., and Harry C. Boyte. *Free Spaces: The Sources of Democratic Change in America.* Chicago: University of Chicago Press, 1992.

Farnham, Christie, ed. *The Impact of Feminist Research in the Academy.* Bloomington: Indiana University Press, 1987.

Fehrér, Ferenc. "The Status of Hope at the End of the Century," pp. 31–42 in Crozier and Murphy (1996).

Felman, Shoshana. "Education and Crisis, or the Vicissitudes of Teaching," pp. 1–56 in Felman and Laub (1992).

Felman, Shoshana, and Dori Laub. *Testimony: Crises of Witnessing in Literature, Psychoanalysis, and History.* New York: Routledge, 1992.

Feminist Teacher. Eau Clair, Wisc.: *Feminist Teacher* Editorial Collective, University of Wisconsin, Eau Clair.

Ferguson, Ann. "Can I Choose Who I Am? And How Would That Empower Me? Gender, Race, Identities and the Self," pp. 108–26 in Garry and Pearsall (1996).

Ferguson, Kathy E. *The Feminist Case Against Bureaucracy.* Philadelphia: Temple University Press, 1984.

Fernandes, Leela. "Beyond Public Spaces and Private Spheres: Gender, Family and Working-Class Politics in India." *Feminist Studies* 23, no. 3 (Fall 1997): 525–47.

Ferree, Myra Marx. "The Political Context of Rationality: Rational Choice Theory and Resource Mobilization," pp. 29–52 in Morris and Mueller (1992).

Ferree, Myra Marx, and Patricia Yancey Martin. "Doing the Work of the Movement: Feminist Organizations," pp. 3–23 in Ferree and Martin (1995).

———, eds. *Feminist Organizations: Harvest of the New Women's Movement.* Philadelphia: Temple University Press, 1995.

Fetterley, Judith. *The Resisting Reader: A Feminist Approach to American Fiction.* Bloomington: Indiana University Press, 1978.

Fine, Michelle. "Sexuality, Schooling, and Adolescent Females: The Missing Discourse of Desire." *Harvard Educational Review* 58, no. 1 (February, 1988): 29–53.

Fine, Michelle, and Adrienne Asch, eds. *Women with Disabilities: Essays in Psychology, Culture, and Politics.* Philadelphia: Temple University Press, 1988.

Fine, Michelle, Lois Weis, Linda C. Powell and L. Mun Wong, eds. *Off-White: Readings on Race, Power and Society.* New York: Routledge, 1997.

Fiol-Matta, Liza. "Litmus Tests for Curriculum Transformation." *Women's Studies Quarterly* 21, nos. 3 & 4 (Fall/Winter 1993): 161–63.

Fiol-Matta, Liza, and Mariam K. Chamberlain, eds. *Women of Color and the Multicultural Curriculum: Transforming the College Classroom.* New York: Feminist Press at the City University of New York, 1994.

Firestone, Shulamith. *The Dialectic of Sex: The Case for Feminist Revolution.* New York: Morrow, 1970.

Fisher, Berenice M. "Enhancing Feminist Pedagogy: Multimedia Workshops on Women's Experience with the Newspaper and Home," pp. 98–113 in Cohee et al. (1998).

———. "Feminist Acts: Women, Pedagogy, and Theatre of the Oppressed," pp. 185–97 in Schutzman and Cohen-Cruz (1994).

———. "Guilt and Shame in the Women's Movement: The Radical Ideal of Action and Its Meaning for Feminist Intellectuals." *Feminist Studies* 10, no. 2 (Summer 1984): 185–212.

———. "The Heart Has Its Reasons: Feeling, Thinking, and Community-Building in Feminist Education." *Women's Studies Quarterly* 21, nos. 3 & 4 (Fall/Winter 1993): 75–87.

———. "The Models among Us: Social Authority and Political Activism." *Feminist Studies* 7, no. 1 (Spring 1981): 100–12.

———. "Philosophy and Education in Feminist Pedagogical Practice." Paper presented at the annual meeting of the National Women's Studies Association, Albuquerque, June 1999.

———. "Professing Feminism: Feminist Academics and the Women's Movement." *Psychology of Women Quarterly* 7, no. 1 (Fall 1982): 55–69.

———. "Wandering in the Wilderness: The Search for Women Role Models." *Signs: Journal of Women in Culture and Society* 13, no. 2 (Winter 1988): 211–33.

———. "What Is Feminist Pedagogy?" *Radical Teacher*, no. 18 (1981): 20–24.

———. "Who Needs Woman Heros?" *Heresies: A Feminist Publication on Art & Politics* 3, no. 1, issue 9, "Women Organized/Women Divided: Power, Propaganda & Backlash" (1980): 10–13.

Fisher, Berenice M., and Roberta Galler. "Friendship and Fairness: How Disability Affects Friendship between Women," pp. 172–94 in Fine and Asch (1988).

Fisher, Berenice M., and Anselm L. Strauss. "Interactionism," pp. 457–98 in Bottomore and Nisbet (1978).

Fisher, Berenice M., and Joan Tronto. "Toward a Feminist Theory of Caring," pp. 35–62 in Abel and Nelson (1990).

Fisher, Roger, William Ury, with ed. Bruce Patton. *Getting to Yes: Negotiating Agreement without Giving In.* 2d ed. New York: Penguin, 1991.

Fishman, Pamela M. "Interaction: The Work Women Do." *Social Problems* 25, no. 4 (April 1978): 397–406.

Flacks, Richard. *Making History: The American Left and the American Mind.* New York: Columbia University Press, 1988.

Flax, Jane. "Postmodernism and Gender Relations in Feminist Theory," pp. 39–62 in Nicholson (1990).

———. *Thinking Fragments: Psychoanalysis, Feminism, and Postmodernism in the Contemporary West.* Berkeley: University of California Press, 1990.

Fonow, Mary Margaret, and Judith A. Cook, eds. *Beyond Methodology: Feminist Scholarship as Lived Research.* Bloomington: Indiana University Press, 1991.

Fonseca, Isabel. *Bury Me Standing: The Gypsies and Their Journey.* New York: Random House, 1995.

Forman, James. *The Making of Black Revolutionaries.* New York: Macmillan, 1972.

Foster, Michèle. *Black Teachers on Teaching*. New York: New Press, 1997.

———. "Constancy, Connectedness, and Constraints in the Lives of African-American Teachers." *NWSA Journal* 3, no. 2 (Spring 1991): 233–61.

———. "Othermothers: Exploring the Educational Philosophy of Black American Women Teachers," pp. 101–23 in Arnot and Weiler (1993).

Foster, Susan Leigh. "Choreographies of Gender." *Signs: Journal of Women in Culture and Society* 24, no. 1 (Autumn 1998): 1–33.

Foucault, Michel. *Power/Knowledge: Selected Interviews and Other Writings, 1972–1977*. Ed. Colin Gordon. New York: Pantheon, 1980.

Frankenberg, Ruth. *White Women, Race Matters: The Social Construction of Whiteness*. Minneapolis: University of Minnesota Press, 1993.

Fraser, Nancy. *Justice Interruptus: Critical Reflections on the "Postsocialist" Condition*. New York: Routledge, 1997.

———. "Rethinking the Public Sphere: A Contribution to the Critique of Actually Existing Democracy," pp. 109–42 in Calhoun (1992).

———. *Unruly Practices: Power, Discourse, and Gender in Contemporary Social Theory*. Minneapolis: University of Minnesota Press, 1989.

Fraser, Nancy, and Linda Gordon. "A Genealogy of 'Dependency': Tracing a Keyword of the U.S. Welfare State," pp. 121–49 in Fraser (1997).

Freedman, Estelle B. "Small-Group Pedagogy: Consciousness Raising in Conservative Times," pp. 35–50 in Garber (1994).

Freeman, Jo (Joreen). *The Politics of Women's Liberation: A Case Study of an Emerging Social Movement and Its Relation to the Policy Process*. New York: McKay, 1975.

———. "The Tyranny of Structurelessness," pp. 285–99 in Koedt, Levine, and Rapone (1973).

Freire, Paulo. *Pedagogy of the Oppressed*. Trans. Myra Bergman Ramos. New York: Herder & Herder, 1971.

———. *The Politics of Education: Culture, Power, and Liberation*. Trans. Donaldo Macedo. Intro. Henry A. Giroux. South Hadley, Mass.: Bergin & Garvey, 1985.

Friedan, Betty. *The Feminine Mystique*. New York: Norton, 1963.

Frye, Marilyn. "The Possibility of Feminist Theory," pp. 59–75 in Frye (1992).

———. *Willful Virgin: Essays in Feminism 1976–1992*. Freedom, Calif.: Crossing, 1992.

Funk, Nanette, and Magda Mueller, eds. *Gender Politics and Post-Communism: Reflections from Eastern Europe and the Former Soviet Union*. New York: Routledge, 1993.

Fuss, Diane. *Essentially Speaking: Feminism, Nature & Difference*. New York: Routledge, 1989.

Galler, Roberta. "The Myth of the Perfect Body," pp. 165–72 in Vance (1992).

Gallop, Jane. *Feminist Accused of Sexual Harassment*. Durham, N.C.: Duke University Press, 1997.

———. "Im-personation: A Reading in the Guise of An Introduction," pp. 1–18 in Gallop (1995).

———, ed. *Pedagogy: The Question of Impersonation*. Bloomington: Indiana University Press, 1995.

Garber, Linda, ed. *Tilting the Tower.* New York: Routledge, 1994.

Gardiner, Judith Kegan, ed. *Provoking Agents: Gender and Agency in Theory and Practice.* Urbana: University of Illinois Press, 1995.

Garry, Ann, and Marilyn Pearsall, eds. *Women, Knowledge, and Reality: Explorations in Feminist Philosophy.* 2d ed. New York: Routledge, 1996.

Gentile, Kathryn A. "Healing through Lyrical Improvisations within the Transitional Space of a Diary." Ph.D. dissertation, New York University, 2000.

Giddings, Paula. *When and Where I Enter: The Impact of Black Women on Race and Sex in America.* New York: Bantam, 1984.

Gilbert, Sandra M., and Susan Gubar. *The Madwoman in the Attic: The Woman Writer and the Nineteenth-Century Literary Imagination.* New Haven, Conn.: Yale University Press, 1979.

Gilligan, Carol. *In a Different Voice: Psychological Theory and Women's Development.* Cambridge, Mass.: Harvard University Press, 1982.

Ginsburg, Faye, and Anna Lowenhaupt Tsing, eds. *Uncertain Terms: Negotiating Gender in American Culture.* Boston: Beacon, 1990.

Giroux, Henry A., ed. *Postmodernism, Feminism, and Cultural Politics: Redrawing Educational Boundaries.* Albany: State University of New York Press, 1991.

———. *Schooling and the Struggle for Public Life: Critical Pedagogy in the Modern Age.* Minneapolis: University of Minnesota Press, 1988.

———. *Theory and Resistance in Education: A Pedagogy for the Opposition.* Foreword by Paulo Freire. South Hadley, Mass.: Bergin & Garvey, 1983.

Glen, John Matthew. *Highlander: No Ordinary School, 1932–1962.* Lexington: University Press of Kentucky, 1988.

Goffman, Erving. *Stigma: Notes on the Management of Spoiled Identity.* Englewood Cliffs, N.J.: Prentice Hall, 1963.

Goldberger, Nancy Rule, Jill Mattuck Tarule, Blythe McVicker Clinchy, and Mary Field Belenky, eds. *Knowledge, Difference, and Power: Essays Inspired by Women's Ways of Knowing.* New York: Basic Books, 1996.

Gore, Jennifer M. *The Struggle for Pedagogies: Critical and Feminist Discourses as Regimes of Truth.* New York: Routledge, 1993.

Gorelick, Sherry. "Contradictions of Feminist Methodology," pp. 23–45 in Gottfried (1996).

———. "Peace Movements," pp. 1033–40 in Hyman and More (1997).

Gornick, Vivian. *The Romance of American Communism.* New York: Basic Books, 1977.

Gornick, Vivian, and Barbara K. Moran, eds. *Woman in Sexist Society: Studies in Power and Powerlessness.* New York: Basic Books, 1971.

Gottfried, Heidi, ed. *Feminism and Social Change: Bridging Theory and Practice.* Urbana: University of Illinois Press, 1996.

Gould, Jane S. *Juggling: A Memoir of Work, Family and Feminism.* New York: Feminist Press, 1997.

Gramsci, Antonio. *Selections from the Prison Notebooks of Antonio Gramsci.* Ed. and trans. Quintin Hoare and Geoffrey Nowell Smith. New York: International, 1971.

Grant, Joanne. *Ella Baker: Freedom Bound.* New York: Wiley, 1998.

Grant, Judith. *Fundamental Feminism: Contesting the Core Concepts of Feminist Theory.* New York: Routledge, 1993.

Green, Rayna. "American Indian Women: Diverse Leadership for Social Change," pp. 61–73 in Albrecht and Brewer (1990).

———. "Magnolias Grow in Dirt: The Bawdy Lore of Southern Women." *Southern Exposure* 4, no. 4 (Winter 1977): 29–33.

Greene, Maxine. *The Dialectic of Freedom.* New York: Teachers College Press, 1988.

Griffin, Susan. "The Way of All Ideology," pp. 273–92 in Keohane, Rosaldo, and Gelpi (1982).

Griffiths, Morwenna. "Feminism, Feelings and Philosophy," pp. 131–51 in Griffiths and Whitford (1988).

Griffiths, Morwenna, and Margaret Whitford, eds. *Feminist Perspectives in Philosophy.* Bloomington: Indiana University Press, 1988.

Griscom, Joan L. "Women and Power: Definition, Dualism, and Difference." *Psychology of Women Quarterly* 16, no. 4 (December 1992): 389–414.

Grumet, Madeleine R. *Bitter Milk: Women and Teaching.* Amherst: University of Massachusetts Press, 1988.

Gutmann, Amy, and Dennis Thompson. *Democracy and Disagreement.* Cambridge, Mass.: Belknap, 1996.

Habermas, Jürgen. *Justification and Application: Remarks on Discourse Ethics.* Trans. Claran Cronin. Cambridge, Mass.: MIT Press, 1993.

———. *Moral Consciousness and Communicative Action.* Cambridge, Mass.: MIT Press, 1990.

Hanisch, Carol. "The Liberal Takeover of Women's Liberation," pp. 163–67 in Redstockings (1978).

———. "The Personal Is Political," pp. 204–5 in Redstockings (1978).

Hansen, Abby J. "Establishing a Teaching/Learning Contract," pp. 123–35 in Christensen, Garvin, and Sweet (1991).

Hansen, Karen V., and Ilene J. Philipson, eds. *Women, Class, and the Feminist Imagination: A Socialist-Feminist Reader.* Philadelphia: Temple University Press, 1990.

Haraway, Donna. "Situated Knowledges: The Science Question in Feminism and the Privilege of Partial Perspective." *Feminist Studies* 14, no. 3 (Fall 1988): 575–99.

Harding, Sandra. "Rethinking Standpoint Epistemology: What Is 'Strong Objectivity?'" pp. 49–82 in Alcoff and Potter (1993).

———. *Whose Science? Whose Knowledge? Thinking from Women's Lives.* Ithaca, N.Y.: Cornell University Press, 1991.

Harkin, Patricia, and John Schilb, eds. *Contending with Words: Composition and Rhetoric in a Postmodern Age.* New York: Modern Language Association of America, 1991.

Harris, Maria. *Women and Teaching: Themes for a Spirituality of Pedagogy.* New York: Paulist, 1988.

Harrison, Cynthia. *On Account of Sex: The Politics of Women's Issues, 1945–1968.* Berkeley: University of California Press, 1988.

Hartmann, Heidi. "The Unhappy Marriage of Marxism and Feminism: Towards a More Progressive Union," pp. 1–41 in Sargent (1981).

Hartsock, Nancy. "Community/Sexuality/Gender: Rethinking Power," pp. 27–49 in Hirschmann and Di Stefano (1996).

———. "Political Change: Two Perspectives on Power," pp. 3–19 in Bunch (1981).

Haywoode, Terry L., and Laura Polla Scanlon. "World of Our Mothers: College for Neighborhood Women." *Women's Studies Quarterly* 21, nos. 3 & 4 (Fall/ Winter, 1993): 133–41.

Hearne, Vicki. *Adam's Task: Calling Animals by Name.* New York: Knopf, 1986.

Heldke, Lisa. "John Dewey and Evelyn Fox Keller: A Shared Epistemological Tradition," pp. 104–15 in Tuana (1989).

Heller, Craig W. "A Paradox of Silence: Reflections of a Man Who Teaches Women's Studies," pp. 228–37 in Mayberry (1996).

Heller, Scott. "Finding a Common Purpose: U. of Chicago Scholar Has Become a Key Advocate of Communitarianism." *Chronicle of Higher Education* (31 March 1995): A10, A16.

Hernández, Adriana. *Pedagogy, Democracy, and Feminism: Rethinking the Public Sphere.* Albany: State University of New York Press, 1997.

Hesford, Wendy S. *Framing Identities: Autobiography and the Politics of Pedagogy.* Minneapolis: University of Minnesota Press, 1999.

Heyward, Carter, and Beverly Wildung Harrison. "Boundaries: Protecting the Vulnerable or Perpetuating a Bad Idea?" pp. 111–28 in Ragsdale (1996).

Hillyer, Barbara. *Feminism and Disability.* Norman: University of Oklahoma Press, 1993.

Hirschmann, Nancy J., and Christine Di Stefano, eds. *Revisioning the Political: Feminist Reconstructions of Traditional Concepts in Western Political Theory.* Boulder, Colo.: Westview, 1996.

Hoagland, Sarah Lucia. *Lesbian Ethics: Toward New Value.* Palo Alto, Calif.: Institute of Lesbian Studies, 1988.

———. "Some Thoughts about Caring," pp. 246–63 in Card (1991).

Hochschild, Arlie Russell. "The Sociology of Feeling and Emotion: Selected Possibilities," pp. 280–307 in Millman and Kanter (1975).

Hoffmann, Frances L., and Jayne E. Stake. "Feminist Pedagogy in Theory and Practice: An Empirical Investigation." *NWSA Journal* 10, no. 1 (Spring 1998): 79–97.

Honig, Bonnie, ed. *Feminist Interpretations of Hannah Arendt.* University Park: Pennsylvania State University Press, 1995.

hooks, bell. *Killing Rage: Ending Racism.* New York: Holt, 1995.

———. *Sisters of the Yam: Black Women and Self-Recovery.* Boston: South End, 1993.

———. *Talking Back: Thinking Feminist, Thinking Black.* Boston: South End, 1989.

———. *Teaching to Transgress: Education as the Practice of Freedom.* New York: Routledge, 1994.

Howe, Florence. "Mississippi's Freedom Schools: The Politics of Education" (1964), in Howe (1984).

———. *Myths of Coeducation: Selected Essays, 1964–1983.* Bloomington: Indiana University Press, 1984.

———. "Women and the Power to Change," pp. 127–171 in Howe (1975).

Howe, Florence, ed. *Women and the Power to Change.* New York: McGraw-Hill, 1975.

Hull, Gloria T., Patricia Bell Scott, and Barbara Smith, eds. *All the Women Are White, All the Blacks Are Men, But Some of Us Are Brave: Black Women's Studies.* Old Westbury, N.Y.: Feminist, 1982.

Humphrey, Karen K. "Theater as Field: Implications for Gestalt Therapy." *Studies in Gestalt Therapy* 8 (1999): 172–81.

Hurtado, Aída. *The Color of Privilege: Three Blasphemies on Race and Feminism.* Ann Arbor: University of Michigan Press, 1996.

Hutchins, Robert Maynard. *The Conflict in Education in a Democratic Society.* New York: Harper, 1953.

———. *The Higher Learning in America.* New Haven, Conn.: Yale University Press, 1936.

Hyman, Paula E., and Deborah Dash More. *Jewish Women in America: An Historical Encyclopedia.* New York: Routledge, 1997.

Jaggar, Alison M. "Introduction: Living with Contradictions," pp. 1–12 in Jaggar (1994).

———. "Love and Knowledge: Emotion in Feminist Epistemology," pp. 145–71 in Jaggar and Bordo (1989).

Jaggar, Alison M., ed. *Living with Contradictions: Controversies in Feminist Social Ethics.* Boulder, Colo.: Westview, 1994.

Jaggar, Alison M., and Susan R. Bordo, eds. *Gender/Body/Knowledge: Feminist Reconstructions of Being and Knowing.* New Brunswick, N.J.: Rutgers University Press, 1989.

James, Joy. "Gender, Race, and Radicalism: Teaching the Autobiographies of Native and African American Women Activists," pp. 234–58 in Cohee (1998).

James, William. *The Will to Believe and Other Essays in Popular Philosophy.* New York: Longmans, Green, 1908.

Jarratt, Susan C. "Feminism and Composition: The Case for Conflict," pp. 105–23 in Harkin and Schilb (1991).

Johnson, Elisabeth J. "Working-Class Women as Students and Teachers," pp. 197–207 in Tokarczyk and Fay (1993).

Johnson, J. Scott, Jennifer Kellen, Greg Seibert, and Celia Shaughnessy. "No Middle Ground? Men Teaching Feminism," pp. 85–103 in Mayberry (1996).

Jones, Hettie. *How I Became Hettie Jones.* New York: Dutton, 1990.

Jones, Kathleen B. "On Authority: Or, Why Women Are Not Entitled to Speak," pp. 152–68 in Pennock and Chapman (1987).

———. *Compassionate Authority: Democracy and the Representation of Women.* New York: Routledge, 1993.

———. "What Is Authority's Gender?" pp. 75–93 in Hirschmann and Di Stefano (1996).

Jordan, June. *On Call: Political Essays.* Boston: South End, 1985.

———. "Report from the Bahamas," pp. 39–49 in Jordan (1985).

Joseph, Gloria I. "Black Mothers and Daughters: Their Roles and Functions in American Society," pp. 75–126 in Joseph and Lewis (1981).

Joseph, Gloria I., and Jill Lewis, eds. *Common Differences: Conflicts in Black and White Feminist Perspectives.* New York: Anchor, 1981.

Karamcheti, Indira. "Caliban in the Classroom," pp. 138–46 in Gallop (1995).

Kaufman, Cynthia. "Postmodernism and Praxis: Weaving Radical Theory from Threads of Desire and Discourse." *Socialist Review* 24, no. 3 (1994): 57–80.

Kaye/Kantrowitz, Melanie. *The Issue Is Power: Essays on Women, Jews, Violence and Resistance.* San Francisco: Aunt Lute Books, 1992.

Keating, AnnLouise. "Heterosexual Teacher, Lesbian/Gay/Bisexual Text: Teaching the Sexual Other(s)," pp. 96–107 in Garber (1994).

Keller, Evelyn Fox. *Reflections on Gender and Science.* New Haven, Conn.: Yale University Press, 1985.

Kelly-Gadol, Joan. "Did Women Have a Renaissance?" pp. 137–64 in Bridenthal and Koonz (1977).

Keohane, Nannerl O., Michelle Z. Rosaldo, and Barbara C. Gelpi, eds. *Feminist Theory: A Critique of Ideology.* Chicago: University of Chicago Press, 1982.

Kittay, Eva Feder, and Diana T. Meyers, eds. *Women and Moral Theory.* Totowa, N.J.: Rowman & Littlefield, 1987.

Klepfisz, Irena. *Dreams of an Insomniac: Jewish Feminist Essays, Speeches and Diatribes.* Portland, Ore.: Eighth Mountain, 1990.

Koedt, Anne, Ellen Levine, and Anita Rapone, eds. *Radical Feminism.* New York: Quadrangle, 1973.

Kolodny, Annette. *Failing the Future: A Dean Looks at Higher Education in the Twenty-First Century.* Durham, N.C.: Duke University Press, 1998.

———. "Paying the Price of Antifeminist Intellectual Harassment," pp. 3–33 in Clark (1996).

Kramarae, Cheris, and Dale Spender, eds. *The Knowledge Explosion: Generations of Feminist Scholarship.* New York: Teachers College Press, 1992.

Krauss, Celene. "Women of Color on the Front Line," pp. 540–51 in Andersen and Collins (1998).

Kravitz, Diane. "Consciousness-Raising Groups in the 1970's." *Psychology of Women Quarterly* 3, no. 2 (Winter 1978): 168–186.

Kristeva, Julia. "Women's Time," pp. 31–53 in Keohane, Rosaldo, and Gelpi (1982).

Kuhn, Thomas. *The Structure of Scientific Revolutions.* Chicago: University of Chicago Press, 1970.

Lantieri, Linda, and Janet Patti. *Waging Peace in Our Schools.* Boston: Beacon, 1996.

Lawrence, Sandra M. "Bringing White Privilege into Consciousness." *Multicultural Education* 3, no. 3 (Spring 1996): 46–48.

Lemons, Gary L. "'Young Man, Tell Our Stories of How We Made It Over': Beyond the Politics of Identity," pp. 259–84 in Mayberry (1996).

Lennox, Sara. "Divided Feminism: Women, Racism, and German National Identity," pp. 123–54 in Arenal (1997).

Lewis, Magda Gere. *Without a Word: Teaching Beyond Women's Silence.* New York: Routledge, 1993.

Lim, Shirley Geok-lin. "'Ain't I a Feminist?': Re-forming the Circle," pp. 450–66 in DuPlessis and Snitow (1998).

Lister, Ruth. "Dialectics of Citizenship." *Hypatia* 12, no. 4, special issue on "Citizenship in Feminism: Identity, Action, and Locale," ed. Kathleen B. Jones (Fall 1997): 6–26.

Long, Priscilla. "We Called Ourselves Sisters," pp. 324–37 in DuPlessis and Snitow (1998).

Longino, Helen E. "Subjects, Power, and Knowledge: Description and Prescription in Feminist Philosophies of Science," pp. 101–20 in Alcoff and Potter (1993).

Lorde, Audre. *Sister Outsider: Essays and Speeches.* Trumansburg, N.Y.: Crossing, 1984.

———. *Zami: A New Spelling of My Name.* Watertown, Mass.: Persephone, 1982.

Lugones, María C. "Playfulness, 'World'-Travelling, and Loving Perception," pp. 159–80 in Allen (1990).

Lugones, María C., and Elizabeth V. Spelman. "Competition, Compassion, and Community: Models for a Feminist Ethos," pp. 234–47 in Miner and Longino (1987).

Luke, Carmen, and Jennifer Gore, eds. *Feminisms and Critical Pedagogy.* New York: Routledge, 1992.

Lyons, Gracie. *Constructive Criticism: A Handbook.* Oakland, Calif.: Issues in Radical Therapy, 1976.

MacIntyre, Alasdair. *After Virtue: A Study in Moral Theory.* 2d ed. Notre Dame, Ind.: University of Notre Dame Press, 1984.

MacKinnon, Catharine A. "Feminism, Marxism, Method, and the State: An Agenda for Theory." *Signs: Journal of Women in Culture and Society* 7, no. 3 (Spring 1982): 515–44.

Macy, Joanna Rogers. *Despair and Personal Power in the Nuclear Age.* Philadelphia: New Society, 1983.

Maher, Frances A., and Mary Kay Thompson Tetreault. *The Feminist Classroom.* New York: Basic Books, 1994.

Malinowitz, Harriet. *Textual Orientations: Lesbian and Gay Students and the Making of Discourse Communities.* Portsmouth, N.H.: Heinemann, 1995.

Mann, Patricia S. "Cyborgean Motherhood and Abortion," pp. 133–51 in Gardiner (1995).

Mannheim, Karl. *Essays on the Sociology of Knowledge.* Ed. Paul Kecskemeti. London: Routledge & Kegan Paul, 1952.

———. "The Problem of Generations," pp. 276–320 in Mannheim (1952).

Marks, Stephen R. "The Art of Professing and Holding Back in a Course on Gender." *Family Relations* 44, no. 2 (April 1995): 142–48.

Marrow, Alfred J. *The Practical Theorist: The Life and Works of Kurt Lewin.* New York: Teacher's College Press, 1977.

Martin, Jane Roland. *Reclaiming a Conversation: The Ideal of the Educated Woman.* New Haven, Conn.: Yale University Press, 1985.

Marx, Karl, and Frederick Engels. *The German Ideology.* Ed. C. J. Arthur. New York: International, 1978.

Mayberry, Katherine J., ed. *Teaching What You're Not: Identity Politics in Higher Education*. New York: New York University Press, 1996.

Mayberry, Maralee, and Ellen Cronan Rose, eds. *Meeting the Challenge: Innovative Feminist Pedagogies in Action*. New York: Routledge, 1999.

McIntosh, Peggy. "White Privilege and Male Privilege: A Personal Account of Coming to See Correspondences through Work in Women's Studies," pp. 94–105 in Andersen and Collins (1998).

McKeachie, Wilbert J. *McKeachie's Teaching Tips: Strategies, Research, and Theory for College and University Teachers*. 10th ed. Boston: Houghton Mifflin, 1999.

McKeon, Richard. "Dialogue and Controversy in Philosophy," pp. 103–25 in McKeon (1990).

———. *Freedom and History, and Other Essays: An Introduction to the Thought of Richard McKeon*. Ed. Zahava K. McKeon. Chicago: University of Chicago Press, 1990.

McNeill, William H. *Hutchins' University: A Memoir of the University of Chicago, 1929–1950*. Chicago: University of Chicago Press, 1991.

McRae, Mary B. "Interracial Group Dynamics: A New Perspective." *Journal for Specialists in Group Work* 19, no. 3 (September 1994): 168–174.

Mead, George. *George Herbert Mead on Social Psychology*. Ed. and intro. Anselm L. Strauss. Rev. ed. Chicago: University of Chicago Press, 1964.

Meijer, Irene Costera, and Baukje Prins. "How Bodies Come to Matter: An Interview with Judith Butler." *Signs: Journal of Women in Culture and Society* 23, no. 2 (Winter 1998): 275–86.

Messer-Davidow, Ellen. "Acting Otherwise," pp. 23–51 in Gardiner (1995).

Meyers, Diana Tietjens. "Emotion and Heterodox Moral Perception: An Essay in Moral Social Psychology," pp. 197–218 in Meyers (1997).

———. *Subjection and Subjectivity: Psychoanalytic Feminism and Moral Philosophy*. New York: Routledge, 1994.

———, ed. *Feminists Rethink the Self*. Boulder, Colo.: Westview, 1997.

Middleton, Sue. *Educating Feminists: Life Histories and Pedagogy*. New York: Teachers College Press, 1993.

Miller, Jean Baker. *Toward a New Psychology of Women*. Boston: Beacon, 1976.

Millett, Kate. *The Loony-Bin Trip*. New York: Simon & Schuster, 1990.

———. *Sexual Politics*. New York: Avon, 1970.

Millman, Marcia, and Rosabeth Moss Kanter, eds. *Another Voice: Feminist Perspectives on Social Life and Social Science*. New York: Anchor, 1975.

Miner, Valerie, and Helen E. Longino. "A Feminist Taboo," pp. 1–37 in Miner and Longino (1987).

———, eds. *Competition: A Feminist Taboo?* New York: Feminist, 1987.

Minnich, Elizabeth Kamarck. "Feminist Attacks on Feminisms: Patriarchy's Prodigal Daughters." *Feminist Studies* 24, no. 1 (Spring 1998): 159–175.

———. *Transforming Knowledge*. Philadelphia: Temple University Press, 1990.

Mitchell, Juliet. *The Longest Revolution: Essays on Feminism, Literature, and Psychoanalysis*. London: Virago, 1984.

Mohanty, Chandra Talpade. "Defining Genealogies: Feminist Reflections on Being

South Asian in North America," pp. 351–58 in Women of South Asian Descent Collective (1993).

————. "Under Western Eyes: Feminist Scholarship and Colonial Discourses," pp. 51–80 in Mohanty, Russo, and Torres (1991).

Mohanty, Chandra Talpade, Ann Russo, and Lourdes Torres, eds. *Third World Women and the Politics of Feminism.* Bloomington: Indiana University Press, 1991.

Molina, Papusa. "Recognizing, Accepting and Celebrating Our Differences," pp. 326–31 in Anzaldúa (1990).

Moraga, Cherríe, and Gloria Anzaldúa, eds. *This Bridge Called My Back: Writings by Radical Women of Color.* Watertown, Mass.: Persephone, 1981.

Morgan, Robin, ed. *Sisterhood Is Powerful: An Anthology of Writings from the Women's Liberation Movement.* New York: Random House, 1970.

Morris, Aldon D., and Carol McClurg Mueller, eds. *Frontiers in Social Movement Theory.* New Haven, Conn.: Yale University Press, 1992.

Morrison, Toni. *Playing in the Dark: Whiteness and the Literary Imagination.* New York: Vintage, 1993.

————, ed. *Race-ing Justice, En-gendering Power: Essays on Anita Hill, Clarence Thomas, and the Construction of Social Reality.* New York: Pantheon, 1992.

Mouffe, Chantal. "Feminism, Citizenship and Radical Democratic Politics," pp. 369–84 in Butler and Scott (1992).

Moulton, Janice. "A Paradigm of Philosophy: The Adversary Method," pp. 11–25 in Garry and Pearsall (1996).

Moynagh, Patricia. "A Politics of Enlarged Mentality: Hannah Arendt, Citizenship Responsibility, and Feminism." *Hypatia* 12, no. 4, special issue, "Citizenship in Feminism: Identity, Action, and Locale," ed. Kathleen B. Jones (Fall 1997): 27–53.

Naples, Nancy A. with Emily Clark. "Feminist Participatory Research and Empowerment: Going Public as Survivors of Childhood Sexual Abuse," pp. 160–83 in Gottfried (1996).

Narayan, Uma. "The Project of Feminist Epistemology: Perspectives from a Nonwestern Feminist," pp. 256–69 in Jaggar and Bordo (1989).

Nelson, Lynn Hankinson. "Epistemological Communities," pp. 121–59 in Alcoff and Potter (1993).

Nestle, Joan. *A Fragile Union: New and Selected Writings.* San Francisco: Cleis, 1998.

Nicholson, Linda J., ed. *Feminism/Postmodernism.* New York: Routledge, 1990.

Noddings, Nel. *Caring: A Feminine Approach to Ethics and Moral Education.* Berkeley: University of California Press, 1984.

————. *The Challenge to Care in Schools: An Alternative Approach to Education.* New York: Teachers College Press, 1992.

Novack, Cynthia J. *Sharing the Dance: Contact Improvisation and American Culture.* Madison: University of Wisconsin Press, 1990.

NOW Guidelines for Feminist Consciousness-Raising. Washington, D.C.: National Organization for Women, 1983.

Nussbaum, Martha C. "Emotions and Women's Capabilities," pp. 360–95 in Nussbaum and Glover (1995).

Nussbaum, Martha C., and Jonathan Glover, eds. *Women, Culture, and Development: A Study of Human Capabilities.* Oxford: Clarendon, 1995.

O'Reilly, Jane. *The Girl I Left Behind.* New York: Macmillan 1980.

Omolade, Barbara. *The Rising Song of African American Women.* New York: Routledge, 1994.

Overall, Christine. *A Feminist I: Reflections from Academia.* Peterborough, Ontario: Broadview, 1998.

Pagano, Jo Anne. *Exiles and Communities: Teaching in the Patriarchal Wilderness.* Albany: State University of New York Press, 1990.

———. "Teaching Women," pp. 101–32 in Pagano (1990).

Pardo, Mary. "Doing it for the Kids: Mexican American Community Activists, Border Feminists?" pp. 356–71 in Ferree and Martin (1995).

Paringer, William Andrew. *John Dewey and the Paradox of Liberal Reform.* Albany: State University of New York Press, 1990.

Patai, Daphne, and Noretta Koertge. *Professing Feminism: Cautionary Tales from the Strange World of Women's Studies.* New York: Basic Books, 1994.

Paul, Ellen Frankel, Fred D. Miller Jr., and Jeffrey Paul, eds. *The Communitarian Challenge to Liberalism.* Cambridge: Cambridge University Press, 1996.

Payne, Charles. "Ella Baker and Models of Social Change." *Signs: Journal of Women in Culture and Society* 14, no. 4, (Summer 1989): 885–99.

Pennock, J. Roland, and John W. Chapman, eds. *Authority Revisited: Nomos XXIX.* New York: New York University Press, 1987.

Perls, Frederick S., Ralph F. Hefferline, and Paul Goodman. *Gestalt Therapy: Excitement and Growth in the Human Personality.* New York: Julian, 1951.

Personal Narratives Group, ed. *Interpreting Women's Lives: Feminist Theory and Personal Narratives.* Bloomington: Indiana University Press, 1989.

Pheterson, Gail. "Alliances between Women: Overcoming Internalized Oppression and Internalized Domination," pp. 34–48 in Albrecht and Brewer (1990).

Phillips, Anne. "Dealing with Difference: A Politics of Ideas, or a Politics of Presence," pp. 140–52 in Benhabib (1996).

Pitkin, Hanna Fenichel. "Conformism, Housekeeping, and the Attack of the Blob: The Origins of Hannah Arendt's Concept of the Social," pp. 51–81 in Honig (1995).

Plaskow, Judith. *Standing Again at Sinai: Judaism From a Feminist Perspective.* San Francisco: HarperCollins, 1990.

Popkin, Ann. "The Personal Is Political: The Women's Liberation Movement," pp. 183–222 in Cluster (1979).

Potter, Elizabeth. "Modeling the Gender Politics in Science," pp. 132–46 in Tuana (1989).

Pratt, Minnie Bruce. "Identity: Skin Blood Heart," pp. 11–63 in Bulkin, Pratt, and Smith (1984).

Radical Teacher: A Socialist and Feminist Journal on the Theory and Practice of Teaching. Cambridge, Mass.: Boston Women's Teachers' Group. Published triannually.

Radicalesbians. "The Woman Identified Woman," pp. 240–45 in Koedt, Levine, and Rapone (1973).

Ragsdale, Katherine Hancock, ed. *Boundary Wars: Intimacy and Distance in Healing Relationships.* Cleveland, Ohio: Pilgrim, 1996.

Rajchman, John, ed. *The Identity in Question.* New York: Routledge, 1995.

Raymond, Janice G. *A Passion for Friends: Toward a Philosophy of Female Affection.* Boston: Beacon, 1986.

Reagon, Bernice Johnson. "Coalition Politics: Turning the Century," pp. 356–68 in Smith (1983).

Redstockings. *Feminist Revolution.* Abridged ed. with additional writings. New York: Random House, 1978.

Rehg, William. *Insight and Solidarity: A Study in the Discourse Ethics of Jürgen Habermas.* Berkeley: University of California Press, 1994.

Reinelt, Claire. "Moving onto the Terrain of the State: The Battered Women's Movement and the Politics of Engagement," pp. 84–104 in Ferree and Martin (1995).

Ressler, Paula. "Queer Issues in Multicultural Teacher Education: Toward an Anti-homophobic Educational Practice." Ph.D. dissertation, New York University, 1999.

Rich, Adrienne. *Blood, Bread, and Poetry: Selected Prose 1979–1985.* New York: Norton, 1986.

———. *The Dream of a Common Language: Poems 1974–1977.* New York: Norton, 1978.

———. *On Lies, Secrets, and Silence: Selected Prose 1966–1978.* New York: Norton, 1979.

Richardson, Laurel. "Sharing Feminist Research with Popular Audiences: The Book Tour," pp. 284–95 in Fonow and Cook (1991).

Riley, Denise. *"Am I That Name?" Feminism and the Category of "Women" in History.* Minneapolis: University of Minnesota Press, 1988.

Rinehart, Jane A. "Feminist Wolves in Sheep's Disguise," pp. 63–97 in Mayberry and Rose (1999).

Rollins, Judith. *Between Women: Domestics and Their Employers.* Philadelphia: Temple University Press, 1985.

Ropers-Huilman, Becky. *Feminist Teaching in Theory and Practice: Situating Power and Knowledge in Poststructural Classrooms.* New York: Teachers College Press, 1998.

Rose, Ellen Cronan. " 'This Class Meets in Cyberspace': Women's Studies via Distance Education," pp. 141–67 in Mayberry and Rose (1999).

Rossman, Michael. *On Learning and Social Change.* New York: Random House, 1972.

Rothenberg, Paula S., ed. *Race, Class, and Gender in the United States: An Integrated Study.* 2d ed. New York: St. Martin's, 1992.

Rousso, Harilyn. "Daughters with Disabilities: Defective Women or Minority Women?" pp. 139–71 in Fine and Asch (1988).

Rowbotham, Sheila. *The Past Is before Us: Feminism in Action since the 1960s.* Boston: Beacon, 1989.

————. *Woman's Consciousness, Man's World.* Middlesex, England: Penguin, 1973.

————. "The Women's Movement and Organizing for Socialism," pp. 21–155 in Rowbotham, Segal, and Wainright (1981).

Rowbotham, Sheila, Lynne Segal, and Hilary Wainright, eds. *Beyond the Fragments: Feminism and the Making of Socialism.* Boston: Alyson, 1981.

Ruddick, Sara. *Maternal Thinking: Toward a Politics of Peace.* Boston: Beacon, 1989.

————. "Reason's 'Femininity': A Case for Connected Knowing," pp. 248–73 in Goldberger, Tarule, Clinchy, and Belenky (1996).

Ruggiero, Chris. "Teaching Women's Studies: The Repersonalization of Our Politics." *Women's Studies International Forum* 13, no. 5 (1990): 469–75.

Sandoval, Chela. "U.S. Third World Feminism: The Theory and Method of Oppositional Consciousness in a Postmodern World." *Genders* 10 (Spring 1991): 1–24.

Sarachild, Kathie. "The Power of History," pp. 13–43 in Redstockings (1978).

————. "A Program for Feminist Consciousness-Raising," pp. 202–03 in Redstockings (1978).

Sargent, Lydia, ed. *Women and Revolution: A Discussion of the Unhappy Marriage of Marxism and Feminism.* Boston: South End, 1981.

Sattler, Cheryl L. *Talking about a Revolution: The Politics and Practice of Feminist Teaching.* Cresskill, N.J.: Hampton, 1997.

Sawicki, Jana. *Disciplining Foucault: Feminism, Power, and the Body.* New York: Routledge, 1991.

Sayres, Sohnya, Anders Stephanson, Stanley Aronowitz, and Frederic Jameson, eds. *The 60s without Apology.* Minneapolis: University of Minnesota Press, 1984.

Scanlon, Jennifer. "Educating the Living, Remembering the Dead: The Montreal Massacre as Metaphor," pp. 224–33 in Cohee et al. (1998).

Scheman, Naomi. *Engenderings: Constructions of Knowledge, Authority, and Privilege.* New York: Routledge, 1993.

————. "Queering the Center by Centering the Queer: Reflections on Transsexuals and Secular Jews," pp. 124–62 in Meyers (1997).

Schniedewind, Nancy. "Teaching Feminist Process in the 1990s." *Women's Studies Quarterly* 21, nos. 3 & 4 (Fall/Winter 1993): 17–30.

Schön, Donald A. *The Reflective Practitioner: How Professionals Think in Action.* New York: Basic Books, 1983.

Schrecker, Ellen. *Many Are the Crimes: McCarthyism in America.* Boston: Little, Brown, 1998.

Schultz, Dagmar. "Anti-Racism: The Challenge to Women's Studies." Trans. Tobe Levin. *WISE [Women's International Studies Europe] Women's News* 1 (1993): 36–44.

Schutzman, Mady, and Jan Cohen-Cruz, eds. *Playing Boal: Theatre, Therapy, Activism.* London: Routledge, 1994.

Schweickart, Patrocinio P. "Speech Is Silver, Silence Is Gold: The Asymmetrical Intersubjectivity of Communicative Action," pp. 305–31 in Goldberger, Tarule, Clinchy, and Belenky (1996).

————. "What Are We Doing? What Do We Want? Who Are We? Comprehending the Subject of Feminism," pp. 229–48 in Gardiner (1995).

Scott, Joan W. "'Experience,'" pp. 22–40 in Butler and Scott (1992).

Seigfried, Charlene Haddock. *Pragmatism and Feminism: Reweaving the Social Fabric*. Chicago: University of Chicago Press, 1996.

Seller, Anne. "Realism versus Relativism: Towards a Politically Adequate Epistemology," pp. 169–86 in Griffiths and Whitford (1988).

Shor, Ira. *Critical Teaching and Everyday Life*. Boston: South End, 1980.

————. *Empowering Education: Critical Teaching and Social Change*. Chicago: University of Chicago Press, 1992.

Showalter, Elaine. ed. *The New Feminist Criticism: Essays on Women, Literature, and Theory*. New York: Pantheon, 1985.

Shreve, Anita. *Women Together, Women Alone: The Legacy of the Consciousness-Raising Movement*. New York: Viking, 1989.

Shrewsbury, Carolyn M. "What is Feminist Pedagogy?" *Women's Studies Quarterly* 21, nos. 3 & 4 (Fall/Winter 1993): 8–16.

Shugar, Dana R. *Separatism and Women's Community*. Lincoln: University of Nebraska Press, 1995.

Silin, Jonathan G. *Sex, Death, and the Education of Children: Our Passion for Ignorance in the Age of AIDS*. New York: Teachers College Press, 1995.

Silko, Leslie Marmon. *Yellow Woman and a Beauty of the Spirit: Essays on Native American Life Today*. New York: Simon & Schuster, 1997.

Simmel, Georg. *The Sociology of Georg Simmel*. Trans. and ed. Kurt H. Wolff. Glencoe, Ill.: Free Press, 1950.

Simone, Timothy Maliqalim. *About Face: Race in Postmodern America*. New York: Autonomedia, 1989.

Singer, Judith Y. "Fighting for a Better World: Teaching in an Inner-City Day Care Center." Ph.D. dissertation, New York University, 1998.

Sleeter, Christine E. *Multicultural Education as Social Activism*. Albany: State University of New York Press, 1996.

Smith, Barbara, ed. *Home Girls: A Black Feminist Anthology*. New York: Kitchen Table: Women of Color Press, 1983.

Smith, Dorothy E. *The Conceptual Practices of Power: A Feminist Sociology of Knowledge*. Boston: Northeastern University Press, 1990.

Sommers, Christina Hoff. *Who Stole Feminism? How Women Have Betrayed Women*. New York: Simon & Schuster, 1994.

Sparks, Holloway. "Dissident Citizenship: Democratic Theory, Political Courage, and Activist Women." *Hypatia* 12, no. 4 (Fall 1997): 74–110.

Spelman, Elizabeth V. *Fruits of Sorrow: Framing Our Attention to Suffering*. Boston: Beacon, 1997.

————. *Inessential Woman: Problems of Exclusion in Feminist Thought*. Boston: Beacon, 1988.

Spender, Dale. *Invisible Women: The Schooling Scandal*. London: Readers and Writers Publishing Cooperative Society, 1982.

Spivak, Gayatri Chakravorty. *Outside in the Teaching Machine*. New York: Routledge, 1993.

Spivak, Gayatri Chakravorty, and David Plotke. "A Dialogue on Democracy." *Socialist Review* 24, no. 3, (1994): 1–22.
Stacey, Judith. "Can There Be a Feminist Ethnography?" pp. 88–101 in Gottfried (1996).
Stack, Carol B. *All Our Kin: Strategies for Survival in a Black Community.* New York: Harper, 1974.
Starhawk. *Dreaming the Dark: Magic, Sex, and Politics.* Boston: Beacon, 1982.
Stone, I. F. *The Haunted Fifties.* New York: Random House, 1963.
Strauss, Anselm L. *Qualitative Analysis for Social Scientists.* Cambridge: Cambridge University Press, 1987.
Sweet Honey in the Rock. *Sweet Honey in the Rock.* Flying Fish Music, BMI, FF022, 1976.
Talaska, Richard A., ed. *Critical Reasoning in Contemporary Culture.* Albany: State University of New York Press, 1992.
Tallen, Bette S. "How Inclusive Is Feminist Political Theory? Questions for Lesbians," pp. 241–57 in Allen (1990).
Tanner, Laurel N. *Dewey's Laboratory School: Lessons for Today.* New York: Teachers College Press, 1997.
Tappan, Mark B., and Lyn Mikel Brown. "Stories Told and Lessons Learned: Toward a Narrative Approach to Moral Development and Moral Education," pp. 171–92 in Witherell and Noddings (1991).
Taylor, Verta, and Leila J. Rupp. "Lesbian Existence and the Women's Movement: Researching the 'Lavender Herring,'" pp. 143–59 in Gottfried (1996).
The Teaching Professor. Madison: Wisc.: Magna (published monthly except July and August).
Thompson, E. P. *The Poverty of Theory and Other Essays.* New York: Monthly Review Press, 1978.
Tokarczyk, Michelle M., and Elizabeth A. Fay, eds. *Working-Class Women in the Academy: Laborers in the Knowledge Factory.* Amherst: University of Massachusetts Press, 1993.
Tompkins, Jane. *Life in School: What the Teacher Learned.* Reading, Mass.: Perseus, 1996.
Trebilcot, Joyce, ed. *Mothering: Essays in Feminist Theory.* Totowa, N.J.: Rowman & Allanheld, 1983.
Trinh, T. Minh-ha. *Woman, Native, Other: Writing Postcoloniality and Feminism.* Bloomington: University of Indiana Press, 1989.
Tronto, Joan C. *Moral Boundaries: A Political Argument for an Ethic of Care.* New York: Routledge, 1993.
Truame, Anneliese. "Tau(gh)t Connections: Experiences of a 'Mixed-Blood, Disabled, Lesbian Student,'" pp. 208–14 in Garber (1994).
Tsui, Kitty. "Breaking Silence, Making Waves and Loving Ourselves: The Politics of Coming Out and Coming Home," pp. 49–61 in Allen (1990).
Tuana, Nancy, ed. *Feminism and Science.* Bloomington: Indiana University Press, 1989.
Vance, Carole S., ed. *Pleasure and Danger: Exploring Female Sexuality.* New York: HarperCollins, 1992.

Walker, Margaret Urban, ed. *Mother Time: Women, Aging, and Ethics*. Lanham, Md.: Rowman & Littlefield, 1999.

———. "Picking Up Pieces: Lives, Stories, and Integrity," pp. 62–84 in Meyers (1997).

Walters, Kerry S., ed. *Re-Thinking Reason: New Perspectives in Critical Thinking*. Albany: State University of New York Press, 1994.

Ware, Cellestine. *Woman Power: The Movement for Women's Liberation*. New York: Tower, 1970.

Weber, Max. *From Max Weber: Essays in Sociology*. Trans., ed., and with introduction by H. H. Gerth and C. Wright Mills. New York: Oxford University Press, 1958.

———. *The Theory of Social and Economic Organization*. Ed. Talcott Parsons. New York: Free Press, 1947.

Weiler, Kathleen. "Freire and a Feminist Pedagogy of Difference." *Harvard Educational Review* 61, no. 4 (November 1991): 449–74.

———. *Women Teaching for Change: Gender, Class and Power*. South Hadley, Mass.: Bergin & Garvey, 1988.

Weiner, Gaby. *Feminisms in Education: An Introduction*. Buckingham, England: Open University Press, 1994.

Weiss, Penny A., and Marilyn Friedman, eds. *Feminism and Community*. Philadelphia: Temple University Press, 1995.

Wendell, Susan. "Oppression and Victimizations; Choice and Responsibility." *Hypatia* 5, no. 3 (Fall 1990): 15–46.

Wernham, James C. S. *James's Will-to-Believe Doctrine: A Heretical View*. Kingston, Ontario: McGill-Queen's University Press, 1987.

Wetzel, Jodi. "Assessment and Feminist Pedagogy," pp. 99–119 in Mayberry and Rose (1999).

Whalen, Mollie. *Counseling to End Violence against Women: A Subversive Model*. Thousand Oaks, Calif.: Sage, 1996.

Wheeler, Charlene Eldridge, and Peggy L. Chinn. *Peace and Power: A Handbook of Feminist Process*. New York: National League for Nursing, 1989.

Whittier, Nancy. *Feminist Generations: The Persistence of the Radical Women's Movement*. Philadelphia: Temple University Press, 1995.

Williams, Patricia J. *The Alchemy of Race and Rights*. Cambridge, Mass.: Harvard University Press, 1991.

Willis, Ellen. "Radical Feminism and Feminist Radicalism," pp. 91–118 in Sayres, Stephanson, Aronowitz, and Jameson (1984).

Wingrove, Elizabeth. "Interpellating Sex." *Signs: Journal of Women in Culture and Society* 24, no. 4 (Summer 1999): 869–93.

Winkler, Barbara Scott. "Raising C-R: Another Look at Consciousness-Raising in the Women's Studies Classroom." *Transformations, a Resource for Curriculum Transformation and Scholarship: The New Jersey Project Journal* 8, no. 2 (Fall 1997): 66–85.

Winnicott, D. W. "The Theory of the Parent–Infant Relationship." *International Journal of Psycho-Analysis* 41 (November–December 1960): part 6, 585–95.

Witenko, Barbara. "Feminist Ritual as a Process of Social Transformation." Ph.D. dissertation, New York University, 1992.

Witherell, Carol, and Nel Noddings, eds. *Stories Lives Tell: Narrative and Dialogue in Education.* New York: Teachers College Press, 1991.

Wollstonecraft, Mary. *A Vindication of the Rights of Women.* Ed. with introduction by Miriam Brody Kramnick. Middlesex, England: Penguin, 1975.

Women and Disability Awareness Project. *Building Community: A Manual Exploring Issues of Women and Disability.* Rev. ed. New York: Educational Equity Concepts, 1989.

Women of South Asian Descent Collective, eds. *Our Feet Walk the Sky: Women of the South Asian Diaspora.* San Francisco: Aunt Lute Books, 1993.

Women's Studies Quarterly. Special issue on "Feminist Pedagogy: An Update." Vol. 21, nos. 3 & 4 (Fall/Winter 1993).

———. "Looking Back, Moving Forward: 25 Years of Women's Studies History." Ed. Elaine Hedges. Anniversary issue, vol. 25, nos. 1 & 2 (Spring/Summer 1997).

Yamada, Mitsuye. "Asian Pacific American Women and Feminism," pp. 71–75 in Moraga and Anzaldúa (1981).

———. "Invisibility Is an Unnatural Disaster: Reflections of an Asian American Woman," pp. 35–45 in Moraga and Anzaldúa (1981).

Young, Iris Marion. *Justice and the Politics of Difference.* Princeton, N.J.: Princeton University Press, 1990.

———. *Throwing Like a Girl and Other Essays in Feminist Philosophy and Social Theory.* Bloomington: Indiana University Press, 1990.

Young-Bruehl, Elisabeth. "The Education of Women as Philosophers." *Signs: Journal of Women in Culture and Society* 12, no. 2 (Winter 1987): 207–221.

Zita, Jacquelyn N. "Gay and Lesbian Studies: Yet Another Unhappy Marriage?" pp. 258–76 in Garber (1994).

Index

abstracting, in consciousness-raising, 31

academia: versus activism, 193–97; caring in, 117; coercion in, 143; heterosexism in, 87, 263n2; legitimacy in, risk to, 198; passion in, 99–100; questioning, 107–8; and social movements, 201. *See also* institution

academic skills, and access to discourse, 47–48

access: in feminist pedagogy, 46–48; questioning, 58

accountability, expanded, 91–93

action: Arendt on, 241n24; and attention, 134; consciousness-raising, 40–41; in discourse work, 185; feeling and thinking, 67–79; forms of, 196; and hope, 196–97; and theory, 75–79. *See also* collaborative action; collective action

activism: versus academia, 193–97; and criticism, 200; and safety, 140; and teachers, 77–78

Addams, Jane, 7

Adler, Mortimer, 11

affinity groups, 183

African Americans: and caring, 128; and class, 180–81; and education, 24; and feminist pedagogy, 47

age, 16, 205–8

agency, political. *See* political agency

agency, women's. *See* women's agency

agreement, authority of, 85–87

Allen, Jeffner, 125

Allen, Pamela, 30–31, 62, 74, 140–41, 238n16

Allen, Paula Gunn, 204

analysis, and experience, 63–65

anger, 70–71, 125, 167

anonymity, and safety, 146–47

Anzaldúa, Gloria, 26, 154, 170, 189

Arendt, Hannah, 85, 93, 103, 195, 241n24, 277n4

argument: common ground in, 180–81; in discussion method, 12; experience as, 64–67

attention: and caring, 119–21, 134; and consciousness, 241n26; to experience, 60; refocusing, 133–34; shift in, 34

authority, 81–109; and caring, 111, 113–14; as command capacity, 84–85; compassionate, 114; of experience, 63–66; as knowledge, 89–96; as passion, 96–102; as position, 102–9; reflection on, 216; sharing, 84–88; as zero-sum game, 92

Baier, Annette C., 86, 255n6

Baker, Ella, 14, 28, 226n15, 236n11

Barber, Benjamin, 223n2

Bartkowski, Frances, 192

Bartky, Sandra Lee, 239n19

Beauvoir, Simone de, 9, 74, 84, 116, 164, 269n2

labor movement, 130–31
leadership, and students, 87–88
lecturing, 148; styles of, 50
legitimacy, risk to, 198
lesbian/gay/bisexual/transgender movement, 160–61
Lewin, Kurt, 236n11
liberal feminism, 17
limits: on caring, 114–16, 123–32; on
discourse, 201–2; on hope, 192–93;
setting, 147; transgressing, 147–48
listening, 92, 185; political, 142–43
Lister, Ruth, 241n23
logic of preparation, 195
Lorde, Audre, 70, 73, 203
Lugones, María, 59, 173, 204

MacKinnon, Catherine, 58
Maher, Frances, 179, 273n19
male students/teachers, in feminist
classroom, 231n34
managerial questions, 216
Mannheim, Karl, 208
marginalization, 20
Marks, Linda Nathan, 18, 229n26
Martin, Patricia Yancey, 159
McKeon, Richard, 11–12
mental illness, 102–3, 105–6
Messer-Davidow, Ellen, 103–4
Meyers, Diana, 172
Minh-ha, Trinh T., 67, 132
Minnich, Elizabeth, 58, 62
Mitchell, Juliet, 21
Mohanty, Chandra, 58–59
Molina, Papusa, 272n18
Moraga, Cherríe, 189
moral development, 116–17
mothering, 48, 57–58, 89–90, 206; and
caring, 116–17, 121, 128; critique
of, 125, 194–95
movement techniques, 18, 67–68, 135–
36, 229n24
multivocality, 228n23
mutual vulnerability, 217, 219–20

naiveté, 202–3
narration, 185

National Organization for Women
(NOW), 30, 237n14
National Women's Studies Association
(NWSA), 9–10, 16
needs, 42, 113, 258n1; asymmetrical,
117–19; discourse on, 130–32; and
limits of caring, 126–30; of stu-
dents, 111–12
Nelson, Lynn Hankinson, 58, 246n4
New York University, 8
Noddings, Nel, 48, 117–18
nonjudgmentalness, in feminist peda-
gogy, 37–38, 216
NOW. See National Organization for
Women
NWSA. See National Women's Studies
Association

objectification, as experience-bearer,
67, 72
O'Malley, Susan, 14
Omolade, Barbara, 47–48
opening up, in consciousness-raising,
31
openness, of teaching structures,
147–49
open workshops, 218–19
oppression: authority of, 65–66, 82;
faces of,181, 20–21, 231n35; naming experiences of, 36; unified theory of, 73–74; use of term, 20
O'Reilly, Jane, 240n20
othermothers, 128–30
outlaw feelings, 69–70

Pagano, Jo Anne, 84
passion, authority as, 96–102
Patai, Daphne, 15, 138
peace movement, 29, 107–8, 155–57
performance, 51, 220, 245n39
Persian Gulf war, 156
personal versus political, 241n27; and
consciousness-raising, 41–44; and
movement visibility, 158–59; second-wave feminism on, 28; and social movements, 28–29
persuasion, 93–96

About the Author

BERENICE MALKA FISHER is professor of educational philosophy at New York University, where she cofounded the School of Education's Women's Studies Commission. She also created and directs the university's faculty development Seminar on Teaching Social Justice and serves as a consultant to individual faculty on their teaching. Her feminist writing includes articles on shame and guilt in the women's movement, the impact of disability on friendships between women, the meaning of role models, the theory and practice of caring, and issues in feminist pedagogy. She pursues feminist education outside academia through workshops and presentations on subjects such as lesbian visibility and aging and activism.